Communications in Computer and Information Science   1800

Rationale

The CCIS series is devoted to the publication of proceedings of computer science conferences. Its aim is to efficiently disseminate original research results in informatics in printed and electronic form. While the focus is on publication of peer-reviewed full papers presenting mature work, inclusion of reviewed short papers reporting on work in progress is welcome, too. Besides globally relevant meetings with internationally representative program committees guaranteeing a strict peer-reviewing and paper selection process, conferences run by societies or of high regional or national relevance are also considered for publication.

Topics

The topical scope of CCIS spans the entire spectrum of informatics ranging from foundational topics in the theory of computing to information and communications science and technology and a broad variety of interdisciplinary application fields.

Information for Volume Editors and Authors

Publication in CCIS is free of charge. No royalties are paid, however, we offer registered conference participants temporary free access to the online version of the conference proceedings on SpringerLink (http://link.springer.com) by means of an http referrer from the conference website and/or a number of complimentary printed copies, as specified in the official acceptance email of the event.

CCIS proceedings can be published in time for distribution at conferences or as post-proceedings, and delivered in the form of printed books and/or electronically as USBs and/or e-content licenses for accessing proceedings at SpringerLink. Furthermore, CCIS proceedings are included in the CCIS electronic book series hosted in the SpringerLink digital library at http://link.springer.com/bookseries/7899. Conferences publishing in CCIS are allowed to use Online Conference Service (OCS) for managing the whole proceedings lifecycle (from submission and reviewing to preparing for publication) free of charge.

Publication process

The language of publication is exclusively English. Authors publishing in CCIS have to sign the Springer CCIS copyright transfer form, however, they are free to use their material published in CCIS for substantially changed, more elaborate subsequent publications elsewhere. For the preparation of the camera-ready papers/files, authors have to strictly adhere to the Springer CCIS Authors' Instructions and are strongly encouraged to use the CCIS LaTeX style files or templates.

Abstracting/Indexing

CCIS is abstracted/indexed in DBLP, Google Scholar, EI-Compendex, Mathematical Reviews, SCImago, Scopus. CCIS volumes are also submitted for the inclusion in ISI Proceedings.

How to start

To start the evaluation of your proposal for inclusion in the CCIS series, please send an e-mail to ccis@springer.com.

Taye Girma Debelee · Achim Ibenthal ·
Friedhelm Schwenker
Editors

Pan-African Conference on Artificial Intelligence

First Conference, PanAfriCon AI 2022
Addis Ababa, Ethiopia, October 4–5, 2022
Revised Selected Papers

 Springer

Editors
Taye Girma Debelee (iD)
Ethiopian Artificial Intelligence Institute
Addis Ababa, Ethiopia

Friedhelm Schwenker (iD)
University of Ulm
Ulm, Germany

Achim Ibenthal (iD)
HAWK University of Applied Sciences
and Arts
Göttingen, Germany

ISSN 1865-0929   ISSN 1865-0937 (electronic)
Communications in Computer and Information Science
ISBN 978-3-031-31326-4   ISBN 978-3-031-31327-1 (eBook)
https://doi.org/10.1007/978-3-031-31327-1

Preface

This volume presents the proceedings of the *Pan-African Conference on Artificial Intelligence 2022 (PanAfriCon AI 2022)*. This artificial intelligence (AI) conference specializing in African topics finds its motivation in the expected AI-related annual turnover increase from USD 390 million to USD 1,414 million in the years 2021 to 2025. AI is listed as a priority in the development plans of 21 out of 32 African countries surveyed by UNESCO.

PanAfriCon AI 2022 aimed at bringing together AI researchers, computational scientists, engineers, entrepreneurs, and decision-makers from academia, industry, and government institutions to discuss the latest trends, opportunities, and challenges of the application of AI in different sectors of the continent. During the conference, attendees were able to exchange the latest information on techniques and workflows used in artificial intelligence for a variety of research fields.

After the call for proposals for the conference and proceedings publication in May 2022, 49 contributions were received by July 3, 2022. Based on a single-blind review by 2 reviewers, 25 of the 49 contributions were accepted for presentation and for the further publication process. Following an update considering reviewer comments and Springer CCIS series requirements, these contributions were single-blind reviewed by 3 peer reviewers per paper, out of which 16 submissions were accepted finally for publication in this volume.

The first day of the conference took place at the new Science Museum in Addis Ababa and was opened by Ethiopia's Prime Minister Abiy Ahmed Ali. Motivational speeches were given by H.E. Dr. Mohamed Al Kuwaiti, Head of Cyber Security, UAE Government and Mr. Antonio Pedro, Acting Executive Secretary United Nations Economic Commission for Africa. Subsequently keynote speeches were given by Abeba Berhane University College Dublin, Ireland, Tommie Meyer, University of Cape Town, South Africa, Herman Kojo Chinery-Hesse, theSOFTtribe, Ghana, and Sabelo Sethu Mhlambi, Bhala AI, UK. A panel discussion with contributions from the keynote speakers, Mercy Ndegwa, Facebook, Kenya, and Achim Ibenthal, HAWK University of Applied Sciences and Arts, Germany concluded the first day. The second day took place in virtual conference rooms and was opened by a keynote address of Friedhelm Schwenker, University of Ulm, Germany. The four sessions featured presentations on AI in public health, algorithmic optimization, IT security & human-machine interaction, and applications.

This conference would not have been possible without the help of many people and organizations. First of all, we are grateful to all the authors who submitted their contributions. We thank the members of the program committee and the peer reviewers for performing the task of selecting the best papers for the workshop proceedings, and we hope that readers may enjoy this selection of papers and get inspired from these excellent contributions.

March 2023

Taye Girma Debelee
Achim Ibenthal
Friedhelm Schwenker

Address of the Prime Minister of the Federal Democratic Republic of Ethiopia

H. E. Dr. Abiy Ahmed Ali
Prime Minister
Federal Democratic Republic of Ethiopia
Peace Nobel Laureate, Addis Ababa, Ethiopia

The advancement of technology has made it possible for us to accomplish great things in innovative ways to tackle humanity's complex problems. We have experienced a complete transformation in the way we do business as a result of several cutting-edge technologies and advancements. One of today's most notable examples of disruptive innovation is artificial intelligence (AI). In addition to helping us automate our factories, automobiles, homes, and electronic gadgets, AI is enabling us to make significant strides toward resolving pressing problems in key sectors like healthcare, education, agriculture, and government.

Since the first industrial revolution, technological advancements have been the main force behind social progress, economic expansion, and gains in productivity. We are once more witnessing the beginning of the next technological revolution. Industry 4.0 is already here thanks to AI, big data, the Internet of Things (IoT), blockchain, 5G, quantum computers, augmented reality, virtual reality, and many more technologies. Although these technologies have the potential to boost economic development, provide employment, and improve living standards for millions of Africans, many African nations are failing to adopt and embrace them, which puts the continent at risk of falling farther behind in the global economic race. The importance of AI technology for Africa's global competitiveness is more than ever as we stand on the cusp of a new age and the world depends more and more on technical breakthroughs. Africa as a whole has made a remarkable progress in recent years with a growing economy, a burgeoning population, and a vibrant youth population. However, we must embrace AI technology and integrate it into our economic and social institutions if we want to maintain our competitiveness on a global scale.

To reap the full benefits of AI, we must address the challenges that come with it. These include the ethical implications of AI, such as bias, transparency, inclusivity, and privacy concerns, and the need to develop a robust regulatory framework to ensure that AI is used for the greater good to all mankind.

We are a continent of ancient civilization. We carved monolithic architectures out of rock. We offered an ancient mathematics that is as sophisticated as the one that is used in today's computer systems. Those testaments clearly show that we Africans have a lot to offer. Let us all contribute our own intellect to the future of AI to keep things moving in the right direction.

Address of the Head of Cyber Security, United Arab Emirates Government

H. E. Dr. Mohamed Al-Kuwaiti
Head of Cyber Security
United Arab Emirates Government
UAE

Relevance of AI to the development of Africa

Artificial Intelligence (AI) has emerged as a transformative technology with the potential to revolutionize various industries across the globe. The relevance of AI to the development of Africa has become increasingly apparent. AI technologies have the potential to address some of the most pressing development challenges facing the continent, from healthcare and education to infrastructure and financial inclusion.

Africa has a unique opportunity to leverage new digital technologies and AI allows to leapfrog traditional development pathways and accelerate progress by transforming various sectors, and drive economic growth and shaping the future for its people.

With a rapidly growing population and development needs, Africa benefits significantly from developing and deploying AI technologies across various sectors, including healthcare, public safety, cyber security, finance, agriculture, education, and infrastructure.

For instance, AI can be used in healthcare to improve diagnosis and treatment outcomes, especially in remote areas with limited healthcare infrastructure. In agriculture, AI can enhance productivity and improve crop yields by providing farmers with timely information on weather patterns, soil quality, and pest control. AI can also improve financial inclusion by providing underserved populations access to financial services and products.

Additionally, it can be used to improve education outcomes in Africa by providing personalized learning experiences for students, identifying areas where students are struggling and providing targeted interventions to help them improve. To maximize the potential benefits of AI in Africa, policymakers, researchers, and practitioners must prioritise developing and deploying AI technologies as part of broader development efforts. This includes investing in AI research and development and fostering collaboration between public and private stakeholders.

In conclusion, AI has the potential to transform various sectors and unlock new opportunities for growth and development in Africa. However, to fully realize the potential of AI, there is a need for adequate infrastructure, digital literacy, and the development of ethical and responsible AI solutions that are responsive to the needs of African communities. Africa can harness the power of AI to achieve sustainable and inclusive development for its people.

Significance of PanAfriCon AI 2022 to Africa

The PanAfriCon AI 2022 event was significant for Africa because it provided a unique forum for AI researchers, computational scientists, engineers, entrepreneurs, decision makers from academia, industry, and government institutions, practitioners, and policymakers from across global, to explore the potential of AI in addressing some of the continent's most pressing development challenges and discuss African strategies towards sustainable development through harnessing AI.

The conference was significant because it promoted collaboration & networking among stakeholders, and was essential in fostering the development and deployment of AI technologies that are responsive to the needs of African communities and that are in a responsible and ethical manner.

Moreover, the PanAfriCon AI 2022 event enabled participants to share insights, ideas, and best practices on the development and deployment of AI in Africa. Through this exchange, participants gained a deeper understanding of the potential applications of AI in various sectors as well as eased the pathways toward full cooperation.

Overall, the PanAfriCon AI 2022 event is a crucial opportunity for Africa to accelerate progress towards achieving Sustainable Development Goals through harnessing the power of AI.

Address of the Director General EAII

Worku Gachena Negera
Director General
Ethiopian Artificial Intelligence Institute (EAII)
Addis Ababa
Ethiopia

Artificial Intelligence (AI) has the power to change a wide range of social constructs, including the cause of Pan-Africanism. The Pan-African movement aims to further the social, economic, and political advancement of Africans on the continent as well as those of African heritage worldwide. One-seventh of the world's population resides in Africa, although the continent has fallen behind other continents in terms of economic and technological advancement. Yet, because to the quick advancement of AI and associated technologies, Africa now has a rare opportunity to leapfrog many of its current issues and accelerate its development.

By facilitating fresh perspectives, discoveries, and innovations that can help address some of the grand challenges African societies are currently grappling with, as well as by stimulating economic growth and improving living standards, AI can significantly contribute to the advancement of a Pan-African cause. However, for the Pan-African cause to be fully realized, governments, corporations, academic institutions, and civil society must all work together. The lack of data infrastructure and poor data quality in many African nations is one of the greatest challenges. Effective AI model development is difficult without access to high-quality data. Lack of knowledge and funding for AI research and development is another issue. It is crucial to make investments in the education and training of AI professionals as well as the creation of the required infrastructure to enable AI growth if we are to fully realize the promise of AI for the Pan-African cause.

Notwithstanding these difficulties, AI has immense potential to advance the Pan-African cause. AI has the potential to boost the economy, advance healthcare, optimize agricultural yield, expand educational opportunities, ensure financial inclusion, advance environmental sustainability, and many more. Yet, for this potential to be realized, all stakeholders will need to make a sustained long-term commitment and work together across the whole continent. AI has the ability to alter the Pan-African movement and provide a better future for all Africans and people of African heritage worldwide with the right investments and policies.

Address of the Core Organizing Committee Member

Solomon Kassa
International Tech Consultant & Strategist
Founder, 1888EC
Author
TV Personality
Public Speaker
Core Organizing Committee Member and MC
PanAfriCon AI 2022

The Ethiopian Artificial Intelligence Institute (EAII) hosted Ethiopia's first Artificial Intelligence (AI) conference, PanAfriCon AI 2022, with a motto "Empowering Africa Through AI," at the newly inaugurated Science Museum in Addis Ababa, Ethiopia from October 4–5, 2022. Addis Ababa, Africa's main diplomatic hub, was a delightful place to host the conference. PanAfriCon AI 2022 featured, keynote remarks, panel discussions, paper presentations and an exhibition. PanAfriCon AI 2022 brought together AI researchers, computational scientists, engineers, entrepreneurs, and decision-makers from academia, industry, and government institutions to discuss the latest trends, opportunities, and challenges of the application of AI in various sectors in the continent. The inaugural conference served as a springboard to discuss African strategies for sustainable development through leveraging AI by exchanging cutting-edge knowledge and applications used across several sectors including agriculture, healthcare, finance, services, Geographic Information System (GIS), manufacturing, and cybersecurity. The conference will continue to be a platform to catalyze Africa's excellence in AI. The 800+ participants engaged in several constructive conversations and interactions that helped make the conference a success. The meeting had a genuinely continental dimension thanks to the participation of nine countries. From the total of 49 research articles that were submitted, 25 of them were accepted and presented on the second day. They served as the conference's centerpiece to offer a wealth of discussion opportunities. Nearly equal numbers of research articles were submitted for each of the major conference topic areas, namely AI in public service, cyber security, in agriculture, in public health, in robotics, in finance, in Geographic Information System, and trustworthy/ethical AI. Of the total number of presented research articles, 16 of these are included in this proceedings volume, the first time that abstracts have been published by EAII, host of PanAfriCon AI 2022.

"By focusing human interactions on several studies, AI is the ability to optimize computerized machines for real solutions using special technology practices. We do not want to cultivate a generation that only observes and adopts the world's industrial revolution from a distance," said Prime Minister Abiy Ahmed (PhD) when he first officially announced his AI vision for Ethiopia in 2020. If used properly, ethically, and responsibly, AI has a huge potential in bringing solutions to the most crucial problems facing the African continent today, both for the public and private sectors. AI applications continue to expand potential for African growth and the achievement of the Sustainable Development Goals (SDGs.)

Generous support for the conference was provided by the Prime Minister Office of Ethiopia, Ethio telecom, and others. I encourage the next PanAfriCon AI conference to seek a higher level of African nations and sectoral involvement and funding from multiple stakeholders to adequately support the involvement of young AI scientists from across the continent. All in all, the inaugural PanAfriCon AI 2022 in Addis Ababa was very successful. The keynote remarks, panel discussion, and abstract presentations brought AI practitioners and stakeholders together and made it possible for AI non-experts to gain insight into the field. The next PanAfriCon AI is expected to take place in Addis Ababa in the 4th quarter of 2023.

Given the speed with which AI is advancing, I anticipate that these future PanAfriCon AI conferences will be as stimulating and fascinating as this most recent one was, as indicated by the contributions presented in this proceedings volume.

Organization

Ethiopian Artificial Intelligence Institute
Addis Ababa, Ethiopia

Conference Patron

H. E. Dr. Abiy Ahmed Ali

Prime Minister, Federal Democratic Republic of Ethiopia, Peace Nobel Laureate, Addis Ababa, Ethiopia

General Chairs

Taye Girma Debelee — Ethiopian Artificial Intelligence Institute, Ethiopia
Achim Ibenthal — HAWK Univ. of Applied Sciences & Arts, Germany
Friedhelm Schwenker — Ulm University, Germany

Program Committee

Worku Gachena Negera — Ethiopian Artificial Intelligence Institute, Ethiopia
Israel Goytom — Chapa, Ethiopia
Solomon Kassa — 1888EC, Ethiopia
Yehualashet Megeresa — Ethiopian Artificial Intelligence Institute, Ethiopia
Samuel Rahimeto — Ethiopian Artificial Intelligence Institute, Ethiopia

Cordula Reisch	HAWK Univ. of Applied Sciences & Arts, Germany
Billene Seyoum	Office of the Prime Minister of Ethiopia, Ethiopia
Girmaw Abebe Tadesse	IBM Research Africa, Kenya

Submission Platform

| Lilsa Benti | Ethiopian Artificial Intelligence Institute, Ethiopia |
| Friedhelm Schwenker | Ulm University, Germany |

Conference Sponsors

Collaborating Partners

Event Organizer

Conference Site

The conference took place in Addis Ababa's new Science Museum, which was inaugurated just one day before the event. Located in the neighborhood of the Freedom Park and the presidential palace, it is likewise close to the African Union headquarters. More conference information can be obtained from https://panafriconai.org/.

Peer Reviewers

Shigeo Abe	Kobe University, Japan
Mesfin Abebe	Adama Science & Technology University, Ethiopia
Sinshaw Bekele Habte	Addis Ababa University, Ethiopia
Stefan Faußer	University of Applied Sciences, Neu-Ulm, Germany
Fraol Gelana	Ethiopian Artificial Intelligence Institute, Ethiopia
Shimelis Getu Assefa	Univ. of Denver, USA
Taye Girma Debelee	Ethiopian Artificial Intelligence Institute, Ethiopia
Beakal Gizachew	Addis Ababa Institute of Technology, Ethiopia
Israel Goytom	Chapa, Ethiopia
Rolf-Rainer Grigat	Technical Univ. Hamburg-Harburg, Germany
Achim Ibenthal	HAWK Univ. of Appl. Sciences & Arts, Germany
Worku Jifara	Adama Science & Technology University, Ethiopia
Simon-Christian Klein	Technical University of Braunschweig, Germany
Adane Leta	University of Gonder, Ethiopia
Getachew Mamo	Jimma University, Ethiopia
Yehualashet Megeresa	Ethiopian Artificial Intelligence Institute, Ethiopia
Henock Mulugeta	Addis Ababa Institute of Technology, Ethiopia
Srinivas Nune	Adama Science & Technology University, Ethiopia

Contents

AI in Public Health

Robust Cough Analysis System for Diagnosis of Tuberculosis Using Artificial Neural Network

Amsalu Fentie Jember[1]($\boxtimes$), Yehualashet Megersa Ayano[2],
and Taye Girma Debelee[2,3]

[1] University of Gondar, Gondar, Ethiopia
amsalu.fentie@uog.edu.et
[2] Ethiopian Artificial Intelligence Institute, Addis Ababa, Ethiopia
[3] Addis Ababa Science and Technology University, Addis Ababa, Ethiopia

Abstract. This research proposed a robust and easily applied method for tuberculosis (TB) screening system based on the analysis of patients' cough sounds. The coughing sound of patients with TB have distinct mathematical features or information that can indicate a disease. For this research, dateset of 6476 cough and non-cough sound events was collected from patients with various respiratory diseases from Bahir Dar Felege Hiwot compressive specialized hospital using three different recorders. An automatic cough detection and classification system were implemented using an artificial neural network (ANN) and a support vector machine. The algorithms used Mel frequency cepstral coefficient (MFCC) features to detect cough sound from the recording, and then classify it as TB or non-TB. The MFCCs are machine-based methods for detecting and classifying sounds by mimic human hearing perception. Audio signal processing was done to extract the robust MFCC features, which were achieved by pre-processing and feature engineering efforts. The ANN outperforms the SVM in cough detection, with a 98.2% accuracy and an F1-score of 98.1%, and in TB/non-TB classification, with a 92.3% accuracy and an F1-score of 87.7%. The result shows the potential of the proposed cough sound analysis framework for the diagnosis of TB. This study contributes to the development of a robust TB diagnosis system that addresses fundamental gaps in the cough sound analysis area and can be transformed into a cost-effective alternative to the existing diagnosis.

Keywords: Neural Network · Tuberculosis · Mel frequency cepstral coefficient

1 Introduction

1.1 Overview of Tuberculosis

Tuberculosis (TB) is a bacterial infection caused by Mycobacterium tuberculosis (MTB) which mainly affects the lungs. It is one of the top 10 killers worldwide.

© The Author(s), under exclusive license to Springer Nature Switzerland AG 2023
T. Girma Debelee et al. (Eds.): PanAfriCon AI 2022, CCIS 1800, pp. 3–26, 2023.
https://doi.org/10.1007/978-3-031-31327-1_1

Provided the correct medication that allows the patient to take antimicrobial drugs for 6 months, TB is a curable and treatable disease [1]. There are various existing tests for TB such as chest radiography, tuberculin skin test, and gene-Xperts, but they are expensive or need highly skilled physicians and laboratory facilities [2,3]. Therefore, there is a need for an inexpensive, quick diagnosis process and easily accessible solution for TB diagnosis in developing countries.

1.2 Diagnosis Using Cough Sound

Cough offers significant information on the health of the airways (vocal track) and is very useful in assessing the disease [4]. Analysis of the cough sound using digital signal processing is to calculate the spectral features of cough sound events, which are then used by intelligent algorithms to diagnose various pulmonary diseases. Detection and classification of cough sounds have been an area of research since 1989 to the diagnosis of different pulmonary diseases [5,6]. In digital signal processing, cough detection is a technique of separating cough events from other sounds, which is useful for obtaining data on the frequency and strength of cough and can provide valuable insight into the treatment of patients and the seriousness of the disease. Cough classification is aimed at diagnosing particular diseases or disorders by analyzing cough sounds. It uses spectral features and is usually used for the analysis of cough frequency, to a specific disease. Several methods were proposed in recent times for the automatic detection [7], counting [8], and classification of cough [9].

A cough detection algorithm for continuous cough counting systems using an event detection algorithm by thresholding a smoothed energy measure has been designed for monitoring patient recovery from pulmonary TB [10]. In [11], automatic cough events detection was constructed using spectral features from acoustic signals using a logistic regression model to classify cough from non-cough signals. The performance of the algorithm was evaluated on 980 coughs and more than 1000 non-cough sounds events, from 43 patients. In [12], a cough detector using a wearable microphone was developed based on neural networks. The model is trained with audio recordings collected from 9 pulmonary disease patients. A frame of 200 ms was split into four windows of 50 ms, and 42 features (13 MFCCs, 13 deltas, 13 delta-delta, and 3 log energy) were computed from each window. For the detection of cough, principal components analysis (PCA) and deep learning networks (DLN) based on TensorFlow were used in [13]. Feature extraction was done using PCA, model training using DLN, and graph model computation was used by TensorFlow, and the PCA+DLN model performed better than the DLN model.

A dry and wet cough sound classifier has been designed with 178 cough events from 46 subjects in [14]. Features like bispectrum score, non-Gaussianity score (NGS), formants frequencies, log energy (LogE), kurtosis, and MFCC were used for classification. In [9], cough sound analysis has been designed for pneumonia and asthma classification using ANN for 18 patients with a total of 674 cough events. In this study, 22 features were computed (13 MFCCs, first five formant frequencies, zero-crossing rate, NGS, and Shannon entropy).

They used an ANN with 1 input layer with linear activation function, 2 hidden layers with sigmoid activation function, and an output layer. In [15], a cough analysis system has been developed to diagnose pertussis by analyzing cough signals using logistic regression. Features like MFCC, crest factor, maximum frequency, spectral roll-off, spectral kurtosis, spectral slope, band power, spectral flatness, the spectral standard deviation are extracted from 38 audio recordings and used to train and test the cough sound, detection model. Automatic detection of TB has been designed to differentiate TB positive from healthy controls using cough sounds analysis, in [7]. The dataset was built from 17 TB-infected individuals and 21 healthy individuals. A total of 746 cough events were extracted and then used for logistic regression classifier training. Features such as log spectral energies and MFCC are used to develop models and reported Sensitivity of 95% and Specificity of 72%.

Despite efforts and promising results in the use of cough sound for diagnosis of various pulmonary diseases, robustness to various recording environments and different types of recorders, as well as fully automating the process by integrating cough sound detection and classification, remains a challenging task. The previous studies for TB diagnosis used data from TB patients and healthy people, but data from patients with diseases similar to TB were not included. The classification between coughs caused by TB and coughs caused by other lung diseases has yet to be investigated. In previous studies for TB diagnosis the cough sounds were recorded in a specially designed facility under controlled environments. There was no background noise, and the silences had a consistent energy level, but this differs from realistic conditions. This study proposes a robust signal pre-processing method for removing background noise and versatile energy level silences from data recorded in noisy environments (clinical settings in real-world environments). The proposed method automatically extracts cough events from recordings and categorizes them as TB or non-TB cough. It is simple and effective to implement into practice.

2   Datasets Preparation

The recordings of sound data (both cough and non-cough sound) were collected from January 2020 to March 2020 from Ethiopia Bahir Dar Felege Hiwot compressive specialized hospital. Table 1, shows several patients with coughs due to different respiratory diseases, that are included in this data collection. The recording data were collected from patients after their cases are identified by the medical experts using clinical diagnoses such as GeneXpert, chest x-ray, computed tomography scan (CT scan), and Bronchoscopy. The dataset is labeled as TB and non-TB for the cough classification model. Pneumonia, asthma, bronchitis, and all other diseases cough listed in Table 1 except TB are all included in the non-TB labeled data. To build a robust system, recordings were collected using three different recorders, a Philips(DVT1200) digital Voice handheld recorder, an HM 1000 microphone, and an Infinix Hot 8 (model-X650C) smartphone. The Philips Digital Voice handheld recorder has a 1 channel built-in microphone,

Table 1. Number of patients who participated in this data collection.

No.	Case	Number of patients
1	TB	15
2	Pneumonia	38
3	Asthma	4
4	Bronchiectasis	6
5	Obstructive airway, Pleural effusion, Rt lung mass, URTI, Cardiomegaly, Lung Cancer, Allergic rhinitis, and Interstitial lung disease (ILD)	1 each

WAV recording formats, and a 24 kHz sample rate. The HM1000 consists with a 10 m (33 ft) cable, a spring steel hanging clamp that precisely aligns the microphone and keeps it fixed in place, and a balanced XLR audio output with WAV formats. Infinix Hot 8 (model-X650C) is a Dirac surround sound and support sound formats of AAC, AAC+, AMR, WAV, eAAC+. There had been variations in the recording instruments, noise levels, and sampling frequencies, associated with each recording. Each recording was loaded into Audacity software and, listening to the audio, and detected the cough events and extracted each cough event with 16 bits per sample and a sampling rate of 44.1 kHz, which is CD standard. Figure 1 shows a raw recording of a patient recorded using an HM 1000 microphone.

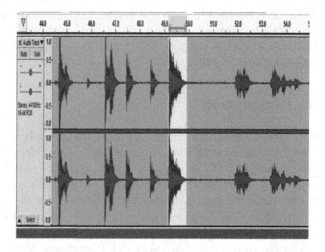

Fig. 1. The waveform of a raw recording of a patient.

Cough Detection and Classification Dataset. A total of 6,476 sound events are extracted and represented in this cough detection dataset (CDD), among them 3,238 events were labeled as cough sounds and 3,238 were non-cough events. This CDD was used for training and testing for the cough detection algorithm. A total of 3,238 sound events are represented in the cough classification dataset (CCD), among them 1,080 cough events were labeled as TB cough sounds and 2,158 were non-TB cough events. The CCD was used for training and testing for the cough classification algorithm. Represented within these cough events are robust data, which is a multitude of different pulmonary diseases recorded by a microphone, handheld recorder, and phone. One aim of this research is to develop a robust system for various recording devices and different pulmonary diseases. Represented within these non-cough events are a multitude of other audio sources such as speech, ceiling fan, footsteps, sounds from the outside environment (ambulance), sounds of closing the doors, sounds typical for walking, motor vehicles, laughter, sounds as the mobile device moved about, recording office sound effects, free tools recording effects and the phone ringing, and other types of background sounds. All cough sound events and other non-cough sounds in this datasets are audible. All data collects were approved by Bahir Dar Felege Hiwot Compressive Specialized Hospital Out-Patient Department.

3   Cough Detection and Classification Methods

3.1   Cough Detection Method

This research aims to develop a robust cough analysis method for different types of recorders in a moderately noisy environment and different lung diseases. It focuses on robust feature extraction for differentiating cough sounds from non-cough sounds within recordings, and then classifying coughs as TB cough or non-TB cough. This was accomplished through pre-processing and feature engineering efforts. This automatic cough detection and classification method have two major steps. The first is cough detection, which involves separating cough events from non-cough sounds in a recording by removing undesirable signals via pre-processing and then extracting features for classifiers. The second stage is cough classification, which extracts discriminating features for classifiers to classify the detected cough events in the first step as TB cough or non-TB cough.

Cough detection is a technique of separating cough events from other sounds. Manual cough detection by listing each recording is very time-consuming. The sound events in CDD were used to train the learning models, which were then used to detect cough automatically, from the newly recorded data. The cough segment detected by the model can then be used as the expected input for subsequent cough classifiers. Before performing the feature extraction, the sound signals were pre-processed, then detection was performed using those extracted features. The cough detector learning algorithms' efficiency depends on both how well the features are extracted and how well the sound signals are pre-processed. The general workflow for automatic cough detection is displayed in Fig. 2. The first step aims at removing background noise and silence within the recordings. Normalization and filtering were performed on the audio recording and then segmenting each recording into short events and features were extracted for each

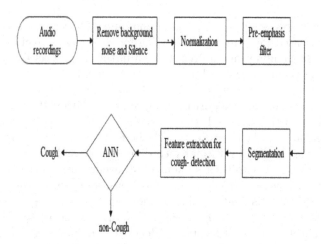

Fig. 2. The general workflow for automatic cough detection system.

sound event. Finally, with those extracted features, the learning models training, and testing were performed. The outcome of each step is highly dependent on the previous steps. To enhance the system's robustness capacity to identify cough events, each processing step was investigated and improved.

3.2   Background Noise and Silence Removal

This research proposes a robust signal preprocessing method for removing background noise and versatile energy level silences from data recorded in noisy environments (clinical settings in real-world environments). This method is advantageous because it is analogous to real-world conditions. Equation (1) below models the discrete-time audio recordings with their components, which are used to demonstrate the changes after pre-processing.

$$x[n] = x_a[n] + x_{bn}[n] + x_s[n] \tag{1}$$

where $x[n]$ is the audio recording, $x_a[n]$ are the audio components (cough sound and non-cough sound), $x_{bn}[n]$ represents the background, and $x_s[n]$ is the silence.

To suppress the background noise $x_{bn}[n]$ from $x[n]$, a Butterworth band-pass filter was used to pass frequencies within a range. The Butterworth filter is a flat band filter at most, and the passband or stopband does not have a ripple. It has a wide region of transition from passband to stopband, and the response of frequency, group delay, the impulse response is much better and more practical than other filters [16]. The filter is bandpass, second order and has a low and high cut-off frequency of $Lf_c = 20$ Hz and of $Hf_c = 20$ kHz respectively, which is the lower and upper boundaries of human hearing.

After eliminating the background noise, the estimated audio recording is given below in Eq. (2).

$$x_e[n] = x_{ea}[n] + x_{es}[n] \qquad (2)$$

where $x_{ea}[n]$ is the estimates of is the audio components (cough sound and non-cough sound), and $x_{es}[n]$ is the estimate of silence.

The next step is removing silence from the estimated audio recording. The removal of silence focuses on the detection of frames that do not contain sound events relative to cough events or other non-cough events. Different methods are used to identify and remove the silence. The audio recordings are conducted at clinics and have moderate levels of noise (versatile or dynamic energy level silences), so this issue must be resolved by the silence removal process. The standard deviation was used to solve this problem since it is the effective method of silence removal for performing under moderate noisy conditions. Standard deviation (σ) is a measure used to quantify a signal's variance or dispersion [17]. It is the square root of variance by evaluating the variation of each data point (amplitude value) relative to the mean. The standard deviation of audio recording is calculated as follows:

1. The first step is to split the audio recording into several short frames.
2. The mean (μ_i) of a frame (Eq. (3)) is determined by summing all the data points and dividing them by the total number (N) of points in a frame.

$$\mu_i = \frac{\sum_{n=1}^{N} x_{en}}{N} \qquad (3)$$

where, x_{en} the data points of estimate frames of audio recording and N is the number of data points in a frame.

3. The variance (σ_i^2) for each data point of a frame i is calculated using Eq. (4), by subtracting the mean (μ_i) from each data point. Then, each of the resulting values is squared and the results are summed up and divided by the number of points minus one.

$$\sigma_i^2 = \frac{\sum_{k=1}^{W} x_{ei}(k) - \mu_i^2}{W-1} \qquad (4)$$

where, $x_{ei}(k)$ are the estimated frames of audio recording, W is the window size, i is the current frame, and k is the current sample.

4. By square rooting the variance resulting in number 3, the standard deviation is obtained.

There is a higher variance within a recording if the data points are further from the mean. For each audio recordings, the audio event and silence were determined using a threshold (T) value as shown in Eq. (5).

$$T = \mu(min_\sigma) + \sigma(min_\sigma) \qquad (5)$$

A higher standard deviation refers to audio bursts and a lower standard deviation would be correlated with silence.

3.3   Amplitude Normalization

Audio recordings have variations in waveform amplitudes due to patients sitting at various distances from the recorders, different recording devices, or the naturally different sound loudness of the patients. Audio normalization can compensate for those differences by boosting the sound to a target level by altering the overall audio recordings by the same amount, without clipping and distorting the peak. For each sound recording event, the normalization was performed as follow:

1. Split the sound event into non-overlapping frames.
2. Compute the energy of each frame. It can be calculated by:

$$E\left(i\right) = \frac{1}{N}\sum_{n=1}^{N}|x_i\left(n\right)|^2 \tag{6}$$

   where N is the length of the frame, i is the current frame, and n is the current sample.
3. Find maximum standard deviation (σ_{max}) of all event energy frames and the energy standard deviation (σ_{energy}) of each frame.
4. Calculate the ratio $r = \frac{\sigma_{energy}}{\sigma_{max}}$ for all samples and multiply all samples with the mean.
5. The waveform has been scaled such that the energy of the events among sound events is normalized.

3.4   Pre-emphasis and Segmentation

A pre-emphasis is used to amplify the magnitude of higher-frequencies components of the sound events, to enhance the Signal to Noise Ratio (SNR). Pre-emphasis reduces the adverse effects of events such as recording device distortion in subsequent parts of the environment and flattens the spectrum. At this stage, Eq. (7) was used on sound events to enhance SNR with a $\varepsilon = 0.96$ which is the cut-off standard for the pre-emphasis [18].

$$x_i\left[n\right] = x_i\left[n\right] - \varepsilon x_i\left[n - 1\right] \tag{7}$$

This process (pre-emphasis) increases the energy of sound signals at a higher frequency and gives more information. After preprocessing, the next step was to segment the filtered sound events into a 100 ms-size non-overlapping block. The energy of each segment was computed after segmentation, and a segment with a pick value was selected. To reduce the computational complexity of processing all segments of a sound event, it is possible to represent a sound event with a pick-value segment. Then, for further processing of the feature extraction, this pick-value segment of a sound event was used.

3.5   Feature Extraction

In cough signal analysis, feature engineering is a central task that is the process of converting raw sound events into features that better represent the underlying problem to enhance the accuracy of machine learning or deep learning model on unseen data. The innovative aspect of feature engineering is to find ways to develop the model by extracting different unique features used to discriminate cough events from other non-cough events and further classification of coughs. It helps the algorithms to understand data and decide patterns that can enhance the learning algorithms' efficiency. Much of the effectiveness of machine learning is the success of the feature engineering process that a learning model can comprehend [19]. The aim of feature extraction is not only dimensionality reduction, but also extracting unique features present in the cough events, as well as to reduce the risk of overfitting, speeding up training, and reducing the complexity of computations.

There are a variety of sound features aimed at the identification and classification of cough signals. In this paper, MFCC was used, because it is the prominent and more robust feature in cough signal processing [20] and it gives consistent and robust results to noise because it is based on human perception of hearing [21]. MFCCs represent the short-term spectral of audio based on the human hearing mechanism [22]. In nature, cough sounds are complex signals, indicating that the respiratory tract (system) carries essential information and provides the tract with cough sound from its substructure. MFCCs produces a sound signal representation, varying from other cepstral features is it use the Mel-scale in the frequency bands. In MFCC the bands are arranged logarithmically, which mimic the human hearing mechanism. The efficacy of MFCCs is their ability to efficiently represent the significant part of the vocal tract (shape of the vocal tract, which originates cough or non-cough sound) [4]. Figure 3 explains the concrete steps of the MFCC.

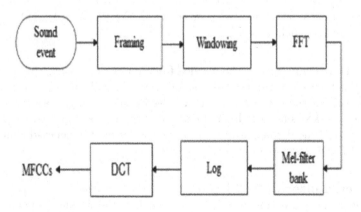

Fig. 3. MFCCs features calculation flow diagram.

Framing. In MFCCs, the selected sound event is split into frames of short length. A spectral-domain analysis (e.g., Fourier transform) yields good results for stationary signals, but not for non-stationary signals. Cough sound signals are volatile and have non-stationary characteristics, so computing a single Fourier transformation to the entire cough event or record is meaningless. But for the frame of short length, the properties of the cough signal are considered stationary, and thus spectral analysis can be applied to it [23]. For this reason, the spectral domain analysis is computed for successive frames of the sound signal. The frame duration is usually between 20–40 ms. Each frame was overlaid on the front frame to smooth the transition by accounts frames at window edges and provide equal weight between frames.

Windowing. The next step in the MFCC is to eliminate discontinuities or spectral leakage at the edges of the frames by windowing all frames. There are several window functions, but the hamming window is used to conduct windowing, which is better to eliminate spectral leakage [24]. Equation (8) is a Hamming window that is used at both edges of a frame to reduce spectral leakage.

$$w(m) = 0.54 - 0.46cos(\frac{2\pi m}{N_m - 1})...0 \leq m \leq N_m - 1 \tag{8}$$

where, $w(m)$ is the window function, N_m is the number of samples within each frame. Overlapping Hamming windows were used to eliminate the degraded events at the boundaries, which improves how well the MFCC can describe different sounds. Before the fast Fourier transform, the framed signals $x(m)$ were multiplied with the hamming function. The output signal after windowing is presented in Eq. (9).

$$y(m) = x(m)w(m) \qquad 0 \leq m \leq N_m - 1 \tag{9}$$

where, $y(m)$ is the output windowed signal, $x(m)$ is the input framed signal, $w(m)$ is the Hamming window shown in Eq. (9), and N_m is the number of samples within each frame.

Fast Fourier Transform. The cochlea function can be considered to be identical to the Fourier transform, transforming raw sound vibrational waves into neural signals in the frequency domain. The frequency distribution of a sound should be assessed since the human ear exercises this skill in hearing [25]. The FFT converts time-domain frames into the spectrum (frequency-domain). The result of FFT is a spectrum or periodogram.

Mel-Filter Banks. In the FFT spectrum, the frequency range is wide and has a linear spectrum (follow a linear scale). But the frequency perception of the human ear follows a non-linear scale, which is linear up to 1000 Hz Hz and logarithmic above. MFCCs use a non-linear frequency scale since it is the perception of human hearing [26]. The filter Bank of melody scale called Mel-Scale, which describes the frequency perception of the human ear was used as a pass-band filter at this stage. The tone of the sound signal with a real frequency is measured in Hz, and the perceptual scale of pitches is measured on Mel-Scale. As mentioned above, the Mel-Scale is linear up to 1000 Hz Hz and logarithmic above, so the following formula approximates each real linear frequency scale to the Mel-Scale.

$$f_m = 2595 \log_{10} \left(1 + \frac{f}{700}\right) \tag{10}$$

where f is the real frequency in Hz, and f_m is the perceptual Mel-Scale frequency in a melody (Mel).

In MFCC processing, Mel-frequency warping is realized by triangular band-pass filter banks in the frequency domain. The spectrum of signals (cough and non-cough sound segments) is passed through the Mel-filter banks, which spaced non-uniformly with Mel scale, then normally obtain the perceptual frequency, that can properly simulate auditory processing [27].

Log. After acquiring the Mel-spectrum, the next step is calculating the logarithm (*log*) of the squared magnitude or power spectrum of the output. The reason for this is that the dynamic range of amplitudes can be compressed by a logarithm. Since the response of the human ear to the sound signal level is logarithmic, it is less sensitive to small-amplitude differences. This makes the estimated frequency less sensitive to small amplitude changes due to the patient mouth being closer or far to the recorders.

Discrete Cosine Transform (DCT). In this step, the DCT was carried out on the log Mel-spectrum to convert it back to the time domain, and the result is called MFCC. Cepstrum is the inverse Fourier transform of the spectrum. The DCT decorrelates the filter bank coefficients and generates a compressed representation of the log filter banks. Then, the DCT of the log Mel-scale of the power spectrum can be estimated by Eq. (11).

$$MfCC_w = \sum_{k=1}^{K} L_{Ms} \cos\left[w(k - \frac{1}{2})\frac{\pi}{K}\right], \quad w = 1, 2, ...W \tag{11}$$

where, W is the required number of MFCC coefficients, L_{Ms} is log Mel-scale of the power spectrum, and K is the number of filters.

Typically, for cough sound analysis the first 13 coefficients are retained for each window and the rest are discarded. The set of 13 MFCC is called acoustic vectors. Therefore, each input sound signal is transformed into a sequence of MFCCs.

3.6 Cough Detection Learning Algorithms

The cough detection phase was carried out after obtaining the feature vector, to discriminate cough sound events from no cough sound events. For cough detection and classification two popular and suitable algorithms in cough analysis fields were trained and tested to select the one with the highest numerical performance. The F1-score and accuracy were used as a metric to choose optimal models and compare results during optimization.

Artificial Neural Network. The ANN operated using an algorithm to interpret nonlinear data which is independent of sequential patterns. The ANN consists of neurons, organized into input, hidden, and output layers between the input and the results, which act like biological neurons, and are learned through a technique of backpropagation [28]. The strength typically offered by ANN is its capability of extracting hidden linear and classified data in complex and high-dimensional data like cough datasets based on a supervised learning technique using non-linear decision boundaries [29]. The learning models have hyperparameters, that can influence the model's performance. Over-fitting can be avoided by optimizing model hyper parameters on a development set (selected from the training set). The hyper-parameters of a model were optimized using a brute force method called grid search to achieve the best results. The procedure begins by separating the datasets into K equal sections, with the validation set being chosen from one of the K folds and the remaining $K - 1$ folds set as the training set. This was performed until all K folds have been tested, and the final evaluation metrics were calculated by averaging all K iterations. The ANN structure consisted of a feed-forward network and all of the layers used the sigmoid transfer function to transform activation levels to output, and the approaches for this study were written in the MATLAB script.

Support Vector Machines. The SVM is a supervised machine learning algorithm for detecting and analyzing relationships. It operates by analyzing data sets using a set of parameters that are used to solve classification and regression problems. SVM determines the desired hyperplane for maximizing the distance between any two classes [30]. The hyperplane is a decision boundary that aid in the classification of data into various classes based on its attributes. The number of features of the data determines the dimension of the hyperplane. The position of the hyperplane is influenced by data points called support vectors that are closer to the hyperplane. SVM aims to find a plane with the greatest distance between support vectors referred to as the maximum margin distance, to both classes.

3.7   Cough Classification

The second phase of this study was classifying the cough events as TB disease and non-TB diseases. The method used to classify cough events as TB and non-TB diseases is extremely similar to the technique of cough detection. There are two differences between the two methods. The first difference is the dataset used for training and testing the classifier model. The dataset used for the classifier model is the cough classifier dataset (CCD). The CCD contains only cough events collected from 71 patients with various lung diseases. There are 3,238 cough events in CCD, of which 1,080 cough events were obtained from patients with TB and 2,158 cough events were obtained from 12 other different pulmonary diseases. The second differences are at the stage of pre-processing and extraction of features. The input for the classifier (cough classification artificial neural network (CC-ANN) system is the pre-processed cough events obtained from the cough detection system, so no further pre-processing is required. The classifier model begins with the extraction of features from cough events, from those previously obtained in cough detection artificial neural network (CD-ANN). Both models (CD-ANN and CC-ANN) use MFCCs features, but the extraction process has changed slightly. Figure 4 demonstrates the general workflow for the automatic cough classification system. The MFCC features were extracted from the cough events obtained from the CD-ANN model. The process of extracting features is almost similar to the technique previously used for cough detection. The differences are, in CC-ANN the frame length is 20 ms instead of 40 ms. The differences are relatively small, but they combine to make the classification neural network complex, which boosts the accuracy.

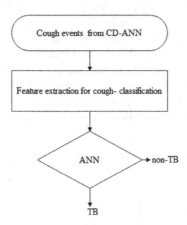

Fig. 4. The general workflow for the cough classification (TB/non-TB).

4   Implementation Result and Discussion

This section presented the results and discussion of this study stage by stage, starting from the prepared input dataset to the final result.

4.1   The Datasets Preparation Result and Discussion

The dataset (CDD and CCD) was used to train and test the models in this study. Using the technique presented in part 2 of this paper, 6476 sound events were labeled in the CDD and 3238 cough events were labeled in the CCD. The datasets were obtained from multiple pulmonary patients in a clinical setting using three different recording devices in moderately noisy environments. This system is robust to differences in recording equipment, noise levels, and sampling frequencies associated with each recording because the sounds were recorded from patients with various lung diseases. The datasets was validated since it was manually segmented using a human scorer. The datasets used in this study is robust and comparable to the previous studies in terms of datasets size, number of patients, diversity of diseases, and also diversity of recording devices.

4.2   Result and Discussion on Pre-processing Phases

The sound signals were pre-processed to eliminate background noise before the features were extracted, and then detection and classification models were developed using the extracted features. The performance of the classifier models was determined by how well the sound signals were pre-processed as well as how well the features were extracted. The recording sound signal was passed through a bandpass Butterworth filter, with low and high cut-off frequencies of 20 Hz and 20 kHz, respectively, to minimize the background noise. The filter suppressed the low and high-frequency noise components of the signal and lies within a fixed boundary. The silence was removed from the recording using the SD method after the noise from audio recording signals was suppressed. Figure 5 shows the audio recording before and after the silence was removed. There was a higher variance within a recording if the data points were further from the mean. For each audio recordings, the audio event and silence were determined using a threshold (T)

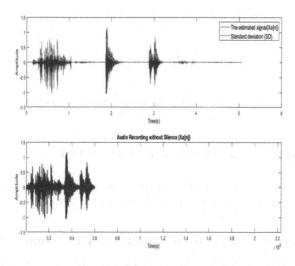

Fig. 5. Waveforms, before silence removal, and after silence removal (The threshold value is determined by Eq. (5)).

value using Eq. (5). A higher standard deviation refers to an audio event and a lower standard deviation would be correlated with silence. The audio recordings were conducted at clinics and have moderate levels of noise, so this issue was solved by the standard deviation silence removal method and it is an effective method for using in real-time conditions.

Waveform amplitudes in audio recordings varied due to patients sitting at different distances from the recorders, different recording devices, or the patients' naturally variable sound loudness. Audio normalization adjusted for these variations by raising the sound to a target level by adjusting the entire audio recordings. The waveform before and after normalization is illustrated in Fig. 6.

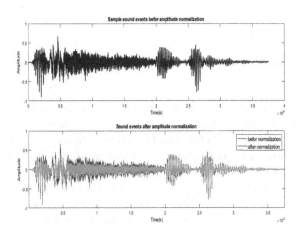

Fig. 6. Sample waveform and its normalization result.

The amplitude of the sound events has been normalized by different scaling factors based on its waveform variation. After normalization, a pre-emphasis was used to enhance the magnitude of the sound events' higher-frequency components. The filtered sound events were segmented into a 100 ms non-overlapping block. After segmentation, the energy of each segment was calculated, and a segment with a pick value was chosen as shown in Fig. 7.

This segmentation process reduces the computational complexity of processing all segments of a sound event, it is possible to represent a sound event with a pick-value segment and feature extraction was performed on this segment.

4.3   Results of Feature Extraction Process

For cough detection, a segment of each input sound event was split into frames of short length (40 ms duration with 50% overlap), considering it as stationary signal and thus spectral analysis was applied to it. The 100 ms segment in Fig. 7 was split into 4 overlapped frames. By taking into account discontinuities at window edges, the frame was overlaid to smooth the transition. The spectral

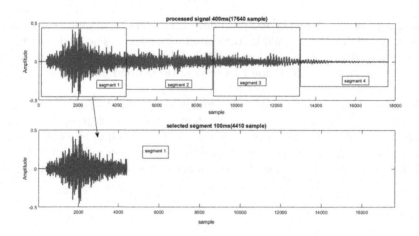

Fig. 7. Sample cough event and segmentation result.

leakages at the edges of the frames were eliminated by windowing all frames using hamming window. A framed signal, as shown in Fig. 8, was multiplied with the Hamming window, before the fast Fourier transform.

Figure 8(d) shows a framed signal after windowing, which reduces the effects of FFT leakage. FFT was calculated after windowing, and the time-domain frames were transformed to the spectrum (frequency-domain). The Fourier transform function is similar to that of the cochlea in the human ear. The function of the cochlea is to transform raw sound vibrational waves into frequency domain neural impulses.

The frequency range in the Fourier spectrum was large and followed a linear scale, whereas the human ear's frequency perception follows a non-linear scale. The Mel-Scale filter Bank, which describes the frequency perception of the human ear was used as a passband filter at this stage. The FFT spectrums of frames were passed through Mel-filter banks, which were spaced non-uniformly with Mel scale (Eq. (10)), to obtain the perceptual frequency, which can accurately mimic auditory processing. The human ear is less sensitive to small-amplitude changes of sound, but the amplitude of the FFT result had a dynamic range. By calculating the logarithm of the spectrum, the dynamic range was compressed, making the estimated spectrum less responsive to small amplitude changes. Finally, the DCT was carried out on the log Mel-spectrum to convert it to cepstrum. The DCT decorrelates the filter bank coefficients and generates a compressed representation of the log filter banks. The set of 13 cepstrum coefficients (MFCCs) for each window were held for cough sound analysis. These MFCCs are used as features for the classifier models. A vector containing $4 \times 13 = 52$ MFCC features was formed from the 100 ms segment of every sound event. This feature vector was then supplied to a classifier for the cough detection system.

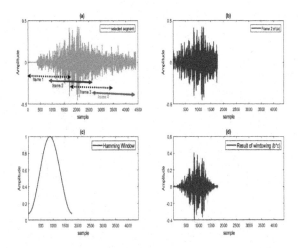

Fig. 8. Waveforms, (a) four overlapped frames of a segment, (b) frame 2 of a segment in (a), (c) Hamming window, and (d) the result of a frame in (b) multiplied by the window in (c)

The second phase of this study was classifying the detected cough event as TB disease and non-TB disease cough. The method used to classify cough events as TB and non-TB diseases used the CCD dataset and it was extremely similar to the technique of cough detection. The MFCC features were extracted from the cough events obtained from the cough detection system. For cough classification, a segment of each input sound event was split into 20 ms frames with 50% overlap. The 100 ms segment was split into nine overlapped frames, because of this parameters used above for cough detection has changed slightly. The modification enhances the effectiveness of classifier models for differentiating Tb coughs from other coughs, but it comes at the cost of increased computational complexity compared to the cough detection system. The 100 ms segment of every (TB/non-TB) cough event was used to create a vector with $9 \times 13 = 117$ MFCC features. This feature vector was then fed into a cough classification system classifier.

4.4   Hyper-parameters Optimization of the Models

The hyper-parameters of ANN were optimized using a brute force method called grid search to achieve the best results. The other hyper-parameters were adjusted or tuned using a variety of parameter combinations, and the validation method was k-fold cross-validation. The first main hyper-parameter for ANN was the number of hidden layers. The scoring method used during hidden layer optimization was root means square error. Figure 9 depicts the optimization surface for the number of hidden layers with their root means square error. The number of hidden layers was selected 28 since it had the minimum root means square error value as shown in Fig. 10.

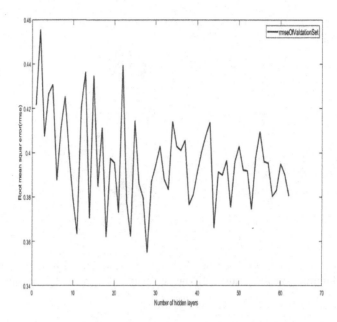

Fig. 9. The rmse value with the number of hidden layers.

The second main hyper-parameter for ANN was the learning algorithm. Table 2 depicts the ANN learning algorithms with their accuracy for both cough detection and classification systems.

Table 2. ANN (Levenberg Marquardt(LM), Gradient Descent(GD), One Step Secant(OSS) and Resilient Backpropagation(RBP)) algorithms with their accuracy.

Systems	LM	GD	OSS	RBP
Cough Detection	98.2%	93.7%	96.2%	96.9%
Cough Classification	92.3%	80.9%	88.0%	92.1%

Levenberg-Marquardt's learning algorithm was selected for both cough detection and classification with high accuracy of 98.2% and 92.3% respectively. Because of its ability to solve difficult nonlinear problems, the Levenberg-Marquardt algorithm outperformed other algorithms. It is a hybrid of Gauss-Newton and the gradient descent method; when the parameters are near to their optimal value, it acts more like the Gauss-Newton, and when they are far from their objective function, it works more like a gradient-descent. The other hyper-parameter is epochs, which represent one complete pass of the data (training data) through the learning algorithm. Figure 10 depicts the optimization surface for the performance of the model with their number of epochs for cough detection model. The best validation performance for cough detection was 0.028 at epoch 9 and the network was trained for 15 epochs. Similarly, Fig. 11 depicts the optimization surface for the performance of the model with their number of epochs for cough classification model. The best validation performance for cough detection was 0.11367 at epoch 7 and the network was trained for 13 epochs.

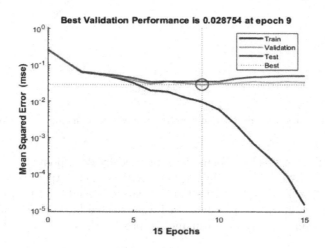

Fig. 10. Optimization for performance with number of epochs for cough detection.

Grid search was also used to optimize the hyper-parameters of SVM. Obtaining the desired hyperplane (kernel) for optimizing the distance between any two classes is the key parameter for SVM. Table 3 lists the SVM:- Linear, Radial Basis Function (RBF), Polynomial power 2 (Poly2), and Polynomial power 3 (Poly3) kernel functions for cough detection and classification systems, along with their accuracy.

Table 3. SVM kernel functions with their accuracy.

Systems	Linear	RBF	Poly2	Poly3
Cough Detection	86.9%	97.1%	91.7%	91.8%
Cough Classification	66.5%	89.4%	75.4%	75.4%

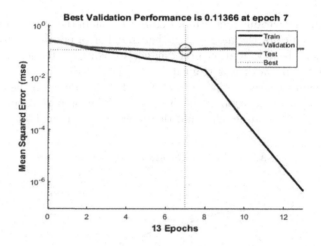

Fig. 11. Optimization for performance with number of epochs for cough classification.

The position of the hyperplane is influenced by data points called support vectors that are closer to the hyperplane. RBF kernel outperforms other kernels as shown in Table 3 due to its function space flexibility in projecting high-dimensional non-linear data. RBF kernel was selected for both cough detection and classification with high performance to project the data.

4.5   Performance Comparison of the Selected ANN and SVM Models

The accuracy and F1-score validation metrics were used to compare the performance of the two models (ANN and SVM with their selected optimal parameters). Based on the ANN and SVM, the full dataset used in the current study has 6,476 and 3,238 sound events for detection and classification respectively, from the datasets 70% were used for training, 15% were used for validation, and 15% were used for the test. The confusion matrix for cough detection ANN is displayed in Fig. 12. The accuracy and F1-score of the models were evaluated on overall sets. Table 4 shows the performance of cough detection and cough classification systems on overall sets for ANN and SVM classifiers.

Table 4. Overall accuracy and F1-score of the models.

Models	Cough Detection		Cough Classification	
	Accuracy	F1-score	Accuracy	F1-score
ANN	98.2%	98.1%	92.3%	87.7%
SVM	97.1%	96.6%	89.4%	82.2%

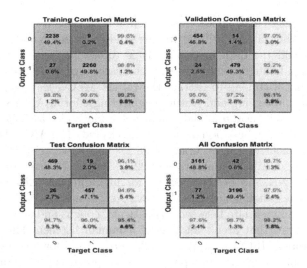

Fig. 12. The confusion matrix for cough detection ANN.

In both cough detection and cough classification, the two models, ANN and SVM, achieved acceptable accuracy and F1-score valuesThis indicates that MFCCs, which are based on perceptual models of the human auditory system, can uniquely represent sound signals using feature engineering effort. Due to its capacity to adjust the size of a network, the ANN outperforms SVM models in solving high dimensionality nonlinear problems.

4.6 Research Contributions

This research contributes to the advancement and novel methods of automatic cough analysis methods for TB diagnosis using cough analysis. The development of a robust cough dataset in this study will be useful for future research in this area. The dataset used in this study was robust in terms of dataset size, the number of patients, diversity of diseases (twelve different pulmonary diseases), and also diversity of recording devices (three different recording devices to record sounds). This study adds a robust technique for signal preprocessing and feature extraction for tuberculosis diagnosis using patients' cough sounds. Another novel contribution of this study is the integration of an automated cough detection system with a TB/non-TB cough classification system. This is the first study in this field to differentiate TB cough from other similar lung diseases cough with high classification accuracy, and the proposed method can help clinicians in resource-limited areas.

5 Conclusion and Recommendation

The use of cough data obtained from patients with various pulmonary diseases and recorded using three different recorders in a clinical setting in a moderately noisy environment to develop a robust system for TB diagnosis was investigated in this study. The dataset utilized in this study was compared to data from other studies, and the data in this study is robust in terms of dataset size, the number of patients, disease diversity, and recording device diversity. Audio signal processing was done to extract the robust MFCC features, which were achieved by pre-processing and feature engineering efforts. An ANN and SVM were used to create an automated cough detection and classification system, and the ANN with the best performance was selected. The ANN algorithms for cough detection achieved an accuracy of 98.2% and F1-score of 98.1%, and for TB/non-TB classification, an accuracy of 92.3% and an F1-score of 87.7%. This indicates that ANN is a better classifier for high-dimensional and non-linear complex data like cough sound classification. As a result, we can conclude that the system can differentiate between TB patients' coughs and coughs caused by other lung diseases that aren't audible by a human listener. This shows that using cough sound MFCCs features as a diagnostic tool for TB testing can be a viable solution. However, before putting the proposed approach into practice, it is important to note that the promising outcomes of this research should be followed up with further research.

To advance this research, the dataset must first be analyzed and given attention. Even if the dataset used in this research was robust and comparable to those used in previous similar studies, the development of the best reliable dateset remains a priority. A comprehensive dataset could be built by increasing the dataset's size, including coughs from patients with other lung diseases such as Coronavirus (COVID-19), including data from pediatric patients, and collecting sound recordings from various settings. In some clinics, the cough recording space is too small, resulting in echo, an echo cancellation algorithm from recordings would be useful to improve the cough processing algorithm. More research should be conducted in the future to resolve these issues, and the method should be developed into a smartphone application.

References

1. World Health Organization: Global Tuberculosis Report, Geneva (2020). ISBN 978-92-4-1565646
2. Horsburgh, R., Barry, C.E., Lange, C.: Treatment of tuberculosis. New Engl. J. Med. **373**, 2149–60 (2015)
3. Singer-Leshinsky, S.: Pulmonary tuberculosis: improving diagnosis and management. Am. Acad. Physician Assistants **29**(2) (2016)
4. Smith, J., Ashurst, H., Jack, S., Woodcock, A., Earis, J.: The description of cough sounds by healthcare professionals. BioMed Centra **2**(1) (2006)
5. Smith, J., Woodcock, A.: New developments in the objective assessment of cough. Lung **186**(1), 48–54 (2007)
6. Piirila, P., Sovijarvi, A.: Differences in acoustic and dynamic characteristics of spontaneous cough in pulmonary diseases. Chest **96**(1), 46–53 (1989)
7. Botha, G., et al.: Detection of tuberculosis by automatic cough sound analysis. Physiol. Measur. **39** (2018)

8. Barry, S.J., Dane, A.D., Morice, A.H., et al.: The automatic recognition and counting of cough. Cough **2**, 8 (2006)
9. Amrulloh, Y., Abeyratne, U., Swarnkar, V., Triasih, R.: Cough sound analysis for pneumonia and asthma classification in pediatric population. In: IEEE 6th International Conference on Intelligent Systems, Modelling and Simulation (2015)
10. Brian, T., Comina, G., Larson, S., Bravard, M., López, J., Robert, H.: Cough detection algorithm for monitoring patient recovery from pulmonary tuberculosis. In: Annual International Conference of the IEEE Engineering in Medicine and Biology Society (2011)
11. Pramono, R., Imtiaz, A., Rodriguez-Villegas, E.: Automatic cough detection in acoustic signal using spectral features, vol. 19. IEEE (2019). ISBN 978-1-5386-1311-5
12. Kadambi, P., et al.: Towards a wearable cough detector based on neural networks. IEEE (2018). 978-1-5386-4658-8/18
13. Khomsay, S., Vanijjirattikhan, R., Suwatthikul, J.: Cough detection using PCA and deep learning. IEEE (2019). 978-1-7281-0893-3/19
14. Swarnkar, V., Abeyratne, U., Amrulloh, Y., Chang, A.: Automated algorithm for wet/dry cough sound classification. In: IEEE Engineering in Medicine and Biology Society, 34th Annual International Conference of the IEEE EMBS (2012)
15. Pramono, R., Imtiaz, S., Rodriguez, V.: A cough-based algorithm for automatic diagnosis of pertussis. PLoS ONE **11**(9) (2016)
16. Rao, E., Muralidhar, P., Raghuramakrishna, S.: Audio equalizer with fractional order Butterworth filter. Int. J. Eng. Manag. Res. **5**(5), 266–272 (2015)
17. Cohen-McFarlane, M., Goubran, R., Knoefel, F.: Comparison of silence removal methods for the identification of audio cough events. IEEE (2019). 978-1-5386-1311-5/19
18. Swarnkar, V., Abeyratne, U., Amrulloh, Y., Hukins, C., Triasih, R., Setyati, A.: Neural network based algorithm for automatic identification of cough sounds. In: Annual International Conference of the IEEE Engineering in Medicine and Biology Society (2013)
19. Nargesian, F., Samulowitz, H., Khurana, U., Khalil, E., Turaga, D.: Learning feature engineering for classification. In: International Joint Conference on Artificial Intelligence, University of Toronto (2017)
20. Sai, P., Rao, N., Kumar, N., Brahmaiah, P., Ajay, D.: Cough classification tool for early detection and recovery monitoring of tuberculosis and asthma. In: 4th International Conference on Computing, Communication and Sensor Network, CCSN 2015 (2015)
21. Prithvi, P., Kumar, K.: Comparative analysis of MFCC, LFCC, RASTA-PLP. Int. J. Sci. Eng. Res. (IJSER) **4**(5) (2016)
22. Mermelstein, S., Davis, P.: Comparison of parametric representations for monosyllabic word recognition in continuously spoken sentences. IEEE Trans. Acoust. Speech Signal Process. **28**, 357–366 (1980)
23. Knocikova, J., Korpas, J., Vrabec, M., Javorka, M.: Wavelet analysis of voluntary cough sound in patients with respiratory diseases. J. Physiol. Pharmacol. **59**, 331–340 (2008)
24. Bhatnagar, A.C., Sharma, L., Kumar, R.: Analysis of hamming window using advance peak windowing method. Int. J. Sci. Res. Eng. Technol. (IJSRET) **1**(4) (2012)
25. Hu, F., Cao, X.: An auditory feature extraction method for robust speaker recognition. In: IEEE 14th International Conference on Communication Technology (2012)

26. Shi, Y., Liu, H., Wang, Y., Cai, M., Xu, W.: Theory and application of audio-based assessment of cough. Hindawi (2018). 9845321/18
27. Muda, L., Begam, M., Elamvazuthi, I.: Voice recognition algorithms using Mel frequency cepstral coefficient (MFCC) and dynamic time warping (DTW) techniques. J. Comput. **2**(3) (2010)
28. Kaushik, A.C., Sahi, S.: HOGPred: artificial neural network-based model for orphan GPCRs. Neural Comput. Appl. **29**(4), 985–992 (2016). https://doi.org/10.1007/s00521-016-2502-6
29. Smitha, Shetty, S., Hegde, S., Dodderi, T.: Classification of healthy and pathological voices using MFCC and ANN. In: Second International Conference on Advances in Electronics, Computer and Communications (ICAECC). IEEE (2018)
30. Cortes, C., Vapnik, V.: Support-vector networks. Mach. Learn. **20**(3), 273–297 (1995)

A Multi-input Architecture
for the Classification of Skin Lesions
Using ResNets and Metadata

Fraol Gelana Waldamichael[1]([✉]) [iD], Samuel Rahimeto Kebede[1] [iD],
Yehualashet Megersa Ayano[1] [iD], Messay Tesfaye Demissie[2],
and Taye Girma Debelee[1] [iD]

[1] Ethiopian Artificial Intelligence Institute, 40782 Addis Ababa, Ethiopia
{fraol.gelana,samuel.rahimeto}@aic.et, taye.girma@aii.et
[2] College of Health Sciences, Department of Dermato-venereology,
Addis Ababa University, Addis Ababa, Ethiopia

Abstract. Skin illnesses are one of the most frequent diseases in the
world, ranking fourth in terms of non-fatal human sickness, with an
annual increase rate of 46.8% from 1990 to 2017. In this paper, we present
a multi-input deep learning architecture for detecting and classifying
Atopic Dermatitis, Papular Urticaria, and Scabies, three non-cancerous
and common skin illnesses affecting children in Ethiopia. The suggested
architecture comprises of a pre-trained ResNet architecture (ResNet101
and ResNet50) that has been fine-tuned on a dataset of 1796 photos
and a convolutional neural network (CNN) that has been trained on
tabular information associated with each image. We present a method
for translating metadata to picture format by leveraging the correlation
between each feature to establish their spatial and intensity values. On
ResNet101, the architecture obtained average precision, recall, f1, and
accuracy of 0.94, 0.94, 0.95, and 0.95, respectively, while on ResNet50,
the architecture achieved average precision, recall, f1, and accuracy of
0.94, 0.92, 0.93, and 0.94, respectively. The lighter ResNet50 architecture was also integrated into an Android application.

Keywords: Skin Lesions · Atopic Dermatitis · Papular Urticaria ·
Scabies · Deep Learning · Skin Disease Detection · Convolutional
Neural Networks

1 Introduction

Skin diseases are one of the most prevalent diseases in the world, affecting almost
one-third of the world's population [1]. According to a 2017 study [2], they are
responsible for 41.6 million disability-adjusted life years (DALYs), which was
1.79% of the total global burden of diseases. This includes 0.03% Scabies,0.19%

Ethiopian Artificial Intelligence Institute.

T. Girma Debelee et al. (Eds.): PanAfriCon AI 2022, CCIS 1800, pp. 27–49, 2023.
https://doi.org/10.1007/978-3-031-31327-1_2

Dermatitis, and 0.009% Urticaria [2]. Skin diseases occur throughout the world at significant levels. Although most skin diseases don't result in death, they lead to a significant reduction in the quality of life, especially in resource-poor regions. Disability and morbidity that is usually chronic are what patients with skin diseases live with. On top of that, patients face social stigma and loss of self-esteem due to deformities and disabilities of various degrees. For one or more of the reasons those living in resource-poor settings become unproductive and leave in poverty to a deeper degree [3].

According to the Global Burden of Disease project, skin diseases continue to be the 4th leading cause of nonfatal disease burden worldwide [2]. Pruritus or itching is the most common symptom of skin diseases, characterized by an unpleasant feeling that causes a desire to scratch. Itching negatively affects the psychological and physical aspects of life [4]. The list of skin diseases presenting with the itch is very long. In Ethiopia, the most predominant skin disease in children that present with itching is mainly due to infestation, infection, and inflammation. Among these Scabies, Papular urticaria, and Atopic dermatitis are the most common with a prevalence of 14.5%, 20.3%, and 19% respectively [5–7].

If not diagnosed and treated promptly each of the skin conditions can lead to significant sequela. Scabies can lead to long-term disfigurement, disability, stigmatization, and socioeconomic loss [8]. Patients with Atopic dermatitis experience poor quality of life and significant psychosocial impact [9]. Childhood atopic dermatitis has a physical, emotional, and social impact on both the child and the parent with physical discomfort from persistent itching and scratching, low self-esteem, and social isolation [10]. The annual costs of atopic dermatitis in the united states were estimated to be $5.297 billion in 2015 [11]. A study comprised of adults with AD from 9 European countries found that out-of-pocket costs accounted for about 900£ per year including the costs for medication and travel expenses [12]. Even though studies regarding the psychological and socioeconomic burden of Atopic dermatitis in Ethiopia are lacking, the increase in prevalence and the low economic status of the country make the burden very huge.

Papular urticaria (PU) is a common chronic skin disorder that occurs mainly in tropical regions, frequencies of 2.4 to 16.3, 4.4, and 5.2% have been observed in Mexico City, Mali, and India, respectively [13]. And current studies show that the prevalence of papular urticaria is 20.3% in children between 1 and 6 years of age [6]. Papular urticaria may lead to serious complications such as local bacterial super-infection or, in rare instances, insect-borne systemic diseases like endemic typhus [13]. The clinical presentations can be difficult to differentiate among the three skin conditions, especially in children living in tropical areas [14]. The underlying causes and their management are so different that it needs a well-trained dermatologist to differentiate between them and give appropriate therapy for each. In this work, we propose a multi-input deep learning architecture for the detection and classification of Atopic Dermatitis, Papular Urticaria, and Scabies; the three non-cancerous and highly prevalent skin diseases affecting children in Ethiopia. The proposed architecture consists of two pre-trained ResNet architectures, namely ResNet101 and ResNet50 which are fine-tuned on a dataset of 2616 clinical images collected from 1796 patient cases. Additionally, each patient's case is accompanied by 19-dimensional metadata describing parameters such as age, sex, rash location, and family history of the patient. We also proposed an approach to converting the metadata to an image format by using the correlation between each feature to define their respective spatial and intensity values. Experimental results were conducted comparing various deep learning architectures on the collected dataset and accordingly, it was found that ResNet101 architecture yields the best performance in terms of accuracy, precision, recall, and f1 score. Additionally, a lighter ResNet50 architecture was incorporated into an Android application.

The rest of the paper is organized into five sections. In Sect. 2, we will discuss related works of literature, and in Sect. 3, we provide the ethical guidelines used in conducting the study. In Sect. 4, we discuss in detail the data collection methods, explore the statistical distribution of the data, and the challenges faced during this phase. In Sect. 5, we discuss the methodology used in conducting this study, the tools and materials used and we discussed in detail the proposed architecture. In Sect. 6, we provide the experimental results of the study and its practical applications.

2   Related Works

Advances in deep learning and the availability of medical data have made AI-assisted medical diagnosis possible [15]. Works on deep learning-based classification and detection of breast cancer from mammography [16–18], deep learning-based brain tumor detection [19]. Consequently, the application of deep learning for skin disease detection has seen a significant rise. Esteva et al. [20] proposed a CNN trained end-to-end on a dataset of 129,450 clinical images. The proposed CNN architecture was performed on par with trained dermatologists in classifying 2,032 different classes of diseases.

Zhu et al. [21] suggested an EfficientNet-b4 technique to the identification and classification of 14 skin illness types. Using a dataset of 13,603 dermatologist-labeled pictures, the authors fine-tuned a pre-trained EfficientNet-b4 model. Kassani et al. [22] examined the performance of different state-of-the-art deep convolutional neural networks for creating an accurate melanoma diagnosis. The authors compared the performance of several architectures, including Xception [23], AlexNet [24], VGG16, and VGG19 [25]. ResNet50 beat the other designs in terms of accuracy and f1-score, with 92.08 and 92.74%, respectively.

Srinivasu et al. [26] proposed a MobileNetV2 and LSTM-based architecture for the detection of 7 classes of skin cancers. The authors evaluated the performance of their proposed architecture with other state-of-the-art architectures on the Ham10000 dataset. Their results showed that their architecture outperforms the other models in accuracy and provides a significant improvement in execution speed. Han et al. [27] proposed a ResNet152 model for the classification of 12 skin diseases. The pre-trained ResNet model was further fine-tuned on the Asan, MED-NODE, and atlas datasets containing a total of 19,398 images.

The above studies have achieved very high accuracy in detecting a variety of skin diseases on controlled datasets, but we found them to be hard to implement in real-life clinical applications. This is due to the datasets used to train the deep learning models being limited in their coverage of ethnical and geographic diversities and also the disease encountered are less common than those occurring in Ethiopia. For example, most of the datasets [28] contain carefully collected dermoscopic images of Benign and Malignant skin cancer data which are very rare in sub-Saharan African countries such as Ethiopia. Additionally, almost all the datasets are compiled from mostly light-skinned people of European or Asian descent.

Therefore, to adapt deep learning-based skin disease detection to the Ethiopian context, we set out to prepare a dataset of the three most commonly occurring skin diseases affecting children in Ethiopia that represents the environment of Ethiopian health centers. The disease types subjected to this study are Atopic Dermatitis (AD), Papular Urticaria (PU), and Scabies. These are highly infectious skin diseases that mostly affect children living in under-resourced and poor communities. Further, these communities have very limited access to a trained dermatologist, because as of the year 2021 Ethiopia has only 170 certified dermatologists available, and the majority of them are found in hospitals around the capital Addis Ababa.

3   Ethical Approval

We conducted this research according to the ethical tenets of the National Ethical Review Committee (NERC). And this study was approved by the ALERT Ethics Review Committee, Protocol number $P0/07/21$. Informed written consent was obtained from all the included adult patients or the guardians of juvenile patients.

4   Dataset

The dataset used for this study was prepared in collaboration with the Ethiopian Artificial Intelligence Institute[1], All African Leprosy Rehabilitation and Training Center (ALERT)[2], and the University of Gondar (UOG) Referral Hospital[3].

---

[1] www.aii.et.

[2] www.alertethiopia.org.

[3] www.uog.edu.et.

Table 1. List of parameters that are used by a dermatologist during diagnosis.

Num	Parameter Name	Description
1	Sex	Sex of the patient
2	Age	Age of the patient
3	Family_history_AAR	Family history of Asthma, allergy or rhinosinusitis
4	Itch_worsens_night	If the Itch worsens during nighttime
5	Family_member_itchy_skin	History of a family member with an itchy skin condition
6	Arm	Locations on the body where the rash is present
7	Abdomen	Locations on the body where the rash is present
8	Buttocks	Locations on the body where the rash is present
9	Back	Locations on the body where the rash is present
10	Chest	Locations on the body where the rash is present
11	Face	Locations on the body where the rash is present
12	Feet	Locations on the body where the rash is present
13	Groin	Locations on the body where the rash is present
14	Hand	Locations on the body where the rash is present
15	Head	Locations on the body where the rash is present
16	Legs	Locations on the body where the rash is present
17	Neck	Locations on the body where the rash is present
18	Popliteal	Locations on the body where the rash is present
19	Thighs	Locations on the body where the rash is present

The dataset consists of 2616 clinical images captured on-site using smartphones of varying camera quality and taken under diverse lighting and background conditions. These images are obtained from a total of 1769 patients mostly children who visited ALERT or UOG and were confirmed pathologically to be diagnosed with either Atopic Dermatitis, Papular Urticaria, or Scabies. The corresponding images are then labeled by the dermatologist with the type of disease present and also with tabular metadata. This metadata has 19 parameters that are used by a dermatologist during diagnosis Table 1. The fourteen rash location groups were created in conjunction with a dermatologist from ALERT and UOG to reduce the dimensionality of the data as some rash locations occur seen in the data rarely. Therefore, the major groups are formed by combining anatomical areas that are close together as one single group, for example, rashes that appear on the waist, flank, or Abdomen are grouped into the category Abdomen as seen in Fig. 1.

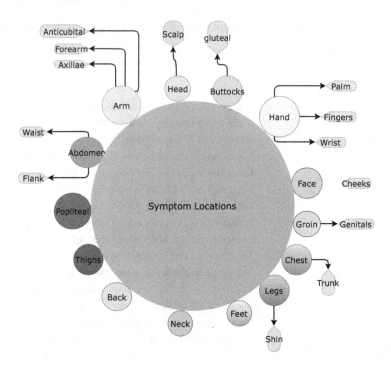

Fig. 1. Grouping of the multiple rash areas into fourteen major groups.

The dataset contains 1016(56.57%), 484(26.94%), and 296(16.48%) cases of Atopic Dermatitis, Papular Urticaria, and Scabies respectively, shown in Fig. 2; of this number 67.31% are male and 32.68% are female. The dataset contains patients of ages ranging from 1 month–20 years old (median age 2.0, mode 1.0, mean 3.71), as depicted in Fig. 3, the majority of the age distribution (67.65%) is between the ages of 1 month–3.7 years. This range is especially significant for Atopic Dermatitis where a majority (63.48%) of the cases happen within this age range.

These metadata features are then encoded according to the type of value they hold. Numeric values such as the age of the patient are all converted into year form and min-max scaling was performed to normalize the values between 0 and 1. That is patients' age given in months is divided by 12. Binary features such as "sex", "family history of asthma, allergy or rhino-sinusitis", "itch worsen at night" and "family member with itchy skin condition" are converted into 1's and 0's. For example, in "Male" and "Female" values of the sex feature are represented as 0 and 1 respectively. Accordingly, the fourteen rash locations are One-Hot encoded as 1 if the rash is seen on a particular location and 0 otherwise. Each image is then cropped and annotated by the dermatologist. This step ensures that the images contain minimal background information and

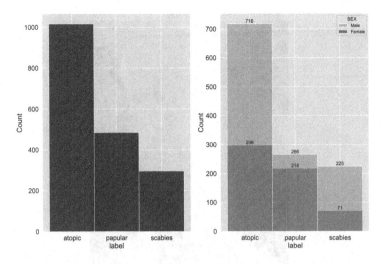

Fig. 2. Disease type distribution of the database with respect to sex.

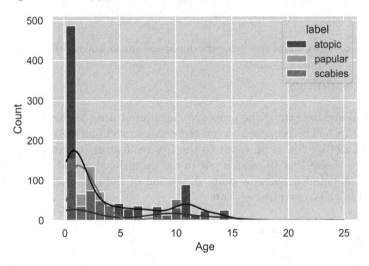

Fig. 3. Patient age distribution across dataset with respect to disease type.

that only the rashes take up a majority of the image. This step also helps increase the size of the dataset, as a single image from a patient might include multiple rashes Fig. 4. After performing this crop operation we manage to increase the size of our dataset from 1796 to 2870 images.

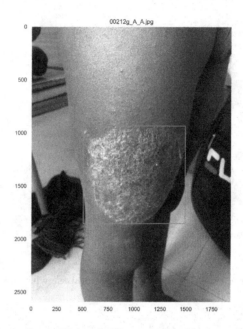

Fig. 4. Bounding rectangle specifying the dimension and location of the crop operation.

5   Methodology

The overall architecture of the proposed multi-input deep learning model is presented in Fig. 5. The proposed architecture takes two inputs; An RGB image of the size of 224 by 224 as an input to the ResNet feature extractor and a grayscale image of size 19×19 as an input to a convolutional neural network feature extractor. A detailed point-by-point discussion of the proposed architecture is presented in the consequent sections.

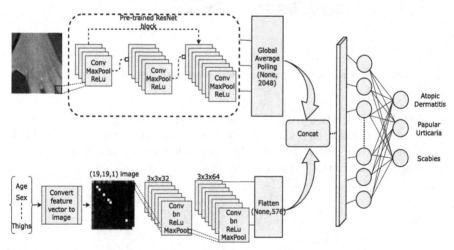

Fig. 5. Architecture of the proposed multi-input model with a pre-trained ResNet image feature extractor and CNN metadata feature extractor.

5.1   Image Pre-processing

The initial step in every image-based deep learning application is to pre-process the picture to meet the criteria of the chosen architecture. This includes resizing the image into the dimensions needed by the architecture, normalizing the intensity values, and performing image augmentation techniques. In this work, we resize all images into a square image of size 224 pixels by 224 pixels which is the dimension required by the ResNet architecture used. Further, each pixels intensity value for the red, green, and blue channels which has a value ranging from 0–255 is normalized according to Eq. 1, where I, μ, and σ are the pixels current intensity value, the mean intensity value and standard deviation respectively. To prevent over-fitting on our relatively small data set, we utilized the image augmentation technique. Image augmentation is used to artificially expand the data by performing various operations on an image during training time. Some of these operations are zoom, shear, rotation, translation, blurring, and so on.

$$\bar{I} = \frac{I - \mu}{\sigma} \tag{1}$$

5.2   ResNet Image Feature Extractor Architecture

ResNet is a deep convolutional neural network architecture developed by Microsoft research [29] back in 2015 to solve the vanishing gradient and degradation problems that occur when training deeper networks. For this, the researchers created a concept of skip connections, in which, instead of letting stacked layers fit the desired mapping they explicitly let these layers fit a residual mapping Fig. 6.

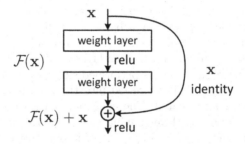

Fig. 6. Building blocks of ResNet [29].

In this work, we utilized the ResNet101 and ResNet50 with 101 and 50 layers respectively Fig. 7. Transfer learning is utilized to train the two models, by fine-tuning convolutional neural networks that are trained to perform different task on our dataset. Transfer learning is an essential way of issue resolution when the training data is significantly less than what is necessary to create a deep learning model [30]. To achieve this, we removed the last fully-connected layer with 1000 neurons intended for the ImageNet dataset from both architectures and replaced it with a *GlobalAveragePooling* layer. We also froze the bottom 75 convolutional layers of the ResNet101 architecture and the bottom 30 convolutional layers of the ResNet50 architecture during training time; we then fine-tuned the remaining top convolutional layers on our dataset.

layer name	output size	18-layer	34-layer	50-layer	101-layer	152-layer
conv1	112×112	7×7, 64, stride 2				
		\multicolumn 3×3 max pool, stride 2				
conv2_x	56×56	$\begin{bmatrix} 3{\times}3,\,64 \\ 3{\times}3,\,64 \end{bmatrix}{\times}2$	$\begin{bmatrix} 3{\times}3,\,64 \\ 3{\times}3,\,64 \end{bmatrix}{\times}3$	$\begin{bmatrix} 1{\times}1,\,64 \\ 3{\times}3,\,64 \\ 1{\times}1,\,256 \end{bmatrix}{\times}3$	$\begin{bmatrix} 1{\times}1,\,64 \\ 3{\times}3,\,64 \\ 1{\times}1,\,256 \end{bmatrix}{\times}3$	$\begin{bmatrix} 1{\times}1,\,64 \\ 3{\times}3,\,64 \\ 1{\times}1,\,256 \end{bmatrix}{\times}3$
conv3_x	28×28	$\begin{bmatrix} 3{\times}3,\,128 \\ 3{\times}3,\,128 \end{bmatrix}{\times}2$	$\begin{bmatrix} 3{\times}3,\,128 \\ 3{\times}3,\,128 \end{bmatrix}{\times}4$	$\begin{bmatrix} 1{\times}1,\,128 \\ 3{\times}3,\,128 \\ 1{\times}1,\,512 \end{bmatrix}{\times}4$	$\begin{bmatrix} 1{\times}1,\,128 \\ 3{\times}3,\,128 \\ 1{\times}1,\,512 \end{bmatrix}{\times}4$	$\begin{bmatrix} 1{\times}1,\,128 \\ 3{\times}3,\,128 \\ 1{\times}1,\,512 \end{bmatrix}{\times}8$
conv4_x	14×14	$\begin{bmatrix} 3{\times}3,\,256 \\ 3{\times}3,\,256 \end{bmatrix}{\times}2$	$\begin{bmatrix} 3{\times}3,\,256 \\ 3{\times}3,\,256 \end{bmatrix}{\times}6$	$\begin{bmatrix} 1{\times}1,\,256 \\ 3{\times}3,\,256 \\ 1{\times}1,\,1024 \end{bmatrix}{\times}6$	$\begin{bmatrix} 1{\times}1,\,256 \\ 3{\times}3,\,256 \\ 1{\times}1,\,1024 \end{bmatrix}{\times}23$	$\begin{bmatrix} 1{\times}1,\,256 \\ 3{\times}3,\,256 \\ 1{\times}1,\,1024 \end{bmatrix}{\times}36$
conv5_x	7×7	$\begin{bmatrix} 3{\times}3,\,512 \\ 3{\times}3,\,512 \end{bmatrix}{\times}2$	$\begin{bmatrix} 3{\times}3,\,512 \\ 3{\times}3,\,512 \end{bmatrix}{\times}3$	$\begin{bmatrix} 1{\times}1,\,512 \\ 3{\times}3,\,512 \\ 1{\times}1,\,2048 \end{bmatrix}{\times}3$	$\begin{bmatrix} 1{\times}1,\,512 \\ 3{\times}3,\,512 \\ 1{\times}1,\,2048 \end{bmatrix}{\times}3$	$\begin{bmatrix} 1{\times}1,\,512 \\ 3{\times}3,\,512 \\ 1{\times}1,\,2048 \end{bmatrix}{\times}3$
	1×1	\multicolumn average pool, 1000-d fc, softmax				
FLOPs		$1.8{\times}10^9$	$3.6{\times}10^9$	$3.8{\times}10^9$	$7.6{\times}10^9$	$11.3{\times}10^9$

Fig. 7. Various ResNet architectures [29].

5.3   CNN Metadata Feature Extractor Architecture

We designed a lightweight convolutional neural network Fig. 8 for the task of feature extraction from the 19×19 images generated from the metadata feature vector. The steps and algorithm used to convert metadata into the image are discussed in detail in Sect. 5.4 below. The architecture consists of just two convolutional layers each followed by a batch normalization layer [31], a ReLu activation layer, and a MaxPooling layer. The output of the last convolutional layer is then fed into the input of a Flatten layer. Training of the ResNet architectures and the CNN architecture is performed simultaneously. Clinical images and their corresponding metadata are fed into the models and the outputs of each model are then concatenated. The concatenated features are then fed as an input to a fully connected layer having an input layer of size 2624 and an output layer of size 3 as shown in Fig. 5. A softmax activation function is used in this layer to generate a class probability for each of the disease classes in the data set.

5.4   Representing Tabular Metadata Feature Vectors as Images

Representation of tabular data as a two-dimensional image is a well-proven method for enabling CNN modeling of tabular data. Work on the representation of gene expression profiles of cancer cell lines and molecular descriptors of drugs into their respective image representation has been undertaken by Zhu et al. [32], in which their algorithm assigns features in the tabular data to a pixel in the image where the pixel intensity reflects the value of the corresponding feature. The algorithm assigns features to pixels by minimizing the difference between the pairwise euclidean distance between features and the ranking of pairwise distances between the assigned pixels. Sharma et al. [33] proposed an algorithm to represent tabular features as images with respect to the Pearson's correlation vector $\rho(X, Y)$ between the input features $X \in \mathbb{R}^{1 \times n}$ and targets vectors $Y \in \mathbb{R}^{1 \times m}$. Where m is the number of samples and n is the number of features.

Given a training dataset $X \in \mathbb{R}^{m \times n}$, where m is the number of samples in the training set and n is the number of features, we find the Cramer's correlation

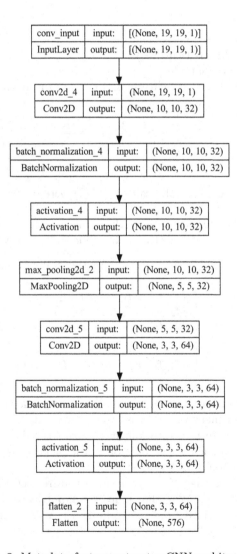

Fig. 8. Metadata feature extractor CNN architecture.

matrix $C \in \mathbb{R}^{n \times n}$ between the features across m samples of the dataset. Cramer's V is a statistical method used to understand the strength of the relationship between two categorical variables. Where a Cramer's V value of 0 indicates no association between the two variables and a 1 indicates a perfect association. Since there are only two unique values for each of the categories in our tabular metadata, we need to use Cramer's v to calculate the correlation between each feature. Cramer's V between two variables is given in Eq. 2 as:

$$V = \sqrt{\frac{\frac{\chi^2}{\eta}}{min(k-1, r-1)}} \tag{2}$$

where:

- $\eta \rightarrow$ Grand total observations.
- $k \rightarrow$ number of columns (features).
- $r \rightarrow$ number of rows (samples).
- $\chi^2 \rightarrow$ The derived Pearson's chi-squared test, and is given in Eq. 3

$$\chi^2 = \sum_{ij} \frac{(n_{ij} - \frac{n_i n_j}{n})^2}{\frac{n_i n_j}{n}} \tag{3}$$

where:

- $n_{ij} \rightarrow$ the number of times the values (x_i, x_j) were observed.
- $n \rightarrow$ the sample size.
- $n_i = \sum_j n_{ij} \rightarrow$ the number of times the value x_i is observed.
- $n_j = \sum_i n_{ij} \rightarrow$ the number of times the value x_j is observed.

For feature vector $F = [f_1, f_2, ..., f_n]$ in X, the cramer's correlation matrix

$$C \in \mathbb{R}^{n \times n} = \begin{bmatrix} \rho(f_1, f_1) & \rho(f_1, f_2) & \rho(f_1, f_3) & \cdots & \rho(f_1, f_n) \\ \rho(f_2, f_1) & \rho(f_2, f_2) & \rho(f_2, f_3) & \cdots & \rho(f_2, f_n) \\ \rho(f_3, f_1) & \rho(f_3, f_2) & \rho(f_3, f_3) & \cdots & \rho(f_3, f_n) \\ \vdots & \vdots & \vdots & \ddots & \vdots \\ \rho(f_n, f_1) & \rho(f_n, f_2) & \rho(f_n, f_3) & \cdots & \rho(f_n, f_n) \end{bmatrix} \tag{4}$$

where, each element of the matrix C is found by taking the cramer's V, $\rho(f_i, f_j)$ of the ith and j^{th} element of F across the training data X. The correlation matrix $C \in \mathbb{R}^{n \times n}$, where $n = 19$ in our case, forms the backbone of our image of size 19×19, Fig. 9. The spatial location of the pixel p_{ij} is obtained from the ith row and the jth column of the matrix C.

Therefore, to get the image for unseen (test) feature vector $\bar{F}$, we need to find a function $M : \mathbb{R}^{1 \times n} \rightarrow \mathbb{R}^{n \times n \times 1}$ that maps the input feature vector $\bar{F}$ and the correlation matrix C derived from the training set X to an image $I \in \mathbb{R}^{n \times n \times 1}$ as expressed in Eq. 5.

$$I = M(C, \bar{F}) = (C \odot \bar{F}) \times 255.0 \tag{5}$$

The intensity of the pixel P_{ij} is therefore proportional to the cramer's co-relation coefficient $\rho(x_i, x_j)$ and is expressed in Eq. 6 as:

$$|P_{ij}| = \rho(x_i, x_j) \cdot \bar{f}_i \cdot 255.0 \qquad (6)$$

where:

- $\rho(x_i, x_j) \rightarrow$ the cramer's correlation coefficient between i^{th} and j^{th} element in the matrix C
- $\bar{f}_i \rightarrow$ the ith feature of the input feature vector $\bar{F}$
- $255.0 \rightarrow$ the scaling factor.

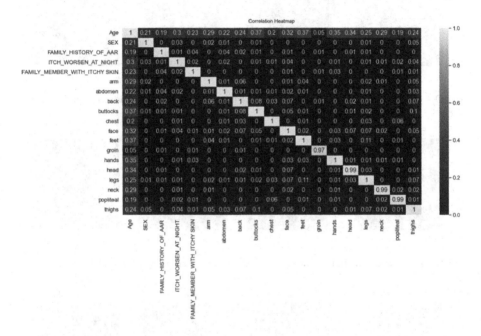

Fig. 9. Correlation matrix between features of our training sample.

For illustration, four samples are selected randomly from each class of skin disease to observe the reoccurring patterns generated when applying the method presented in Eq. 5. The generated images by this algorithm are shown in Fig. 10. The figures are presented in a sequential style color map to better help in visualization. From the presented images we can notice a clear pattern, in generated atopic dermatitis images Fig. 10a on the 10th column of the images, also the 15th column of the papular urticaria images Fig. 10b show distinct and repeated intensity values. For scabies Fig. 10c, pixels along the diagonal and 5th column of the scabies images have the recognizable pattern.

6 Experimental Results

All model training and testing implementation were performed on Google co-laboratory[4] by using the TensorFlow deep learning library[5]. The dataset used for training consists of cropped-out images of rash areas from a particular patient belonging to one of the three disease classes. In total, the dataset consists of 2870 images and their corresponding metadata. A 5-fold cross-validation was

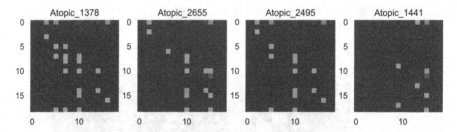

(a) Output image on four randomly picked atopic dermatitis metadata from the test set.

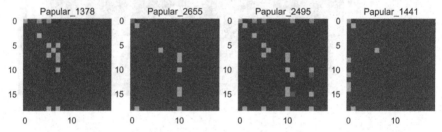

(b) Output image on four randomly picked papular urticaria metadata from the test set.

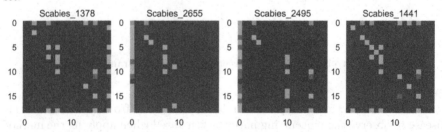

(c) Output image on four randomly picked scabies metadata from the test set.

Fig. 10. An illustration showing the visible patterns generated by the algorithm for each disease class. Notice the reoccurring pattern on the 10th column of the atopic dermatitis images, 15th column of the papular urticaria images, and along the diagonal and 14th column of the scabies images.

---

[4] https://colab.research.google.com.

[5] https://www.tensorflow.org/.

performed, and with each fold, the dataset was randomly split 80/20 into a training set and a testing set. The training images are further split 90/10 into training and validation sets respectively. To address the imbalanced dataset that would otherwise cause over-fitting, we utilized class weighted cross-entropy loss [34] where misclassifications of the minority are penalized more than the majority classes, we also used image augmentations to artificially increase the dataset size and to improve the models' accuracy, a variety of augmentation techniques was implemented. In this work, random zoom, shear, and rotation augmentation techniques were used, Table 2.

Table 2. Image augmentation operations used.

Operation	Values	Description
Augmentation Shear	(−8,8)	Fractional affine shear
Augmentation Translate	(−0.2,0.2)	Minimum and Maximum translation percentage
Augmentation Zoom	0.2	Fractional zoom for image augmentation generator
Augmentation Rotation	(−25,25)	Minimum and Maximum rotation angle
Gaussian Blur	(0,0.5)	Standard deviation of the Gaussian kernel

For this work, we used the f1-score, precision, recall, and execution time metrics to evaluate the performance of our proposed architecture. Precision, Eq. 7 and Recall, Eq. 8 are popular metrics for measuring a machine learning model performance. They measure how often the model is predicting correct classes and the model's positive prediction rate relative to the ground truth respectively. And they are given as:

$$Precision = \frac{TP}{TP + FP} \tag{7}$$

$$Recall = \frac{TP}{TP + FN} \tag{8}$$

TP = True Positve, **FP** = False Positive, **FN** = False Negative

f1-score is defined as the harmonic mean of precision and recall and is given by Eq. 9 as:

$$f_1 = 2 \times \frac{precision \times recall}{precision + recall} \tag{9}$$

We evaluated three pre-trained architectures; ResNet101, ResNet50, and Xception. We experimented with various model hyper-parameters and selected the combination of hyper-parameters that yield the best score on the testing data Table 3. For all the architectures we utilized exponential learning rate decay Algorithm 1 and early stopping of training if there is no significant improvement in validation loss Algorithm 2. The training/validation accuracy and loss of the evaluated models if given in Fig. 11 and 12 respectively.

Algorithm 1. Learning rate exponential decay.

---

procedure LRDECAY(*initialLR*)
    $lr \leftarrow initialLR$ ▷ Initial learning rate
    $epochs \leftarrow 100$ ▷ Training Epochs
    $rate \leftarrow 0.9$ ▷ Decay rate
    $step \leftarrow 10$ ▷ Decay steps
    for $epoch \in$ **range**($epochs$) **do**
        if $(epoch\%step) = 0$ **then**
            $lr = lr \times \exp(-rate)$
        end if
    end for
end procedure

Algorithm 2. Model early stopping criteria.

$loss \leftarrow infinity$ ▷ Initial validation loss
$epochs \leftarrow 100$ ▷ Training Epochs
$patience \leftarrow 10$ ▷ check loss improvement every 10 epochs
$delta \leftarrow 0.001$ ▷ Minimum difference in loss
for $epoch \in$ **range**($epochs$) **do**
    if $(epoch\%patience) = 0$ **then**
        if $(loss - epochLoss) \leq delta$ **then**
            break   ▷ End training
        end if
        $loss = epochLoss$
    end if
end for

Table 3. Model hyper-parameters that yield the best score on the test data.

Arch	Input shape	Initial lr	Optimizer	Batch size
Resnet101	224 × 224	0.01	SGD	32
Resnet50	224 × 224	0.01	SGD	32
Xception	299 × 299	0.001	Adam	32

On a testing data of 533 images belonging to three classes of diseases, the ResNet101-based architecture achieved an average classification accuracy of 95.0% Table 4, while both ResNet50 and Xception-based architectures achieved an average classification accuracy of 94.0% Table 5 and 6. The confusion matrix for the prediction results on the testing set is given in Figs. 13a, 13b, and 13c.

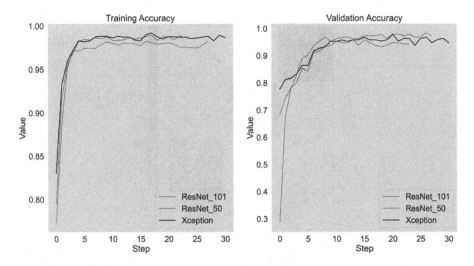

Fig. 11. Training and Validation accuracy of the evaluated models.

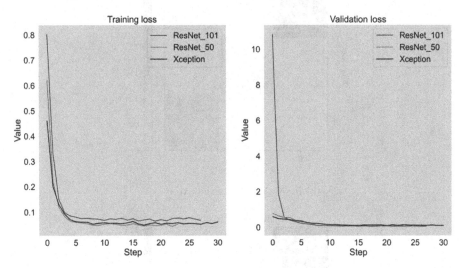

Fig. 12. Training and validation loss of the evaluated models.

Table 4. ResNet101 per-class model performance on testing data.

class (class name)	images/class	precision	recall	f1
0 (Atopic Dermatitis)	334	0.98	1.00	0.99
1 (Papular Urticaria)	167	0.99	0.97	0.98
2 (Scabies)	171	0.99	0.98	0.99

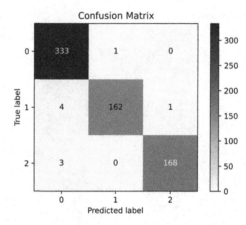

(a) ResNet101 based architecture

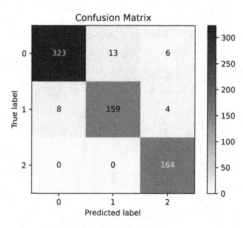

(b) ResNet50 based architecture

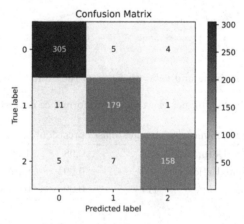

(c) Xception based architecture

Fig. 13. Confusion matrix for the evaluated architectures.

Table 5. ResNet50 per-class model performance on testing data.

class (class name)	images/class	precision	recall	f1
0 (Atopic Dermatitis)	342	0.98	0.94	0.96
1 (Papular Urticaria)	171	0.92	0.93	0.93
2 (Scabies)	164	0.94	1.00	0.97

Table 6. Xception per-class model performance on testing data.

class (class name)	images/class	precision	recall	f1
0 (Atopic Dermatitis)	314	0.95	0.97	0.96
1 (Papular Urticaria)	191	0.94	0.94	0.94
2 (Scabies)	170	0.97	0.93	0.95

The proposed skin disease detection based on ResNets and meta-data is incorporated into an android mobile application for ease of use for doctors to classify diseases based on the data fed. The trained architecture is converted into a format suitable for mobile applications by using the TensorflowLite library. This compact model is then imported into an android application which was made easy in Android Studio. The mobile application is written using Java programming language. The user initially fills in the metadata information of the patient by using the user interface Fig. 14a. After inserting and saving the meta-data the user is then prompted to either capture an image by using the device's camera or upload an existing picture from the device's storage, after capturing the image the user then edits the image (crop, rotate, and zoom) as shown in Fig. 14b. When finished with editing the image the user then saves the image and the application displays the prediction results on a new interface Fig. 14c.

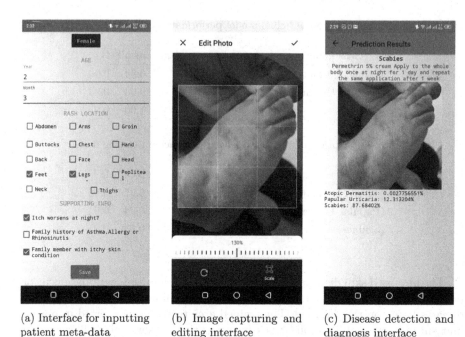

(a) Interface for inputting patient meta-data

(b) Image capturing and editing interface

(c) Disease detection and diagnosis interface

Fig. 14. The interface of the mobile application to gather patients' meta-data and prediction result interface of a mobile application.

7   Conclusion

In this work, we presented a model for the detection of three common skin diseases that affect children in Ethiopia. The model combines image and tabular meta-data associated with each patient to make a prediction. It consists of a ResNet101 or ResNet50 architecture for extracting features from the image data and a CNN for extracting features from the tabular meta-data. To use the tabular meta-data with the convolutional neural network, we proposed an algorithm for converting the one-dimensional meta-data feature vectors into two-dimensional images based on Cramer's v correlation coefficient between each feature. To train the proposed model we collected and prepared a dataset in collaboration with the All African Leprosy Rehabilitation and Training Center (ALERT) and the University of Gondar (UOG) Referral Hospital. We evaluated the proposed model by using three image feature extractor architectures. These architectures are ResNet50, ResNet101, and Xception. We utilized a transfer learning approach when training these architectures and further fine-tuned them on our dataset. For evaluation, we used the precision, recall, f1-score, and accuracy metrics. The ResNet101-based architecture gave the top evaluation results with precision, recall, f1, and accuracy of 0.94,0.94,0.95, and 0.95 respectively.

8   Future Work

The proposed architecture's performance in the detection of certain classes of diseases such as Scabies can be further improved by collecting more data as we had some challenges in collecting balanced data for all classes due to the seasonal nature of some of the diseases. In the future, we plan to identify and include other disease types.

References

1. Flohr, C., Hay, R.: Putting the burden of skin diseases on the global map. Br. J. Dermatol. **184**(2), 189–190 (2021)
2. Karimkhani, C., et al.: Global skin disease morbidity and mortality: an update from the global burden of disease study 2013. JAMA Dermatol. **153**(5), 406–412 (2017)
3. Jamison, D.T., et al.: Disease Control Priorities in Developing Countries (2006)
4. Cevikbas, F., Lerner, E.A.: Physiology and pathophysiology of itch. Physiol. Rev. **100**(3), 945–982 (2020)
5. Azene, A.G., Aragaw, A.M., Wassie, G.T.: Prevalence and associated factors of scabies in Ethiopia: systematic review and meta-analysis. BMC Infect. Dis. **20**(1), 1–10 (2020)
6. Ständer, S., Steinhoff, M., Schmelz, M., Weisshaar, E., Metze, D., Luger, T.: Neurophysiology of pruritus: cutaneous elicitation of itch. Arch. Dermatol. **139**(11), 1463–1470 (2003)
7. Sumino, K., et al. & American Lung Association Asthma Clinical Research Centers: Methacholine challenge test: diagnostic characteristics in asthmatic patients receiving controller medications. J. Allergy Clin. Immunol. **130**(1), 69–75 (2012)
8. Padovese, V., Dassoni, F., Morrone, A.: Scabies coexisting with other dermatoses: the importance of recognizing multiple pathologies in resource-poor settings. Int. J. Dermatol. **59**(12), 1502–1505 (2020)
9. Ng, M.S., Tan, S., Chan, N.H., Foong, A.Y., Koh, M.J.: Effect of atopic dermatitis on quality of life and its psychosocial impact in Asian adolescents. Aust. J. Dermatol. **59**(2), e114–e117 (2018)
10. Meintjes, K.F., Nolte, A.G.: Parents' experience of childhood atopic eczema in the public health sector of Gauteng. curationis **38**(1), 1–9 (2015)
11. Drucker, A.M., Wang, A.R., Li, W.Q., Sevetson, E., Block, J.K., Qureshi, A.A.: The burden of atopic dermatitis: summary of a report for the national eczema association. J. Invest. Dermatol. **137**(1), 26–30 (2017)
12. Zink, A.G., et al.: Out-of-pocket costs for individuals with atopic eczema: a cross-sectional study in nine European countries. Acta Derm. Venereol. **99**(3), 263–267 (2019)
13. Sorvillo, F.J., et al.: A suburban focus of endemic typhus in Los Angeles county: association with seropositive domestic cats and opossums. Am. J. Trop. Med. Hyg. **48**(2), 269–273 (1993)
14. Caraballo, L., et al.: Particularities of allergy in the tropics. World Allergy Organ. J. **9**(1), 1–44 (2016)
15. Debelee, T.G., Schwenker, F., Ibenthal, A., Yohannes, D.: Survey of deep learning in breast cancer image analysis. Evol. Syst. **11**(1), 143–163 (2020)

16. Debelee, T.G., Amirian, M., Ibenthal, A., Palm, G., Schwenker, F.: Classification of mammograms using convolutional neural network based feature extraction. In: Mekuria, F., Nigussie, E.E., Dargie, W., Edward, M., Tegegne, T. (eds.) ICT4DA 2017. LNICST, vol. 244, pp. 89–98. Springer, Cham (2018). https://doi.org/10.1007/978-3-319-95153-9_9
17. Debelee, T.G., Gebreselasie, A., Schwenker, F., Amirian, M., Yohannes, D.: Classification of mammograms using texture and CNN based extracted features. J. Biomimetics Biomater. Biomed. Eng. **42**, 79–97 (2019)
18. Rahimeto, S., Debelee, T.G., Yohannes, D., Schwenker, F.: Automatic pectoral muscle removal in mammograms. Evol. Syst. **12**(2), 519–526 (2019). https://doi.org/10.1007/s12530-019-09310-8
19. Biratu, E.S.S., Schwenker, F., Debelee, T.G.G., Kebede, S.R.R., Negera, W.G.G., Molla, H.T.T.: Enhanced region growing for brain tumor MR image segmentation. J. Imaging **7**(2), 22 (2021)
20. Esteva, A., et al.: Dermatologist-level classification of skin cancer with deep neural networks. Nature **542**(7639), 115–118 (2017)
21. Zhu, C.-Y., et al.: A deep learning based framework for diagnosing multiple skin diseases in a clinical environment. Front. Med. **8**, 626369 (2021)
22. Kassani, S.H., Kassani, P.H.: A comparative study of deep learning architectures on melanoma detection. Tissue Cell **58**, 76–83 (2019)
23. Chollet, F.: Xception: deep learning with depthwise separable convolutions. In: Proceedings of the IEEE Conference on Computer Vision and Pattern Recognition, pp. 1251–1258 (2017)
24. He, K., Zhang, X., Ren, S., Sun, J.: Deep residual learning for image recognition. In: Proceedings of the IEEE Conference on Computer Vision and Pattern Recognition, pp. 770–778 (2016)
25. Simonyan, K., Zisserman, A.: Very deep convolutional networks for large-scale image recognition. arXiv preprint arXiv:1409.1556 (2014)
26. Srinivasu, P.N., SivaSai, J.G., Ijaz, M.F., Bhoi, A.K., Kim, W., Kang, J.J.: Classification of skin disease using deep learning neural networks with MobileNet V2 and LSTM. Sensors **21**(8), 2852 (2021)
27. Han, S.S., Kim, M.S., Lim, W., Park, G.H., Park, I., Chang, S.E.: Classification of the clinical images for benign and malignant cutaneous tumors using a deep learning algorithm. J. Invest. Dermatol. **138**(7), 1529–1538 (2018)
28. Tschandl, P., Rosendahl, C., Kittler, H.: The HAM10000 dataset, a large collection of multi-source dermatoscopic images of common pigmented skin lesions. Sci. Data **5**(1), 1–9 (2018)
29. He, K., Zhang, X., Ren, S., Sun, J.: Deep residual learning for image recognition (2015)
30. Waldamichael, F.G., Debelee, T.G., Ayano, Y.M.: Coffee disease detection using a robust HSV color-based segmentation and transfer learning for use on smartphones. Int. J. Intell. Syst. **37**(8), 4967–4993 (2021)
31. Ioffe, S., Szegedy, C.: Batch normalization: accelerating deep network training by reducing internal covariate shift. In: International Conference on Machine Learning, pp. 448–456. PMLR (2015)
32. Zhu, Y., et al.: Converting tabular data into images for deep learning with convolutional neural networks. Sci. Rep. **11**(1), 1–11 (2021)

33. Sharma, A., Vans, E., Shigemizu, D., Boroevich, K.A., Tsunoda, T.: DeepInsight: a methodology to transform a non-image data to an image for convolution neural network architecture. Sci. Rep. **9**(1), 1–7 (2019)
34. Xu, Z., Dan, C., Khim, J., Ravikumar, P.: Class-weighted classification: trade-offs and robust approaches. In: International Conference on Machine Learning, pp. 10544–10554. PMLR (2020)

Data Management Strategy for AI Deployment in Ethiopian Healthcare System

Shimelis Assefa(✉)

University of Denver, Denver, CO 80208, USA
shimelis.assefa@du.edu

Abstract. This paper reviewed data management practices in healthcare system in Ethiopia. Through the lens of strategic approach for good data management practices, the extent to which healthcare data is leveraged for AI applications was assessed. As the main body for collecting, archiving, managing, and sharing health data in Ethiopia, the national data management center for health (NDMC) at the Ethiopian public health Institute (EPHI) is considered for this study. To guide the study, the FAIR (Findability, Accessibility, Interoperability, and Reusability) principles; the key elements of data strategy by Inner City Fund (ICF) International Inc: data governance, data architecture, needs assessment, future state vision and roadmap, organizational analytics maturity assessment; and data from Papers with Code (data in Meta Artificial Intelligence (AI) Research), more specifically, State-of-the-Art (SOTA) benchmarks, AI models, use cases, libraries, and frameworks, were used to assess the extent to which NDMC data activities support deployment of AI applications. From the analysis of primary and secondary sources, as well as based on the principles and frameworks, the following key findings were reported: NDMC by and large pursues data strategy as outlined by ICF International, except two key elements that could not be detected from the review and an in-person discussion and these are: future state vision and roadmap, organizational analytics maturity assessment. When the FAIR principle is used as a guide, the data and metadata at NDMC do not strictly adhere to community standards in bio-medical sciences that promote findability, accessibility, interoperability, and reusability. In regard to the SOTA benchmarks, NDMC, data analytics and reporting being one of its core charges, mainly relies on descriptive and inferential statistical methods to generate data reports and no AI, Machine Learning (ML), or Deep Learning (DL) applications were identified that could offer more predictive and prescriptive insights.

Keywords: Data Management · Data Strategy · Ethiopian Healthcare · National Data Management Center · Healthcare Data · AI Applications

© The Author(s), under exclusive license to Springer Nature Switzerland AG 2023
T. Girma Debelee et al. (Eds.): PanAfriCon AI 2022, CCIS 1800, pp. 50–66, 2023.
https://doi.org/10.1007/978-3-031-31327-1_3

1   Introduction

The volume of data produced in the world is growing rapidly, from 33 zettabytes in 2018 to an expected 175 zettabytes in 2025 [33]. One of the leading sectors that is awash with large explosion of data is healthcare. From globally scoped general-purpose data repositories such as Dataverse, FigShare, Dryad, Zenodo, to focused and special-purpose data repositories in healthcare such as GeneBank, Worldwide Protein data Bank, and Sequence Read Archive (SRA), data is everywhere [44]. Broadly the stakeholders of data in healthcare are varied - from medical centers, hospitals, laboratories, research centers, public health institutions, pharmaceutical industries, insurance, government agencies, patients and the general public at large.

The diversity of data in healthcare is rich and it comes from different sources - i.e., electronic medical records, vital statistics, national public health surveys, social media streams, medical- and bio- images, wearable devices and sensors, and Internet of Things (IoTs) (e.g., [1]). While robust and open healthcare data is largely missing in developing countries such as Ethiopia, it is not uncommon to find such datasets on a number of cases in advanced countries. A case in point is - the freely accessible massive collections of physiological and clinical data including cardiopulmonary, neural, and other biomedical signals from healthy subjects and patients with a variety of conditions and related open-source software from PhysioNet [15].

The application of data in healthcare is equally far and wide - whether it is to reduce the risk of medical errors through deep learning technologies (e.g., [46]), or to enhance and augment public health and medical decisions through clinical predictive modeling (e.g., [24]), or using AI for chemoinformatics or drug discovery (e.g., [8]); precision medicine as in genetic disease detection ([21]); web and social media data for digital disease detection or epidemic prediction (e.g., [43]), or medical image analysis for breast cancer detection (e.g., [2,42]); analysis of electrical signals generated by the brain and muscles acquired through appropriate sensors such as electroencephalogram (EEG), magnetoencephalography (MEG), functional magnetic resonance imaging (fMRI), functional near infrared spectroscopy (fNIRS) (e.g., [12]), the biomedical domain is a fertile ground for data application employing different methods and technologies.

With such diverse data types coming from disparate places, and multitude of internal and external entities having a stake for data use, establishing a mechanism to collect, organize, manage, share, and access such a valuable resource is very critical. This is even more complex when the task is to build a mechanism at institutional and inter-institutional level, as well as zonal, regional, and national levels across the board is considered. Without such processes and procedures to perform curatorial and management activities for the invaluable asset that healthcare data has become, the quality of data suffers and that in turn makes it difficult and expensive to deploy analytical methods and applications such as machine learning algorithms.

1.1 Data Management

Data management, often referred to as research data management or scientific data management, can be broadly described by sets of activities such as - data policies, data planning, data element standardization, information management control, data synchronization, data sharing, and database development, including practices and projects that acquire, control, protect, deliver and enhance the value of data and information [3]. It is imperative that the different stakeholders and the wide range of datasets generated are easily managed, accessed, and used across the span of the patient, for example, or the life cycle of the medical research project.

While comprehensive standard principles or account for data management is hard to come by, there are certain practical guideposts that serve as baselines for good data management practices. One such guidepost is the foundational principles that goes by the acronym FAIR - for Findability, Accessibility, Interoperability, and Reusability [44], the notion that data should be findable, accessible, interoperable, and reusable. Each of the facets in FAIR require extensive background work to fulfill that data is FAIR. Data extracted from an extensive article that appeared in Nature Scientific data, the following table captures the FAIR principle very well.

Table 1. The description of FAIR principle, based on [44].

Principle	Explanation	Example in human genetics and genomics
Findable	Datasets should be described, identified and registered or indexed in a clear and unequivocal manner	BBMRI-ERIC Directory
Accessible	Datasets should be accessible through a clearly defined access procedure, ideally using automated means. Metadata should always remain accessible	European genome-phenome archive
Interoperable	Data and metadata are conceptualized, expressed and structured using common, published standards	GA4GH Genomic Data Toolkit
Reusable	Characteristics of data and their provenance are described in detail according to domain relevant community standards, with clear and accessible conditions for use	BRCA Exchange

In addition to the technical description of the FAIR principles, an internationally recognized consulting firm in digital services provider that also worked with the Ethiopian Public Health Institute (EPHI) to carry out demographic and health survey (DHS), states the following as the key elements of data strategy: data governance, data architecture, needs assessment, future state vision and roadmap, organizational analytics maturity assessment; and it also outlines what is involved by data management activities as: developing application program interface (APIs), infrastructure planning, backup and recovery, logging, access management, data security and cloud analytics [18].

1.2 Data Management and AI Applications

A robust data management infrastructure is critical to take advantage of advances made in AI. It can be safely argued that the precursor for AI readiness and AI-enabled applications across any sector including healthcare is the data pipeline that supports data management and data transformation before machine learning or deep learning model training proceeds. Data and AI are closely connected so much so that without data, AI applications cannot be deployed. For example, in the famous strategy document by European Union (EU) on data strategy and AI [10], the following definition clearly states this fact - "Simply put, AI is a collection of technologies that combine data, algorithms and computing power. Advances in computing and the increasing availability of data are therefore key drivers of the current upsurge of AI".

While the connection between data and AI is clear, the challenge is to make sure that these data-intensive activities do not happen in an ad hoc, fragmented, and sporadic way, but rather are integrated into the culture of the healthcare system across the board and become standard practice including - health ministry, research institutions, health referral systems, clinics, health stations and health posts at national and sub-national levels, and academic institutions across Ethiopia. The purpose of this study is to investigate the current state of data infrastructure and data strategy in healthcare systems and services in Ethiopia with a view to propose activities and strategies that leverage data for AI applications. Data strategy across the healthcare system is considered including public health (e.g., disease surveillance) and clinical services (e.g., screening, diagnosis, and treatment). A strategic approach to identify methods and processes that guide activities around data management and use across healthcare facilities, healthcare research centers, relevant ministry agencies, etc., is pursed. Specific focus areas for this study include: policies that govern data collection, data management, data storage; responsible units and/or centers that coordinate data management activities across and between relevant healthcare institutions; the current state of workforce expertise engaged in data management activities; data integration strategies exist; data storage technologies in use; the metadata specifications developed to describe and document data; ethical guidelines and finally what kinds of analytic tools and use cases in AI applications exist in Ethiopian healthcare system.

In addition to the different facets of data management strategies described above, data from Papers with Code (data in Meta AI Research) in the biomedical and health sciences domain will be used to identify proven and tested State-of-the-Art (SOTA) benchmarks, AI models, use cases, libraries, and frameworks.

2 Data Management in Ethiopian Healthcare

The Ethiopian healthcare system, for the size of the country and its population, while still lags behind from comparable low-middle income countries, has made impressive strides in various areas including skilled workforce development, improving existing health facility infrastructure, building new health facilities including expansion of rural health centers, improving universal access and coverage, and improving the IT and information system infrastructure. In 2018, health worker density was estimated at 1.0 per 1,000 population (considerably lower than 4.5 per 1000 population standard proposed by WHO to achieve UHC, Universal health Coverage) [45]. Or, By the end of 2011 Ethiopian fiscal year (2018/19),17,550 HPs, 3,735 health centers and 353 hospitals were available; and 425 health posts, 96 health centers, and 107 hospitals were under construction in Ethiopia. In addition, during HSTP-I, special purpose facilities, including warehouses, trauma centers, mini blood banks and laboratory infrastructures were constructed [13].

According to the 2018 service availability and readiness assessment (SARA) survey, only of the 764 health facilities surveyed have the seven amenity tracer elements (i.e., water, electricity, sanitation facilities, emergency transport, consultation room, computer with internet, and communication equipment) and the mean availability of these tracer items for all facilities assessed was 39% with referral hospitals scoring the highest and health posts the lowest (30%) (FMOH and EPHI. 2018). In addition, the WHO global health workforce statistics database (WHO, 2022) was queried to get a quick snapshot of the numbers for medical doctors and nursing and midwifery personnel for the years 2018-2020. The following table provides the result of the query of how Ethiopia compares to neighboring countries as well as countries in the south, west, and north Africa.

In regards to the specific focus of this study around data infrastructure and digital services, the HSTP II (Health Sector Transformation Plan II of 2020/21 - 2024/25) reports encouraging initiatives and accomplishments around quality data use, digitization of priority health information system (HIS), and governance of HIS that resulted in the implementation of eCHIS (Community Health Information System) at 6,320 rural health posts, and DHIS2 (District Health Information System) at 95% of the health institutions [29,30]. The fact that DHIS2 penetration is reported at 95% of Ethiopian Health Institutions, it can be taken as a huge success. DHIS2 is an open source, web-based software platform for data collection, management, and analysis [40].

With such great successes and promises, when it comes to data infrastructure and AI applications, there are still persisting challenges that the Ethiopian healthcare system face as in many developing countries, and these include lack

Table 2. Comparison of healthcare workforce data.

Workforce	Country	Per 10,000	Number	Generalist	Specialist
Medical Doctors	Ethiopia	1.06	12174	9361	2813
	Kenya	1.57	8042	5602	2440
	Sudan	2.62	10683		
	Senegal	0.88	1435	353	1082
	Algeria	17.19	72604	32774	39830
	Rwanda	1.34	1648	1114	534
Nursing and Midwifery	Ethiopia	7.84	90179	69824	20355
	Kenya	11.66	59901	59901	
	Sudan	11.46	47882	47882	
	Senegal	5.40	8807	6151	2656
	Algeria	15.48	95359	56411	8948
	Rwanda	9.48	11970	10409	1561

of representative, reliable, and robust data coupled with the infrastructure to collect, organize, analyze, and use big data [9, 14]. Vital statistics such as births, deaths and causes of death are not often registered in uniform, standardized manner and across health centers and facilities in Ethiopia [16]. Electronic medical records are not uniformly implemented in the majority of the healthcare facilities. Other than the ministry of health and select health research centers, dedicated units with data science professionals that work in data management and AI applications are largely absent. The data analytics largely involves descriptive statistics that summarizes and reports on the current situations without offering much predictive or prescriptive insights. The data are mostly survey-based, a chief example of which is the popular demographic and health survey (DHS)- that involves community and public health data on various indicators such as infant and maternal mortality rates, nationally representative data on fertility, family planning, maternal and child health, gender, HIV/AIDS, malaria, and nutrition.

The Ethiopian Public Health Institute (EPHI) and Armature Hansen Research Institute (AHRI) are the exceptions and have relatively well-organized units staffed by qualified professionals to handle data management tasks. This author visited with the national data management center for health at the EPHI and spoke at length with two great professionals running the center. The NDMC is a great center staffed with 17 professionals with expertise in public health, epidemiologists, statistics, and computer science - organized around case team that are the stewards of the country's health data and conduct advanced analytics and modeling. The recent national 'health atlas' report outlining the burden of disease at national and sub-national level produced by NDMC in collaboration with the Institute of Health Metrics and Evaluation (IHME) at the University of Washington is an excellent example [5].

The National Data Management Center for health (NDMC) at the Ethiopian Public Health Institute (EPHI) is responsible to centrally archive health and health related data, process and manage health research, apply robust data analytic techniques, synthesize evidence and to ensure evidence utilization for decision making by the Federal Ministry of Health (FMoH). In the 120p document of HSTP II, it picked up from HSTP I to strengthen studies such as SARA and DQR (Data Quality Review) and further positions EPHI/NDMC as the coordinating center for Ethiopia when it comes to data activities. The planned data center to be built inside the NDMC with 50TB HPC is another opportunity for NDMC to continue its work with great efficiency - in data stewardship, governance, and data sharing for the wider healthcare community and academic institutions, as well as government policy makers at national and regional levels.

In addition to the heavy survey-based data collected and analyzed, there are a few examples with potential to expand - for example - data submitted to the global Health Data Exchange at the Institute for Health Metrics and Evaluation (IHME), there are about 1003 datasets (https://ghdx.healthdata.org/geography/ethiopia) deposited and the breakdown of these datasets by the type of data is as follows.

Table 3. Datasets deposited to health data exchange.

Data type	Number	Data type	Number
Administrative data	11	Geospatial data	2
Census	7	Intervention study	1
Demographic surveil-	11	Legislation	0
lance	6	Modleed data	0
Disease registry	6	Report	61
Environmental monitor-	49	Scientific literature	676
ing	50	Survey	118
Epi surveillance	6	Vital registration	0
Estimate	0		
Event data			
Financial record			

The majority of these datasets are provided by international organizations such as the WHO and/or in some of the cases Ethiopia is included in the aggregate as part of a regional data collection effort. A few interesting notes in these data collection is that there is no 'vital registration' or 'modeled data' datasets for Ethiopia and all the six 'disease registry' datasets are for Addis Ababa city select hospitals. The disease registry (by the Addis Ababa City Cancer Registry (AACCR) is the first population-based cancer registry in Ethiopia. It collects data from 17 selected health institutions with cancer diagnostic and/or treatment services in Addis Ababa. Epi surveillance - Environmental monitoring - geospatial data (FB Data for Good, e.g.) GPS Coordinates - Demographic surveillance (mostly, again, in Addis Ababa - one in Butajira).

3   Study Design

From the broader foundational guideposts in data management such as the FAIR principles [4] to government agency frameworks in Science Data Lifecycle Model (SDLM) [11], and data management strategy recommendations by global consultancy firms [18], to a more health and life sciences data management and sharing policies [25], there are several often overlapping policies and frameworks that guide in establishing a sound data management and access governance. In this study, for its wider adoption and appeal the FAIR principles is chosen to frame the investigation how NDMC at EPHI addresses healthcare data management and sharing. Figure provides an encapsulated summary of the FAIR principles [35].

Figure 1 Together with FAIR principles, key data strategy elements such as: data governance, data architecture, needs assessment, future state vision and roadmap, organizational analytics maturity assessment [18] are considered to evaluate the degree to which Ethiopian healthcare system leverages a strategic approach to data management and access activities.

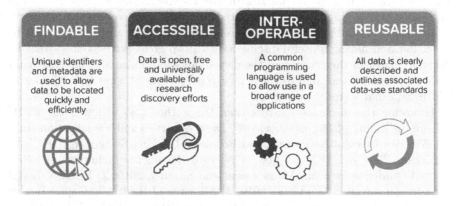

Fig. 1. FAIR principles [https://kidsfirstdrc.org/about/drc_impact/, accessed August 7, 2022].

In regard to the degree to which AI applications leverage healthcare data in the context of Ethiopia, existing data use cases were looked through the prism of the State-of-the-Art (SOTA) use cases, tasks, and benchmarks. Using data from Papers with Code - that is: data from Meta AI Research [28], this study presents top-performing tasks, benchmarks and AI models, use cases, libraries, and frameworks that received SOTA status. Currently, there are 9,199 benchmarks, 3,665 tasks, 78,490 papers with code including 6,827 machine learning datasets, 1,972 machine learning components/methods, and 944 machine learning models/Libraries that received SOTA status. In medical sciences alone, there are 264 benchmarks, 212 tasks, 150 datasets, and 3056 papers with code. The benchmarks in the medical sciences that received SOTA status are large to review them all, so this study considered 5 task areas in image segmentation, cell segmentation, drug discovery, medical diagnosis, and mortality prediction.

Additional data points for the study comes from a review of important documents and an in-person conversation with the director/lead coordinator and software engineer, both at the National Data Management Center (NDMC). The documents reviewed were: 1) EPHI Revised Guideline for Data Management and Sharing, 2019; 2) EPHI National Data Implementation Guideline, 2019; 3) Ministry of Health. Ethiopia: Health Sector Transformation Plan II, HSTP II; and 3) Ethiopia Health Atlas, 2021.

4   Results and Discussion

The National Data Management Center for Health (NDMC) is the lead entity under EPHI that is charged with coordination and stewardship of health research data in Ethiopia. Working with different directorates across federal and regional-level ministry of health organs, health facilities at all levels, and international partners such as the Institute for Health Metrics and Evaluation (IHME) at the University of Washington, it is mandated to collect, receive, archive, manage, analyze, share and disseminate health related data. After an in-person visit to the center and having a useful discussion with two great professionals - that is, the coordinator of the center and the data analysis and visualization case team leader, the author was able to get a very good picture of what NDMC does in health data management and access.

Following the in-person conversation, the author also reviewed the EPHI website (including platforms such as the Data Analytics and Visualization Hub, H-DAV; Health Data Repository and Research Tracking System, RTDS; Data Collection Platform, DCP as well as relevant documents including: 1) EPHI Revised Guideline for Data Management and Sharing, 2019; 2) EPHI National Data Implementation Guideline, 2019; 3) Ministry of Health. Ethiopia: Health Sector Transformation Plan II, HSTP II; and 3) Ethiopia Health Atlas, 2021.

Organized into four units, that is: 1) data repository and governance; 2) data analytics and visualization; 3) data to action; and 4) burden of diseases - the NDMC has 17 diverse and very qualified professionals with expertise ranging from public health, international health, computer science/computer engineering, statistics, and linguistics. Data is received from various directorates at EPHI such as Food Science and Research Directorate; Health System and Reproductive Health; National Laboratory; Public Health Emergency Management; Bacteriology, Parasitology and Zoonosis; as well as non-EPHI sources, chief among them is the Ethiopian Statistics Service, and NGOs. Currently the repository has

416 datasets including published articles and reports. The bulk of the datasets, about 85%, are survey data. The datasets can be publicly queried via the RTDS platform - Heath Data Repository and Research Tracking System with advanced search options. However, one has to submit a request to download the associated dataset returned from the search result.

The data repository is described on the RTDS portal as a platform designed and implemented with the FAIR principles considered. However, more work remains to achieve open and FAIR repository and access system. For example, inspecting the search results and the metadata description associated with any item in the result set, it is difficult to find a persistent or unique identifier for the data (hence posing a challenge to future discoverability), or from the platform there is no option for API-based query to the datasets, data citation information, description of tools and software used and README files to describe project level and file level details are not available - together limits consolidating data into a single place and view, and hence challenge for interoperability. Equally, it is not clear what standard vocabulary language is used, whether there is a codebook and/or data dictionary to document and describe data and metadata and all the granular level variable - that in turn will impact accessibility and reusability of data.

Overall, when evaluated through the FAIR principles, the data management activities by NDMC can be summarized as follows. It is to be noted that the FAIR principles is a high-level guideline and is not a specific technical specification.

- Findable - 'unique id' and 'rich metadata' are core attributes for universal findability. The data at NDMC repository use internal ID's such as 'EPHI-DS0072' and it is not helpful for long-term archiving and identification of networked resources. Unique digital resource identifiers such as DOI number or persistent handles should be made public when the data is published. The metadata provided by NDMC, while helpful for Ethiopian researchers, it is not consistent with community standards for a global audience. Instead, standard metadata vocabularies that map with standards such as DataCite metadata schema is required.
- Accessible - core attributes in this dimension A in FAIR include 'open', 'free', 'searchable'. NDMC metadata can be searched and freely accessible via the RTDS (Health Data Repository and Research Tracking System) platform [https://rtds.ephi.gov.et/public/]. However, the data can not be downloaded automatically. Instead, a request should be submitted to get the dataset and it is not clear if who will be granted permission to access the dataset. This limits 'openness,' one of the key attributes of Accessibility in FAIR. The datasets at NDMC are not publicly published. Even when the data is restricted, the common practice is to allow data and metadata to be searched and accessed using API key/tokens.
- Interoperable - here the key attributes to be used as measure are 'data format' and 'common programming language or tools' used. At NDMC, data formats are largely '.csdb' for census data sources, and processed using SPSS

'.SAV' format. These formats don't allow easy integration with other systems. Machine-readable formats such as JSON, RDF, XML, CSV, are required. Good data stewardship requires preparing the data for machine discovery at the data repository level.

- Reusable - 'data documentation' 'data code books' 'data and metadata use standards' are attributes that suggest reusability. Associating data and metadata with detailed provenance and publishing data and metadata with clear data use license statements are cardinal principles that promote R in FAIR. At NDMC, limited details are provided that permit stakeholders and downstream researchers to access and use the data. For example, other than 'title' and 'description' attributes, little details are given such as citation information in case of reuse. In addition, there is no accompanying documentation or code that describes the data and analysis methods to understand the data better.

The data collection platform, DCP, uses a mix of well known and robust tools and software including REDCap, DHIS2 (District Health Information System), ODK (Open Data Kit), CSPro (Census and survey processing). While internal documentation may exist, it is important that NDMC take the lead to coordinate efforts in providing training to responsible entities, as well as developing standard templates to ensure quality data, reduce human error, improve consistency, and avoid missing values that will save significant time down the road. In addition, it is pertinent to expand the data collection effort to clinical records across healthcare facilities on priority disease conditions following privacy preserving protocols. Often, enrolling representative and select individuals based on priority areas into a multi-year, longitudinal data collection programs is beneficial.

NDMC had worked with ICF International, a global consulting and digital services company, to conduct demographic and health survey (DHS). Because of this connection and the rich portfolio of work the company undertook in African healthcare service improvement through digital technology, this study considered ICF International's key elements of data strategy, that is: - data governance, data architecture, needs assessment, future state vision and roadmap, organizational analytics maturity assessment. Accordingly, there are plenty of evidence that suggest NDMC has a well-thought out 'data governance' articulation and to a degree 'data architecture' and 'needs assessment' specifications. Through documents reviewed such as 'Data Implementation Guidelines,' and 'Data Management and Sharing Guideline,' it is evident that the database organization plan is a good marker for data architecture. To the contrary, the review did not find any details that pertain to the other two key elements of data strategy, and these are - 1) future state vision and roadmap, and 2) organizational analytics maturity assessment.

The next major component reviewed was NDMC's National health data analytics and visualization (H-DAV) dashboard. The data analytics and visualization case team lead the task of cleaning, preparing, and analyzing the data in the repository with a goal to disseminate useful insight for decision-making at all levels of the health sector and government policy makers. A closer look into the visualization artefacts and analysis methods reveal that most fall in the area of report generation, data summary and synthesis using descriptive statistics and, in a few exceptions, modeled and estimate data. For example, the perinatal mortality rate by region as shown in the following bar chart, while useful to make comparisons across regions and changes every 5 years from 2000 to 2016, doesn't give us much insights why certain regions are doing better or worse. The method used is also a simple average to find early neonatal death rate per 1000. The data source for the bar chart shown below is from the Ethiopian Demographic Health Survey (EDHS) 2000,2005,2011 and 2016 dataset.

Figure 2 To meet the objectives of this study, the SOTA benchmarks, tasks, and methods were used to showcase the kinds of use cases that are currently dominating the field of AI applications in healthcare. The goal is to suggest the idea that NDMC should leapfrog through its strategy for data management and analysis pipeline by employing more cutting-edge AI methods to get more powerful insights (such as predictive insights). NDMC through a more broad-based redefining or roles and capacity building need to start to go beyond descriptive and inferential statistical methods that won't help explain the underlying causes why certain results are the way they are.

From papers with code (https://paperswithcode.com/sota), by focusing on biomedical categories, only a few tasks and use cases were selected to demonstrate the kinds of task (sub-task), dataset used, model, and the names of the metrics with their performance score. The most implemented papers for each of the tasks shown in table 4 with their descriptions are:

– Medical image segmentation task - segmentation of polyps in colonoscopy images for lesion detection - on Kvasir-SEG dataset (https://datasets.simula. no/kvasir-seg/) - using Fully Convolutional Branch- TransFormer (FCB-Former) model - the performance of the model was evaluated with respect to mDICE (average DICE metric, that assesses the quality of classification) - achieved a metric value of 0.9385 (the dice coefficient ranges from 0 to 1, with 1 signifying the greatest similarity between predicted and truth).
– Cell segmentation task -microscopy cell segmentation - on DIC-C2DH-HeLa dataset (Differential Interference Contrast microscopy images of HeLa cells on flat glass, HeLa cell populations included in the Cell Tracking Challenge database http://celltrackingchallenge.net/2d-datasets/)- using the encoder section with C-LSTM layers (referred to as EncLSTM Convolutional Long-Short Term Memory) model - segmentation accuracy (SEG) of the average intersection over union (mean IoU) evaluation measures in the Cell Segmentation Benchmark - achieved an IoU of 79.3%.
– Drug discovery task to discover new candidate drugs - on Tox21 dataset (Toxicology in the 21st Century https://tripod.nih.gov/tox/) - using SSVAE (Semi-supervised Sequential Variational Autoencoder) model defined over multiple SMILES (Simplified Molecular Input Line Entry System, a chemical structure line notation for entering and representing molecules) - evaluated with the area under the receiver operating characteristic curve (AUC-ROC)

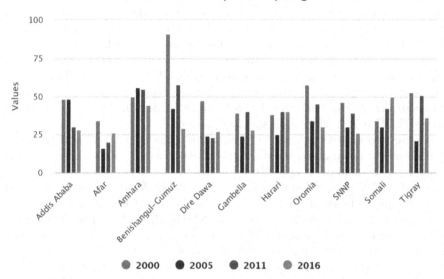

Fig. 2. FAIR principles [Perinatal mortality rate by regional states in Ethiopia. [https://vizhub.ephi.gov.et/pages/perinatalmortality/index.php, Accessed August 12, 2022].

- fully supervised regression averaged over all 12 toxicity types resulted in 0.871 score.
- Mortality prediction task for patients admitted to critical care units at a large tertiary care hospital - on Medical Information Mart for Intensive Care (MIMIC-III) dataset (a large, de-identified and publicly available collection of medical records https://mimic.mit.edu/) - using random forest classifier achieved 97% performance across all three measures, that is, precision (the correctness achieved in positive prediction), recall (calculates how many of the actual positives our model capture through labeling it as positive (True Positive), and F1-Score (a weighted average of the recall and precision).
- Medical diagnosis task, the process of identifying the disease a patient is af-fected by, based on the assessment of specific risk factors, signs, symp-toms and results of exams - on clinical admission notes from Medical Infor-mation Mart for Intensive Care (MIMIC-III) dataset (a large, de-identified and publicly available collection of medical records https://mimic.mit.edu/) - using the CORe model (Clinical Outcome Representations) - results in perfor-mance score of 83.54% area under the receiver operating characteristic curve (AUROC) averaged over all 10 disease conditions and procedures.

The table below summarizes these benchmarks and the metric score.

Table 4. Select examples of AI applications in biomedical field.

Task	Dataset	Model	Metric name	Metric value
Medical image segmentation	KVASIR-SEG	FCBFormer	mean DICE	0.9385
Cell segmentation	DIC-C2DH-HeLa	EncLSTM	SEG (Mean IoU)	0.793
Drug discovery	Tox21	SSVAE with multiple SMILES	AUC-ROC	0.871
Mortality prediction	MIMIC-III	Random Forest	F1 Score, Precision, Recall	0.97
Medical diagnosis	Clinical admission notes from MIMIC-III	CORe	AUROC	83.54

5   Conclusion

This study sets out to investigate data management practices and activities by Ethiopian healthcare system through the lens of strategic approach. In so doing, the goal was to determine the extent to which good data management practices leverage AI applications in healthcare. Initially three institutions viz. 1) Ethiopian Public Health Institute; 2) Ethiopian Biotechnology Institute; and 3) Tikur Anbessa Specialized Hospital (TASH), the leading teaching hospital in the College of Health Sciences (CHS) at Addis Ababa University (AAU) - were identified to assess data management, data access, data sharing, data governance, data security, data preservation, data use, and overall infrastructure that exist to support these sets of activities.

Once it was determined that the national data management center for health (NDMC) was the lead coordinating body mandated with health data management and sharing, the other two institutions were dropped to place more focus on NDMC. NDMC is very well positioned and has the underlying infrastructure and skilled personnel to take on the charge of coordinating data collection, data analysis, data sharing, data governance, training, and data preservation and security. As discussed in the results section above, the center, however, needs to be strengthened to build onto what it is currently doing. For example, to add more diverse and heterogenous data such as biomedical images, more genomic sequence data, modeling data, or clinical and vital registration data, in addition to public health survey data. The center needs to employ more predictive and prescriptive types of analytic methods such as in AI/ML/DL to better predict health phenomena, in addition to describing and reporting on what is happening. The center needs to build a more open and FAIR repository system so that healthcare researchers, academicians, students, and government policymakers can access, download, and manipulate the data in various ways that further spurs discovery. This also promotes machine readable and accessible data platform.

In addition, NDMC should take the strategic approach by taking the whole-Ethiopia view to develop capacity at national, regional, woreda, and rural health posts and centers level. This could involve strengthening NDMC to build both public health and clinical data management capacities, work with academic institutions, play a coordinating role to establish data management teams at regional and woreda level. Coordinate continuous professional development, allow both vertical and horizontal integration between and among all the data management teams in the country, developing a robust metadata with standard vocabularies that permit humans as well as machine-to-machine communication through API access, developing a data dictionary that describes data elements and variables at a granular level, developing consistent templates and frameworks for data collection, access, and sharing, including frameworks for ethics, license for use, and different toolkits for data management for the entire lifecycle, for security, for management, and for quality assurance.

To take the strategic approach - the two key elements missing from ICF International recommendations, namely: 1) future state vision and roadmap, and 2) organizational analytics maturity assessment should be looked into. This could take the form of developing a 'data management strategy' roadmaps and conducting digital readiness and maturity assessment at each level of the health-care system. With the institutional framework in place, units and teams will be deployed to pursue best practices in data management and use. A diverse group of talent is needed to staff units and centers at national and regional levels with expertise in computer science and statistics, public health, clinical service, bioinformatics, etc. For the existing staff, data upskilling in a form of continuous professional development could be offered in a coordinated manner.

References

1. Alonso, S.G., de la Torre Diez, I., Rodrigues, J.J., Hamrioui, S., Lopez-Coronado, M.: A systematic review of techniques and sources of big data in the healthcare sector. J. Med. Syst. **41**(11), 1–9 (2017)
2. Aswathy, M.A., Jagannath, M.: Detection of breast cancer on digital histopathology images: Present status and future possibilities. Inform. Med. Unlocked **8**, 74–79 (2017)
3. Baker, D., et al.: Research data management in Canada: a backgrounder. Genève, Switzerland, Zenodo (2019)
4. Boeckhout, M., Zielhuis, G.A., Bredenoord, A.L.: The FAIR guiding principles for data stewardship: fair enough? Eur. J. Hum. Genet. **26**(7), 931–936 (2018)
5. Burden of Disease Unit (BoD). National Data Management Center (NDMC) for health. Ethiopia Public Health Institute. Ethiopia Health Atlas, 2021. Addis Ababa, Ethiopia (2021). https://ndmc.ephi.gov.et/download/national-health-atlas-2021/
6. Chatterjee, S.: AI strategy of India: policy framework, adoption challenges and actions for government. Transforming Gov.: People Process. Policy **14**(5), 757–775 (2020)
7. Chen, P.T., Lin, C.L., Wu, W.N.: Big data management in healthcare: adoption challenges and implications. Int. J. Inf. Manag. **53**, 102078 (2020)

8. David, L., Thakkar, A., Mercado, R., Engkvist, O.: Molecular representations in AI-driven drug discovery: a review and practical guide. J. Cheminformatics **12**(1), 1–22 (2020)
9. Easterly, W.: How the millennium development goals are unfair to Africa. World Dev. **37**(1), 26–35 (2009)
10. European Commission. A European strategy for data. Shaping Europe's digital future (2022). https://digital-strategy.ec.europa.eu/en/policies/strategy-data
11. Faundeen, J.L., et al.: The United States geological survey science data lifecycle model. US Department of the Interior, US Geological Survey, Reston, VA, USA (2013)
12. Faust, O., Hagiwara, Y., Hong, T.J., Lih, O.S., Acharya, U.R.: Deep learning for healthcare applications based on physiological signals: a review. Comput. Methods Programs Biomed. **161**, 1–13 (2018)
13. The Federal Democratic Republic of Ethiopia (FDRE). Ministry of Health. HSTP: Health Sector Transformation Plan. 2015/16-019/20, p. 184 (2015)
14. Fehling, M., Nelson, B.D., Venkatapuram, S.: Limitations of the millennium development goals: a literature review. Glob. Public Health **8**(10), 1109–1122 (2013)
15. FMOH and EPHI: Service Availability and Readiness Assessment (SARA). Addis Ababa, Ethiopia (2018)
16. Gebremedhin, L.T.: Investment in health data can drive economic growth. Nat. Med. **28**, 2000 (2022). https://doi.org/10.1038/s41591-022-02022-8
17. Holmström, J.: From AI to digital transformation: the AI readiness framework. Bus. Horiz. **65**(3), 329–339 (2022)
18. ICF International Inc. Analytics, AI, and Impact (2022). https://www.icf.com/work/analytics
19. Jiang, F., et al.: Artificial intelligence in healthcare: past, present and future. Stroke Vasc. Neurol. **2**(4) (2017)
20. Jöhnk, J., Weißert, M., Wyrtki, K.: Ready or not, AI comes-an interview study of organizational AI readiness factors. Bus. Inf. Syst. Eng. **63**(1), 5–20 (2021)
21. Johnson, K.B., et al.: Precision medicine, AI, and the future of personalized health care. Clin. Trans. Sci. **14**(1), 86–93 (2021)
22. Kazim, E.: Innovation and opportunity: review of the UK's national AI strategy. Discover Artif. Intell. **1**(1), 1–10 (2021)
23. Lin, S.Y., Mahoney, M.R., Sinsky, C.A.: Ten ways artificial intelligence will transform primary care. J. Gen. Intern. Med. **34**(8), 1626–1630 (2019)
24. Lipton, Z. C., Kale, D. C., Elkan, C., Wetzel, R.: Learning to diagnose with LSTM recurrent neural networks (2015). arXiv preprint arXiv:1511.03677
25. Martone, M.E., Nakamura, R.: Changing the culture on data management and sharing: overview and highlights from a workshop held by the national academies of sciences, engineering, and medicine. Harvard Data Sci. Rev. **4**(3) (2022). https://doi.org/10.1162/99608f92.44975b62
26. Mathers, C.D., Loncar, D.: Projections of global mortality and burden of disease from 2002 to 2030. PLoS Med. **3**(11), e442 (2006). https://doi.org/10.1371/journal.pmed.0030442
27. Medeiros, M.M.D., Maçada, A.C.G., Freitas Junior, J.C.D.S.: The effect of data strategy on competitive advantage. Bottom Line **33**(2), 201–216 (2020). https://doi.org/10.1108/BL-12-2019-0131
28. Meta AI. Papers with Code. https://paperswithcode.com/sota
29. Ministry of Health (2022). eCHIS. https://www.moh.gov.et/site/projects-3-col/echis

30. Ministry of Health (2022). DHIS2. https://www.moh.gov.et/site/projects-3-col/dhis2

31. MIT Laboratory for Computational Physiology. PhysioBank, PhysioToolkit, and PhysioNet: Components of a New Research Resource for Complex Physiologic Signals (2022). https://www.physionet.org/about/

32. Neumann, J.: FAIR data infrastructure. Adv. Biochem. Eng. Biotechnol. **182**, 195–207 (2022). https://doi.org/10.1007/10_2021_193

33. Reinsel, D., Gantz, J., Rydning, J.: The digitization of the world from edge to core. IDC white paper, **13** (2018)

34. Roberts, H., Cowls, J., Morley, J., Taddeo, M., Wang, V., Floridi, L.: The Chinese approach to artificial intelligence: an analysis of policy, ethics, and regulation. AI Soc. **36**(1), 59–77 (2021)

35. Sansone, S.A., et al.: FAIRsharing as a community approach to standards, repositories and policies. Nat. Biotechnol. **37**(4), 358–367 (2019)

36. Schmeiss, J., Friederici, N.: Understanding 'AI Made in Germany': a report on the german startup landscape. Delphi **2**, 87 (2019)

37. Schneider, D.F.: Machine learning and artificial intelligence. In: Dimick, J.B., Lubitz, C.C. (eds.) Health Services Research. SAS, pp. 155–168. Springer, Cham (2020). https://doi.org/10.1007/978-3-030-28357-5_14

38. Shaheen, M.Y.: Applications of artificial intelligence (AI) in healthcare: a review. ScienceOpen Preprints (2021)

39. Topol, E.: Deep medicine: how artificial intelligence can make healthcare human again. Hachette UK (2019)

40. UiO. University of Oslo (2022). About DHIS2. https://dhis2.org/about/

41. Väänänen, A., Haataja, K., Vehviläinen-Julkunen, K., Toivanen, P.: AI in healthcare: a narrative review. F1000Research, **10**(6), 6 (2021)

42. Veta, M., Pluim, J.P., Van Diest, P.J., Viergever, M.A.: Breast cancer histopathology image analysis: a review. IEEE Trans. Biomed. Eng. **61**(5), 1400–1411 (2014)

43. Wang, P., Zheng, X., Li, J., Zhu, B.: Prediction of epidemic trends in COVID-19 with logistic model and machine learning technics. Chaos Solitons Fractals **139**, 110058 (2020)

44. Wilkinson, M.D., et al.: The FAIR guiding principles for scientific data management and stewardship. Sci. Data **3**, 160018 (2016). https://doi.org/10.1038/sdata.2016.18

45. World Health Organization. The Global Health Observatory: Explore a world of health data. Global Health Workforce Statistics Database (2022). https://www.who.int/data/gho/data/themes/topics/health-workforce

46. Zemouri, R., Zerhouni, N., Racoceanu, D.: Deep learning in the biomedical applications: recent and future status. Appl. Sci. **9**(8), 1526 (2019)

AI-Based Heart Disease and Brain Stroke Prediction Using Multi-modal Patient Data

Gizeaddis Lamesgin Simegn[1,2]([✉])[ID] and Mizanu Zelalem Degu[2,3][ID]

[1] Biomedical Image Unit, School of Biomedical Engineering, Jimma Institute of Technology, Jimma University, Jimma, Ethiopia
gizeaddis.lamesgin@ju.edu.et
[2] AI and Biomedical Imaging Research Unit, Jimma Institute of Technology, Jimma University, Jimma, Ethiopia
[3] Faculty of Computing and Informatics, Jimma Institute of Technology, Jimma University, Jimma, Ethiopia

Abstract. Heart disease and stroke are among the major causes of death and disabilities globally causing numerous social or economic difficulties. Neurological damage is the primary cause of most deaths following a stroke, with cardiovascular issues being the second leading cause. Research findings, both from clinical and experimental studies, indicate a cause-and-effect connection between damage to the brain and the development of heart disease. If left untreated at early stages, stroke, and heart disease can lead to death. Therefore, Early diagnosis and monitoring of these diseases are crucial for the reduction of morbidity and mortality. In this research electronic medical records of patients' symptoms, body features, clinical laboratory test values, and brain images were used to analyze patterns, and train and validate different machine learning and deep learning models to predict heart disease and brain stroke. Three types of modules including machine learning-based heart disease, brain stroke prediction using clinical data, and a deep learning-based brain stroke prediction using brain MRI image data were designed and deployed into a user-friendly custom-made user interface. The heart disease and brain stroke prediction models were found to be 100% and 97.1% accurate in predicting heart disease and brain stroke, respectively, based on clinical and patient information, while the MRI image-based deep learning stroke prediction model was 96.67% accurate. Our experimental results suggest that the proposed systems may have the potential to impact clinical practice and become a decision support system for physicians to predict heart disease and brain stroke from a set of risk factors and laboratory tests improving diagnosis accuracy for better treatment planning.

Keywords: Brain stroke · Clinical data · Deep learning · Heart disease · Machine learning · Prediction

T. Girma Debelee et al. (Eds.): PanAfriCon AI 2022, CCIS 1800, pp. 67–78, 2023.
https://doi.org/10.1007/978-3-031-31327-1_4

1   Introduction

Currently, heart disease (HD) is a widespread ailment that can be attributed to various factors, including high blood pressure, diabetes, fluctuations in cholesterol levels, fatigue, and several other causes [1]. Similarly, stroke is a major health-related challenge and the second leading cause of death and disability globally [2,3]. The primary cause of heart attacks and strokes is the obstruction of blood flow to the heart or brain. This is commonly due to the accumulation of fatty deposits on the inner walls of the blood vessels that provide blood to these organs, which can cause the blood vessels to become narrower and less flexible. A stroke takes place when a section of the brain loses its blood supply, and as a result, it stops functioning. Blood flow is essential for the brain to function properly. There are two significant blood vessels located on each side of the neck that supplies blood from the heart to the brain. As these blood vessels branch out and become smaller, they ultimately provide oxygen and nutrients to all areas of the brain. When a stroke happens, the area of the body controlled by the affected part of the brain ceases to function [4,5]. A stroke, which is also known as a cerebrovascular accident or brain attack, is a medical condition that affects the brain and can occur due to blockage or bleeding in the brain's arteries. It often causes a range of motor and cognitive problems, which can vary from person to person and limit their ability to function normally [6].

Heart disease and stroke are frequently occurring conditions that have many similarities in their underlying physiological processes. They both typically result from a blockage that hinders the flow of blood to either the heart or the brain [7,8]. Arteriosclerosis, a condition where the arteries harden, can greatly impact a patient and put them at risk for both acute coronary syndrome (ACS) and acute stroke. In both cases, there is a sudden interruption of blood flow, leading to a decrease in circulation to the heart or brain. A stroke is sometimes referred to as a "brain attack" because it is similar to a heart attack but in the brain. As a result, there are similarities between ACS and acute stroke in terms of their epidemiology, risk factors, causes, and treatment options. Furthermore, studies have shown that stroke patients often have coronary artery disease and that having chronic coronary artery disease also increases the likelihood of experiencing a stroke [9,10]. The primary risk factors for heart disease and stroke are hypertension, high levels of low-density lipoprotein (LDL) cholesterol, diabetes, smoking or being exposed to secondhand smoke, obesity, unhealthy eating habits, and a lack of physical activity [11,12]. Hypertension is particularly concerning because it can harm the artery lining, rendering it more vulnerable to plaque accumulation. This can lead to a constriction of the arteries that transport blood to the heart and brain, posing a significant risk for heart disease and stroke [12,13].

The identification and management of heart disease and stroke can be challenging in developing countries due to limited access to diagnostic equipment, healthcare professionals, and other resources. As a result, it is often difficult to diagnose and treat patients with heart disease and stroke, resulting in fewer opportunities for disease prevention and management [14,15]. Lack of effective treatment complicates the curing of heart disease and stroke patients. On the

other hand, even if patients with heart disease and stroke are treated successfully, they may still experience long-term consequences such as permanent disability, reduced ability to perform daily tasks, and decreased participation in
social activities. This puts a significant burden on the patient, the healthcare
system, and society as a whole. Additionally, research suggests that there may
be a period of time before the onset of a stroke where warning signs are present
but not yet noticeable, known as the "eclipse period" [16–18].

Early detection can help reduce the incidence rate of the diseases. In this
regard, different machine learning and deep learning-based heart disease and
brain stroke prediction systems have been proposed in literature [19–25]. However, it is challenging to predict brain stroke and heart disease easily because
the data related to the disease are multi-modal or multi-source. To achieve high
accuracy of prediction and combine the stroke and heart disease risk predictors,
a method for predicting the probability of stroke and heart disease occurrence
based on multi-source data is required. To resolve these complexities an integrated decision support system based on machine learning and deep learning
predictive models has been proposed in this study, for the prediction of heart
disease and brain stroke.

2 Methods

In this paper, three modules were designed and developed for heart disease and
brain stroke prediction. To develop the first module, which involves predicting
heart disease, machine learning models were trained and tested using structured
patient information such as age, gender, and hypertension history, as well as real-
time clinical data like heart rate and blood pressure. The second module, brain
stroke prediction, was developed based on laboratory data and patient information. For the third module, brain stroke prediction using MRI data, MRI image
data was used to train and validate deep learning models. Finally, a user-friendly
web-based system was developed for ease of use of the developed subsystems for
the diagnosis of heart disease and brain stroke. Figure 1 demonstrates the summary of the general framework of the proposed system.

2.1 Heart Disease Prediction Model

To the prediction of heart disease, a dataset of 1190 observations was collected
from the University of California Irvine (UCI) Machine Learning Repository [26].
This dataset contains different attributes such as age, sex, chest pain type, blood
pressure, cholesterol level (in mg/dL), blood sugar, and maximum heart rate.
The data were originally obtained from 5 separate datasets, including the Cleve-
land V.A. Medical Center (303 observations), Hungarian (294 observations),
Switzerland (123 observations), Long Beach V.A. Medical Center (200 observations), and Stalog dataset (270 observations).

The data was used to train and test three different machine learning models: XGBoost, Random Forest, and an artificial neural network (ANN) model.

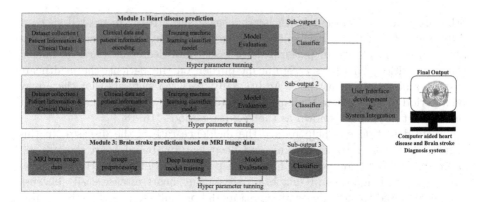

Fig. 1. General framework of the proposed system.

XGBoost is a type of ensemble machine-learning algorithm that is based on decision trees and uses a gradient-boosting framework. It is optimized for distributed computing and designed to be highly efficient, flexible, and portable. XGBoost provides a parallel tree-boosting technique that can handle large datasets efficiently [27]. It is a versatile machine learning algorithm that can be used for prediction tasks involving unstructured data such as images and text, as well as for a range of applications such as regression, classification, ranking, and user-defined prediction problems. For this study, the XGBoost model was configured with specific parameters, including a learning rate of 0.01, an L1 regularization value of 5, an L2 regularization value of 2, and a total of 2000 estimators or learning iterations for the model.

Random forest is a popular supervised machine learning algorithm that can be used for both classification and regression tasks [28]. It is an ensemble method that consists of multiple decision trees. For this study, the random forest algorithm was configured to use 600 decision trees (estimators) and default parameter settings.

For the heart disease prediction model training, initially, the data were randomly split into an 8:2 training-test ratio. After that, a 10-fold cross-validation method was used on the training dataset, which involved dividing the dataset into 10 equal parts. During each iteration, 9 parts were used for training the model and 1 part was used for validation. This process was repeated 10 times, and the average accuracy was calculated as the expected prediction accuracy.

A standard feed-forward back-propagation neural network (BPNN) model was utilized for the ANN. The ANN model consisted of three layers, which included an input layer of 13 neurons, a hidden layer with 11 neurons, and an output layer with 1 neuron. During the training process, a uniform kernel initializer, ReLu activation function in the input and hidden layer, sigmoid activation function in the output layer, an Adam optimizer, and a binary cross entropy (to compare the predicted probabilities to actual class output) were used. The model was trained with a batch size of 10 and 100 epochs. The dataset was divided into 80% for training and 20% for testing.

2.2 Brain Stroke Prediction Using Patient Information and Laboratory Data

For the brain stroke prediction, a total of 5110 observations containing patient information (gender, age, marital status, smoking status, etc.) and laboratory data such as hypertension, heart disease status, body mass index, and average glucose level were used to train, validate and compare different machine learning models. A total of 9 models including XGBoost, Random Forest, AdaBoost, Decision tree, BernoulliNB, KNeighbors, Logistic regression, GaussianNB, and Support vector machines were trained and validated on the same datasets. The best-performing model was selected and deployed to the custom-designed web-based system for the prediction of brain stroke.

2.3 Brain Stroke Prediction Using MRI Image Data

A total of 2251 MRI image data were also used to train and validate deep learning models, EfficientNetB2 and ResNet50 for brain stroke prediction. The data was acquired from an online public dataset, Kaggle. To avoid class imbalance, a technique called the Synthetic Minority oversampling technique (SMOTE) was applied to the original dataset before model training. SMOTE is a technique for oversampling the minority class in which synthetic examples are created instead of simply over-sampling the existing examples with replacement. After applying SMOTE the total dataset was increased to 2852 (1426 normal and the rest 1426 Stroke).

3 Results

3.1 Heart Disease Prediction

The evaluation and comparison of the models were conducted using several performance metrics such as accuracy, precision, recall, F1-score, and Receiver Operating Characteristic (ROC) curve. These metrics were calculated based on the actual and model-predicted true positive, false positive, false negative, and true negative values. Table 1 summarizes the models' performances on the test data, while Figs. 2 and 3 show the ROC curves of XGBoost, ANN, and random forest models that were trained using patient information and clinical data for heart disease prediction. The AUC values obtained for the XGBoost, ANN, and random forest models were 0.98, 0.95, and 1, respectively. Based on Table 1, the random forest model performed better than the other models in predicting heart disease using the given data, achieving an accuracy of 100%. Therefore, the random forest model was chosen and implemented in our system for heart disease prediction.

3.2 Brain Stroke Prediction Using Clinical Data

Amon the 9 machine learning models trained using laboratory data and patient information for brain stroke prediction, the random forest model resulted in the

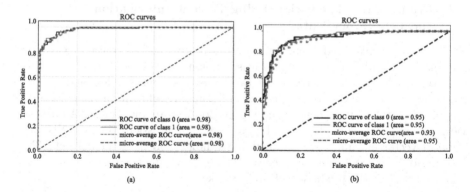

Fig. 2. ROC curves of (a) XGBoost and (b) ANN models trained on patient information and clinical data for heart disease prediction.

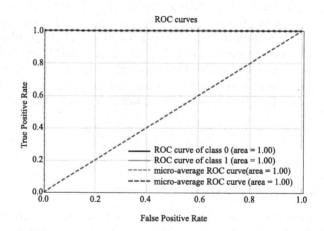

Fig. 3. The ROC curve generated for the random forest model trained on patient information and clinical data for heart disease prediction.

Table 1. A summary of the performance of models on test data for predicting heart disease.

Performance metrics/Models	ANN	XGBoost	Random Forest
Area under the curve (AUC)	0.95	0.98	1
Precision (%)	94.07	91.35	100
Recall (%)	79.19	91.15	100
F1-score(%)	86.16	91.15	100
Accuracy(%)	85.71	92.19	100

highest test accuracy (97.12%) followed by XGBoost (96.93%) and AdaBoost (95.19%) classifiers. Hence, the random forest model was selected for deployment into the custom-made web-based user interface. Figure 4 demonstrates the ROC curve of the selected Random Forest model.

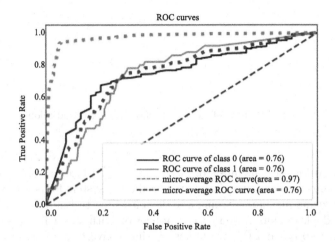

Fig. 4. ROC curve of Random Forest model trained for brain stroke prediction using patient information and laboratory data.

3.3 Brain Stroke Prediction Using MRI Brain Image Data

For the brain stroke prediction using MRI brain image data, ResNet 50 model resulted in better test performance with a precision of 96.67%, F1-score of 96.67%, recall of 96.67%, and accuracy of 96.67%. Hence, the model was selected for deployment into the integrated web-based user interface for the prediction of brain stroke based on MRI image data. Figure 5 demonstrates the model's training and validation accuracy and loss curves.

4   Discussion

Heart disease and stroke are life-threatening illnesses that are becoming increasingly prevalent in both resource-rich and resource-poor countries. An accurate and precise diagnosis of the risks associated with these conditions is essential to reduce potential harm and improve the safety of the heart and brain. Early detection of these diseases, coupled with effective treatment, can prevent fatalities or slow down the disease's progression. Typically, laboratory tests, imaging techniques, and non-invasive procedures are required for efficient treatment planning. However, traditional manual diagnosis procedures can be complicated and subjective, potentially leading to misdiagnosis. In low-resource settings, the limited availability of medical diagnostic tools and professionals can further complicate the diagnosis and treatment of these diseases [20,29]. AI-based predictive techniques are capable to provide quick results and help physicians make informed

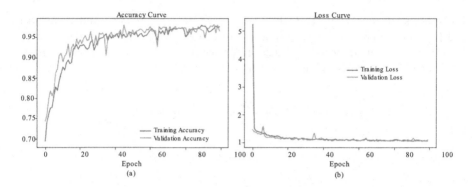

Fig. 5. (a) Accuracy and (b)Loss of the ResNet 50 Model for prediction of brain stroke based on MRI data.

decisions regarding the diagnosis of heart disease and brain stroke. This study involved the development of an integrated prediction system for heart disease and brain stroke using machine learning and deep learning techniques. The resulting system was deployed into a web-based application with a user-friendly interface. Streamlit, a web-based Python framework that converts data scripts into web applications, was used to create the web-based user interface (UI) for the system.

The developed user interface has three parts (pages), (1) heart disease prediction, (2) brain stroke prediction using clinical data and patient information, and (3) brain stroke prediction using MRI brain image data.

The system for predicting heart disease requires the input of various attribute information, such as age, sex, chest pain type, blood pressure, cholesterol level, fasting blood sugar, maximum heart rate, exercise-induced angina, ST segment depression, the slope of the peak exercise ST segment, number of major vessels, and a blood disorder called thalassemia. Once the necessary patient information and clinical data have been entered, the system analyzes the attributes and makes a prediction about whether or not the individual has heart disease. Figure 6 provides sample observations from a person with heart disease, a healthy individual, and the system's predictions. Similarly, the brain stroke prediction module (using clinical data and patient information) accepts 10 attributes consisting of age, gender, marital status, smoking habit, hypertension, blood glucose level, etc., and predicts whether the patient has a brain stroke or note with prediction percentile (Fig. 7). The third module: brain stroke prediction using brain MRI data allows the user to upload an Image and automatically predicts the presence of a brain stroke (Fig. 8).

The proposed system is intended to overcome the challenges of current manual heart disease and brain diagnosis by providing physicians with dependable support, reducing workload pressure while increasing efficiency, and allowing experts to make informed patient-specific diagnosis and treatment decisions. This work can also serve as a foundation for future AI-based heart disease and brain stroke diagnosis decision support system developments in the context of clinical computer-aided diagnosis adoption. However, further experiments on simultaneously acquired patient information and image data labeled with multi-disease are required for efficient detection and classification of heart disease and brain stroke.

5 Conclusion

This paper presents a machine learning and deep learning system for the prediction of heart disease and brain stroke. Multiple models were trained, evaluated, and compared using various data sources, and the best-performing models were selected for deployment in a custom-made web-based interface. The heart disease prediction model achieved 100% accuracy, while the brain stroke prediction models achieved accuracies of 97.1% and 96.67% for structured patient data and MRI image data, respectively. This approach has the potential to improve clinical diagnosis accuracy, save time and resources, and aid in rapid decision-making and treatment planning for heart disease and brain stroke.

Acknowledgements. The resources required for this study were provided by the AI and Biomedical Imaging research unit, the school of Biomedical Engineering, and the faculty of Computing and informatics of Jimma institute of Technology, Jimma University.

A   Appendix: User Interface

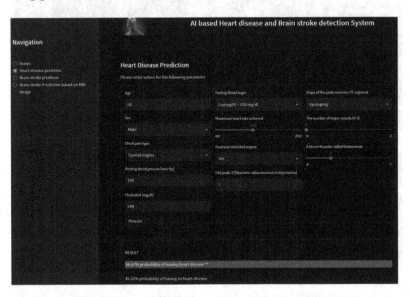

Fig. 6. Heart-disease prediction user interface demonstrating typical observations of patients with heart disease and system's prediction.

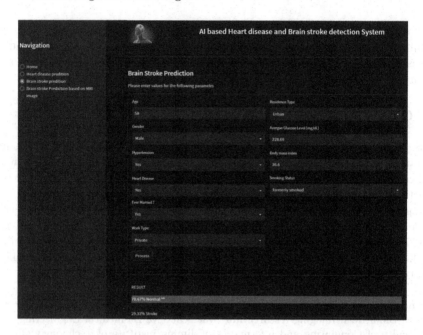

Fig. 7. Brain stroke prediction using clinical data user interface demonstrating typical observations of patients with no brain stroke and system's prediction.

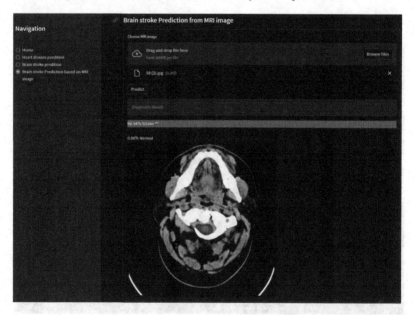

Fig. 8. Brain stroke prediction using MRI brain image data user interface demonstrating typical observations of patients with brain stroke and system's prediction.

References

1. Almustafa, K.M.: Prediction of heart disease and classifiers' sensitivity analysis. BMC Bioinf. **21**(1), 1–18 (2020)
2. Thrift, A.G., et al.: Global stroke statistics. Int. J. Stroke **12**(1), 13–32 (2017)
3. Katan, M., Luft, A.: Global burden of stroke. Semin. Neurol. **38**(2), 208–211 (2018)
4. Koh, S.-H., Park, H.-H.: Neurogenesis in stroke recovery. Transl. Stroke Res. **8**(1), 3–13 (2017)
5. Kuriakose, D., Xiao, Z.: Pathophysiology and treatment of stroke: present status and future perspectives. Int. J. Mol. Sci. **21**(20), 7609 (2020)
6. Boehme, A.K., Esenwa, C., Elkind, M.S.: Stroke risk factors, genetics, and prevention. Circ. Res. **120**(3), 472–495 (2017)
7. Palomeras Soler, E., Casado Ruiz, V.: Epidemiology and risk factors of cerebral ischemia and ischemic heart diseases: similarities and differences. Curr. Cardiol. Rev. **6**(3), 38–149 (2010)
8. Alistair, D.G.: Hypertensive cerebral small vessel disease and stroke. Brain Pathol. **12**(3), 358–370 (2002)
9. Gongora-Rivera, F., et al.: Autopsy prevalence of coronary atherosclerosis in patients with fatal stroke. Stroke **38**(4), 1203–1210 (2007)
10. Touzé, E., et al.: Coronary risk stratification in patients with ischemic stroke or transient ischemic stroke attack. Int. J. Stroke **2**(3), 177–183 (2007)
11. Mackay, J., Mensah, G.A., Greenlund, K.: The atlas of heart disease and stroke: World Health Organization (2004)
12. Lackland, D.T., Weber, M.A.: Global burden of cardiovascular disease and stroke: hypertension at the core. Can. J. Cardiol. **31**(5), 569–571 (2015)
13. Kakadiya, J.: Causes, symptoms, pathophysiology and diagnosis of atherosclerosis-a review. PharmacologyOnline **3**, 420–442 (2009)
14. Coca, A., et al.: Predicting stroke risk in hypertensive patients with coronary artery dis-ease: a report from the INVEST. Stroke **39**(2), 343–8 (2008)
15. Peer, N., Baatiema, L., Kengne, A.-P.: Ischaemic heart disease, stroke, and their car-diometabolic risk factors in Africa: current challenges and outlook for the future. Expert Rev. Cardiovasc. Ther. **19**(2), 129–140 (2021)
16. Liu, Y., Yin, B., Cong, Y.: The probability of ischaemic stroke prediction with a multi-neural-network model. Sensors **20**(17), 4995 (2020)
17. Faura, J., et al.: Stroke-induced immunosuppression: implications for the prevention and prediction of post-stroke infections. J. Neuroinflammation **18**(1), 1–14 (2021)
18. Carod-Artal, F.J.: Post-stroke depression: can prediction help prevention? Future Neurol. **5**(4), 569–580 (2010)
19. Das, R., Turkoglu, I., Sengur, A.: Effective diagnosis of heart disease through neural networks ensembles. Expert Syst. Appl. **36**(4), 7675–7680 (2009)
20. Yang, H., Garibaldi, J.M.: A hybrid model for automatic identification of risk factors for heart disease. J. Biomed. Inform. **58**(Suppl), S171–S182 (2015)
21. Patel, J., TejalUpadhyay, D., Patel, S.: Heart disease prediction using machine learning and data mining technique. Heart Dis. **7**(1), 129–137 (2015)
22. Gudadhe, M., Wankhade, K.K., Dongre, S.S.: Decision support system for heart disease based on support vector machine and artificial neural network. In: 2010 International Conference on Computer and Communication Technology (ICCCT), pp. 741–745 (2010)

23. Simegn, G.L., Gebeyehu, W.B., Degu, M.Z.: Computer-aided decision support system for diagnosis of heart diseases. Res. Rep. Clin. Cardiol. **13**, 39–54 (2022)
24. Sirsat, M.S., Fermé, E., Câmara, J.: Machine learning for brain stroke: a review. J. Stroke Cerebrovasc. Dis. **29**(10), 105162 (2020)
25. Lee, E.-J., et al.: Deep into the brain: artificial intelligence in stroke imaging. J. stroke. **19**(3), 277 (2017)
26. Dua, D., Graff, C.: UCI machine learning repository. University of California, School of Information and Computer Science, Irvine, CA (2019)
27. Chen, T., Guestrin, C.: XGBoost: a scalable tree boosting system. In: Proceedings of the 22nd ACM SIGKDD International Conference on Knowledge Discovery and Data Mining (2016)
28. Breiman, L.: Random forests. Mach. Learn. **45**(1), 5–32 (2001)
29. Allen, L.A., et al.: Decision making in advanced heart failure: a scientific statement from the American Heart Association. Circulation **125**(15), 1928–1952 (2012)

Lung Tumor Detection and Recognition Using Deep Convolutional Neural Networks

Shehabeldin Solyman[1]([⊠])[iD] and Friedhelm Schwenker[2][iD]

[1] Faculty of Media Engineering and Technology, German University in Cairo,
Cairo, Egypt
shehabeldin.solyman@student.guc.edu.eg
[2] Institute of Neural Information Processing, Ulm University, 89081 Ulm, Germany
friedhelm.schwenker@uni-ulm.de

Abstract. Cancer with the greatest fatality rate, lung cancer, requires
a biopsy to define its type to select the best course of treatment. For
decades scientists have been working on a method to detect tumors earlier
than the current procedures. This research proposes an approach using
artificial intelligence to predict a tumor's presence and malignancy using
only computed tomography (CT) scans. This is by using the techniques
of deep learning, transfer learning, and ensemble learning. This research
made use of two different datasets, one with only benign, malignant, and
normal cases called the IQ-OTH/NCCD dataset and another dataset
with 3 carcinoma classes and a normal class. Applying convolutional
neural networks (CNN)s architecture in VGG-16 using only the dataset
with 3 classes, this experiment achieved a very satisfying result of 89%
test accuracy with relatively low computational power. Then applying
ensemble learning techniques in a VGG-16, ResNet50, InceptionV3, and
EfficientNetB7 majority voting architecture to classify not only CT scans
being malignant, benign, or normal, but also to classify different types
of lung carcinomas, this architecture outperformed every other trial and
achieved a 92.8% test accuracy.

Keywords: CNN · Lung tumor Detection · Transfer Learning ·
Ensemble Learning · Tumor · Carcinoma · Deep Convolutional Neural
Networks

1 Introduction

Lung tumors are one of the hardest and most severe types of cancer to treat
especially if not detected early. There are two types of lung tumors. A benign,
which is a harmless tumor, is just a node present inside the lung. Malignant,
which is the cancerous one that spreads and causes harm to the lungs and in
some cases neighboring organs too. There are three types of malignant tumors
that have different methods of treatment. These are Adenocarcinoma, large cell

T. Girma Debelee et al. (Eds.): PanAfriCon AI 2022, CCIS 1800, pp. 79–91, 2023.
https://doi.org/10.1007/978-3-031-31327-1_5

carcinoma, and squamous cell carcinoma. We aim to find a way to speed up the diagnosis process using *CNN* and deep neural network techniques such as transfer learning and ensemble learning using only Computed Tomography (*CT*) scans [14].

2 Background and Literature Review

2.1 Deep Learning

Deep learning techniques are representation-learning techniques that use multiple levels of representation. They are built by combining simple but non-linear modules that each convert a representation at one level (starting with the raw input) into a representation at a higher, marginally more abstract level. Very complex functions can be learned if enough of these transformations are combined. Higher layers of representation for classification problems increase characteristics of the input crucial for discrimination and decrease irrelevant variations. The key aspect of deep learning is that, as opposed to being designed by engineers, these layers of features are learned from data using a general-purpose learning algorithm [9].

Transfer Learning. Transfer learning is a technique in deep learning where a previously trained model is used as the foundation for a model on a new task. Simply said, a model developed for one activity is applied to another, similar work as an optimization to enable quick progress when modeling the second task. One can accomplish a new task with considerably improved performance by using transfer learning as opposed to training with just a small amount of data. It is uncommon to train a model from scratch for tasks linked to images or natural language processing because transfer learning is so widespread. Instead, data scientists and academics prefer to begin with a model that has already been trained to recognize general properties in photos, such as edges and curves, and to classify things [16]. This can be visualized in Fig. 1 on page 3.

Ensemble Learning. By combining the key characteristics of two or more models, ensemble learning is a technique for arriving at predictions that are in agreement. Because grouping together minimizes the variation in the prediction errors, the final ensemble learning framework can be more robust than the individual models that make up the ensemble. A framework for ensemble learning works best when the contributing models are statistically varied since it aims to capture complementing information from each of them [12].

One of the earliest and simplest ensemble techniques in the literature is majority and soft voting. These approaches select several contributing classifiers and then compute the classifiers' predictions for each sample. The class that draws the greatest amount of data from the classifier pool is then known as the ensemble's predicted class [12].

A presentation of the flow of the utilization of transfer learning and ensemble learning in our research is in Fig. 2.

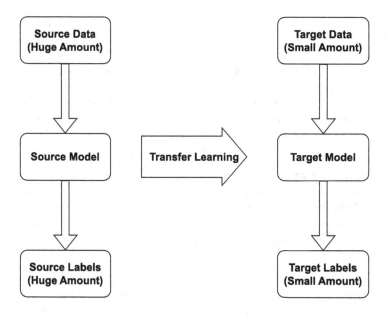

Fig. 1. Knowledge of extensively trained model passed to target model.

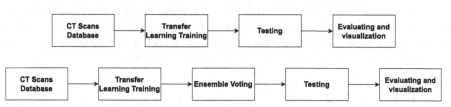

Fig. 2. Flow of training process using two approaches.

2.2 Tumors

When cells grow and divide too quickly to make new cells in a disorderly and uncontrolled manner, the consequence is a swelling or pathological enlargement that is known as a tumor [10].

Benign Tumor. A benign tumor is not malignant. Benign tumors do not spread throughout the body or infiltrate neighboring healthy tissue. Meningiomas are an illustration of a benign tumor. The membranes covering the brain and spinal cord are where meningiomas develop. The majority of meningiomas are benign, but there are occasional occurrences of malignant or atypical meningiomas, which are tumors that fall midway between benign and malignant [6].

Adenomcarcinoma. The most frequent primary lung cancer diagnosed in the United States is lung adenocarcinoma. It is classified as non-small cell lung cancer

($NSCLC$) and has a close connection to prior smoking. Although incidence and mortality have decreased, it continues to be the primary cause of cancer-related death in the United States. About 40% of all lung cancers are adenocarcinomas, which typically develop from the mucosal glands. It is the most typical sub-type to be identified in non-smokers. Lung adenocarcinoma typically develops at the lung periphery and is frequently discovered in scars or regions of persistent inflammation. Additionally, these cells have the potential to spread to other parts of your body and harm healthy tissues [15].

Squamous Cell Carcinoma. A type of $NSCLC$ lung cancer, is squamous cell lung cancer, is characterized by squamous cell carcinoma (SCC) of the lung $NSCLC$. Adenocarcinoma is the most prevalent type of $NSCLC$, followed by lung squamous cell carcinoma, particularly in females. There is speculation that this is related to a shift in smoking habits, although there is no concrete proof [3].

Large Cell Carcinoma. One of the various types of $NSCLC$ is large cell lung carcinoma ($LCLC$). As opposed to some other types of lung cancer, $LCLC$ frequently starts in the outer parts of the lungs and spreads quickly. The key early signs of $LCLC$ are weariness and shortness of breath. Around 85% of all lung, malignancies are $NSCLC$, with $LCLC$ making up about 10% of the total. Because of the size of the cancer cells that can be seen when the tumor is studied under a microscope, $LCLC$s are also known as large cell lung cancers (as opposed to the tumor size, which also tends to be quite large) [5].

2.3   Related Work

In [8], the authors used a combination of CT scans and chest X-ray images to detect COVID-19, pneumonia, and lung cancer. This combination has been employed because a chest CT scan can precisely detect the aberrant features that are found in images, whereas a chest X-ray is less effective in the early stages of the disease. Additionally, using these two kinds of scans will expand the dataset, improving classification precision. The authors used 4 different ML architectures. These are VGG19-CNN, ResNet152V2, ResNet152V2 + Gated Recurrent Unit GRU, and ResNet152V2 + Bidirectional GRU Bi-GRU. The results were, the VGG19 +CNN model outperformed the three other suggested models. Based on X-ray and CT images, the VGG19+CNN model had 99.66% area under the curve AUC, 98.05% area under the curve ACC, 98.05% recall, 98.43% precision, 99.5% specificity SPC, 99.3% negative predictive value NPV, 98.24% F1 score.

Another approach taken by Brahim Ait Skourt, Abdelhamid El Hassani, and Aicha Majda [1] was to detect the presence of cancer nodes in CT scans using a U-net architecture. But before that, a pre-processing step took place that consists of cropping the images to simply remove any information that does not feed the machine with useful information. Part of the pre-processing involved was to increase contrast in images to filter out unwanted details that can cause classification errors. This attempt led to an accuracy level of 95.02%.

In another study [11], the authors used a dataset of *CT* images from 125 patients of lung cancer in the early stage to identify different pathology types. Namely, invasive lung adenocarcinoma, squamous cell carcinoma, small cell lung cancer, and adenocarcinoma in situ. After extracting the lesion information, a boosting strategy is used to combine various classification results to enhance the performance of the proposed VGG16-T neural network. The result of this experiment was VGG16-T performed with an accuracy of 85% by identifying 20 random *CT* images from the dataset, while two respiratory doctors from Grade 3A level hospitals obtain an accuracy of 55% and 65%, respectively.

On a dataset of 311 patients with early-stage *NSCLC* undergoing surgical care at Massachusetts General Hospital *MGH*, the authors of this research paper [4] trained and validated *CNN*s with a focus on the two most prevalent histological types: adenocarcinoma *ADC* and squamous cell carcinoma *SCC*. With an area under the curve (*AUC*) of 0.71(p=0.018), the *CNN*s were able to predict the histology of tumors. Additionally, they discovered that applying support vector machine *SVM* and k-nearest neighbors *kNN* classifiers to CNN-derived quantitative radiomics features produced equivalent discriminative performance, with *AUC*s up to 0.71 (p = 0.017). In heterogeneous test sets, their top-performing *CNN* served as a reliable probabilistic classifier with qualitatively understandable visual justifications for its predictions.

3   Specifications and Experimental Methods

3.1   Datasets

In this study we made use of the ImageNet database as transfer learning training along with two other datasets, IQ-OTH/NCCD [2] and Kaggle's Chest CT-Scan [7] images Dataset.

IQ-OTH/NCCD. In the first phase of experimenting, the Iraq-Oncology Teaching Hospital/National Center for Cancer Diseases IQ-OTH/NCCD dataset has been used. This lung cancer dataset was gathered across three months in the aforementioned specialty hospitals in the fall of 2019. It includes *CT* scans of both healthy volunteers and patients with lung cancer in various stages of the disease. 1190 pictures in all, taken from slices of 110 cases' *CT* scans, make up the dataset. These cases are divided into three categories: benign, malignant, and normal. Of them, 40 cases have been determined to be malignant, 15 to be benign, and 55 to be normal cases.

Kaggle's Chest CT-Scan Images Dataset. This dataset was created on Kaggle.com in 2020. It contains around 1000 images which are in jpg or png format. Data contain 3 chest cancer types which are Adenocarcinoma, Large cell carcinoma, Squamous cell carcinoma, and one folder for the normal case.

Combined Dataset. By our second study titled Transfer learning on the advanced dataset, instead of using only the IQ-OTH/NCCD dataset to recognize normal, benign, or malignant cases. A trial to make this project more advanced by creating a new dataset consisting of the normal cases of both datasets, benign cases from the IQ-OTH/NCCD dataset, and adenocarcinoma, large cell carcinoma, and squamous cell carcinoma from the Kaggle dataset. This new dataset will be used to detect and recognize cancer malignancy types. Samples are visualized in Fig. 3.

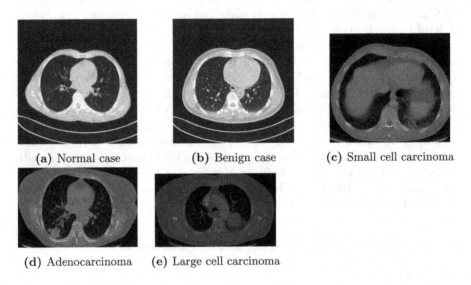

    (a) Normal case   **(b)** Benign case   **(c)** Small cell carcinoma

(d) Adenocarcinoma   **(e)** Large cell carcinoma

Fig. 3. Samples from the combined dataset showcasing all the cases.

3.2 Data Augmentation

Data augmentation is the technique of creating additional data points from current data to artificially increase the amount of data. This includes improving the dataset by making minor adjustments to the data or by using machine learning models to add additional data points to the original data's latent space. In this project, we augmented using three types of augmentation techniques.

Flip and Rotation. A mirror reflection of the original image is produced by random flipping along one (or more) chosen axes. The horizontal axis of natural pictures may typically be reversed, but the vertical axis cannot because up and down portions of an image are not always 'interchangeable.' Similar characteristics apply to MRI images of the lungs; lungs can be regarded as anatomically symmetrical in the axial plane. The left lung is switched with the right lung when the body is turned along the horizontal axis, and vice versa [13].

Scaling and Cropping. The deep network can learn useful deep features independent of the original scale by including scaled replicas of the original images in the training set [13].

Shearing. With the shear transformation, every point in an image is moved in a certain direction. This displacement is proportional to how far it is from the line that parallels this direction and passes through the origin [13].

3.3 Models

This project relied heavily on the premises of transfer learning. Using mainly 4 pre-built models which are Oxford university's *VGG*16, ResNet50 by He et al., Google's InceptionV3, and EfficientNetB7 created by AutoML MNAS. At the end of each *CNN* 5 extra layers are added, these are:

- Global Average pooling layer to replace the original fully connected layer.
- Dense layer of 1024 units with activation function ReLu.
- Dense layer of 1024 units with activation function ReLu.
- Dense layer of 512 units with activation function ReLu.
- Dense Softmax layer of as many units as there are classes (depending on the study).

4 Studies

4.1 Study 1: Transfer Learning

Study 1.1. In the first study, only VGG16 architecture is used as a baseline test using the transfer deep learning model (built with the 5 NN layers stated earlier) along with the IQ-OTH/NCCD dataset. This attempted to classify three classes, namely: Normal, Benign, and Malignant cases. This model uses two callback functions, Early Stopping (ES) (with the patience of 4 epochs) and Model Checkpoint (MC). The optimizer used is Adam. After pre-processing, the data is split into a test set consisting of 50 samples from each class, and the augmented total of approximately 1000 (330 from each class) images are split into training and validation sets, of which 80% are for training and the rest are for validation. Then, the model is fitted with 20 epochs and the best model file is loaded to be evaluated.

Study 1.2. In the earlier study, we used a VGG16 model for transfer learning, in this experiment to give the compiler more data to learn, instead of augmenting data 330 samples per class, this study augments to 1000 per class (3000 total samples). And to let the model run for more epochs and utilize the ES property, the number of epochs is increased to 200. Finally, the best model file is loaded and tested on the test set.

4.2   Study 2: Transfer Learning on the Advanced Dataset

This study involves upgrades applied to study 1.2 (Transfer Learning) These are: To make the VGG16 model classify not only the tumor presence but also malignancy type the combined dataset is used instead of IQ-OTH/NCCD alone. An increase in augmentation size to 1500 per class (7500 total samples). And to remove anomalies in the number of epochs, ES has been omitted and the model is fitted to a consistent 50 epochs, this number of epochs has been chosen since ES best performing runs finished around 50 epochs before the early stopping callback is activated. Afterward, the best model from MC is loaded and evaluated.

4.3   Study 3: Majority Voting Ensemble Learning

In this study, the VGG16 model from study 1.2 (Transfer Learning) works along with 3 other models in an ensemble deep learning model. These are ResNet50, InceptionV3 and EfficientNetB7. All the models in this study are built with the 5 NN layers stated earlier, use model checkpoint as the only callback function, and are fitted to 50 epochs. The optimizers used are Adamax for VGG16, Nadam for ResNet50, and Adam for InceptionV3 and EficientNetB7. The dataset used is the combined dataset with a test sample size of 50 samples and augmented data for training and validation of approximately 7500, split 80% and 20% respectively.

The predictions of each model on the test set are collected and used in the voting algorithm using the majority voting ensemble learning technique. Then, the ensemble predicted classes are acquired and studied.

4.4   Study 4: Soft Voting Ensemble Learning

The last trial is similar to trial 3 but instead of majority voting soft voting technique is applied. This ensemble learning method chooses the prediction with the highest overall probability rather than the prediction with the most votes. It accomplishes this by adding the probabilities of each prediction in each model.

5   Results and Discussions

5.1   Study 1: Transfer Learning

Study 1.1 results were under fitted and the model failed to classify the test set.

In study 1.2, with training accuracy and validation accuracy averaging around 54% and training and validation loss above 0.8, this result is very low but is considered a step in the right direction compared to the earlier study. Even though the training and validation accuracies are low, the test accuracy was 89% which is very satisfying. Visualized in Fig. 4.

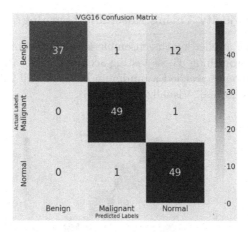

Fig. 4. Study 1.2 "Transfer Learning" Confusion matrix.

Here it can be observed that both normal and malignant cases had an almost perfect score but the accuracy dropped with the benign case with 12 out of 50 samples being misclassified as normal which is not a huge issue given that both are non-threatening situations.

5.2 Study 2: Transfer Learning on Advanced dataset

The testing phase yielded an accuracy of 87.2%, combined with the training and validation performance, this trial is considered successful. It can be observed in the confusion matrix in Fig. 5 that the aim of the project has been achieved, since malignant tumors are not being misclassified as benign or normal, except for one instance where large cell carcinoma has been mislabelled as benign. It can also be observed that almost a quarter of benign cases are being mislabelled as normal and there are some noticeable misclassifications between carcinomas.

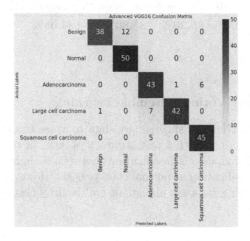

Fig. 5. Study 2 "Transfer learning on advanced dataset" Confusion matrix.

5.3 Study 3: Majority Voting Ensemble Learning

The majority voting applied by the ensemble learning technique showed impressive results, with astonishing 92.8% testing accuracy. One can notice that confusion between carcinomas reached a minimum however still 24% of benign cases are misclassified as normal. Visualized in Fig. 6.

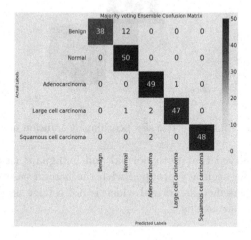

Fig. 6. Study 3 "Majority voting ensemble learning" Confusion matrix.

In Table 1, test performance shows VGG16's superiority compared to ResNet50, InceptionV3 and EfficientNetB7.

Table 1. Study 3 models' test accuracies comparison.

VGG16	ResNet50	InceptionV3	EfficientNetB7
87.90%	85.20%	85.60%	86.05%

5.4 Study 4: Soft Voting Ensemble Learning

Performance in this trial was surprisingly slightly worse than study 3 (Majority voting ensemble learning) with a test accuracy of 90%. In the confusion matrix of Fig. 7, there are obvious misclassifications between malignant classes, and the benign class misclassification as normal class persists. However, this architecture eliminated mislabelling between malignant and healthy classes.

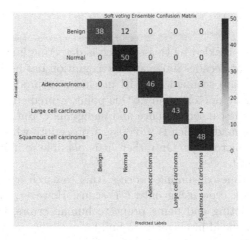

Fig. 7. Study 4 "Soft voting ensemble learning" Confusion matrix.

5.5 Discussions

The research results concluded that study 3, Majority voting ensemble learning, showed the best performance compared to the rest of the studies which is due to the high computational effort exerted. Also, Study 1 (Transfer Learning), using only IQOTH/NCCD dataset, had a high test accuracy. Thus it is inferred that to recognize only normal, benign, and malignant cases, only one transfer learning model can be used to achieve high results (Table 2).

Table 2. Studies' Test accuracies comparison.

Study 1	Study 2	Study 3	Study 4
89.00%	**87.20%**	**92.80%**	**90.00%**

Limitations. One of the main limitations faced in this project was that datasets provided on the internet are very scarce. This led to an overuse of data augmentation, but this can only get us so far. This is believed to limit the project's accuracy.

Another issue faced was the imbalanced distribution of classes in the dataset. The main issue faced here was that the benign class had so few images that it was often mislabelled as normal to an extent of 24% of the test set, which is an obvious case of under-fitting.

Another limitation encountered was the fact that the computer running this project has a GPU of NVIDIA RTX 3070 with 16 GB of RAM. And, to process a sufficient amount of data with enough epochs takes a lot of time on such capabilities. This limitation stopped us from using K-fold cross-validation. However, to compensate for this, the studies had rerun sessions and the results were always similar in performances.

6   Conclusions

The central problem tackled by this research is detecting lung tumors and their malignancy type. For decades lung cancer recognition has been a very long procedure where lungs are scanned by MRI machines to produce CT scans these are then examined by doctors, and at this point, a prediction can be made by the doctors about the cancer presence and malignancy. But, a final step of confirmation has to be made which is a biopsy, a procedure where sample cells are examined under a microscope. Only then, it is possible to infer cancer presence and malignancy level.

To tackle this time-consuming process, this research exploited the idea of predicting a tumor's type using only CT scans. However, instead of a medical oncologist predicting and being prone to human errors, these studies were conducted using artificial intelligence to build a machine to recognize a tumor's presence and existence is a concrete solution. This machine's algorithm has been built successfully in 5 months in this project with a 92.8% accuracy using transfer learning and ensemble learning.

Compared to the related papers, our initial studies to find out only the presence of a tumor and whether or not it is malignant or benign got a test accuracy lower than that of the two research papers that tackle only that, nevertheless we used small computational power with only VGG16 compared to the first research paper's VGG19 or the second research paper's pre-processing steps. The third study was the only one that considered studying the type of malignancy, which our research outperformed its 85% test accuracy with a 92.8% accuracy.

References

1. Ait Skourt, B., El Hassani, A., Majda, A.: Lung CT image segmentation using deep neural networks. Procedia Comput. Sci. **127**, 109–113 (2018). Accessed 01 Aug 2022
2. Alyasriy, H.: The IQ-OTHNCCD lung cancer dataset, Mendeley Data, V1 (2020). https://doi.org/10.17632/bhmdr45bh2.1. Accessed 01 June 2022
3. Anjum, B.R.S.F.: Squamous Cell Lung Cancer (2021). Accessed 29 July 2022
4. Chaunzwa, T.L., et al.: Deep learning classification of lung cancer histology using CT images. Sci. Rep. **11**(1), 1–12 (2021). Accessed 01 Aug 2022
5. Eldridge, L.: What is large cell carcinoma of the lungs? April 2022. Accessed 29 July 2022
6. Goldstraw, P., et al.: Non-small-cell lung cancer. Lancet **378**(9804), 1727–1740 (2011)
7. Hany, M.: Chest CT-Scan images Dataset (2021). Accessed 01 June 2022
8. Ibrahim, D.M., Elshennawy, N.M., Sarhan, A.M.: Deep-chest: multi-classification deep learning model for diagnosing COVID-19, pneumonia, and lung cancer chest diseases. Comput. Biol. Med. **132**, 104348 (2021). Accessed 01 Aug 2022
9. LeCun, Y., Bengio, Y., Hinton, G.: Deep learning. Nature **521**(7553), 436–444 (2015). Accessed 30 July 2022
10. Lemjabbar-Alaoui, H., Hassan, O.U., Yang, Y.W., Buchanan, P.: Lung cancer: biology and treatment options. Biochim. Biophys. Acta **1856**(2), 189–210 (2015)

11. Pang, S., et al.: VGG16-T: a novel deep convolutional neural network with boosting to identify pathological type of lung cancer in early stage by CT images. Int. J. Comput. Intell. Syst. **13**(1), 771 (2020). Accessed 01 Aug 2022

12. Polikar, R.: Ensemble Learning, pp. 1–34. Springer, US, Boston, MA (2012). https://doi.org/10.1007/978-1-4419-9326-7_1

13. Shorten, C., Khoshgoftaar, T.M.: A survey on image data augmentation for deep learning. J. Big Data **6**(1), 1–48 (2019). Accessed 31 July 2022

14. U.S. National Institute Of Health, National Cancer Institute: Seer cancer statistics review (2015). Accessed 01 Aug 2022

15. Wallen, D.J.M.J.M.: Lung Adenocarcinoma, September 2021. Accessed 29 July 2022

16. Zhuang, F., et al.: A comprehensive survey on transfer learning. Proc. IEEE **109**(1), 43–76 (2021). https://doi.org/10.1109/JPROC.2020.3004555

Agriculture

Tomato Leaf Disease Detection and Classification Using Custom Modified AlexNet

Dereje Hinsermu Senbatu⬤, Birhanu Shimelis Girma$^{(\boxtimes)}$⬤, and Yehualashet Megersa Ayano⬤

Ethiopian Artificial Intelligence Institute, Addis Ababa, Ethiopia
birhanu.shimelis@aic.et

Abstract. Tomatoes are used in almost every kitchen worldwide and are produced in large quantities. The productivity of tomato crops, both qualitatively and quantitatively, suffers from various infections. Besides, most tomato diseases commonly affect the leaves of the plant. The existing technique in tomato disease detection needs high human involvement and laborious tasks. Hence, this study designs and implements a convolutional neural network based on a robust autonomous tomato disease detection and classification system that fits the computational capabilities of resource-constrained devices. A custom-modified AlexNet architecture is used to detect diseases in tomato leaves. This approach relies on an automatic feature extraction process for classifying input images into respective disease classes. The model is trained and evaluated using Plant Village's dataset, which contains approximately 14,000 diseased and healthy leaf photos separated into ten classifications. An average training classification accuracy of 99.67% and an average test classification accuracy of 98.43% were achieved in nine diseases and one healthy class by following different neural layer arrangements.

Keywords: Tomato · Classification · Convolutional Neural Network · AlexNet · Plant Village's dataset · automatic feature extraction

1 Introduction

The agriculture industry provides a significant income stream for the vast majority of Ethiopians. Tomatoes are one of the most common vegetables eaten in Ethiopia. In every family, it is consumed in a variety of ways, but it is mostly manufactured in huge amounts in places like Wollo, Hararge, Shewa, Jimma, and Wallaga. Nationally, around 34,947 tons of tomatoes were produced in 2019 [1]. Tomatoes are rich in antioxidants such as vitamins E, C, and beta-carotene and contain minerals essential for a healthy diet [2]. A combination of crop sensitivity and climatic conditions has resulted in widespread disease in the tomato crop throughout its development. Infested plants account for 50–100% of the crop losses [3].

Supported by Ethiopian Artificial Intelligence Institute.

To avoid such a huge loss of productivity, early diagnosis of tomato leaf diseases is crucial [4]. It is challenging to monitor infections in plants with manual labor because of its complexity and taking a long time. Furthermore, many farmers make inaccurate assumptions due to visual obstructions, resulting in ineffective and sometimes harmful prevention mechanisms [5]. Since visual obstruction, and inaccurate assumptions are difficult to look at; thus, many farmers make mistakes in prediction about the conditions. In the absence of a professional' s consultations about guidelines for dealing with harvest infestations, farmers typically come together and implement common disease prevention strategies [6]. All these challenges necessitate automating the tomato leaf disease detection and classification task while ensuring accuracy and reducing computational complexity. This study used techniques to recognize tomato leaves and disease symptoms by examining leaf pictures. Our activity will solve the producer' s obstacles by identifying plant diseases without having to run after plant scientists. In addition, automating the tomato leaf disease detection and classification will aid farmers in timely identifying and seamlessly protecting their farmland from loss-causing diseases. Thus, early detection, accurate identification of tomato leaf diseases, and performing proper diagnosis will increase farm productivity and thus increase farmers' profit.

The emergence of machine learning, data analytics methods, and supercomputing has led to additional chances to break down and evaluate complex data-concentrated procedures within farming operations. As machine learning continues to spread, it is widely applied in several sectors like robotics [17,18], agriculture [8–11], meteorology [12,13], economic sciences [14–16], health [7] and aquaculture [19,20]. In the health sector, machine learning has been applied in breast cancer detection and classification [21–23], breast cancer segmentation [24–26], and brain tumor segmentation [27,28].

The most common diseases of tomato plants leaf include bacterial spot, late blight leaf, early blight leaf, tomato Leaf Mold septoria leaf spot, spider mites leaf, target Spot leaf, mosaic virus, and yellow leaf curl virus leaf. To train and test our proposed model, we used the tomato leaf dataset from the plant village. More than 14,000 tomato leaf photos from the dataset of a plant village are grouped into nine disease groups and one healthy class. The proposed model is a custom-designed Convolution Neural Network having nine convolutional layers. The convolutional layer uses automatic feature extraction, while the fully connected layer uses classification, followed by softmax activation. The rest of the work is structured as follows; Sect. 2 provides a brief summary of the Literature. The methods used to build the tomato disease detection and classification is discussed in Sect. 3. Furthermore, the dataset and materials used for the proposed method's training, testing, and implementation are presented. The fourth part contains the results and discussion. The fifth section concludes with a discussion of future research.

2   Related Works

Plant diseases pose a significant challenge in obtaining quality agricultural products while maintaining an acceptable yield. Thus, early disease detection is the best way to counteract the reduction in productivity. As a result, various research was conducted on reducing pests and diseases in plants by automating the existing manual techniques. The related research presented in this section is discussed below.

Using Image Processing techniques, Y, M. Qo et al. [29] proposed a plant leaf disease detection and classification method that can accurately classify diseased leaves and provides a means to guide robots in disease management. Various approaches were used, including image acquisition, image preprocessing, segmentation using K-means clustering, feature extraction using Grey Level Co-occurrence Matrices (GLCM) and Local Binary Patterns (LBP), and classifying sample images with SVM. The author used high-resolution cameras and repositories to collect 560 sample images of the dataset, divided into different groups. A median filter is used for image smoothing. SVM is used to analyze four classes of plant diseases and calculate the confusion matrix, and this system has a confusion matrix of 98.2% and an error rate of 1.8%. Similarly, the evaluation model metrics generated using k-nearest neighbors algorithm classification is 80.2% accurate and 19.8% error rate, whereas the confusion matrix generated using the ensemble classifier is 84.6% accurate and 15.4% error rate. The drawback of K-Means clustering for picture segmentation is that it is only partially automatic because the user must manually choose the cluster that contains the sick area.

Durmus et al. [30] utilized deep learning to detect diseases on tomato leaves that were more accurate than precision farming. They used a pre-trained model of AlexNet and SqueezeNet, which included a few changes to the architecture of SqueezeNet for the mobile app. Thus, SqueezeNet is a lightweight architecture that works well with mobile apps. As part of the study, the plant village dataset, which contained 54,309 images of fourteen (14) different crops and tomato leaves, was extracted from a plant village dataset, and the model was optimized using the SGD optimizer. Nine diseases and one health class are randomly separated into 80% for training and 20% for testing in the tomato leaves images. Experimentally tested Using AlexNet and SqueezeNet, they got a 0.9565 and a 0.943 accuracy, respectively. They compared the AlexNet model size of 227.6Mbytes with the SqueezeNet model size of 2.9 Mbytes. They also tested the inference time, which for SqueezeNet is 50ms and for AlexNet is 150ms.

L. Aversano et al. [31] proposed a trainable deep neural network algorithm to detect leaf disease automatically by adjusting parameters to enable a faster training process while using minimal computing power. Their study was based on an image dataset of a plant village containing nine different types of diseases and taking one health class of tomato from a comprehensive collection of over 16000 images. A rebalancing technique was applied in some unequal classes, along with different deep learning neural networks already made, including a convolutional neural network with 19 layers, 71 layers, and 50 layers deep. Based on their experiments, the 0.97 precision for a convolutional neural network with 19 layers deep model performed somewhat more reliably than the 0.95 precision for Xception and significantly better than the 0.60 precision for ResNet-50. The accuracy remains good, but it should be improved, and some classes need to be correctly classified. The study didn' t explain why ResNet-50 performed poorly on both training and validation. However, it suggested that extending the dataset and utilizing a larger quantity of groups will enhance the precision of the model.

The Deep-CNN model developed by E. K. Nithish et al. [32] for detecting tomato leaf disease has been implemented in PyTorch. Random Rotation, Random Resize Crop, and a combination of both Random Rotation and Random Resize Crop are augmentation techniques used to amplify the proportion of the original training dataset by four times. This type of augmentation technique is capable of better generalizing what has been learned in the training dataset. The study uses the following steps to develop the model. (i) Dataset collection from plant village repository, (ii) enhancement of the dataset using different techniques. (iii) the CNN approach was utilized for making the model, (iv) creating training data, and (v) classifying groups of the dataset by applying a convolutional neural networks method was used. After applying data augmentation techniques, experiments with the Resnet-50 model show it can better classify healthy and diseased leaf classes with 97.01% accuracy.

This paper used the LeNet architecture for training and testing the model on a publicly available plant village dataset. The paper has used LeNet architecture to train and test the model on a publicly available Plant Village dataset. In [33], the authors have used a convolutional neural network to categorize input photos into different classes using feature extraction automatically. Each group averaged 94–95% accuracy. Researchers successfully illustrate the model's effectiveness and the minimal computing effort needed. Because the collection comprises photos of many forms of tomato leaf disease, data enhancement is employed to improve the model's generalization [32] and to make the classes balanced. Model training and enhancing the numerical condition of the optimization problem, the pictures in the dataset were shot with a high camera resolution.

Francis. M et al. [34] created a CNN model that recognizes and categorizes an apple and tomato to detect and classify plant diseases using the leaves of the two plants. They used 3663 images with a training dropout rate of 0.2 and achieved an accuracy of 87%. Convolutional neural networks are used to execute a binary classification, and the results of the analysis are provided.

In this paper, we have developed a method to identify tomato diseases after analyzing images of leaves by experimenting with different neural network arrangements resulting in higher accuracy than other related works. Farmers' problem of identifying plant diseases will be solved through this research without waiting for plant disease experts. This will result in higher quality and greater quantity of food crops for them and higher profits.

3   Materials and Methods

3.1   Dataset

There are roughly 50,000 images in the plant village collection, with approximately 11 distinct types of crops. Figure 1 depicts nine groups of leaves with health issues and a healthy class of tomato leaves. In our dataset, we chose

Fig. 1. Nine tomato leaf diseases and one healthy class.

tomato as our target crop [35]. The proposed work contains a training dataset with 12801 images, a validation dataset with 2397 images, and a testing dataset containing 796 images. About 1000 pictures are assigned to each tomato disease category, with 1271 images belonging to the healthy group among many of the 12801 training images. Each class in the validation set has an average of 237 photos, whereas each class in the test set has an average of 50 images. For testing, we randomly selected 50 images from each training class and erased them from their respective files. The entire training dataset was created by adding photos to each class randomly and then enhancing the dataset approach to produce new pictures when the number of images in any class dropped below 1000. The data enhancement was performed to build similar new images by twisting, inverting, altering width and height, and resizing the original images. This type of augmentation technique is essential in building a model that has a better generalization capability [32]. Each class was made to have 500 images on the validation dataset, and this procedure prevents bias or any particular class from being underrepresented during the training stage.

3.2 Methodology

The proposed approach involves three phases: Data Acquisition, Pre-processing, and Classification.

Data Acquisition: Among the dataset collected from the Plant Village repository are images of major tomato leaf diseases and healthy tomato leaves that might have a detrimental impact on the crop.

Data Pre-processing: The dataset contains images of different types of tomato leaf disease, so data enhancement methods like dimensionality reduction, feature engineering, data cleaning, and data transformation are applied to improve the model's generalization [32] and to make the classes balanced. Considering that the model's input is a tensor representation of the image' s pixel data. Hence, by using data augmentation, where an image undergoes several alterations but still maintains the meaning, simply changing the pixel values at random (to add more input records) can completely change the meaning of the picture. The image transformations include rescaling, width and height shifting, horizontal flipping, padding, and rotation changes. Doing so can create a vast image dataset with just a single image. The images in the dataset were taken with a high-resolution camera to speed up model training and improve the optimization problem's numerical condition. Furthermore, it guarantees that a number of default settings used during initialization and termination are appropriate.

Model Architecture: A modified AlexNet model is developed in this paper from scratch with nine layers of convolutional neural networks. The detailed architecture of the model is shown in Fig. 4, with a total trainable parameter of around 50 million. The convolutional layers at each layer autonomously extract features in HSV color space, as shown in Fig. 5. The suggested architecture has five convolutional layers, followed by a batch normalization layer, three max-pooling layers, three fully connected dense layers, and a softmax layer with a dropout on each. Dropout necessitates some hyperparameter modifications [36]. The major modifications are as follows:

Enlarge the Network's Size: Dropout eliminates units from the network during training, limiting network capacity. The dropout rate must modify the number of units. i.e., It is essential to multiply the number of units by 1/ (dropout rate). If the dropout rate is 0.3, the number of units will be doubled.

Boost the Learning Rate and Momentum: Dropout introduces noise into the gradients, causing them to sometimes cancel out. This effect can be mitigated by raising the learning rate by 10–100x and increasing momentum between 0.95 and 0.99.

Integrate Maximum-Norm Regularization: High weight values may be the result of increased learning momentum and velocity. The use of maximum-norm regularization mitigates this impact.

Dropping out has the disadvantage of increasing training time. A dropout network increases training time by 200%–300% times longer than a typical neural network of a similar architecture [37]. So, to reduce the effect of the dropout layer, the network has been updated with batch normalization to support the significant hyperparameter changes that are required by the dropout layer and worked effectively [38–40]. On each layer, a different number of filters were implemented. The following steps are followed to develop the proposed model. Data gathering is the first step. Data can be collected by traveling to tomato farms and capturing tomato leaves, and domain experts can annotate the dataset. Data preprocessing is applied in step three. Testing the model steps is necessary to understand how generalized it is. If the model works well, then it should be validated by domain experts and deployed. If performance is not optimal, the model can be retrained until it performs better.

Convolutional layers were utilized in the first layer, then batch normalization and max pooling, respectively. The filter size is an 11 * 11-pixel window with a stride of 4 with a depth of 96 in the first layer, 5 * 5 kernel size with a depth of 256 in the second, 3 * 3 with 384 depths in the third and fourth layer, and in the fifth layer the filter size is 3 * 3 with depth 256 is used. We have reduced the image dimension by adding a max-pooling 3 * 3-pixel window with a stride of 2 pixels in the previous convolutional layer, which reduces the number of pixels in the output. Furthermore, they are optional to be followed by max-pooling. The fifth convolutional layer has three fully-connected layers at the end, two of which have 4096 nodes each, and the third has 1000 as it conducts the 10-way classification using softmax. The details A visual representation of the proposed neural network is shown in Fig. 3. The ReLU activation function, which connects the input and output layers, is applied to each of the five convolutional layers. The existence of the activation layer has an impact on the network's overall performance. The ReLU activation function provides the highest accurate classification rate [41], which treats negative values as zero and positive ones as one. Resolving the exploding/vanishing gradient issue is also another advantage of the rectified linear unit (RELU) activation function [42,43] (Fig. 2).

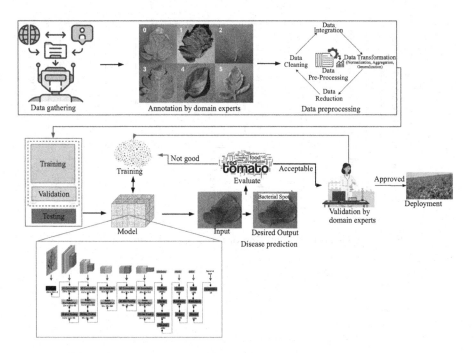

Fig. 2. Overall workflow of the proposed method.

Deep learning, to improve the convergence properties of the network, not only input data normalization but also the network weights/activations of initial layer values are commonly used. Batch normalization occurs when the output of a layer's activation function is normalized and supplied as input to the next layer. The selected layer' s value is normalized using the mean and standard deviation (or variance) of the values in the current batch, which is why it is termed "batch" normalization.

Classification: In order to solve problems involving class prediction, or the likelihood that a given input will be categorized into a specific class, convolutional neural networks are essential. Given that the issue is a multi-class classification problem, the softmax activation function is utilized. Categorical cross-entropy is a loss function used in creating our custom model for detecting and classifying tomato leaf diseases. In categorical cross-entropy, the probability of one class belonging to a particular category is 1, while that of belonging to another is 0. There are tasks in which classes can belong to only one of many possible categories, and the model must decide which category to assign them. Softmax and cross-entropy are, therefore, standard choices for developing neural network classifiers [44]. The proposed model was developed using the hyper-parameters listed in Table 1.

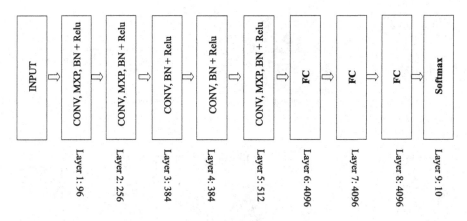

Fig. 3. A visual representation of the proposed neural network.

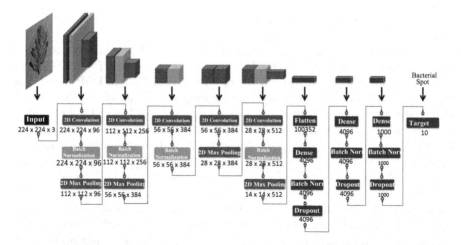

Fig. 4. The proposed custom modified AlexNet architecture.

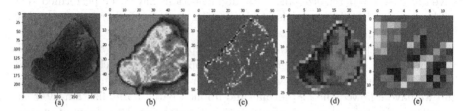

Fig. 5. (a) An image passed to the Input layer, (b), (c), (d), (e) Feature extraction at the first, Second, third, and fourth hidden layers respectively.

Table 1. Hyper-parameters for the proposed model.

Hyper-parameters	Descriptions
Number of convolution layers	5
Number of max pooling layers	3
Number of batch normalization	5
Drop out rate	0.5, 0.2
Activation function	ReLU
Batch size	32
Number of epochs	300
Momentum	0.99
Learning rate	0.001
Optimizer	Adam, SGD

4   Results and Discussions

Model Execution is conducted on an HP Z8W4 workstation computer. The model is trained using the NVIDIA Quadro P4000, which has 1792 CUDA cores, 243 Gbps of memory bandwidth, 8 GB of GDDR5, and 5.3 TFLOPs of processing power. The model's efficiency was measured in terms of training, validation, testing accuracy, confusion matrix, precision, recall, and F1 score, along with training-related parameter optimization. Identifying plant diseases early by detecting symptoms in tomato leaves is critical to diagnosing them accurately and maximizing production. Agriculture is highly specialized, and most farmers lack the necessary professional knowledge. For them, it is challenging to distinguish between plant diseases, and they cannot meet modern agricultural production demands. The objective of this study is to detect and classify diseases of tomato leaves using a convolutional neural network. Three hundred epochs were applied to train the model to a dataset that was split up into 80% training, 15% validation, and 5% testing, respectively. Furthermore, 32 samples have been used in batch size, and data augmentations have been performed. The model described in Sect. 3 is also trained using a categorical cross-entropy loss function with an Adam optimizer.

X. Li et al. [38] gave the statistical and experimental analysis that there is a variance shift when the practitioners use Dropout before batch normalization. Thus, [38] recommend applying Dropout after all batch normalization layers, and we have followed the [38] format and applied batch normalization after the convolution layers. Batch normalization eliminates the need for Dropout in some cases because batch normalization provides similar regularization benefits as Dropout intuitively. Architects like ResNet and DenseNet do not apply Dropout. Since most of the neurons that have the decision power are found at the fully connected (dense) layers, we have applied a dropout of 0.5 and 0.2, respectively, to those layers. The proposed model is trained with a different arrangement, as indicated in Tables 2, 3, 4, and 5. with their training, validation, and test accuracy and loss.

4.1   Results for Different Experimental Setup

Table 2. Experiment result of the first model arrangement.

Experiment (1) Conv -> Relu -> Dropout -> BatchNorm -> Maxpool						
Parameters	Results					
Optimizer = SGD Batch_size = 32	Training		Validation		Test	
Learning rate = 1e−4	Acc	Loss	Acc	Loss	Acc	Loss
epochs =50	83.10%	48.67%	74.11%	92.70%	72.50%	94.12%

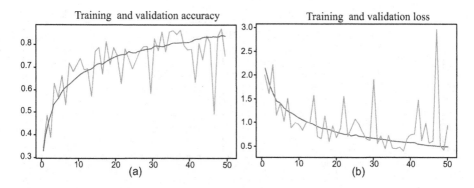

Fig. 6. (a) Training and validation accuracy plot, (b) training loss and validation loss plot.

Figure 6 illustrates how the network arrangement given in Table 2 leads to poor validation and test accuracy, followed by high validation and test loss when trained using an SGD optimizer with a learning rate of le−4. It indicates that the model is learning only the training data rather than gaining generalization capability. Besides, the model has encountered an over-fitting problem. It is evident since the training and validation graphs cross each other, as shown in Fig. 6.

As seen in Fig. 7 using Adam optimizer with learning rate le−3 and the above network arrangement results in high training and validation accuracy, respectively, followed by insufficient validation and test loss. This indicates that the model is learning the training data and gaining generalization capability. Since the training and validation graphs are becoming closer but not overlapping (crossing) each other, it implies that the model is performing as expected.

Table 3. Experiment result of the second model arrangement.

Experiment (2) Conv -> Relu -> BatchNorm -> Dropout -> Maxpool						
Parameters	Results					
Optimizer = Adam Batch_size = 32	Training		Validation		Test	
Learning rate = le−3	Acc	Loss	Acc	Loss	Acc	Loss
epochs = 50	94.98%	13.79%	91.11%	25.85%	91.15%	23.27%

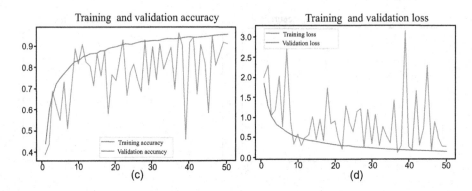

Fig. 7. (c) Training and validation accuracy plot, (d) training loss and validation loss plot.

Table 4. Experiment result of the third model arrangement.

Experiment (3) Conv -> Relu -> Maxpool -> Dropout						
Parameters	Results					
Optimizer = Adam Batch_size = 32	Training		Validation		Test	
Learning rate = 1e−3	Acc	Loss	Acc	Loss	Acc	Loss
epochs = 50	53.57%	139.86%	56.88%	127.66%	54.00%	132.37%

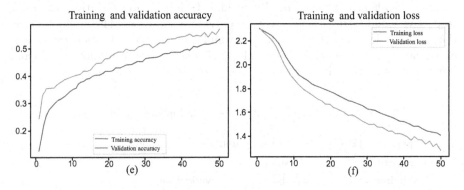

Fig. 8. (e) Training and validation accuracy plot, (f) training loss and validation loss plot.

As seen in Fig. 8, the plot looks smooth because of the absence of a batch normalization layer. However, it results in inadequate training and validation accuracy, respectively, followed by high validation and test loss.

Table 5. Experiment result of the fourth model arrangement.

Experiment (4) Conv -> Relu -> BatchNorm -> Dropout -> Maxpool						
Parameters	Results					
Optimizer = Adam Batch_size = 32	Training		Validation		Test	
Learning rate = 1e−3	Acc	Loss	Acc	Loss	Acc	Loss
epochs = 300	99.67%	1.17%	98.18%	9.56%	98.43%	7.06%

Finally, from Experiments 1, 2, and 3 training the model using the network arrangement mentioned in experiment 2 would be the best practice recommended by our research. Thus, the final result is shown in Fig. 9. After training, the entire dataset was used to generate stable estimates of the variable statistics, which are subsequently fixed at prediction time. The result of batch normalization is different when it is used during training and when it is used during testing. The same is valid for dropouts.

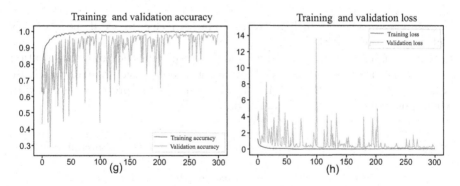

Fig. 9. (a) Training and validation accuracy plot, (b) training loss and validation loss plot.

4.2 Evaluation of Experimental Results

In the custom-modified AlexNet model, previously unknown leaf diseases can be recognized and predict the disease image, producing results comparable to those achieved in human evaluation. This step gives us a sense of one of the model's strengths and limitations and helps us understand the effects of the dataset and other variations that make up a poor or best model. The best model can identify a disease accurately, detect diseases it has never encountered before, and recognize diseases it has never encountered before. A total of 796 samples were used to test the trained model. The testing accuracy has a slight variation in the 95% to 100% range for different disease classes, as shown in Fig. 10. We also evaluated and visualized the performance model using the confusion matrix

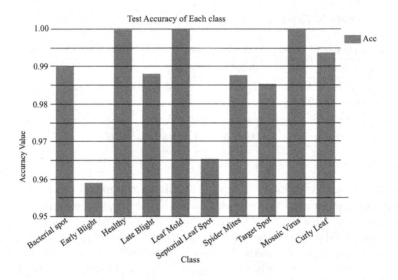

Fig. 10. Testing accuracy for the 10 classes.

for each class, as shown in Fig. 11. This makes it easy to see if the system is confusing for different classes.

The most important parameters to measure the efficiency of a classification model are accuracy, F1-score, recall, precision, and confusion matrix, which are explained in Table 6 and Fig. 11. Table 7 compares the proposed model with other approaches trained on a similar dataset.

Table 6. Performance of the proposed model on each class and overall mean.

Class	Precision	Recall	F1 Score
Bacterial Spot	0.97	0.99	0.98
Early Blight	0.98	0.96	0.97
Healthy	1	1	1
Late Blight	0.97	0.98	0.97
Leaf Mold	1	1	1
Spetoria Leaf Spot	0.98	0.95	0.97
Spider mite	1	0.99	0.99
Target Spot	0.97	0.99	0.98
Mosaic Virus	0.94	1	0.97
Yellow Leaf Curl Virus	1	0.99	1
Mean	0.981	0.985	0.983

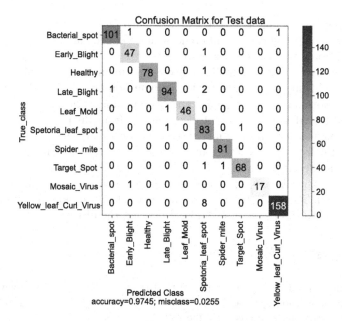

Fig. 11. Confusion Matrix for the proposed model.

Table 7. Comparison of the proposed and pre-trained model approaches.

S.No	Model	Dataset	Test Accuracy	Total Parameters
1	LeNet [33]	PlantVillage	94–95%	60K
2	Xception [31]	PlantVillage	95%	22.8M
3	VGG 19 [31]	PlantVillage	97%	143M
4	ResNet-50 [32]	PlantVillage	97.01%	25.6M
5	SqeezeNet [30]	PlantVillage	95.65%	421K
6	AlexNet [30]	PlantVillage	94.30%	60M
7	Proposed model	PlantVillage	98.43%	50M

5   Conclusion

There are wide varieties of tomatoes grown in many parts of the world and consumed in significant quantities. Nationally, around 34,947 tons of tomatoes were produced in 2019. Early detection of leaf diseases of tomatoes is crucial to prevent a considerable loss in yields. Using a custom-modified AlexNet architecture, a model has been developed for detecting and classifying diseases affecting tomato leaves. The proposed model consists of five convolutional layers, five batch normalization layers, three layers of max-pooling with different numbers of filters, and three fully connected layers. The softmax activation function was applied to the output layer using a categorical cross-entropy loss function. Optimal performance was obtained using a different layer arrangement for the parameters of the convolutional neural network model.

Different layer arrangements have been experimented with, and the arrangement that yields higher efficiency is the convolution layer followed by the ReLu, then Batch Normalization, Dropout, and Max-pooling. The proposed model was trained and tested using the tomato leaf dataset from the plant village. To classify input images into appropriate disease classes, features from input images are automatically extracted using an automatic feature extraction process. Upon testing the model, it was observed that the accuracy ranges from 95% to 100%, depending on the disease type. The model has an average testing accuracy of 98.43% as well. The next step is to tweak the model with more images using the local tomato leaf disease dataset and segmenting the diseased areas.

References

1. Tomatoes, production quantity (tons) for Ethiopia - Tilasto. https://www.tilasto.com/en/topic/geography-and-agriculture/crop/tomatoes/tomatoes-production-quantity/ethiopia. Accessed 25 June 2021
2. LeCun, Y., Bottou, L., Bengio, Y., Haffner, P.: Gradient-based learning applied to document recognition. Proc. IEEE **86**(11), 2278–2324 (1998). https://doi.org/10.1109/5.726791
3. Quintin, G., Abu, T., Teddy, T.: Tomato production in Ethiopia challenged by pest. GIAN report, Adiss Ababa, Ethiopia (2013)
4. Tm, P., Pranathi, A., SaiAshritha, K., Chittaragi, N.B., Koolagudi, S.G.: Tomato leaf disease detection using convolutional neural networks. In: Precedings of the Eleventh International Conference on Contemporary Computing (IC3), pp. 1–5. IEEE (2018). https://doi.org/10.1109/IC3.2018.8530532
5. Agarwal, M., Singh, A., Arjaria, S., Sinha, A., Gupta, S.: ToLeD: tomato leaf disease detection using convolution neural network. J. Proc. Comput. Sci. **167**, 293-301 (2020). International Conference on Computational Intelligence and Data Science, ISSN 1877-0509. https://doi.org/10.1016/j.procs.2020.03.225, https://www.sciencedirect.com/science/article/pii/S1877050920306906
6. Khirade, S.D., Patil, A.B.: Plant disease detection using image processing. In: 2015 International Conference on Computing Communication Control and Automation, pp. 768–771. IEEE (2015). https://doi.org/10.1109/ICCUBEA.2015.153
7. Debelee, T.G., Kebede, S.R., Schwenker, F., Shewarega, Z.M.: Deep learning in selected cancers' image analysis–a survey. J. Imaging **6**(11) (2020). https://doi.org/10.3390/jimaging6110121
8. Afework, Y.K., Debelee, T.G.: Detection of bacterial wilt on enset crop using deep learning approach. Int. J. Eng. Res. Afr. **51**, 131–146 (2020). https://doi.org/10.4028/www.scientific.net/JERA.51.131
9. Yebasse, M., Shimelis, B., Warku, H., Ko, J., Cheoi, K.J.: Coffee disease visualization and classification. Plants **10**(6) (2021) https://doi.org/10.3390/plants10061257. ISSN 2223-7747
10. Cravero, A., Sepúlveda, S.: Use and adaptations of machine learning in big data–applications in real cases in agriculture. Electronics **10**(5) (2021). https://doi.org/10.3390/electronics10050552. ISSN 2079-9292

11. Liakos, K.G., Busato, P., Moshou, D., Pearson, S., Bochtis, D.: Machine learning in agriculture: a review. Sensors **18**(8) (2018). https://doi.org/10.3390/s18082674. ARTICLE-no.2674, ISSN 1424-8220
12. Cramer, S., Kampouridis, M., Freitas, A.A., Alexandridis, A.K.: An extensive evaluation of seven machine learning methods for rainfall prediction in weather derivatives. Expert Syst. Appl. **85**, 169–181 (2017). https://doi.org/10.1016/j.eswa.2017. 05.029. ISSN 0957-4174
13. Rhee, J., Im, J.: Meteorological drought forecasting for ungauged areas based on machine learning: using long-range climate forecast and remote sensing data. Agric. For. Meteorol. **237–238**, 105–122 (2017). https://doi.org/10.1016/j.agrformet. 2017.02.011. ISSN 0168-1923
14. Barboza, F., Kimura, H., Altman, E.: Machine learning models and bankruptcy prediction. Expert Syst. Appl. **83**, 405–417 (2017). https://doi.org/10.1016/j.eswa. 2017.04.006. ISSN 0957-4174
15. Zhao, Y., Li, J., Yu, L.: A deep learning ensemble approach for crude oil price forecasting. Energy Econ. **66**, 9–16 (2017). https://doi.org/10.1016/j.eneco.2017. 05.023. ISSN 0140-9883
16. Bohanec, M., Borštnar, M.K., Robnik-Šikonja, M.: Explaining machine learning models in sales predictions. Expert Syst. Appl. **71**, 416–428 (2017). https://doi. org/10.1016/j.eswa.2016.11.010. ISSN 0957-4174
17. Takahashi, K., Kim, K., Ogata, T., Sugano, S.: Tool-body assimilation model considering grasping motion through deep learning. Robot. Auton. Syst. **91**, 115–127 (2017). https://doi.org/10.1016/j.robot.2017.01.002. ISSN 0921-8890
18. Gastaldo, P., Pinna, L., Seminara, L., Valle, M., Zunino, R.: A tensor-based approach to touch modality classification by using machine learning. Robot. Auton. Syst. **63**, 268–278 (2015). https://doi.org/10.1016/j.robot.2014.09.022. ISSN 0921-8890
19. López-Cortés, X.A., et al.: Fast detection of pathogens in salmon farming industry. Aquaculture **470**, 17–24 (2017). https://doi.org/10.1016/j.aquaculture.2016. 12.008. ISSN 0044-8486
20. Zhou, C., et al.: Near infrared computer vision and neuro-fuzzy model-based feeding decision system for fish in aquaculture. Comput. Electron. Agric. **146**, 114–124 (2018). https://doi.org/10.1016/j.compag.2018.02.006. ISSN 0168-1699
21. Debelee, T.G., Schwenker, F., Ibenthal, A., Yohannes, D.: Survey of deep learning in breast cancer image analysis. Evol. Syst. **11**(1), 143–163 (2020). https://doi. org/10.1007/s12530-019-09297-2. ISSN 1868-6486
22. Debelee, T.G., Amirian, M., Ibenthal, A., Palm, G., Schwenker, F.: Classification of mammograms using convolutional neural network based feature extraction. In: Mekuria, F., Nigussie, E.E., Dargie, W., Edward, M., Tegegne, T. (eds.) ICT4DA 2017. LNICST, vol. 244, pp. 89–98. Springer, Cham (2018). https://doi.org/10. 1007/978-3-319-95153-9_9. ISBN 978-3-319-95153-9
23. Debelee, T.G., Gebreselasie, A., Schwenker, F., Amirian, M., Yohannes, D.: Classification of mammograms using texture and CNN based extracted features. J. Biomimet. Biomater. Biomed. Eng. **42**, 79–97 (2019). https://doi.org/10.4028/ www.scientific.net/JBBBE.42.79
24. Debelee, T.G., Schwenker, F., Rahimeto, S., Yohannes, D.: Evaluation of modified adaptive k-means segmentation algorithm. Comput. Vis. Media **5**(4), 347–361 (2019). https://doi.org/10.1007/s41095-019-0151-2. ISSN 2096-0662
25. Rahimeto, S., Debelee, T.G., Yohannes, D., Schwenker, F.: Automatic pectoral muscle removal in mammograms. Evol. Syst. **12**(2), 519–526 (2021). https://doi. org/10.1007/s12530-019-09310-8. ISSN 1868-6486

26. Kebede, S.R., Debelee, T.G., Schwenker, F., Yohannes, D.: Classifier based breast cancer segmentation. J. Biomimet. Biomater. Biomed. Eng. **47**, 41–61 (2020). https://doi.org/10.4028/www.scientific.net/JBBBE.47.41

27. Megersa, Y., Alemu, G.: Brain tumor detection and segmentation using hybrid intelligent algorithms. Africon 1–8 (2015). https://doi.org/10.1109/AFRCON.2015.7331938

28. Biratu, E.S., Schwenker, F., Debelee, T.G., Kebede, S.R., Negera, W.G., Molla, H.T.: Enhanced region growing for brain tumor MR image segmentation. J. Imaging **7**(2) (2021). https://doi.org/10.3390/jimaging7020022. ISSN 2313-433X

29. Oo, Y.M., Htun, N.C.: Plant leaf disease detection and classification using image processing. Int. J. Res. Eng. **5**(9), 516–523 (2018)

30. Durmuş, H., Güneş, E.O., Kırcı, M.: Disease detection on the leaves of the tomato plants by using deep learning. In: 6th International Conference on Agro-Geoinformatics, pp. 1–5 (2017). https://doi.org/10.1109/Agro-Geoinformatics.2017.8047016

31. Aversano, L., Bernardi, M.L., Cimitile, M., Iammarino, M., Rondinella, S.: Tomato diseases classification based on VGG and transfer learning. In: IEEE International Workshop on Meteorology for Agriculture and Forestry (MetroAgriFor), pp. 129–133. IEEE (2020). https://doi.org/10.1109/MetroAgriFor50201.2020.9277626

32. Nithish Kannan, E., Kaushik, M., Prakash, P., Ajay, R., Veni, S.: Tomato leaf disease detection using convolutional neural network with data augmentation. In: 5th International Conference on Communication and Electronics Systems (ICCES), pp. 1125–1132 (2020). https://doi.org/10.1109/ICCES48766.2020.9138030

33. Irmak, G., Saygili, A.: Tomato leaf disease detection and classification using convolutional neural networks. In: Innovations in Intelligent Systems and Applications Conference (ASYU), pp. 1–5 (2020). https://doi.org/10.1109/ASYU50717.2020.9259832

34. Francis, M., Deisy, C.: Disease detection and classification in agricultural plants using convolutional neural networks-a visual understanding. In: 6th International Conference on Signal Processing and Integrated Networks (SPIN), pp. 1063–1068. IEEE (2019). https://doi.org/10.1109/SPIN.2019.8711701

35. PlantVillage Dataset | Kaggle. https://www.kaggle.com/abdallahalidev/plantvillage-dataset

36. Garbin, C., Zhu, X., Marques, O.: Dropout vs. batch normalization: an empirical study of their impact to deep learning. Multimed. Tools Appl. **79**(19–20) (2020). https://doi.org/10.1007/s11042-019-08453-9

37. Srivastava, N., Hinton, G., Krizhevsky, A., Sutskever, I., Salakhutdinov, R.: Dropout: a simple way to prevent neural networks from overfitting. J. Mach. Learn. Res. **15**(56), 1929–1958 (2014). http://jmlr.org/papers/v15/srivastava14a.html

38. Li, X., Chen, S., Hu, X., Yang, J.: Understanding the disharmony between dropout and batch normalization by variance shift. In: IEEE/CVF Conference on Computer Vision and Pattern Recognition (CVPR), pp. 2677–2685. IEEE (2019). https://doi.org/10.1109/CVPR.2019.00279

39. Alzubaidi, L., et al.: Review of deep learning: concepts, CNN architectures, challenges, applications, future directions. J. Big Data **8**(1), 1–74 (2021). https://doi.org/10.1186/s40537-021-00444-8

40. Ioffe, S., Szegedy, C.: Batch normalization: accelerating deep network training by reducing internal covariate shift. In: Proceedings of the 32nd International Conference on Machine Learning. Proceedings of Machine Learning Research, Lille, France, vol. 37, pp. 448–456. PMLR (2015). http://proceedings.mlr.press/v37/ioffe15.html

41. Ertam, F., Aydın, G.: Data classification with deep learning using Tensorflow. In: International Conference on Computer Science and Engineering (UBMK), pp. 755–758. IEEE (2017). https://doi.org/10.1109/UBMK.2017.8093521
42. Xu, B., Wang, N., Chen, T., Li, M.: Empirical evaluation of rectified activations in convolutional network. arXiv preprint arXiv:1505.00853 (2015)
43. Philipp, G., Song, D., Carbonell, J.G.: The exploding gradient problem demystified-definition, prevalence, impact, origin, tradeoffs, and solutions. arXiv preprint arXiv:1712.05577 (2017)
44. Qin, Z., Kim, D., Gedeon, T.: Rethinking Softmax with cross-entropy: neural network classifier as mutual information estimator (2020). eprint 1911.10688

Wheat Yield Prediction Using Machine Learning: A Survey

Taye Girma Debelee[1,2] [iD], Samuel Rahimeto Kebede[1] [iD],
Fraol Gelana Waldamichael[1(✉)] [iD], and Daniel Moges Tadesse[1] [iD]

[1] Ethiopian Artificial Intelligence Institute, 40782 Addis Ababa, Ethiopia
tayegirma@gmail.com, taye.girma@aii.et,
{samuel.rahimeto,fraol.gelana}@aic.et
[2] Addis Ababa Science and Technology University, College of Electrical
and Mechanical Engineering, 120611 Addis Ababa, Ethiopia

Abstract. Wheat is one of the most important and most produced
cereal crops in the world with over 600 million tonnes harvested annually. Accurate yield prediction of this important crop plays a huge role
in the nation's plan for achieving sustainable food security. In this work,
we performed a systematic review of research works conducted on the
application of machine learning in wheat yield prediction. The reviewed
papers are acquired from multiple digital libraries based on a defined
article selection requirement and the primary research question we hope
to answer. In total, we filtered 24 relevant research articles conducted
between the years 2019 and 2022, and identified the state-of-the-art
machine learning algorithms currently adopted and the types of datasets
used. As such, we found that random forest and gradient boosting are
efficient and reliable choices for the task of wheat yield prediction. We
also observed the rising popularity of deep learning algorithms, such as
deep convolutional neural networks and LSTMs for remote sensing and
time series-based wheat yield prediction. We also identified the lack of a
large public dataset as a major challenge as it makes the reproduction
and comparison of different model performances very difficult.

Keywords: Yield Prediction · Crop · Wheat · Machine Learning ·
Deep Learning

1 Introduction

In the disciplines of academia, business, and particularly in healthcare for early
detection, diagnosis, prediction, and classification [4,5,9–12], machine learning is
used to address a number of difficulties. The development of efficient algorithms
and reasonably priced yet powerful technology has made it viable to use machine
learning and deep learning in the agriculture sector [1]. Machine learning and
deep learning have several uses in the agricultural sector. Early diagnosis of plant

T. Girma Debelee et al. (Eds.): PanAfriCon AI 2022, CCIS 1800, pp. 114–132, 2023.
https://doi.org/10.1007/978-3-031-31327-1_7

diseases has been successfully accomplished by machine learning [37], We have demonstrated this in our previous work [37] where we proposed an algorithm for detecting coffee leaf diseases using HSV color segmentation and deep learning that will enable farmers to monitor the health of their coffee farm using a smartphone. Similarly, Afework and Debelee [1] utilized deep learning for the detection of bacterial wilt on the Enset crop which is the main food for around 20 Million people in the southern part of Ethiopia.

Crop yield estimation is an essential factor in sustainable agriculture [21], and machine learning has been used to predict yields of various crops with success [27] of which one is the main focus of this review work. Wheat, being one of the most important crops being harvested with over 600 million tones of wheat harvested annually [29] is counted as among the "big three" kinds of cereal crops. The success of wheat is due to its adaptability and range of cultivation, growing in a wide range of geographic locations and weather conditions. Accurate yield prediction of this important crop is an immense economic and research interest. Much research around the use of machine learning in yield prediction of various crops has been done in recent years. Nevavuori et al. [24] performed crop yield prediction by using data from UAVs and deep learning. Here, the authors' collected their data during the growing season by UAVs, the collected RGB image is then processed and fed into a deep learning algorithm to get the yield prediction. They showed that deep learning performed better than NDVI data and that the approach is suitable for predicting wheat and barley yield in a specific climate. Accurate prediction of yield patterns and identification of extreme yield loss causes in maize crops was successfully undertaken by Zhong et al. [41]. The authors developed a multi-task learning model that was used to achieve region-specific pattern recognition. The model takes in information about the environment and yields information and uses it to cluster the Corn Belt in the United States into several homogeneous regions. The proposed model then extracts temporal and soil patterns separately according to the specific input and network structure. In this work, we conducted a comprehensive systematic literature review of studies conducted on the application of machine learning in crop yield prediction especially focusing on wheat yield prediction; where we try to identify the most effective and state-of-the-art algorithms that are being applied and also the appropriate features required to enable an accurate yield prediction using the learning algorithms.

2   Related Works

There have been several reviews conducted on general crop yield projections. Finding review articles done exclusively for wheat yield prediction, on the other hand, proved problematic. As a result, we employed reviews of crop production projections using wheat as one of the recognized crop kinds. Oikonomidis et. al.

[25] performed a systematic literature review on predicting crop yield using deep learning techniques. They have identified 44 papers, of which only eight articles focus on wheat yield prediction. They also noted that CNN's are most used architecture for yield prediction.

Bali and Singla [3] explored various machine-learning techniques used in crop yield prediction and discussed the efficiency of hybrid models formed by combining multiple machine-learning techniques. The authors discussed the two crop yield estimation approaches, namely the crop growth model and the data-driven model. The authors implied that the mathematical crop growth models are efficient and can yield good results in the yield prediction of specific crops, but noted that these models are expensive to develop and are impractical for large-scale agricultural planning. On the contrary, the authors discussed that data-driven models are cheaper to develop and easier to deploy.

Klompenburg et al. [35] conducted a survey of machine learning techniques and features that are used in crop yield prediction. The authors reviewed 50 studies conducted on crop yield prediction using machine learning techniques and identified the most used features and algorithms. According to their study, the authors identified temperature, rainfall, and soil type as the most used features. Additionally, they identified convolutional neural networks as the most applied learning algorithm, followed by LSTM'S.

Muruganantham et al. [23] conducted a systematic review on the fusion of remote sensing and deep learning for the application of crop yield prediction. The review study was motivated by the desire to examine the influence of vegetation indices and discover how environmental conditions affect agricultural productivity. The authors set out to find the most regularly used features and deep learning architectures, and discovered that vegetation indices and meteorological data are the most commonly used features, while CNN and LSTM-based models are the most commonly used deep learning architectures.

Table 1. Summary of related works.

Authors	Contribution	Limitation
Oikonomidis et al. [25]	The review work concisely summarizes identified research works from different search engines on deep learning-based crop yield predictions	Since its focuses are the general crop yield prediction and it doesn't include a summary of each reviewed research work, determining which algorithms or datasets were suitable for wheat yield prediction is indeterminate
Bali and Singla [3]	The authors performed in detail discussion on the various crop yield estimation techniques, on the various factors affecting yield estimation and held a broad discussion on the deep learning in crop yield prediction	The work lacks a proper summary of the reviews, which makes it hard for the reader to grasp what kind of machine learning or deep learning approaches are effective and what type of data is mostly used in crop yield estimation
Klompenburg et al. [35]	Feature diagram enables the researchers to know the major features used in crop yield prediction, and the way the discussion section is organized	Each paper is not discussed well, instead, the paper explained different machine learning approaches
Muruganantham et al. [23]	The paper covered most deep learning-based wheat yield prediction using remote sensing data	The paper doesn't give an idea of how the yield prediction models and remote sensing data are efficient among different crop types

3   Methods

This systematic review (SLR) [20] work is intended to highlight new works on wheat yield prediction using machine learning approaches, including both classic machine learning algorithms and deep learning methods. The SLR stresses the need of having a well defined methodology for creating research questions, search methodologies for discovering relevant literature, and establishing the required exclusion and inclusion criteria for selecting the appropriate studies.

3.1   Research Questions

In this study, we want to pinpoint machine learning methods used for crop yield prediction, particularly in the previous four years. Thus, the main research topic that we hope to address is:

PRQ: *"What cutting-edge machine learning methods have been employed in the last four years to forecast wheat yields?"*

In order to further assist in focusing the intended response to the core research question, secondary research questions are also prepared. These are:

- SRQ1: *What was the key motivation for applying machine learning for wheat yield prediction?*
- SRQ2: *What categories of data are utilized and accessible?*
- SRQ3: *Which key evaluation metrics are used to measure yield prediction?*
- SRQ4: *Which machine learning algorithm and dataset performed better for wheat yield prediction?*

3.2   Search Strategies

We need to identify the right search strategies [20] in order to identify as many pertinent primary studies as possible that attempt to respond to the primary research question posed. We have defined our search strategy as follows:

- Choose different search databases for the recent publications related to the title.
- Decompose research questions for better search output.
- Create the keywords related to the title [20]
- Build **search strings** using "AND" and "OR" boolean.

The approach used to search for the primary studies was focused on five known search databases that include: Springer Link[1], Science direct[2], Wiley online library[3] and IEEE Xplore[4]. These databases were selected because they contain most machine learning-related papers.

To get the most out of the databases, an optimized and simplified search string need to be defined as indicated in Algorithm 1. Further, additional inclusion and exclusion criteria were defined as presented in Table 2.

---

[1] https://link.springer.com/.

[2] https://sciencedirect.com/.

[3] https://onlinelibrary.wiley.com/.

[4] https://ieeexplore.ieee.org/.

Algorithm 1. Pseudo-code for defining search string.

Search_String = ("Crop Yield" **OR** "Wheat yield")
AND
("Prediction" **OR** "Estimation" **OR** "Forecasting")
AND
("Machine Learning" **OR** "Deep Learning" **OR** "Artificial Intelligence")

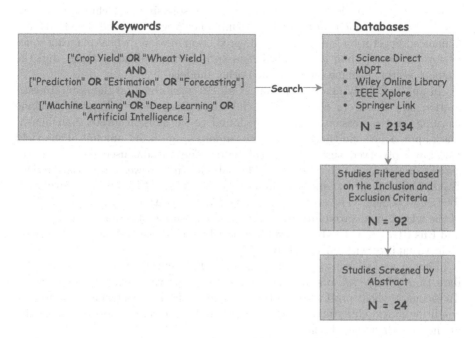

Fig. 1. Methodology for systematic literature review.

Table 2. Paper selection criteria.

Inclusion criteria (IC)	Exclusion criteria (EC)
IC1: Studies that focused on wheat yield prediction	**EC1**: Duplicate publications
IC2: Studies carried out from 2019 to 2022.	**EC2**: Studies performed other than the English language
IC3: The article should be in reputable journals or recognized Conference proceedings.	**EC3**: MSc and Ph.D. thesis, Posters, Seminar, and Case studies
IC4: Publishing Journals should be indexed in web of science or Scopus	**EC4**: Studies that do not use either machine learning or deep learning

4   Machine Learning in Wheat Yield Prediction

4.1   Remote Sensing Based Wheat Yield Prediction

In order to estimate wheat yield in China, Zhou et al. [42] investigated the potential of nine climate factors, three metrics obtained from remote sensing, and three machine learning techniques. They discovered that the northern winter and spring wheat planting zones had the best results. Climate variables connected to water performed better than those related to temperature. In terms of predicting crop yield, they also found that solar-induced chlorophyll fluorescence outperformed the Normalized Difference Vegetation Index (NDVI) and Enhanced Vegetation Index (EVI). The prediction in winter wheat planting zones performed better than the prediction in spring wheat planting zones, and the support vector machine outperformed other models.

In another study made by Kamir et al. [19] performed on the accurate estimation of yields from wheat across the Australian wheat belt using machine learning, and regression models were found to be more accurate than benchmark approaches and they were able to explain a significant amount of the yield variability observed across statistical units. The authors used data on yield, satellite images, and climate data. The satellite images were from the MODIS "MOD13Q1" data set, and the climate data from SILO (Scientific Information for Land Owners). The authors found the SVM algorithm which explained 77% of the wheat yield variability to be the best performing of the regression models and Ens.BDF to be the best ensemble model which explained 76% of the wheat yield variability with an RMSE of 0.57.

Tian et al. [34] built a model using an LSTM neural network technique and data from remote sensors and meteorology to improve wheat yield estimation. To estimate wheat production in the Guanzhong Plain, vegetation temperature condition index, climatic data, and leaf area index are very important, especially at the growth stages of wheat.

The model used several time steps to capture time series data with LSTM. The results showed that the best yield estimation accuracy (RMSE = 357.77 kg/ha and R^2 = 0.83) was achieved with two-time steps and the input combination of meteorological data and two remote sensing indices. The authors compared the best LSTM model performance with BPNN and SVM for yield estimation accuracy. The LSTM model outperformed BPNN (R^2 = 0.42 and RMSE = 812.83 kg/ha) and SVM (R^2 = 0.41 and RMSE = 867.70 kg/ha) because of its recurrent neural network structure that can handle nonlinear relationships between multi-features inputs and yield. The authors also tested the optimal LSTM method on irrigation sites and rain-fed sites from 2008 to 2016 to check its robustness. The results showed that the proposed model was effective for different types of sampling sites and adaptable to inter-annual variations of climate.

Tesfaye et al. [33] undertook a study with the goal of developing a technique for remote sensing-based wheat production prediction in smallholding and heterogeneous agricultural settings. The study used vegetation indices from high-resolution optical and SAR sensors to derive predictions. Five SAR indices were derived from the data of the S1 sensor, and eight vegetation indices from the S2 optical sensors. Data mining techniques were used, which fall into three major categories: statistical, machine learning, and deep learning. These techniques were used because of the intricate interaction between the predictors and response variables. Due to the limited availability of the response variable (field-collected wheat grain yield), this study used data mining techniques instead of the more typical approaches to machine learning and deep learning implementation. According to the study, networks with one or two hidden layers fared worse than deep neural networks with three hidden layers. The best models discovered using the three data mining techniques make use of phenological data, particularly data from the post-grain-filling period.

Vanli et al. [36] proposed a method of using satellite images to predict wheat yields in southeastern Turkey. The study found that the satellite images were accurate in predicting wheat yields, with an error of less than 200 kg/ha. In order to employ the optimum model for the geographical distribution of wheat crops, a total of eight machine-learning algorithms were evaluated and tuned for the categorization of satellite images. The machine learning algorithms produced outcomes with an accuracy of more than 90%. The random forest was chosen for picture categorization as the best model. With a root mean square error (RMSE) of 198 kg/ha, the tested model's observed and anticipated yields were relatively near to one another.

Fei et al. [15] applied five ML algorithms for fusing data from multiple sensors to predict crop yield more accurately. The ML algorithms were Cubist, SVM, DNN, RR, and RF. They used them for multi-sensor data fusion and ensemble learning for wheat grain yield prediction. The study showed that multi-sensor data was better than single-sensor data for prediction accuracy. The ensemble learning predictions had R^2 values up to 0.692, which was higher than individual ML models with multi-sensor data. The RMSE, RPD, and RPIQ were 9160 kg/ha, 1.771, and 2.602, respectively. Their results indicated that low-altitude UAV-based multi-sensor data can be used for early grain yield prediction with data fusion and ensemble learning.

Another study in [14] examined the two machine learning methods of Bootstrapped Regression Trees (BRR) and Convolutional Neural Networks (CNN) and examined how they may be applied for predicting wheat yield. According to the study, local electromagnetic induction surveys or gamma radiometric surveys combined with BRR modeling utilizing publically available Sentinel data gave the most accurate estimates. With the addition of openly accessible data from related disciplines, the CNN models' outcomes improved.

Yang et al. [39] use the CERES wheat model to generate training samples for the training of their random forest model. Using the CERES wheat model simulations, they identified the leaf area index (LAI) and leaf nitrogen content (LNC) as the most sensitive parameters. These features were extracted from UAV's hyperspectral images and used as input into the CW-RF model to estimate winter wheat yield. The model (CERES wheat model) is not accurate enough to be used as a ground truth for training the CW-RF model and needs further improvements.

Shidnal et al. [30] used machine learning to analyze how nutrient levels affect crop yield. They trained a neural network with Tensor Flow to recognize images of crops with different nutrient deficiencies (nitrogen, potassium, phosphorous) or healthy ones. They also used a clustering algorithm to measure the severity of the deficiency. Then they used a rule matrix to estimate the yield of the cropland based on the deficiency level. Their method was 76–77% accurate in predicting the yield.

Qiao et al. [28] developed a method for estimating crop yield using multi-spectral images. The method uses a 3-D convolutional neural network to extract features from the images that capture spatial and spectral information. Then, it uses a multi-kernel learning technique to combine the features from different domains. Finally, it uses a kernel-based method to get the probability distribution of the yield estimates. The method is tested on wheat yield prediction in China and compared with other methods. The results show that the method has R^2 and RMSE values of 0.8 and 730 kg/ha respectively.

Table 3. Summary of papers on remote sensing-based wheat yield prediction.

Author	Method	Dataset	Acc	R^2	RMSE
Zhou et al. [42]	SVM	Remote sensing and climate data	-	0.63–0.74	1100 kg kg/ha
Kamir et al. [19]	SVM	Satellite and climate data	-	0.77	550 kg/ha
Tian et al. [34]	LSTM	Meteorological and remote sensing data	-	0.42	812.83 kg/ha
Tesfaye et al. [33]	DNN	Optical and radar data	-	-	1360 kg/ha
Vanli et al. [36]	Random Forest	Satellite image	90%	-	198 kg/ha
Fei et a. [15]	Ensemble learning	Multi-sensor data	-	0.692	916 kg/ha
Fajardo et al. [14]	Bootstrapped Regression Trees (BRR) and CNN	publicly available Sentinel data with the addition of local electromagnetic induction surveys or gamma radiometric surveys	-	-	600 kg/ha
Yang et al. [39]	Random Forest	UAV's Hyperspectral Imagery & Synthetic Data from CERES wheat model	-	-	1,008.08 kg/ha
Shidnal et al. [30]	k-means clustering	Crop images	76–77%	-	-
Qiao et al. [28]	3-D convolutional neural network	Multispectral images	-	0.8	730 kg/ha

4.2   Environmental Factors Based Wheat Yield Prediction

Zhang et al. [40] proposed a generative adversarial networks (GANs) approach for increasing the precision of winter wheat yield estimation. GANs were proposed by the authors to deal with small datasets and a limited number of annotated samples. The training set consists of data from 2012 to 2015, while the validation set consists of data from 2016. The test set is made up of data from 2017. GANs are used to supplement the training and validation sets. The CNN includes VTCI, LAI, and meteorological data. The CNN is better at predicting yield than previous models, according to the authors, because it can account for the interplay between several sorts of input characteristics.

Chergui [7] conducted durum wheat yield forecasting using machine learning and data augmentation to improve predictions and results. The author employed a dataset containing data on annual yields and acreage for harvest seasons ranging from 1991 to 2019. The study discovered that the data augmentation approach improved overall performance, with the Deep Neural Network producing the best results.

Pang et al. [26] proposed regional and local-scale wheat yield prediction using random forest regression (RFR). The Bureau of Meteorology provided data for this study, and collaborating farmers provided yield for the year 2018. The random forest regression technique was found to be accurate, with a high R^2 value of 0.86 and a low RMSE of 0.18. The study also discovered that the technique was robust and worked well across a variety of paddocks with varying conditions.

Han et al. [18] investigated the use of several data sources and machine learning algorithms to estimate the winter wheat output in China, one or two months before harvest, they discovered that county-level models can forecast yield with good accuracy ($R^2 > 0.7$ and error $< 10\%$). They discovered that training intervals and agricultural zones have an impact on prediction accuracy. They made use of GEE and ArcGIS-processed remote sensing data. For the purpose of predicting yield, they examined three machine learning models (RF, GPR, and SVM). They claimed that RF outperformed GPR in terms of computation speed and accuracy.

Wang et al. [38] developed a method for estimating winter wheat yield within-season using various data sources in the US. The method tries to address the drawbacks of empirical models based on satellite images by using machine learning and multi-source data. The authors tested four machine learning models (SVM, RF, AdaBoost, and DNN) and reported that AdaBoost was the best. They also reported that decreasing the input factors enhanced the neural network's performance by preventing over-fitting and improving generalization ability.

The ABSOLUT v1.2 algorithm, which is used to forecast agricultural yields, was put forth by Tobias Conradt in [8]. The program uses correlations between time-aggregated meteorological indicators and agricultural yields to produce predictions. The method is used in Germany to predict the yields of important crops including winter wheat and silage maize. Separate training and testing years should be used when choosing features because the algorithm can make out-of-sample predictions (based only on data other than the target year to forecast).

In order to anticipate crop yields, Cao et al. [6] developed and used a hybrid skillful ML-dynamical model that blends ML with a global dynamical atmospheric prediction system. In their research, they examined multiple linear regression (MLR) models as well as XGBoost, RF, and SVR. For the period of 2005 to 2014, they projected the production of winter wheat using three datasets: satellite data from MOD13C1, observational climate data from CRU, and S2S atmospheric prediction data from IAP CAS. With the S2S prediction as inputs, XGBoost outperformed the other four evaluated models, scoring R^2 of 0.85 and RMSE of 780 kg/ha within 3–4 months before the winter wheat harvest. Their findings demonstrate that S2S dynamical forecasts outperform observational climate data for agricultural yield forecasting. Furthermore, their findings showed that integrating ML and S2S dynamical atmospheric prediction would be an advantageous yield forecasting tool, which might direct agricultural practices, policy, and agricultural insurance.

Murakami et al. [22] investigated meteorological limitations on winter wheat yield in Hokkaido, Japan's northernmost island, and compared ML models to a null model that returns the municipalities average yield to, neural network (NN), random forest (RF), support vector machine regression (SVR), partial least squares regression (PLS), cubist regression (CB), and multiple linear regression model (MLR). This island has a wet climate due to higher annual precipitation and an abundant snow-melt water supply in spring when compared to other wheat-producing areas. Their research discovered that precipitation, daily minimum air temperature, and irradiance had major effects on yield across the island during the grain-filling period. The study used 10-day mean meteorological data from seeding to harvest as predictor variables, as well as a one-year leave-out cross-validation procedure. The PLS, SVR, and RF had root means square errors of 872, 982, and 1,024 kg/ha, respectively, which were less than MLR (1,068 kg/ha) and the null model (1,035 kg/ha). Other metrics, such as Pearson's correlation coefficient and Nash-Sutcliffe efficiency, showed that these models outperformed the controls. The findings corroborated the authors' understanding of meteorological effects on wheat yield, implying the utility of explainable machine learning in meteorological crop yield prediction in wet climates.

Elavarasan and Vincent [13] proposed a reinforced random forest model for improved crop yield prediction by integrating agrarian parameters. The study describes a new algorithm developed to predict crop yield based on climate, soil, and water parameters. The Reinforcement Random Forest algorithm is a hybrid of regression and machine learning. Because it employs reinforcement learning, this new algorithm is expected to outperform other traditional machine learning techniques. This means that the algorithm learns from its errors and improves over time. The algorithm is also said to perform better with sparse data structures. The results showed that the proposed approach performs better, with lower error measures and an improved accuracy of 92.2%.

Using machine learning and multilayered, multifarm data sets, Filippi et al. developed a method to predict grain crop yield [17]. The authors outlined how crop yield models may be created using machine learning using data from various fields, farms, and years. In a case study, they used yield data from three seasons (2013-2015) spanning hundreds of hectares on substantial farms in Western Australia. For modeling, the yield data were cleaned up and combined into a grid of 100 m. Based on pre-sowing, mid-season, and late-season circumstances, they projected wheat, barley, and canola yields using random forest models. They discovered that as additional within-season data became available, the models' accuracy increased (e.g. rainfall).

Ali et al. [2] suggested a two-phase universal ML model for predicting wheat yield. The model was based on online sequential extreme learning machines and ant colony optimization, and it utilised data from 27 counties in the agroecological zone. The ACO-OSELM model projected future yield at six test sites using yield data from a prior year as an input. Using a feature selection technique, ACO assisted in locating suitable data stations for the model's training and testing. In regions where historical crop data was substantially correlated, the hybrid ACO-OSELM model proved beneficial as a system for predicting crop yield.

Table 4. Summary of papers on environmental factors based wheat yield prediction.

Author	Method	Dataset	Acc	R^2	RMSE
Zhang et al. [40]	CNN with GAN	Environmental and remote sensing data	–	0.5	591.46 kg/ha
Nabila Chergui [7]	DNN	Historical yield data and climate data	–	0.96	4 kg/ha
Pang el al. [26]	Random forest regression	Meteorological data	–	0.45	250 kg/ha
Han et al. [18]	Random Forest	Soil data	–	0.75	6.89 kg/ha
Wang et al. [38]	AdaBoost	Historic yield records, remote sensing images, climate data, and soil maps.	–	–	510 kg/ha
Conrad. [8]	ABSOLUT v1.2 algorithm	Temperature, precipitation, and sunshine duration weather variables that are aggregated over different seasonal periods preceding the harvest	87.8%	–	115 kg/ha
Cao et al. [6]	MHCF v1.0	MOD13C1 satellite data, 225 CRU observational climate data, and IAP CAS S2S atmospheric prediction data	–	–	780 kg/ha
Murakami et al. [22]	partial least squares regression model	meteorological data	–	0.76	872kg/ha
Elavarasan and Vincent [13]	Reinforcement Random Fores	climate, soil and water data	92.2%	0.87	230kg/ha
Filippi et al. [17]	Random Forest	Multi fields, multi-farm and multi-seasonal data	–	0.85 to 0.92	0.36 to 420 kg/ha
Ali et al. [2]	Online sequential extreme learning machines coupled with ant colony optimization (ACO-OSELM)	27 agricultural counties' data within the Agro-ecological zone	–	0.968	155.86 kg/ha

4.3   Genomic and Phenology Based Wheat Yield Prediction

Feng et al. [16] present a mix of machine learning and bio-physical modeling to solve the typical constraints of frequently utilized statistical approaches for seasonal yield forecasting. This author investigated two methods for predicting wheat yields, multiple layer regression (MLR) and random forest (RF) models, and discovered that the RF model predicted observed yields better than the MLR model, especially in years with atypical yields, and provided better forecasts at earlier growth stages. The research was carried out in the New South Wales wheat area, which is located in southern Australia. The scientists integrated a crop simulation model with a statistical regression-based model in this work to dynamically anticipate wheat production at various stages throughout the growing season. APSIM is the crop simulation model, whereas RF is the regression-based model. The authors discovered that their hybrid model, which takes use of the strengths of each model, produced good yield prediction results. This was due mostly to the hybrid model's ability to utilize biophysical processes among crop, soil, management, and climate information, as well as a machine learning approach to account for climatic extremes and remote sensing data. Also, the machine learning technology utilized in the study outperformed standard regression methods.

Using genetic markers, genomic prediction (GP) is a technique for figuring out complex phenotypes. Increased grain production is essential for feeding the world, especially for basic crops like rice and wheat. Recently, machine learning (ML) models have started to be used in general practice (GP), although it isn't always clear which algorithms are best or how feature selection (FS) methods affect the results.

While estimating wheat crop production using a number of different FS techniques, Sirsat et al. [31] compared ML and deep learning (DL) algorithms against traditional Bayesian models (in three datasets). They found that compared to the FS method, the prediction algorithm had a bigger effect on model performance. Traditional Bayesian techniques and tree-based ML techniques (random forests and gradient boosting) outperformed all other models in terms of performance. The latter, however, was prone to fitting problems. The only Bayesian FS method used in this work, models built with features selected using Bayes, likewise showed this issue. However, the other three FS techniques generated models with comparable performance but no fitting problems. The authors contend that choosing the prediction algorithm is more important than choosing the FS approach when building highly predictive models as a result. Also, they got to the conclusion that gradient boosting and random forests offer GP models for wheat grain yield that are very reliable and predictive.

Table 5. Summary of papers on Genomic and Phenology based wheat yield prediction.

Author	Method	Dataset	Acc	R^2	RMSE
Feng et al. [16]	Random Forest	Biophysical data	–	0.62	1000.01 kg/ha
Sirsat et al. [31]	Gradient boosting	Genomic and phenotypic data	–	–	–
Srivastava et al. [32]	CNN	Weather, soil, and crop phenology variables	-	0.65	-

A convolutional neural network model was proposed by Srivastava et al. [32] to anticipate winter wheat yield from environmental and phenological data. The researchers used a dataset of meteorological, soil, and crop phenology characteristics from 1999 to 2019 to investigate the effectiveness of machine learning and deep learning methods for predicting the production of winter wheat. They used RMSE, MAE, and correlation coefficient metrics to assess the prediction power of eight supervised machine learning baseline models. Their findings demonstrated that nonlinear models outperformed linear models in capturing the link between crop yield and input data, including the proposed CNN model, DNN, and XGBoost. For the prediction of winter wheat yield, the suggested CNN model outperformed all previous baseline models (7 to 14% lower RMSE, 3 to 15% lower MAE, and 4 to 50% higher correlation coefficient than the baseline that performed the best across test sets).

5   Discussion

We want to discover the many cutting-edge machine learning trends and methodologies used for a precise prediction of wheat output in this literature review. We conducted a systematic evaluation of the literature on research works published within the last four years for this endeavor, and we found 24 articles that addressed the research questions we were looking to answer for Fig. 2. This review's major research goal is to determine the response to the following research question: **"What cutting-edge machine learning methods have been employed in the last four years to forecast wheat yields?"**

In our review of 24 research articles, we found the Random Forest algorithm and Deep neural network to be the most popular for use in the application of wheat yield prediction with 60% of the reviewed articles utilizing the two machine learning algorithms. These two algorithms are usually applied to remote sensing and time series type of data. The third most used algorithms are families of Gradient boosting algorithms such as AdaBoost, XGboost, and LightGBM,

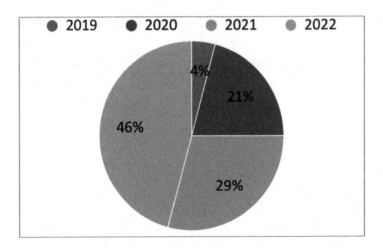

Fig. 2. Distribution of reviewed articles with respect to year of publication.

with 19% Fig. 3. We also observed the popularity of the LSTM algorithm for datasets consisting of historical yield prediction records.

As shown in the summary Tables 3, 4, and 5 of the reviewed articles which are presented in Sects. 4.1,4.2,4.3; we have identified and discussed the state of the art machine learning techniques used to predict crop yield. This gives the full answer to our primary research question and can give a summarized clue for future researchers in the area.

In addition, our survey explores to address the secondary research questions. Based on this we found that accurate prediction of wheat yields is a crucial factor in minimizing yield loss and ensuring food security. We found these reasons are the key motivation for the increased research interest in the application of machine learning in crop yield prediction. We discovered that the main driver for using ML approaches for wheat yield prediction is to improve prediction accuracy while reducing RMSE losses as we reviewed the majority of studies in the field. To minimize output losses and preserve food security, this is vital for farmers and policymakers to consider when making decisions. Many different dataset types are utilized in various studies. Some of them are satellite data, observational climate data, sub-seasonal to seasonal atmospheric prediction data, genetic data, and phenology data. Based on our survey we found that most studies use only one type of dataset(some papers use only satellite data while others use only climate data or genomic and phenology data). Only a few studies used fused datasets (e.g. satellite image, observational climate, and sub-seasonal to seasonal atmospheric prediction data). Our survey result indicates that merging that dataset would give a better result. In most studies, the primary evaluation metrics used for measuring yield accuracy are R^2 and RMSE values. Based on our survey we found that using a fused dataset and a set of ML models with ensemble learning would give a better result. One of the main challenges identified in this review paper is the lack of a large public dataset, which makes reproducibility and comparison of model performances very difficult. Most of the data used in the research articles are geographically specific, which decreases the model's generalization performance and complicates models' performance comparisons. In Addition, we observed the authors using a variety of measurement metrics which causes challenges in comparing prediction performances.

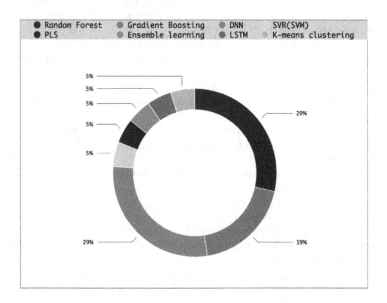

Fig. 3. Distribution of methodologies used in the reviewed articles.

6   Conclusion

For the purpose of this review, we searched through and choose N = 24 journal articles that discuss the various machine-learning approaches used to estimate crop yields over the last five years. This study provides a thorough analysis of yield prediction models that employ machine learning methods. The study issues pertaining to the various machine learning methods/algorithms, the dataset used, the assessment metrics, and the outcomes of each evaluated article are addressed in the paper's presentation. In addition, our survey explores to address the secondary research questions. Based on this we found that accurate prediction of wheat yields is crucial a crucial factor in minimizing yield loss and ensuring food security. We determined that these factors were the primary driving forces for the growing amount of research on the use of machine learning to estimate crop yields. We have observed that dependable and effective options for the task at hand include gradient boosting and Random forest, two machine learning methods. For remote sensing and time series-based wheat production prediction, we also noticed the growing use of deep learning methods like deep convolutional neural networks and LSTMs. In order for the various suggested machine-learning models to be evaluated and contrasted accurately, the research community needs a single common benchmark dataset.

References

1. Afework, Y.K., Debelee, T.G.: Detection of bacterial wilt on enset crop using deep learning approach. In: International Journal of Engineering Research in Africa. vol. 51, pp. 131–146. Trans Tech Publ (2020)
2. Ali, M., et al.: Coupled online sequential extreme learning machine model with ant colony optimization algorithm for wheat yield prediction. Sci. Rep. **12**(1), 1–23 (2022)
3. Bali, N., Singla, A.: Emerging trends in machine learning to predict crop yield and study its influential factors: a survey. Arch. Comput. Methods Eng. **29**(1), 95–112 (2022)
4. Biratu, E.S., Schwenker, F., Ayano, Y.M., Debelee, T.G.: A survey of brain tumor segmentation and classification algorithms. J. Imaging **7**(9), 179 (2021)
5. Biratu, E.S.S., Schwenker, F., Debelee, T.G.G., Kebede, S.R.R., Negera, W.G.G., Molla, H.T.T.: Enhanced region growing for brain tumor MR image segmentation. J. Imaging **7**(2), 22 (2021)
6. Cao, J., Wang, H., Li, J., Tian, Q., Niyogi, D.: Improving the forecasting of winter wheat yields in northern china with machine learning-dynamical hybrid subseasonal-to-seasonal ensemble prediction. Remote Sens. **14**(7), 1707 (2022)
7. Chergui, N.: Durum wheat yield forecasting using machine learning. Artif. Intell. Agric. **6**, 156–166 (2022)
8. Conradt, T.: Choosing multiple linear regressions for weather-based crop yield prediction with ABSOLUT v1. 2 applied to the districts of Germany. Int. J. Biometeorol. **66** 1–14 (2022)
9. Debelee, T.G., Amirian, M., Ibenthal, A., Palm, G., Schwenker, F.: Classification of mammograms using convolutional neural network based feature extraction. In: Mekuria, F., Nigussie, E.E., Dargie, W., Edward, M., Tegegne, T. (eds.) ICT4DA 2017. LNICST, vol. 244, pp. 89–98. Springer, Cham (2018). https://doi.org/10.1007/978-3-319-95153-9_9
10. Debelee, T.G., Kebede, S.R., Schwenker, F., Shewarega, Z.M.: Deep learning in selected cancers' image analysis-a survey. J. Imaging **6**(11), 121 (2020)
11. Debelee, T.G., Schwenker, F., Ibenthal, A., Yohannes, D.: Survey of deep learning in breast cancer image analysis. Evol. Syst. **11**(1), 143–163 (2020)
12. Debelee, T.G., Schwenker, F., Rahimeto, S., Yohannes, D.: Evaluation of modified adaptive k-means segmentation algorithm. Comput. Vis. Media **5**(4), 347–361 (2019)
13. Elavarasan, D., Vincent, P.M.D.R.: A reinforced random forest model for enhanced crop yield prediction by integrating agrarian parameters. J. Ambient. Intell. Humaniz. Comput. **12**(11), 10009–10022 (2021). https://doi.org/10.1007/s12652-020-02752-y
14. Fajardo, M., Whelan, B.: Within-farm wheat yield forecasting incorporating off-farm information. Precision Agric. **22**(2), 569–585 (2021)
15. Fei, S., et al.: Uav-based multi-sensor data fusion and machine learning algorithm for yield prediction in wheat. Precision Agric. **24**, 1–26 (2022)
16. Feng, P., et al.: Dynamic wheat yield forecasts are improved by a hybrid approach using a biophysical model and machine learning technique. Agric. For. Meteorol. **285**, 107922 (2020)

17. Filippi, P., et al.: An approach to forecast grain crop yield using multi-layered, multi-farm data sets and machine learning. Precision Agric. **20**(5), 1015–1029 (2019). https://doi.org/10.1007/s11119-018-09628-4

18. Han, J., et al.: Prediction of winter wheat yield based on multi-source data and machine learning in china. Remote Sens. **12**(2), 236 (2020)

19. Kamir, E., Waldner, F., Hochman, Z.: Estimating wheat yields in Australia using climate records, satellite image time series and machine learning methods. ISPRS J. Photogramm. Remote. Sens. **160**, 124–135 (2020)

20. Keele, S., et al.: Guidelines for performing systematic literature reviews in software engineering. Technical report, ver. 2.3 EBSE (2007)

21. Lischeid, G., Webber, H., Sommer, M., Nendel, C., Ewert, F.: Machine learning in crop yield modelling: a powerful tool, but no surrogate for science. Agric. For. Meteorol. **312**, 108698 (2022)

22. Murakami, K., Shimoda, S., Kominami, Y., Nemoto, M., Inoue, S.: Prediction of municipality-level winter wheat yield based on meteorological data using machine learning in hokkaido, japan. PLoS One **16**(10), e0258677 (2021)

23. Muruganantham, P., Wibowo, S., Grandhi, S., Samrat, N.H., Islam, N.: A systematic literature review on crop yield prediction with deep learning and remote sensing. Remote Sens. **14**(9), 1990 (2022)

24. Nevavuori, P., Narra, N., Lipping, T.: Crop yield prediction with deep convolutional neural networks. Comput. Electron. Agric. **163**, 104859 (2019)

25. Oikonomidis, A., Catal, C., Kassahun, A.: Deep learning for crop yield prediction: a systematic literature review. New Zealand J. Crop Hortic. Sci. 1–26 (2022). https://doi.org/10.1080/01140671.2022.2032213

26. Pang, A., Chang, M.W., Chen, Y.: Evaluation of random forests (RF) for regional and local-scale wheat yield prediction in southeast Australia. Sensors **22**(3), 717 (2022)

27. Paudel, D., et al.: Machine learning for large-scale crop yield forecasting. Agric. Syst. **187**, 103016 (2021)

28. Qiao, M., et al.: Exploiting hierarchical features for crop yield prediction based on 3-d convolutional neural networks and multikernel gaussian process. IEEE J. Sel. Top. Appl. Earth Observations Remote Sens. **14**, 4476–4489 (2021)

29. Shewry, P.R.: Wheat. J. Exp. Bot. **60**(6), 1537–1553 (2009)

30. Shidnal, S., Latte, M.V., Kapoor, A.: Crop yield prediction: two-tiered machine learning model approach. Int. J. Inf. Technol. **13**(5), 1983–1991 (2021)

31. Sirsat, M.S., Oblessuc, P.R., Ramiro, R.S.: Genomic prediction of wheat grain yield using machine learning. Agriculture **12**(9), 1406 (2022)

32. Srivastava, A.K., et al.: Winter wheat yield prediction using convolutional neural networks from environmental and phenological data. Sci. Rep. **12**(1), 1–14 (2022)

33. Tesfaye, A.A., Awoke, B.G., Sida, T.S., Osgood, D.E.: Enhancing smallholder wheat yield prediction through sensor fusion and phenology with machine learning and deep learning methods. Agriculture **12**(9), 1352 (2022)

34. Tian, H., Wang, P., Tansey, K., Zhang, J., Zhang, S., Li, H.: An LSTM neural network for improving wheat yield estimates by integrating remote sensing data and meteorological data in the guanzhong plain, pr china. Agric. For. Meteorol. **310**, 108629 (2021)

35. van Klompenburg, T., Kassahun, A., Catal, C.: Crop yield prediction using machine learning: a systematic literature review. Comput. Electron. Agric. **177**, 105709 (2020). https://doi.org/10.1016/j.compag.2020.105709, https://www.sciencedirect.com/science/article/pii/S0168169920302301

36. Vanli, Ö., Ahmad, I., Ustundag, B.B.: Area estimation and yield forecasting of wheat in southeastern turkey using a machine learning approach. J. Indian Soc. Remote Sens. **48**(12), 1757–1766 (2020)

37. Waldamichael, F.G., Debelee, T.G., Schwenker, F., Ayano, Y.M., Kebede, S.R.: Machine learning in cereal crops disease detection: a review. Algorithms **15**(3), 75 (2022)

38. Wang, Y., Zhang, Z., Feng, L., Du, Q., Runge, T.: Combining multi-source data and machine learning approaches to predict winter wheat yield in the conterminous united states. Remote Sens. **12**(8), 1232 (2020)

39. Yang, S., et al.: Integration of crop growth model and random forest for winter wheat yield estimation from UAV hyperspectral imagery. IEEE J. Sel. TopicsAppl. Earth Observations Remote Sens. **14**, 6253–6269 (2021)

40. Zhang, J., Tian, H., Wang, P., Tansey, K., Zhang, S., Li, H.: Improving wheat yield estimates using data augmentation models and remotely sensed biophysical indices within deep neural networks in the Guanzhong plain, PR china. Comput. Electron. Agric. **192**, 106616 (2022)

41. Zhong, R., et al.: Detect and attribute the extreme maize yield losses based on spatio-temporal deep learning. Fundam. Res. (2022)

42. Zhou, W., Liu, Y., Ata-Ul-Karim, S.T., Ge, Q., Li, X., Xiao, J.: Integrating climate and satellite remote sensing data for predicting county-level wheat yield in china using machine learning methods. Int. J. Appl. Earth Obs. Geoinf. **111**, 102861 (2022)

Algorithmic Optimization

Small Training Datasets for Deep Learning Based Medical Diagnosis

David Härer$^{(\boxtimes)}$, Konrad Kraft, and Achim Ibenthal

HAWK University of Applied Sciences and Arts, Göttingen, Germany
`david@haerer.dev, achim.ibenthal@hawk.de`

Abstract. In a computer-aided diagnosis framework binary, patch-based classification of malaria from thick blood smear images is investigated. Following a state-of-the-art study on malaria, deep learning and transfer learning, classical networks like ResNet are being adapted and optimized for training by the public dataset of the Automated Laboratory Diagnostics project of John A. Quinn et al. at Makerere University, Uganda. The dataset comprises 2,703 thick blood smear images treated with Fields stain. Furthermore models are cross-validated on other thick and thin blood smear datasets treated with Giemsa stain.

Data augmentation with zoomed-in versions of the image tiles in the training dataset and the use of shallow models with relatively few network parameters is evaluated as a solution to the problem of small training databases. Using grid search, optimum hyperparameters for learning rate scheduling are found empirically for each network architecture.

The self-developed deep learning models achieve a TP (True-Positive) rate of 98% at a FP (False-Positive) rate of 0.9% on the thick blood smear images and a TP rate of 90% at a FP rate of 8% on the thin blood smear images. The maximum validation accuracy over the set of models and hyperparameters is 99.3%.

Keywords: classification · deep learning · hyperparameters · malaria · neural networks · small dataset

1 Introduction

Malaria is a disease caused by the protozoan parasite Plasmodium. It is transmitted through the bite of female Anopheles mosquitoes causing infection of patient's RBCs (Red Blood Cells), cf. [13]. For 2020 the WHO reports 241 Million global cases and 627.000 deaths, which is a slight increase compared to the previous years [25]. More than 260.000 malaria-caused deaths occur among children in Africa. The disease is curable and there are various drugs to prevent it. Until recently malaria vaccines were not available. In October 2021 the WHO for the first time recommended the widespread use of the RTS,S vaccine against Plasmodium falciparum [1] for children.

Especially in Africa's rural areas diagnosis methods are limited not only by the availability of laboratory equipment but also by a lack of trained health

© The Author(s), under exclusive license to Springer Nature Switzerland AG 2023
T. Girma Debelee et al. (Eds.): PanAfriCon AI 2022, CCIS 1800, pp. 135–153, 2023.
https://doi.org/10.1007/978-3-031-31327-1_8

professionals. CAD (Computer Aided Diagnosis) is a viable tool to provide analytic expertise and to increase the detection rate, hence potentially saving lives. The target of this work is the binary classification of blood smear image tiles into the classes *benign* and *Plasmodium-infected*. Image tiles are extracted from blood smear images treated with a staining method. The classification is implemented via deep learning models trained on an annotated dataset. A specific focus of the investigation is the reduction of requirements for the size of the training database, especially to make it suitable for the quick adaptation of other diseases that can be diagnosed by image analysis. Examples are Tuberculosis and Leishmania.

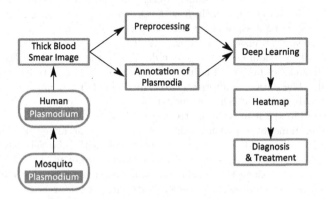

Fig. 1. System description as a block diagram. It shows the biological route of infection, classical diagnosis and subject of this work.

Figure 1 gives a basic system description as a block diagram. Plasmodium causing malaria is transmitted from mosquitoes to humans. The gold standard for diagnosis is microscopic examination [2,27]. If an infection is suspected, a blood sample is taken from the patient, applied to a glass slide and treated with a staining method. Through analog or digital microscopy the resulting blood smear images can be evaluated by trained medical staff. This is a time-consuming and error-prone process. By using a dataset of annotated blood smear images with additional preprocessing steps, a deep learning model can be trained to perform a patch-based classification of the blood smear images. Evaluating the predictions of the neural network, a heatmap with the location of Plasmodia can be created. The heatmap can assist medical staff with the diagnosis and hence indicate the need for medical treatment.

2   State-of-the-Art

In this section the classification problem is detailed, limits of contemporary diagnosis are outlined and a selection of recent publications are reviewed.

2.1 Plasmodium Variants and Classification Task

There are five species of Plasmodium that cause malaria in humans: *P. falciparum*, *P. vivax*, *P. malariae*, *P. ovale* and *P. knowlesi*. The two most common species are *P. falciparum* and *P. vivax*. *P. falciparum* causes the most severe symptoms and is responsible for the majority of malaria-related deaths. All five species are developing through four stages,

- *ring stage,*
- *trophozoite stage,*
- *schizont stage* and
- *gametocyte stage.*

The cycle takes 48 h per stage and causes the Plasmodium to look different at each stage [27]. Hence, related to a blood smear based CAD system there are four possible classification tasks,

- binary classification, i.e. *benign* and *Plasmodium-infected* for a given type,
- classification of *malaria type* at a given stage,
- classification of *stage* at a given malaria type,
- classification of *stage and malaria type.*

The latter classification task is the most difficult one, not only because of the number of classes but also due to the similarities of visual features for the different Plasmodium types [20]. In case the classifier training is limited by a small training data base, binary classification is a suitable option. This can be justified because usually there is a predominant Plasmodium type in a local region such as e.g. *P. falciparum* in Ethiopia.

2.2 Limits of Classical Malaria Diagnosis

The gold standard in diagnosing malaria is to evaluate the presence of Plasmodium through microscopy of blood smear samples [2,27]. Frisch notes in [13] that less than 0.1% infected blood cells may lead to fatalities, but also there are cases where more than 40% of infected blood cells are not leading to death. This means that the disease progression is also influenced by other factors such as patient age, constitution, additional pathogens. The development stage is a general indicator of the progress of the infection.

The contemporary malaria diagnosis method requires the generation of blood smear images, i.e. taking blood samples, preparing the glass target, staining and microscopy. Trained experts have to count the number of infected blood cells which is time-consuming and error prone. In [11] Alemu et al. report an overall agreement between a reference analyst and laboratory staff of just 79% for a case study in Tigray, North Ethiopia. Hence CAD-based malaria detection at sufficient accuracy can serve as a life-saving diagnostic tool and convey its expertise by training laboratory practitioners. This requires a digital image of the microscopic blood smear. Depending on the type of the image (*thin* or *thick blood smear*), the software can also help to identify the species and stage of the parasite [27].

2.3 Malaria CAD

Surveys on malaria CAD algorithms are found in *"Image Analysis and Machine Learning for Detecting Malaria"* by Poostchi et al. [27] and in *"A review on automated diagnosis of malaria parasite in microscopic blood smears images"* by Jan et al. [20]. Methods comprise classical segmentation techniques, clustering, fuzzy methods and various machine learning approaches. For binary classification the reported accuracy ranges between 96 and 99.46%, for 3 up to 6 classes the accuracy is found between 86 and 96.3%. A trend towards deep learning based classification is predominant, whereas in general the strive for higher accuracy is accompanied by higher computational costs. This problem will be addressed through network architecture and hyperparameter optimization in Sects. 5, 6 and 7, after reviewing more recent work subsequently.

2.4 Binary Classification

For mobile phone applications Fuhad et al. used knowledge distillation, data augmentation, an autoencoder and CNN-based feature extraction with subsequent clustering for classification at an accuracy of 99.5% [14]. Their algorithm is based on 28×28 image tiles depicting one blood cell. As of the small image size, classification of 1 tile requires just 4600 flops.

Much work is focusing on CNNs. In [30] three convolutional layers and fully connected layers each are devised for binary classification, reaching an accuracy of 95%. Kapoor compares the VGG-19 and ResNet-50 networks on the malaria data, where ResNet-50 achieved the better accuracy of 97% [21]. Also Chakradeo et al. use a customized VGG-based model, achieving an accuracy of 99.3% in [12].

Among CNNs, DAGCNNs (Directed Acyclic Graph CNNs) and DACNNs (Data Augmentation CNNs), Oyewola et al. achieved best results for the DACNN architecture at an accuracy of 94.79% [26]. The authors are reporting susceptibility to overfitting and question the suitability for data deviating from the training set. The overfitting problem in CNNs is encountered by Negi et al. by data augmentation reaching 95.7% accuracy for a network containing 4 convolution and pooling layers each, followed by several dropout and dense layers [24].

In [3] Abubakar et al. use six different features from VGG16, VGG19, ResNet-50, ResNet101, DenseNet121, and DenseNet201 networks, followed by a decision tree, SVM (Support Vector Machine) Naïve Bayes, and K-Nearest Neighbour classifiers. The accuracy achieved "more than" 94%.

From these results it can be observed that networks featuring a large amount of training parameters naturally tend to overfitting. Hence we conclude that the generation of a network with an optimized set of parameters is able to counter this effect, at the same time reduces computational complexity. This requires design of a simplified network architecture and due to the requirement to cope with a small training dataset also calls for the application of data augmentation techniques.

2.5   Multi-stage Classification

Li et al. dealt with multi-stage malaria classification using DTGCNs (Deep Transfer Graph Convolutional Networks). The DTGCN consists of a CNN (Convolutional Neural Network) for feature learning, source transfer graph building and a GCN (Graph Convolutional Network) for the unsupervised correlation of deviating source and target distributions [23]. They report a peak accuracy of 98.5% for 6 classes.

3   Malaria Datasets

This section describes the training, validation and test datasets used in this work.

3.1   Training, Validation and Test Dataset

The training and validation data used in this work are taken from the PLASMODIUMMOTIC dataset provided publicly by the AUTOMATED LABORATORY DIAGNOSTICS project of John A. Quinn et al. at Makerere University, Uganda [28]. It consists of 2,703 thick blood smear images treated with *Fields* stain. The images are taken from 133 thick blood smears with a Motic MC1000 camera on a microscope at 1000× magnification at a size of 768 × 1024 pixels. The annotation of objects judged to be a parasite was performed by a team of four experienced laboratory technicians [28]. In total, the dataset is annotated with 49,000 bounding boxes. The majority of the Plasmodia are *P. falciparum* in the *trophozoite* stage. This work uses 70% of the images for training data and 20% for validation.

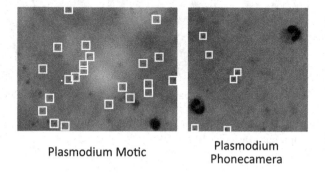

Plasmodium Motic   Plasmodium
                                      Phonecamera

Fig. 2. Thick blood smear image of the PLASMODIUMMOTIC dataset (left) and the PLASMODIUMPHONECAMERA dataset (right) [4,5].

To establish an independent test dataset the remaining 10% of the PLASMODIUMMOTIC dataset is extended by the PLASMODIUMPHONECAMERA dataset also provided by Quinn et al. [29]. It consists of 1,182 thick blood smear images treated with *Giemsa* stain and captured by a smartphone camera at a size of 750 × 750 pixels. In total, the dataset annotates 7,628 bounding boxes around Plasmodia. The color hue of the images is redder than the images of the PLAS-MODIUMMOTIC dataset. Figure 2 shows sample images of both datasets [29].

3.2 Thin Blood Smear Dataset

Through cooperation with Mekelle University, Jimma University Hospital and the Tigray Health Research Institute in Ethiopia, 5,173 *thin* blood smear images of size 768 × 956 pixels could be obtained. The thin blood smears are treated with *Giemsa* stain and captured through a microscope with 1000× magnification. Plasmodia contained in the dataset are of multiple species in multiple development stages. In comparison to *thick* blood smear images, the *thin* blood smears feature more variation in color hue and size of Plasmodia. The dataset annotates 8,740 regions of Plasmodia occurrence by bounding boxes. It is used to test if the developed networks can be applied to *thin* blood smear images. Figure 3 gives a sample overview of the different images contained in the dataset [15].

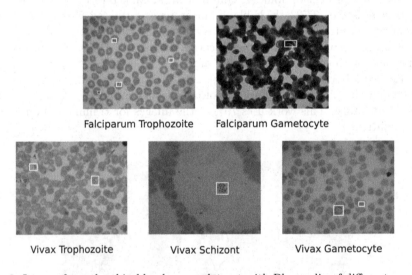

Falciparum Trophozoite   Falciparum Gametocyte

Vivax Trophozoite   Vivax Schizont   Vivax Gametocyte

Fig. 3. Images from the thin blood smear dataset with Plasmodia of different species in multiple development stages [6–10].

4   Data Preprocessing

The deep learning experiments in this work include transforming the RGB image dataset into grayscale and augmenting the training dataset by adding zoomed-in versions of the image tiles. The following sections explain the general preprocessing steps used in this work, how the images are transformed into grayscale and how the training dataset is augmented by zooming into the image tiles.

4.1 General Preprocessing Steps

The image tiles containing Plasmodia are resized to the desired tile size of 50 × 50 pixels and moved to be contained in the image. The Plasmodium tiles are permutated by rotation and flipping, increasing the number of positive samples by a factor of eight. The control tiles are picked from the image between the Plasmodium tiles with a margin of 20 pixels. Figure 4 shows an image from the PLASMODIUMMOTIC dataset with the corrected bounding boxes in black and the control boxes in white. The number of control tiles is equalized to the number of Plasmodium tiles by either permutating or dropping some of the control samples. The last preprocessing step consists of shuffling the data with the corresponding labels to ensure a uniform distribution of positive and negative classes in each training batch.

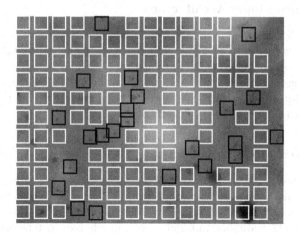

Fig. 4. Image of the PLASMODIUMMOTIC dataset showing the corrected bounding boxes around Plasmodium (black) with control boxes in between (white) [4].

Transforming the images to grayscale is done by the `color.rgb2gray()` method of the SCIKITIMAGE package.

4.2 Data Augmentation by Zooming

The augmentation applied in this work consists of adding two zoomed-in versions of each image tile to the training dataset, augmenting the training dataset by a factor of three. After the image tiles are extracted from the images, zooming is applied on the image tile basis. The additional image tiles are zoomed-in randomly from 100% to up to 66% of the original tile. Since zoom ranges between 0 and 1 are allowed only, zooming into the image tile corresponds to upsampling the tile. Therefore, the zoomed-in versions of an image tile only contain a subset of the information in the original tile, and no fill mode like zero padding or duplicating pixels is needed for the edges. Zooming the image tiles is done by the `transform.rescale()` method of the SCIKITIMAGE package. It uses spline interpolation and takes care of anti-aliasing with the `anti_aliasing` flag set to True [32].

5   Deep Learning Models

This works aims to further improve the previously developed models MYCNN by Härer [19] and DEEPCNN by Kraft [22]. The resulting architecture MYC-NNv2 will be discussed below. Furthermore by using a RESNET architecture pre-trained on the IMAGENET dataset, a comparison to a classical transfer learning method is established.

5.1   Reference Model Architectures

The DEEPCNN developed by Kraft is described in [22]. It uses two convolutional layers with a kernel size of 6 × 6 and has a total of only **11,172** trainable network parameters. The MYCNN architecture of Härer uses four convolutional layers with a kernel size of 3 × 3 and has a total of **337,450** trainable network parameters. Both architecture designs have been guided by the need to reduce model parameters as discussed in Sect. 2.4.

5.2   Improved Model Architecture

The goal of developing the MYCNNv2 architecture consists in further reducing the number of network parameters compared to the MYCNN model. As shown in [19], this can be achieved by global average pooling. In total, the MYCNNv2 model has **19,002** trainable and 256 non-trainable parameters, which is a 94% reduction in comparison to MYCNN. Further differences between MYCNN and MYCNNv2 are explained in [19]. Table 1 shows the individual layers of the MYCNNv2 architecture in detail.

5.3   Transfer Learning Architecture

This work explores network-based transfer learning for malaria detection. It uses the RESNET50 architecture developed by Kaiming He et al. [17] that has been pre-trained on the IMAGENET dataset of natural images. The IMAGENET dataset consists of images in 1000 classes, so the top layer of the RESNET50 architecture has 1000 output neurons. Since this work only deals with binary classification, this top layer is not required. Instead, it is replaced by a dropout layer with a dropout rate of 20% and a fully-connected output layer with two neurons. The

Table 1. Layers of the MyCNNv2 network architecture in detail. Abbreviation BN (Batch Normalization) is used for brevity.

Layer	Activation	Output Shape	Param #
2× Convolution 3 × 3 + BN	ELU(·)	(50, 50, 8)	872
Max Pooling 3 × 3 stride 2 + Dropout 20%		(24, 24, 8)	0
2× Convolution 3 × 3 + BN	ELU(·)	(24, 24, 16)	3,616
Max Pooling 3 × 3 stride 2 + Dropout 20%		(11, 11, 16)	0
2× Convolution 3 × 3 + BN	ELU(·)	(11, 11, 32)	14,144
Max Pooling 3 × 3 stride 2 + Dropout 20%		(5, 5, 32)	0
Global Average Pooling + Dropout 20%		(32)	0
Fully Connected + BN	ELU(·)	(16)	592
Fully Connected	Softmax(·)	(2)	34

transition from the base model of residual units and convolutional layers to the fully connected layer is done via global average pooling. This version of RESNET has **23,538,690** trainable and 53,120 non-trainable parameters. However, since the base model with the majority of trainable parameters is already pre-trained on IMAGENET, these parameters don't have to be determined from scratch. By reducing the learning rate the base model is only fine-tuned, and only the top fully-connected layer is trained with the full learning rate. Table 2 gives a detailed view of the RESNET architecture. The internal structure of the residual units is described in [19] and visualized by Kaiming He et al. in [17,18].

Table 2. Layers of the RESNET network architecture in detail. Abbreviations ZP (Zero Padding) and BN are used for brevity.

Layer	Activation	Output Shape	Param #
Input + ZP		(56, 56, 3)	0
Conv. 7 × 7 stride 2 + BN + ZP	ReLU(·)	(27, 27, 64)	9,728
Max Pooling 3 × 3 stride 2		(13, 13, 64)	0
3× Residual Unit	ReLU(·)	(13, 13, 256)	220,032
4× Residual Unit	ReLU(·)	(7, 7, 512)	1,230,032
6× Residual Unit	ReLU(·)	(4, 4, 1,024)	7,129,088
3× Residual Unit	ReLU(·)	(2, 2, 2,048)	14,998,528
Global Average Pooling + Dropout 20%		(2,048)	0
Fully Connected	Softmax(·)	(2)	4098

6 Neural Network Training

This work conducts several deep learning experiments. Each experiment is referred to as a *training session*. The following sections describe the hyperparameters evaluated and training sessions conducted in this work. The optimizer and its parameters used for training are explained and the training time of the different deep learning models in the individual training sessions is evaluated. The details of the training environment are described in [19].

6.1 Training Environment

All models are trained on a GeForce GTX 1080 Ti graphics cards on a sever with an Intel Xeon Silver 4114 @ 40x 3 GHz processor and 128 GB of RAM, running Ubuntu 18.04. The Python programming language is used with its various packages. In particular, this work leverages the TensorFlow framework with the high-level Keras API.

6.2 Hyperparameters

This work explores an initial learning rate $\eta_0 \in \{\ 0.01;\ 0.1\ \}$ and its decay $\delta \in \{\ 0;\ 2.5 \cdot 10^{-4};\ 2.5 \cdot 10^{-3}\ \}$. These hyperparameters determine the learning rate $\eta(i)$ for each training iteration by Eq. 1 [31]

$$\eta(i) = \frac{\eta_0}{1 + \delta \cdot i}\ . \tag{1}$$

6.3 Training Sessions

A training session consists of training the four deep learning models on a specific training dataset with several hyperparameters. This work conducts the following training sessions:

- ColorImages: The training dataset is used with no additional changes. This aims to reproduce the results of [19] for the DeepCNN and MyCNN architectures and to show whether the new architectures result in higher test accuracies.
- ZoomedColorImages: The training dataset is augmented by zoomed-in versions of the image tiles. This aims to test the hypothesis, that augmenting the training dataset will result in higher test accuracies.
- GrayscaleImages: The RGB images of the training dataset are transformed into grayscale. This aims to test the hypothesis, that normalizing the color values will improve the test accuracies across datasets of different staining methods.
- ZoomedGrayscaleImages: The RGB images of the training dataset are transformed to grayscale and augmented by zoomed-in versions of the image tiles. This aims to evaluate the effects of combining both hypotheses.

6.4   Duration of Training

Training is allowed for a maximum of 100 epochs. However, if a network does not improve the validation accuracy by at least 0.5% over a patience window of 10 epochs, the training process is stopped. By stopping the training, the network parameters from the epoch with the highest validation accuracy are restored. This technique of early stopping is a common practice and well explained in [16]. Figure 5 shows the training time for each network in each training session. For all architectures, training takes longer on the augmented training dataset. The plot also reveals a correlation between the training time and the number of trainable parameters of the network. With over 23 million trainable network parameters, the RESNET architecture takes the longest to train.

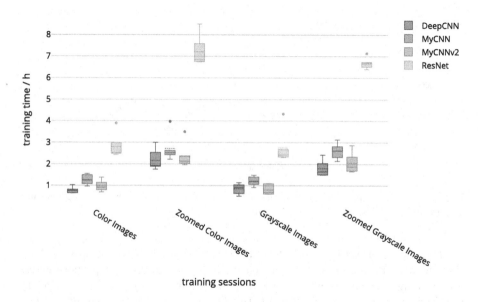

Fig. 5. Duration of the training process of the different architectures in the different training sessions. The mean value is shown as a dotted line.

7   Results

This section presents the test results of the four training sessions described in Sect. 6.3. By calculating box-plots for the test accuracy over the hyperparameters in each training session, the training sessions are compared for each model. Calculating box-plots for the test accuracy over the four training sessions, optimum hyperparameters can be determined for each model. The models are compared across training sessions by the FP rate at a TP rate of 98%.

7.1   Comparison of the Training Sessions

Figure 6 shows a box-plot with the test accuracies of the models for the different training sessions. Each box is calculated from the test accuracies of the model for the different hyperparameters per training session. Table 3 shows the best validation and test accuracies of each model across the different datasets.

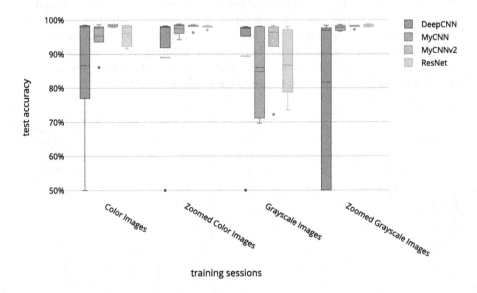

Fig. 6. Box-plot with the test accuracies of the models for the different training sessions. The mean value is shown as a dotted line.

The low mean test accuracy of the DEEPCNN model is explained by the fact, that in each training session for at least one configuration of hyperparameters the training process of the network does not converge. For the other models, the mean test accuracy is lowest in the GRAYSCALEIMAGES training session. Comparing the ZOOMEDCOLORIMAGES and ZOOMEDGRAYSCALEIMAGES training sessions shows no significant difference. Therefore, the hypothesis that using grayscale images improves the test accuracy on a dataset with different staining methods can be refuted. For the MYCNNV2 and RESNET models, augmenting the training dataset with zoomed-in versions of the image tiles does improve the test accuracy on average. This supports the hypothesis of augmenting the training dataset.

7.2   Optimum Hyperparameters

Figure 7 shows a box-plot with the test accuracies of the models for the different hyperparameter configurations. Each box is calculated from the test accuracies of the model for the different training sessions per hyperparameter configuration. This gives insight on the optimum deep learning hyperparameters for each

Table 3. Best validation accuracy (first entry) and test accuracy (second entry) of the models across training sessions.

Training Session	DEEPCNN	MYCNN	MYCNNv2	RESNET
COLORIMAGES	98.5%; 98.5%	97.7%; 98.7%	99.3%; 98.7%	99.2%; 98.5%
ZOOMEDCOLORIMAGES	98.7%; 98.3%	99.1%; 98.8%	99.2%; 98.7%	99.2%; 98.4%
GRAYSCALEIMAGES	98.6%; 98.0%	98.2%; 98.2%	98.8%; 98.3%	99.0%; 98.0%
ZOOMEDGRAYSCALEIMAGES	98.5%; 98.3%	98.9%; 98.6%	99.0%; 98.4%	99.0%; 98.8%

model independent of the structure of the training dataset. Table 4 shows the best validation and test accuracies of each model across the different hyperparameters.

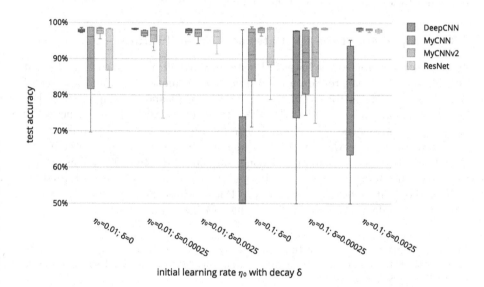

Fig. 7. Box-plot with the test accuracies of the models for the different hyperparameter configurations. The mean value is shown as a dotted line.

RESNET, pre-trained on the IMAGENET dataset of natural images performs best with an initial learning rate of $\eta_0 = 0.1$ and a decay of $\delta = 0.00025$. The DEEPCNN architecture performs overall better with an initial learning rate of $\eta_0 = 0.01$. The MYCNN architecture performs best with an initial learning rate of $\eta_0 = 0.1$ and its decay at $\delta = 0.0025$. With a *lowest* mean test accuracy of 91.8%, the self-developed MYCNNv2 architecture is the most robust against change in hyperparameters.

Table 4. Best validation accuracy (first entry) and test accuracy (second entry) of the models across hyperparameters.

Learning Rate	Decay	DEEPCNN	MYCNN	MYCNNV2	RESNET
$\eta_0 = 0.01$	$\delta = 0$	98.6%; 97.7%	99.2%; 93.6%	99.1%; 98.6%	99.2%; 91.6%
$\eta_0 = 0.01$	$\delta = 0.00025$	98.7%; 98.3%	98.9%; 98.0%	99.1%; 98.7%	99.1%; 92.3%
$\eta_0 = 0.01$	$\delta = 0.0025$	98.5%; 98.1%	98.6%; 98.1%	98.6%; 97.9%	98.7%; 91.4%
$\eta_0 = 0.1$	$\delta = 0$	98.1%; 98.1%	99.2%; 97.8%	99.3%; 98.7%	99.2%; 98.5%
$\eta_0 = 0.1$	$\delta = 0.00025$	97.8%; 97.8%	99.2%; 74.4%	99.3%; 72.2%	99.1%; 98.6%
$\eta_0 = 0.1$	$\delta = 0.0025$	97.0%; 95.2%	99.0%; 97.5%	99.2%; 97.4%	98.8%; 97.7%

Finally, the optimum over the set of architectures and hyperparameters reached a validation accuracy of 99.3% for MYCNNV2.

7.3 Comparison of the FP Rates at a Fixed TP Rate

Table 5 shows a tuple of the lowest FP rates at fixed TP rates of each model and training session for the test datasets of *thick* blood smear images and *thin* blood smear images. This enables comparison across models and training sessions. For the *thick* blood smear dataset, the TP rate is set to 98%. Since the networks are not trained on the *thin* blood smear dataset, the TP rate is only set to 90% respectively. For the DEEPCNN, augmenting the training dataset in the ZOOMEDCOLORIMAGES training session results in a FP rate of 99%. This means, that to predict 90% of the Plasmodia as such, the DEEPCNN network predicts 99% of the control boxes as containing Plasmodium. So the model performs worse than random and is not a fit for the 90% TP rate.

Table 5. Tuples of FP rates of the models across training sessions at a fixed TP rate of 98% (*thick* blood smear dataset, first entry) and 90% (*thin* blood smear dataset, second entry) respectively.

Training Session	DEEPCNN	MYCNN	MYCNNV2	RESNET
COLORIMAGES	1.3%; 17%	1.0%; 25%	1.0%; 42%	1.3%; 67%
ZOOMEDCOLORIMAGES	1.6%; 99%	**0.9%**; 18%	1.1%; **8%**	1.6%; 22%
GRAYSCALEIMAGES	1.4%; 36%	1.7%; 19%	1.1%; 9%	1.4%; 45%
ZOOMEDGRAYSCALEIMAGES	1.5%; 33%	1.2%; 43%	1.6%; **8%**	1.0%; 19%

At a FP rate of only 0.9% in the ZOOMEDCOLORIMAGES training session, the self-developed MYCNN architecture performs best. The model is trained at an initial learning rate of $\eta_0 = 0.1$ and a decay of $\delta = 0$ on the RGB image dataset augmented by zoomed-in versions of the image tiles. The best result on the *thin* blood smear dataset is achieved by the MYCNNV2 architecture. It reaches 90% TP rate on the *thin* blood smear dataset at only 8% FP rate. This is achieved at an initial learning rate of $\eta_0 = 0.1$ and a decay of $\delta = 0.00025$ in the ZOOMEDCOLORIMAGES training session. This supports the hypothesis, that improving the MYCNN architecture by using global average pooling does increase the test accuracy. In general, the RESNET architecture achieves similar results to the self-developed architectures. This supports the hypothesis, that using transfer learning on a small dataset does work, even if the source task of natural image classification is very different from the target tasks of computer-aided medical diagnosis.

8 Application

For the application of this work, the task is to show the user on a given blood smear image where Plasmodia are located. This work follows the approach of K. Kraft in [22] of calculating a heatmap for a given image to highlight the presence of plasmodia. The approach is further developed by using this heatmap as a mask for alpha-blending with the original blood smear image.

8.1 Application on Thick Blood Smear Images

Figure 8 shows two images from the PLASMODIUMMOTIC and PLASMODIUM-PHONECAMERA datasets as an example with the applied alpha-blending. The corresponding heatmap is shown with the original bounding boxes in black on the left for orientation. The margin of 25 pixels with zero-padding on the heatmap is visible. While false positives can be seen on the heatmap as bright artifacts with no black bounding box, TP hotspots have the shape of a square with smoothed corners with the Plasmodium in the center.

8.2 Application on Thin Blood Smear Images

Figure 9 shows five images from the *thin* blood smear dataset containing *Plasmodium falciparum* in the *trophozoite* and *gametocyte* stage and *Plasmodium vivax* in the *trophozoite, schizont* and *gametocyte* stage with the alpha blending applied. On the image containing *Plasmodium falciparum* in the *gametocyte* stage, the classifier performs poor and no correlation between hotspots and the black bounding box is visible. On the other images, the black bounding boxes are all marked as bright hotspots. This indicates a high TP rate. The hotspots not coinciding with a black bounding box explain the higher FP rates on the *thin* blood smear dataset. Whether these parts of the images are classified incorrect or bounding boxes are missing needs to be evaluated by medical experts.

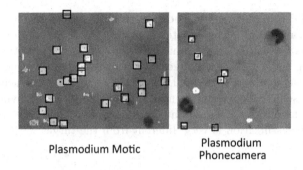

Plasmodium Motic   Plasmodium
                          Phonecamera

Fig. 8. Images from the thick blood smear datasets with alpha-blending and corresponding heatmaps with original bounding boxes in black [4,5].

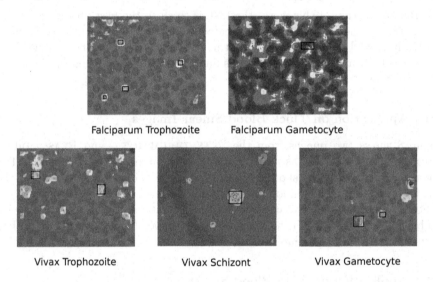

Falciparum Trophozoite   Falciparum Gametocyte

Vivax Trophozoite   Vivax Schizont   Vivax Gametocyte

Fig. 9. Images from the *thin* blood smear dataset containing different Plasmodia species in multiple development stages. Images are shown with alpha-blending and corresponding heatmaps with original bounding boxes in black [6–10].

9   Conclusions

This work uses a small dataset of thick blood smear images treated with *Fields* stain to train deep learning models to classify image tiles on the presence of Plasmodia. Four approaches for achieving higher test accuracies on a test dataset containing thick blood smear images treated with *Fields* and *Giemsa* stain are explored. The models are also tested on a dataset of *thin* blood smear images containing Plasmodia of different species in multiple development stages. The first approach consists of transforming the RGB images into grayscale to normalize the data regarding the staining method. The second approach is augmenting the small training dataset by using zoomed-in versions of the image tiles to make the models robust against small variations in the size of the Plasmodia in the test datasets. The third approach is improving the self-developed MYCNN architecture of the project in [19] to use fewer network parameters. This is done by designing the MYCNNV2 architecture that uses global average pooling and a third pair of convolutional layers with a small kernel size. The fourth approach is exploring transfer learning with the RESNET model pre-trained on the IMAGENET dataset of natural images. The DEEPCNN architecture developed by Kraft [22] is used as a reference model.

The approaches are tested with four deep learning experiments, referred to as training sessions. Comparing the training sessions regarding the training dataset, the hypothesis of transforming the RGB images into grayscale to normalize the staining method can be refuted. Augmenting the training data with zoomed-in versions of the image tiles does lead to better performance of the MYCNN and RESNET architecture. On average, the improved MYCNNV2 architecture shows the best performance across training sessions except for the augmented grayscale training dataset.

The test accuracies of the RESNET architecture are on-par with the test results of the remaining three architectures. This confirms the hypothesis that transfer learning is a viable option for deep learning with a small training dataset. Through global hyperparameter optimization, maximum accuracy reached 99.3%, comparable to best-in-class algorithms at a considerably reduced computational effort compared to standard architectures like RESNET. This balance in terms of validation accuracy between RESNET and the shallow networks also shows, that small models with relatively few trainable network parameters can be used to tackle the problem of small training datasets with low feature variance.

On the test dataset of thick blood smear images, the self-developed MYCNN model achieves a TP rate of 98% at a FP rate of only 0.9%. On the *thin* blood smear dataset, the improved MYCNNV2 model achieves a TP rate of 90% at a FP rate of 8%.

The predictions of the developed deep learning models can be used to create a heatmap indicating the location of Plasmodia on a blood smear image.

References

1. Who recommends groundbreaking malaria vaccine for children at risk. News release October 6, 2021, World Health Organization, Geneva. https://www.who.int/news/item/06-10-2021-who-recommends-groundbreaking-malaria-vaccine-for-children-at-risk. Accessed 25 July 2022
2. Malaria diagnostic tests. CDC Centers for Disease Control and Prevention (2022). https://www.cdc.gov/malaria/diagnosis_treatment/diagnostic_tools.html. Accessed 27 July 2022
3. Abubakar, A., Ajuji, M., Yahya, I.U.: DeepFMD: computational analysis for malaria detection in blood-smear images using deep-learning features. Appl. Syst. Innov. **4**(4) (2021). https://www.mdpi.com/2571-5577/4/4/82

4. J.A.Q., et al.: File: plasmodium-0754.jpg and file: plasmodium-0754.xml (2014). https://github.com/jqug/mobile-microscopy/issues/3. Accessed 08 Sep 2019. contained in the Plasmodium Motic dataset
5. J.A.Q., et al.: File: plasmodium-phone-0001.jpg and file: plasmodium-phone-0001.xml (2016). https://github.com/jqug/mobile-microscopy/issues/3. Accessed 08 Sep 2019. contained in the Plasmodium Phonecamera dataset
6. Y.G.G., et al.: File: 002_0001.png and file: 002_0001.xml. private communication (2019). contained in the Plasmodium Vivax Schizont dataset
7. Y.G.G., et al.: File: 134_0001.png and file: 134_0001.xml. private communication (2019). contained in the Plasmodium Vivax Gametocyte dataset
8. Y.G.G., et al.: File: 13796_0001.png and file: 13796_0001.xml. private communication (2019). contained in the Plasmodium Falciparum Trophozoite dataset
9. Y.G.G., et al.: File: 23517_0001.png and file: 23517_0001.xml. private communication (2019). contained in the Plasmodium Vivax Trophozoite dataset
10. Y.G.G., et al.: File: 89_0001.png and file: 89_0001.xml. private communication (2019). contained in the Plasmodium Falciparum Gametocyte dataset
11. Alemu, M., et al.: Performance of laboratory professionals working on malaria microscopy in tigray, north ethiopia. J. Parasitol. Res. **2017** (2017). https://doi.org/10.1155/2017/9064917
12. Chakradeo, K., Delves, M., Titarenko, S.: Malaria parasite detection using deep learning methods. Int. J. Comput. Inf. Eng. **15**(2), 175–182 (2021). https://publications.waset.org/vol/170
13. Frischknecht, F.: Malaria: Tödliche Parasiten, spannende Forschung und keine Impfung (essentials). Springer Spektrum, Wiesbaden (2019). https://doi.org/10.1007/978-3-658-25300-4
14. Fuhad, K., Tuba, J., Sarker, M., Momen, S., Mohammed, N., Rahman, T.: Deep learning based automatic malaria parasite detection from blood smear and its smartphone based application. Diagnostics (Basel) **10**(5) (2020). https://doi.org/10.3390/diagnostics10050329
15. Gezahegn, Y.G.: E-mail correspondence. private communication (2019)
16. Géron, A.: Hands-On Machine Learning with Scikit-Learn and TensorFlow: Concepts, Tools, and Techniques to Build Intelligent Systems. O'Reilly Media, Sebastopol (2017)
17. He, K., Zhang, X., Ren, S., Sun, J.: Deep Residual Learning for Image Recognition. ArXiv e-prints (2015). https://arxiv.org/pdf/1512.03385
18. He, K., Zhang, X., Ren, S., Sun, J.: Netscope: Resnet-50 (2019). http://ethereon.github.io/netscope/#/gist/db945b393d40bfa26006. Accessed 11 Sep 2019
19. Härer, D.: Deep Learning on Small Image Datasets for Computer Aided Medical Diagnosis - Binary Patch Based Classification and Localization of Plasmodia. Bachelor's thesis, HAWK University of Applied Sciences and Arts, Göttingen, Germany (2019)
20. Jan, Z., Khan, A., Sajjad, M., Muhammad, K., Rho, S., Mehmood, I.: A review on automated diagnosis of malaria parasite in microscopic blood smears images. Multimed. Tools Appl. **77**(8), 9801–9826 (2018). https://doi.org/10.1093/gigascience/giab040, https://doi.org/10.1007/s11042-017-4495-2
21. Kapoor, R.: Malaria Detection Using Deep Convolutional Network. Master's thesis, University of Cincinnati (2020)
22. Kraft, K.: Automatic Plasmodium Highlighting in Thick Blood Smear Images Using Deep Learning. Bachelor's thesis, HAWK University of Applied Sciences and Arts, Göttingen, Germany (2019)

23. Li, S., Du, Z., Meng, X., Zhang, Y.: Multi-stage malaria parasite recognition by deep learning. GigaScience **10**(6) (2016). https://doi.org/10.1093/gigascience/giab040, https://doi.org/10.1093/gigascience/giab040
24. Negi, A., Kumar, K., Chauhan, P.: Machine Learning for Healthcare Applications, chap. 12: Deep Learning-Based Image Classifier for Malaria Cell Detection, pp. 187–197. Scrivener Publishing, Beverly, MA, April 2021. https://doi.org/10.1002/9781119792611.ch12
25. Organization, W.H.: World Malaria Report 2021. World Health Organization, Geneva (2021). https://apps.who.int/iris/rest/bitstreams/1398397/retrieve, licence: CC BY-NC-SA 3.0 IGO
26. Oyewola, D.O., Dada, E.G., Misra, S., Damaševičius, R.: A novel data augmentation convolutional neural network for detecting malaria parasite in blood smear images. Appl. Artif. Intell. **36**(1), 2033473 (2022). https://doi.org/10.1080/08839514.2022.2033473
27. Poostchi, M., Silamut, K., Maude, R.J., Jaeger, S., Thoma, G.: Image analysis and machine learning for detecting malaria. Transl. Res. **194**, 36–55 (2018). https://doi.org/10.1016/j.trsl.2017.12.004
28. Quinn, J.A., Andama, A., Munabi, I., Kiwanuka, F.N.: Automated blood smear analysis for mobile malaria diagnosis. In: Mobile Point-of-Care Monitors and Diagnostic Device Design, pp. 115–135 (2014). http://cit.mak.ac.ug/staff/jquinn/papers/AutomatedMalariaDiagnosisChapter.pdf
29. Quinn, J.A., Nakasi, R., Mugagga, P.K.B., Byanyima, P., Lubega, W., Andama, A.: Deep Convolutional Neural Networks for Microscopy-Based Point of Care Diagnostics. ArXiv e-prints (2016). https://github.com/keras-team/keras/blob/510f9f0b1d97ca3567c858e0300c913a4bc2bf53/keras/optimizers.py#L189-L192
30. Shah, D., Kawale, K., Shah, M., Randive, S., Mapari, R.: Malaria parasite detection using deep learning : (beneficial to humankind). In: 2020 4th International Conference on Intelligent Computing and Control Systems (ICICCS), pp. 984–988 (2020). https://doi.org/10.1109/ICICCS48265.2020.9121073
31. Team, K.: keras/optimizers.py at keras-team/keras (2019). https://github.com/keras-team/keras/blob/master/keras/optimizers.py#L186. Accessed 22 May 2019
32. Team, S.I.: rescale at module:transform (2019). https://scikit-image.org/docs/dev/api/skimage.transform.html?highlight=rescale#skimage.transform.rescale. Accessed 18 Aug 2019

Using Generative Adversarial Networks for Single Image Super-Resolution

Marwan Farag[1]($\boxtimes$) and Friedhelm Schwenker[2]

[1] German University in Cairo, New Cairo, Egypt
marwan.farag@student.guc.edu.eg
[2] Institute of Neural Information Processing, Ulm University, Ulm, Germany
friedhelm.schwenker@uni-ulm.de

Abstract. In digital image processing, retrieving a high-resolution image from its low-resolution version is considered to be a major topic. Super-resolution *SR* is a problem that has direct applications in numerous disciplines like medical diagnosis, satellite imagery, face recognition and surveillance. The choice of the optimization function has been a major factor in previous super-resolution approaches. Optimizing metrics that are determined based primarily on pixel-level variance is the most common objective for supervised super-resolution algorithms. Nevertheless, these approaches do not output perceptually satisfactory images. This paper adopts an idea in which depending on only pixel-space similarity is avoided. Instead, the major goal is to utilize a content loss based on perceptual resemblance using feature maps of the VGG network in conjunction with Generative Adversarial Networks *GAN*. This depends on training two networks: a generator and a discriminator. In an adversarial game, they compete to outperform each other with an ultimate objective of producing super-resolution images that are identical to the real high-resolution images that already exist in the dataset. This paper's main contribution is a comparison of the effects of taking the VGG-19 content loss from various layers. On public benchmarks, super-resolution *GAN* was successful in recovering detailed textures from highly downsampled images. *SRGAN* reveals large gains in perceptual quality in a mean opinion score *MOS* test.

Keywords: super-resolution · *SRGAN* · content loss · perceptual loss · *HR* · *LR* · *SRResNet*

1 Introduction

Single Image Super Resolution, also known as *SISR*, is a technique that is focused on enhancing the clarity of a poor quality image. In general, the expression *super-resolution* refers to extracting knowledge from an existing low-resolution signal and use it to reach a high-resolution signal. Depending on the application, the relationship between the high-resolution *HR* image and the low-resolution *LR* version may differ. This paper presents addresses case that the *LR* image is a

T. Girma Debelee et al. (Eds.): PanAfriCon AI 2022, CCIS 1800, pp. 154–168, 2023.
https://doi.org/10.1007/978-3-031-31327-1_9

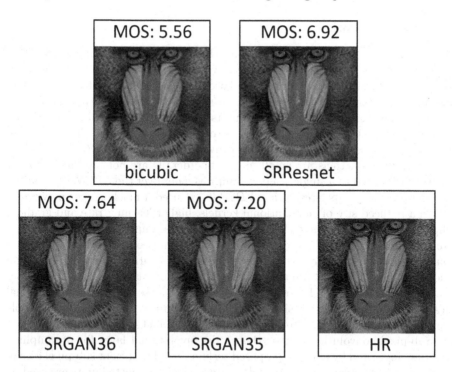

Fig. 1. Mean Opinion Scores *MOS* for *Set14* [16] using bicubic interpolation, *SRRes-Net*, *SRGAN36* (VGG loss taken before 36th layer) and *SRGAN35* (VGG loss taken before 35th layer) in comparison to the ground-truth *HR* image [×4 upscaling].

bicubic downscaled counterpart of the corresponding *HR* image is adopted. The method used to extract and use the data from the *LR* image influences how well the image is recreated. Due to the fact that a large number of *HR* photos can be downscaled into a single *LR* image, single image super resolution continues to be an unsolved and demanding challenge in the field of computer vision.

Super-resolution is involved in many applications. First, it can be used in surveillance systems for a better face recognition in the images obtained from surveillance cameras [4]. Second, it is beneficial for diagnostic imaging, particularly for magnetic resonance imaging *MRI* [11]. By reducing cost of scan time, spatial coverage, and signal-to-noise ratio, it becomes more convenient to use *SR* techniques to output super-resolved *MRI* scans by processing their corresponding low-resolution ones. Third, data transmission and storage can be a relevant application [9], as one may send a low-resolution signal, and upscale it on the fly, rather than sending the high-resolution one, reducing cost. Finally, using super-resolution satellite imagery can help in finding and determining the number of elephants in African environments [3].

1.1   Related Work

A very early solution was to interpolate the values of the missing pixels. This typically results in solutions with excessively smooth textures. Dong et al. [2] proposed the first preprocessing interpolation method that consisted of three layers: feature extraction layer, then feature mapping to high-dimensional feature vectors by using 1×1 convolutional filters that add some non-linearity, then a final reconstruction layer that constructs the final target high-resolution images. However, because this super-resolution convolutional network $SRCNN$ is shallow and convolution kernels are small, image fine details are not obtained and the network is limited to a single scale. An improvement over the $SRCNN$ was utilizing the very-deep-super-resolution $VDSR$ [6]. It used a much deeper network in which a reduced size of convolutional kernels, higher learning rate and gradient clipping were used. This speeded up convergence and improved training stability. Nevertheless, both $SRCNN$ [2] and $VDSR$ [6] were pre-upsampling techniques that accomplished feature extraction in the high-resolution space. $FSRCNN$, on the other hand, does not use an interpolation method at the beginning but does feature extraction in the low-resolution space [11]. It uses multiple convolutional layers with reduced kernel size which in turn reduces the count of learnable weights. Deconvolutional filtering is used in the final step of upsampling.

Sub-pixel convolution, rather than a deconvolutional layer for upsampling, was first suggested by another proposed technology, the efficient sub-pixel convolutional neural network, or $ESPCN$ [12]. Recursively connected units are used by the deeply-recursive convolutional network $DRCN$ [7] to make the convolutional layer much deeper and enhance the fine details of the recounstructed image. The training difficulty of the deep network's parameters can be mitigated through weight sharing while also improving the model's capacity for generalization.

The main objective of SR optimization techniques is to reduce the mean squared error MSE between retrieved HR images and dataset original images. This is beneficial because it optimizes the peak signal-to-noise ratio, or $PSNR$, a typical measure for assessing SR approaches. There are severe limitations on $PSNR$'s capacity to detect perceptual dissimilarity because this metric is calculated depending on pixel-level numeric differences. The lowest $PSNR$ may not always indicate a perceptually enhanced super-resolved image outcome [8].

Generative Adversarial Networks. As described by Goodfellow et al. who were the first to propose the concept of GAN [5], the final aim of GAN is to produce data that has the same distribution as an input dataset. The idea of GAN is based on a rivalry between these generator and discriminator networks which play an adversarial game to beat each other. In this case, the generator's target is to produce fake output that looks very similar to the original dataset examples, trying to fool the discriminator and make it unable to recognize the difference between the real and generated data. On the other side, the discriminator is to be trained to become a reliable judge that can accurately detect the fake output from the generator and tell them apart from the real data. This

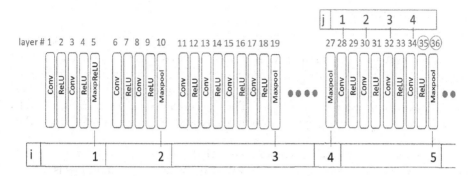

Fig. 2. These are the layers of the VGG19 architecture [13]. In [8], they said that taking an *MSE* loss between the feature maps at $i = 5$ and $j = 4$ after the ReLU activation gives the best results. In [15], however, they took the feature maps before the ReLU activation.

adversarial game will improve both the generator and the discriminator, resulting in the final goal which is to make the generator a well-founded one that can generate accurate images or any kind of data. The target function of *GAN* is:

$$V(\theta^{(D)}, \theta^{(G)}) = E_{x \sim p_{data}(x)} \log(D(x)) + E_{z \sim p_z(z)} \log(1 - D(G(z)) \qquad (1)$$

in which the probability that an input example, x, is real or not is represented by (D(x)), while the generated samples are represented by (G(z)). [5].

The value function $V(\theta^{(D)}, \theta^{(G)})$ can be viewed as a payoff: the aim is to maximize its value with regard to the discriminator (D), while reducing its value with respect to the generator (G), that is, $\min_{G} \max_{D} (V(\theta^{(D)}, \theta^{(G)}))$.

GAN was used to solve the problem of *SISR* for the first time by Ledig et al. [8] in 2017. Their proposed solution made use of residual blocks to enhance the output. Wang et al. [15] improved the work of [8] by employing the fundamental unit known as the Residual-in-Residual Dense Block. In addition, they removed batch-normalization and altered the content loss by changing the VGG layer from which they compared the outputs.

Another method for *SR* reconstruction [11] has been presented using self-attention *GAN* or *SRAGAN*. To enhance the fine details of the recovered image, the generator network assigns higher weights and makes use of the attention mechanism model to create a more complex architecture. Another recently proposed image reconstruction technique called SwinIR [10] makes use of the well-known Swin Transformer network. Their architecture consists of layers for shallow feature extraction, deep feature extraction, and high-quality image reconstruction.

1.2   Contribution

To not rely on the *MSE* loss function, *GAN*s for image super-resolution *SRGAN* [8] have been used in this paper. A perceptual loss function that consists of an adversarial loss and a content loss is used to achieve this. The adversarial loss pushes the output images to look more like the original high-resolution images using a discriminator network. The discriminator has been trained to tell apart between generated super-resolved images and existing ground-truth in the dataset.

As presented in Fig. 2, an enhancement that [15] has done over the original *SRGAN* paper was changing the VGG layer from which the content loss is taken. Nevertheless, this was one of many changes thay have made over *GAN*'s implementation [8]. Evaluating the results of changing the content VGG loss alone has not been done. For this reason, this paper's main contribution is to evaluate the results of taking the content loss of the VGG19 network from different layers. It was discovered that taking the VGG-loss at the 4th convolution (after activation) before the 5th maxpooling layer in the VGG19 network yielded more perceptually fulfilling results compared to taking it before the activation. Figure 1 shows a sample of the *MOS* test result to show a comparison between taking the VGG loss from different layers. On public benchmarks, Super-Resolution *GAN* was able to restore fine texture details from ×4 downscaled images. *SRGAN* reveals large gains in perceptual quality in a mean opinion score *MOS* test as shown in Fig. 1.

2   Methods

2.1   Generator and Discriminator Networks

This paper is adopting the same generator and discriminator structures described by Ledig et al. [8], who were the first to employ a perceptual-based objective function for a real-looking *SISR* output using the notion of *GAN*.

Generator Structure. As shown in Fig. 3, the generator network G is composed of identically designed N residual blocks. In the experiments of this paper, number of residual blocks $N = 16$ was used. Two layers of convolution are employed with small 3×3 filters and a count of 64. Since deep structures like these were found to be challenging to train, batch-normalization is employed to mitigate the internal co-variate shift in order to train these deeper network structures quickly. After that, parametric ReLU is used as the activation function. Finally, the input image's resolution has been increased using two layers of sub-pixel convolution.

Discriminator Structure. As previously mentioned, the discriminator is used as a judge to tell apart between produced images from high-resolution images in the dataset. LeakyReLU is used as an activation function with $\alpha = 0.2$ while

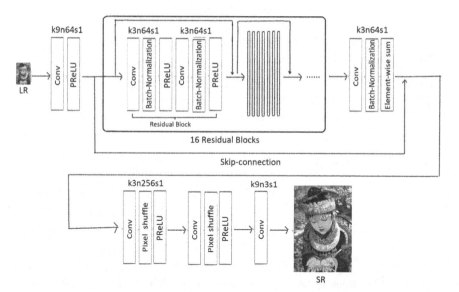

Fig. 3. The architecture of the generator is based on [8], with k denoting the filter size, n denoting representing the count of feature maps, and s denoting the stride for each layer. The generator uses 16 residual blocks, then sub-pixel convolution has been used to increase the image's resolution.

max-pooling is not utilized. The network architecture is composed of eight convolutional layers of a kernel size 3×3. The count of kernels in each layer are (64, 64, 128, 128, 256, 256, 512, 512) respectively. At the final stages, two dense layers and a sigmoid activation functions are employed that output a probability that represents classifying an input image as real or generated. The architecture layers details are depicted in Fig. 4.

2.2   Loss Function

Following the loss function that was suggested by Goodfellow et al. [5], to resolve the adversarial optimization problem that was mentioned in Eq. 1, the generator and discriminator networks are alternately optimized. This formulation enables the training of a generator to mislead a discriminator taught to differentiate between generated images and real ones. The final objective function to determine the perceptual quality of generated images is a summation of the content loss and the adversarial loss, each multiplied by some hyperparameter. This objective function can be represented as follows:

$$l^{SR} = l_X^{SR} + 10^{-3}l_{Gen}^{SR} \tag{2}$$

where l_X^{SR} represents the content loss and l_{Gen}^{SR} represents the adversarial loss and they both add up to the perceptual loss l^{SR} [8]. For the content loss,

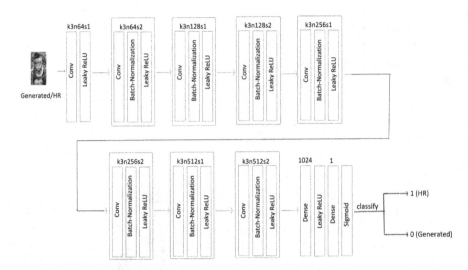

Fig. 4. The Discriminator network adopted from [8] is composed of eight convolutional filters proceeded by dense layers and a final sigomid activation layer to output probability of input being real.

the mean-squared-error *MSE* is the one that is conventionally used. The *MSE* loss in pixels is calculated as follows:

$$l_{MSE}^{SR} = \frac{1}{r^2 WH} \sum_{x=1}^{rW} \sum_{y=1}^{rH} (I_{x,y}^{HR} - G(I_{x,y}^{LR}))^2 \tag{3}$$

such that r represents the factor with which the image is to be upscaled, W represents the image's width, H represents the image's height and (x, y) represent the indices of the pixels [8].

Many modern solutions depend on this objective as it is the most often used image *SR* optimization target. *MSE* optimization approaches mostly lack the fine details, which leads to perceptually unpleasant solutions, despite the fact that they often produce high *PSNR*.

The authors of *SRGAN* [8] use an objective function that is more related to perceptual relevance rather than pixel-wise losses. In their experiments, they use the ReLU activation layers of the pre-trained VGG network to calculate the VGG content loss. The feature map acquired by the jth convolution prior to the ith maxpooling layer within the VGG19 network, which is pre-trained, is indicated by $\phi_{i,j}$ (See Fig. 2). The VGG loss is then specified as the euclidean distance between the feature maps of the super-resolved image by the generator $G(LR)$ and the original *HR* image:

$$l_{VGG/i.j}^{SR} = \frac{1}{W_{i,j} H_{i,j}} \sum_{x=1}^{W_{i,j}} \sum_{y=1}^{H_{i,j}} (\phi_{i,j}(I^{HR})_{x,y} - \phi_{i,j}(G(I^{LR}))_{x,y})^2 \tag{4}$$

where $W_{i,j}$ and $H_{i,j}$, respectively, describe the widths and heights of different feature maps within the VGG network [8].

In [8], they claim that setting $i = 5$ and $j = 4$ gives the most visually compelling output, that they credit to the capacity of deeper architectures to capture elements of higher abstraction. They take the output after the activation (before layer 36 in the *VGG* network) in all of their experiments. However, in [15], they state that applying Eq. 4 before the activation (before layer 35 in the VGG network) is one of the steps to enhance the work the authors of [8] have done. One of the contributions of this paper is to compare the results of training the same network using varying layers of the VGG network to better understand the effect of relying on the VGG content loss.

For the adversarial loss, it depends on the output classification the discriminator $D(G(I^{LR}))$ on the training data, the generative loss l_{Gen}^{SR} is defined as:

$$l_{Gen}^{SR} = \sum_{n=1}^{N} -\log D(G(I^{LR})) \tag{5}$$

2.3   Training Details

The two experiments have been conducted on a NVIDIA GeForce GTX 1650 GPU. Before training, the *LR* images were acquired by downsampling the *HR* counterparts in a bicubic kernel with a factor $r = 4$. A batch size of 16 images was used, where each high-resolution image is a 96×96 randomly cropped image from a distinct training image from the dataset. However, It is essential to keep in mind that the generator can accept images of any size since it is based on convolution layers.

Before training, low-resolution images were rescaled to the range $[0, 1]$ while the high-resolution images were rescaled to the range $[-1, 1]$. The same has been applied in the experiments of this paper. Adam optimizer was used with $\beta_1 = 0.9$ and $\beta_2 = 0.99$ in all experiments. The *SRResNet* model that was trained with the *MSE* loss was utilised as a start for the generator while training the *GAN*-based generator to prevent undesirable local optima.

In each update iteration, both the adversarial models were optimized once in an alternative fashion, which means that $k = 1$ as defined by authors of *GAN* [5]. The residual blocks in the generator network are all identical, where the generator consists of 16 residual blocks in all the conducted experiments ($B = 16$). Pytorch was used to construct and train all the models in the experiments. Datasets were organized in a data loader, where each batch (16 examples) contained $24 \times 24 \times 3$ *LR* images and their corresponding $96 \times 96 \times 3$ *HR* images. Outdoor Scenes *OST* dataset [14] is the main dataset that was used for training in the experiments.

2.4   Training Experiments

Experiment 1: *SRResNet* and *SRGAN36* training on *OST* dataset [14]

– The generator has been trained alone (without training the discriminator) for 440 epochs (270,000 update iterations) using a learning rate $\eta = 1 \times 10^{-4}$. The loss that was used is an *MSE*-based loss between super-resolved images and HR ground truth images. This trained generator phase will be referenced as the *SRResNet* in the course of this paper.
– The *SRResNet* model (trained with *MSE* loss) was used as a start model for the generator in the next training phase, *SRGAN* [8]. The generator was trained using $\eta = 1 \times 10^{-5}$, while the discriminator was trained using a $\eta = 1 \times 10^{-6}$. Both networks were trained for 165 epochs (100,000 update iterations). The VGG loss has been taken with $i = 5$ and $j = 4$ **after the activation**. This takes feature maps of the VGG architecture before the 36th layer. Hence, this phase will be referenced as *SRGAN36* in the course of this paper.
– Finally, the content loss Eq. 4 was multiplied by a factor of 0.006. This is to make the content loss scale comparable to the scale of the adversarial loss.

Experiment 2: *SRResNet* and *SRGAN35* training on OST dataset [14]

– The generator has been trained alone (without training the discriminator). This trained generator phase is exactly similar to the *SRResNet* training phase that was mentioned in Experiment 1.
– The *SRResNet* model (trained with *MSE* loss) was used as a start model for the generator in the next training phase, *SRGAN* [8]. The generator was trained using a $\eta = 1 \times 10^{-5}$, while the discriminator was trained using a $\eta = 1 \times 10^{-6}$. Both networks were trained for 165 epochs (100,000 update iterations). The VGG loss has been taken with $i = 5$ and $j = 4$ **before the activation**. This takes feature maps of the VGG architecture before the 35th layer. Hence, this phase will be referenced as *SRGAN35* in the course of this paper.

2.5   Testing Details

Set5 [1] and *Set14* [16], the testing sets, are two commonly used benchmark datasets on which tests were conducted. As shown in Fig. 5, between low- and high-resolution images, a scaling factor of 4 is used in all tests. This translates to a ×16-pixel reduction in image size. Generated images from other *SR* techniques, including nearest neighbor interpolation, bicubic interpolation, *SRCNN* [2] were obtained from online supplementary materials to do a comparison with

LR image

HR (x4) image

Fig. 5. The left image is the low-resolution bicubic downsampled version that is input to the generator. The right image is the high-resolution real image with a scaling factor ×4. Both images are sample from the *Set14* dataset [16].

the generated *SRGAN36* and *SRGAN35* images.[1]. The following are all the 6 methods on which the tests have been done:

1. Nearest Neighbor Interpolation
2. Bicubic Interpolation
3. Super Resolution Using Deep Convolutional Networks or *SRCNN* [2]
4. Super Resolution Residual Network or *SRResNet* that was trained as initialization for experiments 1 and 2
5. Super Resolution *GAN* or *SRGAN36* of experiment 1
6. Super Resolution *GAN* or *SRGAN35* of experiment 2

The following has been done to test the above different super-resolution algorithms:

- For all the 6 methods, *PSNR* [dB] was calculated for all *Set5* [1] and *Set14* [16] for fair comparison.
- For all the 6 methods, *SSIM* was calculated for all *Set5* [1] and *Set14* [16] for fair comparison.
- For all the 6 methods, a Mean Opinion Score (*MOS*) has been calculated for 3 random images from the *Set5* [1] dataset and 6 random images from the *Set14* [16] dataset. This has been done by creating a google form. For each question, two images are presented beside each other, the first was a *Set14* [16] or *Set5* [1] generated output of one of the reference methods or one of the experiments of this paper, and the second was the *HR* ground-truth image. The quality of the output image has been rated by the participants with a number between 1 (bad quality) and 10 (excellent quality) compared to the *HR* original image from the dataset.
The form consisted of 9 pages (each for a test image). Each page contained 6 comparison questions to compare the 6 corresponding methods to be compared. Consequently, each participant rated 6 versions of 9 images that were presented in a random order, summing up to 54 images to be rated.

---

[1] https://www.kaggle.com/datasets/ll01dm/set-5-14-super-resolution-dataset.

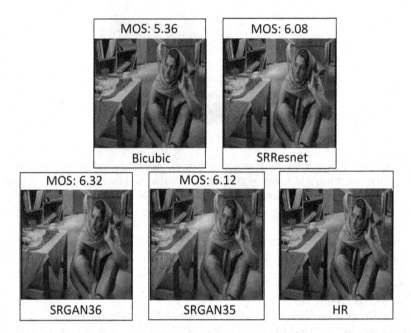

Fig. 6. Results for *Set14* [16] using bicubic interpolation, *SRResNet*, *SRGAN36* and *SRGAN35* in comparison to the ground-truth *HR* image [×4 upscaling].

Table 1. This table shows comparison of the 6 tested methods on *Set14* [16] dataset. Highest measures of average *PSNR*, *SSIM*, and Mean Opinion Score *MOS* are in bold.

Results on *Set14* [16] dataset						
	Nearest	Bicubic	SRCNN	SRResnet	SRGAN36	SRGAN35
PSNR	22.6	23.8	**24.72**	23.64	22.18	21.24
SSIM	0.64	0.68	**0.71**	0.70	0.62	0.58
MOS	4.68	5.29	6.36	6.23	**6.48**	6.07

3   Results and Analysis

This section will go over the *PSNR*, *SSIM*, and *MOS* numerical results that the trained generators of the two conducted experiments produced, beside showing the results of nearest neighbor interpolation, bicubic interpolation, and *SRCNN* [2] for comparison.

In the *MOS* test, 25 raters have participated in grading the *SR* techniques output images from ×4 downsampled images with a score between 1 (poor quality) and 10 (great quality). Of these images, 6 images were obtained from the *Set14* [16] dataset and 3 images were obtained from the *Set5* [1] dataset. The outcomes of the *MOS* test are presented in Tables 1 and 2.

Table 2. This table shows comparison of the 6 tested methods on *Set5* [1] dataset. Highest measures of *PSNR*, *SSIM*, and Mean Opinion Score *MOS* are in bold.

Results on *Set5* [1] dataset						
	Nearest	Bicubic	SRCNN	SRResnet	SRGAN36	SRGAN35
PSNR	24.37	26.45	**27.9**	25.87	23.57	22.42
SSIM	0.71	0.77	**0.81**	0.79	0.71	0.67
MOS	3.92	5.32	6.12	**6.21**	5.84	5.53

3.1   Investigating the Perceptual Loss

Basically, the goal of training an *SRGAN36* model in experiment 1 and an *SRGAN35* model in experiment 2, with the same *SRResNet* initialization, was to compare the effect of taking the VGG-loss before and after the activation. Tables 1 and 2 show the performance of both networks on the *PSNR*, *SSIM* and *MOS* metrics. It can be observed that *SRGAN36* outperformed *SRGAN35* on all metrics. This might make sense given the notion that taking VGG-loss deeper in the network yields the most convincing results [8]. It is also important to mention that the authors of [15] enhanced on [8] by taking the VGG-loss before the activation and achieved better results. However, this was accompanied by some changes in the structure of the generator itself. For example, they removed all

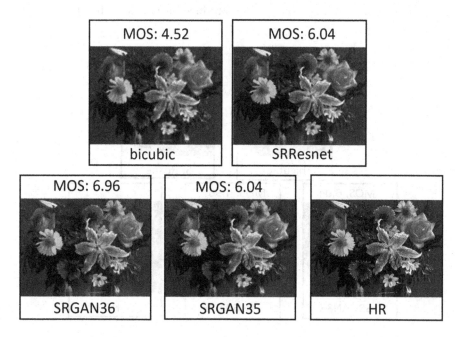

Fig. 7. Results for *Set14* [16] using bicubic interpolation, *SRResNet*, *SRGAN36* and *SRGAN35* in comparison to the *HR* image from the dataset [×4 upscaling].

the batch-normalization layers and increased the number of residual connections. These changes, however, were not employed in experiment 2 since the aim was to see the effect of only taking the VGG-loss before the activation but with the same generator structure that was used in the other experiments.

3.2   Investigating the Performance of Final Networks

SRResNet, *SRGAN36* and *SRGAN35* are compared to nearest neighbor interpolation, bicubic interpolation, and one of the modern algorithms, *SRCNN* [2]. Tables 1 and 2 summarize the quantitative results while Fig. 1, 6, 7, 8 summarize the qualitative results. These results show that *SRResNet* and *SRGAN36* establish a new state-of-the-art on *Set14* [16] and *Set5* [1] datasets. Compared to nearest neighbor interpolation and bicubic interpolation, *SRResNet* had higher *PSNR* and *SSIM* results on mostly all test images. *SRGAN36* and *SRGAN35*, on the other side, could not accomplish superior *PSNR* and *SSIM* results. Despite that, participants in the form gave *SRGAN36* and *SRGAN35* (and *SRResNet*) much higher scores than nearest neighbor and bicubic interpolations, on average.

Moreover, *SRCNN* [2] had the best *PSNR* and *SSIM* results. However, *SRGAN36* was able to do better than it on the average *MOS* on *Set14* [16] as shown in Table 1. This shows the limited potential of metrics like *PSNR* and *SSIM* to recover the image's perceptual quality, taking into account the fine texture details. This might be reasoned by the fact that these metrics are mostly based on pixel-level resemblance between two images. Hence, the weighted average of adversarial loss and content loss produced a new loss that has shown a

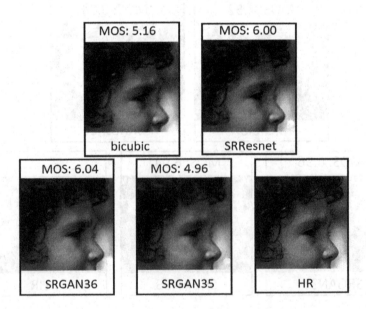

Fig. 8. Results for *Set5* [1] using bicubic interpolation, *SRResNet*, *SRGAN36* and *SRGAN35* in comparison to the *HR* image from the dataset [×4 upscaling].

great performance in capturing the fine details of images. This gave *SRGAN* [8] the ability to produce images that are relatively of higher quality.

4 Conclusion

After conducting two training experiments, an *SRResNet* model and two *SRGAN* models were trained and proven to be competitive with both conventional and cutting-edge super-resolution methods. With *MOS* testing, *SRGAN*'s satisfactory perceptual performance was confirmed. Images generated by the trained *SRResNet* and *SRGAN* models had the highest *MOS* scores on two benchmark datasets compared with interpolation techniques and one of the modern techniques, *SRCNN*. It was also demonstrated that typical performance measures like *PSNR* and *SSIM* do not always succeed in effectively judging image quality like how the perception of a human does. Despite the fact that traditional interpolation methods achieved higher *PSNR* and *SSIM* than *SRGAN* methods, *SRGAN* methods outperformed them in the average mean opinion score. However, It is essential to keep in mind that the *MOS* is quite subjective and the result can be different depending on the individuals who participated in the evaluation, the conditions in which the images are shown to the evaluators, and even the order of the images were shown. While attempting to output perceptually convincing result to solve the *SR* problem, the selection of perceptual loss is especially important. Taking the VGG-loss exactly before the 5*th* max pooling layer and after the activation, as opposed to taking it before the activation, yielded more perceptually appealing results for the participants in the *MOS* test on the *OST* dataset.

References

1. Bevilacqua, M., Roumy, A., Guillemot, C., Alberi-Morel, M.L.: Low-complexity single-image super-resolution based on nonnegative neighbor embedding (2012)
2. Dong, C., Loy, C.C., He, K., Tang, X.: Image super-resolution using deep convolutional networks. IEEE PAMI **38**(2), 295–307 (2015)
3. Duporge, I., Isupova, O., Reece, S., Macdonald, D.W., Wang, T.: Using very-high-resolution satellite imagery and deep learning to detect and count African elephants in heterogeneous landscapes. Remote Sens. Ecol. Conserv. **7**(3), 369–381 (2021)
4. Gohshi, S.: Real-time super resolution algorithm for security cameras. In: ICETE, vol. 5, pp. 92–97. IEEE (2015)
5. Goodfellow, I., et al.: Generative adversarial nets. In: Advances in Neural Information Processing Systems, vol. 27 (2014)
6. Kim, J., Lee, J.K., Lee, K.M.: Accurate image super-resolution using very deep convolutional networks. In: CVPR (2016)
7. Kim, J., Lee, J.K., Lee, K.M.: Deeply-recursive convolutional network for image super-resolution. In: CVPR (2016)
8. Ledig, C., et al.: Photo-realistic single image super-resolution using a generative adversarial network. In: CVPR (2017)

9. Li, H., Zheng, Q., Yan, W., Tao, R., Qi, X., Wen, Z.: Image super-resolution reconstruction for secure data transmission in internet of things environment. Math. Biosci. Eng. **18**(5), 6652–6672 (2021)
10. Liang, J., Cao, J., Sun, G., Zhang, K., Van Gool, L., Timofte, R.: Swinir: image restoration using swin transformer. In: CVPR, pp. 1833–1844 (2021)
11. Liu, Y., Qiao, Y., Hao, Y., Wang, F., Rashid, S.F.: Single image super resolution techniques based on deep learning: status, applications and future directions. J. Image Graph. **9**(3) (2021)
12. Shi, W., et al.: Real-time single image and video super-resolution using an efficient sub-pixel convolutional neural network. In: CVPR (2016)
13. Simonyan, K., Zisserman, A.: Very deep convolutional networks for large-scale image recognition. arXiv preprint arXiv:1409.1556 (2014)
14. Wang, X., Yu, K., Dong, C., Loy, C.C.: Recovering realistic texture in image super-resolution by deep spatial feature transform. In: CVPR (2018)
15. Wang, X., et al.: ESRGAN: enhanced super-resolution generative adversarial networks. In: Leal-Taixé, L., Roth, S. (eds.) ECCV 2018. LNCS, vol. 11133, pp. 63–79. Springer, Cham (2019). https://doi.org/10.1007/978-3-030-11021-5_5
16. Zeyde, R., Elad, M., Protter, M.: On single image scale-up using sparse-representations. In: Boissonnat, J.-D., et al. (eds.) Curves and Surfaces 2010. LNCS, vol. 6920, pp. 711–730. Springer, Heidelberg (2012). https://doi.org/10.1007/978-3-642-27413-8_47

Model Compression Techniques in Deep Neural Networks

Mubarek Mohammed Yesuf[1,2] and Beakal Gizachew Assefa[2]

[1] Information Network Security Agency, Addis Ababa, Ethiopia
mubarek.mohammed@aait.edu.et
[2] Addis Ababa Institute of Technology, AAU, Addis Ababa, Ethiopia
beakal.gizachew@aait.edu.et

Abstract. With the current set-up, the success of Deep Neural Network models is highly tied to their size. Although this property might help them improve their performance, it makes them difficult to train, deploy them on resource-constrained machines, and iterate on experiments. There is also a growing concern about their environmental and economic impacts. Model compression is a set of techniques that are applied to reduce the size of Neural Network (NN) models while maintaining their performance. This survey presents state-of-the-art model compression methods, discusses how they are hybridized, highlights the changes they could cause beyond size reduction, and puts forward open research problems for further study.

Keywords: Artificial Intelligence · Neural Networks · Deep Learning · Model compression · Pruning · Knowledge Distillation · Quantization

1 Introduction

Breakthrough advances in AI algorithms are consequences of Neural Networks which are the foundations for Deep Learning (DL), a family of Machine Learning (ML) algorithms behind successful Artificial Intelligence (AI) innovation in tasks like Voice Recognition, Image Classification [47], Human Language understanding [19], etc. DL algorithms are based on a theorem, named the Universal Approximation Theorem [38], which guarantees that Neural Networks, grouped in some way, can compute any continuous function, and the hierarchical representation of information inspired from the human brain [6]. On the other the exact number of parameters a specific DL model needs for a certain problem is still a hyper-parameter, a choice of the designer. These ideas stimulated overparameterization in an attempt to increase a model's representation capacity and thus performance, as the tasks they are being applied to grows in complexity [8]. How complex a model is commonly measured by the total number

Supported by Ethiopian Artificial Intelligence Institute.

T. Girma Debelee et al. (Eds.): PanAfriCon AI 2022, CCIS 1800, pp. 169–190, 2023.
https://doi.org/10.1007/978-3-031-31327-1_10

of parameters which is useful to measure its memory consumption, and floating point operations per second(FLOPs), useful in fields of computations that require floating-point calculations.

Most benchmark models are related to Computer Vision, a sub-fields of AI that tries to mimic the human vision, and Natural Language Processing, another sub-fields of AI that aims to replicate the human language capability. Computer Vision related models are mostly based on Convolutional Neural Net-work (CNN)s, a type of DL architecture designed for spatial data such as an image. Prominent examples are, Alexnet [47] and VGG16 [73], which are variants of CNNs, are winners of Imagenet [47], a dataset with more than 14 million well labeled images intended to serve as a benchmark in Computer Vision applications. Natural language related models are getting bigger and bigger recently so much that they are now being referred to as Large Language Models. State of the art and benchmark model architectures for language models are based on the transformers [79]. Prominent examples are BERT, GPT, BART, DitillBERT. Figure 1 below shows the evolution of some benchmark computer vision models and their computational burdens expressed in Giga FLoating-point OPerations (GFLOPs) along with their Top-1(left) and Top-2 accuracy.

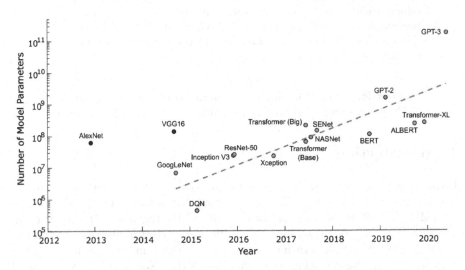

Fig. 1. Size of benchmark vision and language models over the past years [7].

However, there is a trade-off: large models perform well at a cost of increased complexity. Challenges of such big models include longer training, inference and iteration time, difficulty to deploy on resource constrained and edge machines, and economic and environmental impact [66]. This raises the question if there is a way to work around the trade-off. This is where Model Compression comes in, it is the idea of making models small without losing performance. A review of model compression methods for deep-learning are presented here.

Model Compression is a set of techniques [11] for reducing the size of large models without a notable performance loss. Its necessity is increasing in parallel with the advancement and complexity of models. Even though there recent attempts to train a smaller networks from the beginning [22], mostly, Model Compression is applied after training a bigger model as the model needs much less parameters for inference than for learning. Model Compression methods in literature can be classified in four major parts: Pruning, Knowledge Distillation (KD), Quantization, and other methods. Pruning is removing an unwanted structure from a trained network. KD is a mechanism to pass along the knowledge of a bigger model onto a smaller model. Quantization is reducing the number of bits model parts require to be represented. It is similar to approximation. The rest of Model Compression methods other than Pruning, KD and Quantization are can be organized in one section and are referred to as Other methods. Weight decomposition methods deserve to have their own section, but this arrangement makes the paper simpler for the reader.

The contributions of the paper are as follows

- Conduct a review of deep learning Model Compression methods.
- Systematically compare, and discuss each method along with their consequences beyond size reduction, their combinations and selection considerations.
- Discuss open research problems for further study on the topic of Deep Neural Network Model Compression.

The rest of the paper is organized as follows. The next section, section two, reviews prominent works in Model Compression. Section three is on Hybrid Model Compression techniques which is about methods that combine existing ones for a better outcome. The effect of Model Compression beyond size reduction is discussed in section four. Discussions, factors affecting choice of methods, and open research problems are presented in sections, section five, six, and seven respectively. Finally, a conclusion is presented (Fig. 2).

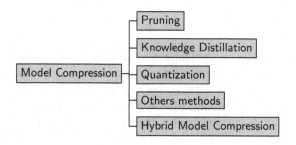

Fig. 2. The taxonomy and categories of Deep Learning model compression methods.

2   Model Compression Methods

2.1   Generic Paradigms

Over the development of Model Compression methods, certain key characteristics keep on reappearing. These characteristics are generic and can be organized as a paradigms of Model Compression. Understanding them gives how the
general view of towards the approaches in Model Compression methods in an
agnostic way, assist in selection, and stimulate research questions. Unlike past
works, here they are organized in one stand alone subsection. Not all of them are
applied for all Compression methods and some can be found in one method at
the same time. They form important trade-offs wherever they appear and extend
the default method which is usually static, deterministic, and post-training.

- **Random or Stochastic.** Sometimes certain aspects (parameters, hyper-
  parameters, etc.) of a certain model are selected at random. The stochasticity
  brings the analogous benefits that it brings to the Stochastic Gradient descent,
  it enables exploration in the space. In fact, sometimes, they can be used as a
  benchmark for comparison against the other methods [9].
- **Data free, Zero-shot, one shot, or few shot.** The data the original models
  were trained on might not be always available or it might be expensive to
  work with the it. But some other information such as the meta data might
  be available. In such cases, a data and iteration sceptic paradigms are used
  [15,76].
- **Dynamic.** The dynamic approach to model compression dynamically decides
  different parts of the process [49].
- **Online.** Compression of the model is done while it is being trained [41].
- **Auto-ML.** Instead of adjusting hyper-parameters by hand, this paradigm
  encourages using Auto-ML methods where certain parts of the process of
  compression is automatically decided by an external algorithm [30,36].
- **Differentiable.** These paradigm's turn hyper-parameters introduced by the
  compression method into a parameters and learn them on the process [43].

2.2   Pruning

The oldest, most studied and intuitive method of reducing model size is pruning. It is literally removing a weight or a node from a network based on how
important it is. The vanilla pruning method has three main stages: initializing,
training, pruning and retraining (fine tuning). Hyperparameters introduced by
the Pruning include compression rate, magnitude to prune with when it is magnitude weight, type of saliency metric to use, etc. The approach towards these
hyperparamters categorize the pruning methods in literature.

The earliest methods were of mainly: Saliency based, where node or weight
is checked for importance, penalty based [48,57], where the a penalty (regularization) term is added on the loss(objective) function to induce weight decay
[70], magnitude based pruning, simply removing the smallest link (weight) in

each iteration. Prominent early works are Optimal Brain Damage (OBD) [48], Optimal Brain Surgeon [35] and Skeletonization [57].

An intuitive direction of development for Pruning is to determine what is important. There were attempts to identify them with statistical methods, and works arounds via following recent advances in the area Explainability, a notion trying to undersand, explain the 'decision' of a model [87] (Fig. 3).

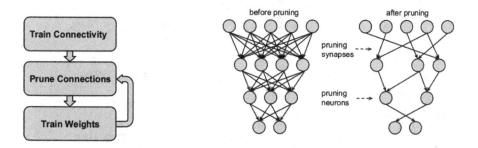

Fig. 3. Iterative Pruning (left) [33] and Pruning (right) [33].

Modern approaches vary not just in the Saliency metrics they use or other approach, but also in the overall pipeline of pruning. The 'lottery ticket hypothesis' [22], whose stronger version was supported in [55], states that random initialization of a network contains a small subnetwork ("the winning tickets") that, when trained in separately, can compete with the performance of the original model. A rather bold finding in by [68] states that there is a randomly initialized subnetwork that even without training can perform as good as the original. The recent work [84], termed pruning from scratch, questions the need for training the network and proposes a different pipeline as: random initialization, pruning and then training. The work in [50], raises the question why train a big model to convergence while it is possible to attain better performance by training it for free iterations and prune it.

Rather than design designing manually the hyperparamters introduced by Pruning, Reinforcement Learning (RL) based methods are emerging to formulate the problem of removing ad node or a weight as a Markov Decision Process [30]. Neural Architecture Search, based methods formulate the Pruning as a search in the space of sub-networks emerging area of study in the study of neural network's [21].

2.3   Knowledge Distillation

Knowledge Distillation is a relatively new compression procedure originally introduced in [11] and reinvented in [37]. A bigger model and well performing model, which is termed as the teacher model, provides labels for a smaller network to train with. For each observation x and its label y out of the dataset the original network was trained on, the smaller network will use the predictions of the bigger network as a label for x instead of just y. The predictions of the teacher model which are termed as soft labels are not ones and zeros like hard labels. These soft labels are termed as the Dark Knowledge. The intuition is an image of a dog has a larger chance of being mistaken as a cat than as a car.

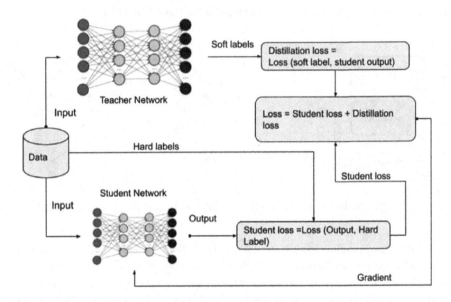

Fig. 4. Knowledge Distillation (KD) [20].

Under normal conditions the output values of a trained classification network, which are termed as Logits, are too small to make a computational difference. Thus, KD uses a constant value named Temperature, T, which magnifies these small values before they are changed to probability values by the softmax function. So, each output of from the teacher with the i-th class in training, logits z_i and a temperature T, is computed as:

$$p(z_i, T) = \frac{exp(z_i/T)}{\sum exp(z_j/T)} \tag{1}$$

Hyper-parameters introduced by KD include the architecture type of the student network, the temperature T, and the distillation loss which measures the divergence between the student model and the teacher model [37]. Different approaches and improvements in these hyper-parameters create variants of KD including variations mentioned in the generic paradigms. For example, there can be improvements in the loss [77,92], or an assistant network with a size that is less than the teacher and smaller than the student, to help out the small student network can be introduced as well [56].

A powerful adaptation of KD, Fitnets [71], trains a student, deeper and thinner than the teacher which is unlike [37], using the intermediate representations, features, learned by the teacher as hints to improve the training process and final generalizing capacity of the student. This work opened a whole new subcatagory of KD termed as Feature Distillation making the original to be called response based distillation [28]. Response-based distillation, is also limited to the supervised learning as the logits, the soft labels, are probability distributions. Relationship distillation extends feature distillation by using outputs of specific layers in the teacher model and exploring the relationships between different layers or data samples [65].

At core level, KD is a knowledge transfer mechanism [54]. Thus, it is extremely versatile and model agnostic, any model can be used as teacher or a student. Thus, it has usage for other purposes including faster optimization [88], defence against adversarial attacks [62], explainable networks [42,63], even to improve the original network itself [24].

2.4   Quantization

Quantization, in simple terms discretization, is mapping numbers from the space of continuous values to discrete values. A good example is rounding up a number. The concept is old and has been used in various settings in information theory and other sciences as well, but in Neural Networks setting, it is about rounding up the networks parameters and decrease the number of bits required for representation [26]. For example from 32 bits floating point representations, to limited precision, commonly in 8 bits or lower representations. It's foundation is related with how a human brain stores and encodes information in a discrete way [25].

Normally, what is known as the clipping range, a range to make sure the individual weights will lie in, is determined before hand. The common formula is given by:

$$Q(w) = Int(\frac{w}{S}) - Z \qquad (2)$$

where w is a real number representing the value of a single parameter in a network, S is a scaling factor, Z is an integer, and Int is the integer function that maps its input to the integer. A quantized number can be recovered with the reverse quantization, Dequantization. These variables are part of the hyperparameters introduced by Quantization.

In literature, the variants of quantization differ according to which parameters to quantize, how to quantize, whether to do it in training time or after training time, and other factors which correspond to the variables S, Z in Eq. 2. S itself is determined by the boundary values of the clipping range. Depending on whether the clipping range is calculated for each dynamically or statically, quantization can be dynamic or static. The work on [41] made sure only 8-bit integers are used in the network at inference time.

The basic method of quantization is to train a model under normal setup and then to quantize each parameter, activation or even input, using some sort of function or mapping, which is sometimes referred to as a quantization operator [25]. When fine tuning is needed after quantization, Quantization Aware Training is used where a re-training is done with floating point propagation but after every gradient update the parameters are quantized again. Post Training Quantization is quantization without retraining [5, 12]. It is preferred when QAT is too complex to implement. Mixed precision quantization methods try to assign varying precision of bits for parameters in the network with an additional burden of searching the right combinations of hyper-parameters [80].

The ideal Quantization is, Binarization, making the parameters of a network binary [17] for memory and compute efficiency. In fact, the most appealing feature of this method, is that it can potentially get rid of the need of multiplication at inference time by replacing the dot product in the network with bitwise operators [18] to train networks with binary weights. In [69], the researchers showed CNNs with only binary weights and demonstrated a binary quantized version of Alexnet [47], with 32 times smaller, with comparable accuracy as the original version. Beyond binarization, an alternative network is a ternary network, where the weights of the network are limited to three values instead of two as in binary. Neither binary nor ternary Quantization methods are trainable with back-propagation with gradient descent.

Recent advances introduce Differentiable Quantization in order to learn the hyper-parameters of Quantization [91].

2.5   Summary of Model Compression Against Generic Paradigms

Once basic Model Compression methods and generic paradigms development is established, they can be effectively summarized in the Table 1 below.

Table 1. Summary of Model Compression paradigms.

Paradigm	Pruning	Quantization	Knowledge Distillation
Random or Stochastic	[76]	[31]	[52, 53]
Data free, Zero, One, or few shot	[15, 76]	[34]	[52, 53, 59]
Dynamic	[83]	[91]	[49]
Online	[48]	[41]	[93]
AutoML (RL, NAS)	[30, 36],	[80]	[2]
Differentiable	[43]	[91]	[29]

2.6   Other Compression Methods

In general, the goal of compression is intuitive: reduce size. In reduce size with accuracy. Thus, people have tried whatever they think would work to achieve that goal. Listed in this section are methods that are both common, Tensor Decomposition, and rare, like Information theoretic.

Tensor decomposition is a popular method to reduce a model size. A tensor is just a matrix in higher dimension. Tensor decomposition is a scaled up version of the common matrix decomposition in linear algebra. Matrix decomposition methods like Singular Value Decomposition and Principal component analysis, have their analogous versions. To make compression, these methods take the weights of a model to form a Tensor. Tensor decomposition, the core of these methods, is an existing approach in other fields and common decomposition methods Canonical Polyadic, Tensor Train, and the Tucker decomposition are applied to compress models. The works in [13,60] and [46] are iconic examples of these methods. These are almost always applied in Multi Layer Perceptrons or Fully connected layers of CNNs. Large scale matrix manipulation involved is their disadvantages. They are also applied on specific architectures.

Weight sharing approaches are somehow ways of making CNN variants efficient. The works [75], Inception [90], MobileNet [39] and SqueezNet [40] are examples of these methods. One of the most influential work [40] achieved Alexnet [47] level accuracy with 50 times fewer parameters on the ImageNet dataset [47]. These family of compression methods are more of careful design choices that turned out to be efficient.

An unique method is presented in [85] used the then state of the art lossless video encoding and compression technique to compress a model. It is an information theoretic approach that formulated the model compression problem as an information source coding one. It used Context-Adaptive Binary Arithmetic Coding (CABAC) a video coding standard H.264/AVC to encode and quantize the networks parameters.

3   Hybrid Model Compression Methods

Fortunately, Model Compression methods are not disjoint: they can be combined. The resulting method would be more complex than the individual ones but in cases where that is not an issue, combining hybrid methods is beneficial. In fact, a symbiotic relationship where the problems of one is addressed by the other can be achieved. This section highlights prominent works in that combine compression methods.

3.1   Pruning and Quantization

Pruning and Quantization the most related ones especially unstructured Pruning where it is simply setting a parameter zero. The most prominent work not just in hybrid paradigm but also in the area of Model Compression is Deep Compression

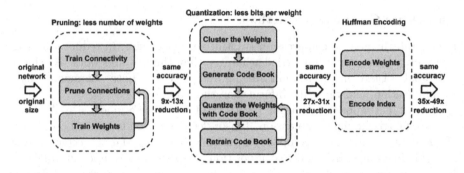

Fig. 5. An example of hybrid Compression is the Deep Compression framework [32].

framework [32] where iterative Pruning, Qauntization and Encoding are applied one after the other. Its Pruning part is the same as [33] (Fig. 5).

The intuitive relationship between Pruning and Quantization is being backed by a recent advances in Quantization that study differentiable hyperparamters in Quantization as a means to unify them [78,82].

3.2   Pruning and Knowledge Distillation

There is also a positive relationship between Pruning and Knowledge Distillation and it has been recognized relatively early in [45] where Pruning is applied on distilled student networks on the task of Neural Machine Translation. Recent works are more generic than applied. A work demonstrated in [64] showed, a student can learn better from pruned teacher which serves as a better regularizer than otherwise in the context of KD. The converse of it has also been shown in [14] where the authors argue that the accuracy of a pruned model is well restored when the student is fine-tuned with KD than vanilla training. A good example of a symbiotic relationship between the two is [1] where unprunable parameters are compressed with KD and potentially redundancy is addressed by Pruning [1].

3.3   Quantization and Knowledge Distillation

An early major work in the combination of Quantization and Knowledge Distillation is the application of Quantization for the choice of a student model for KD [67] where a the knowledge of a Quantized teacher model is transferred to a Quantized student. In this setting, KD helps Quantization restore better performance. Conversely, Quantization also benefits KD as in [10] where it has been used to enable on device KD by introducing noise that mimic the existence of a bigger teacher model. This addresses the problem of missing teacher on edge devices to do vanilla KD and might even put the need of the teacher in the first place in question. Their bond is strengthened by Quantization Aware KD

[44] that aims to solve the problem of performance degradation in Quantized distillation [67] (Table 2).

Table 2. Summary of Hybrid Model Compression.

Hybrid Compression	Remark
Pruning and Quantization	They are applied together almost everywhere [32] and are so similar there are work that attempt to unify them [78,82]
Pruning and Knowledge Distillation	Mutually beneficial result. One solves the challenges of the other [1,45,64]
Quantization and Knowledge Distillation	Distillation restores performance damaged by Quantization [67]. Quantization helps mimic a non existent teacher [10]

As it can be seen on the table, model compression methods can benefit each other when they are combined but at a cost of complexity. The number of hyper-parameters that have to be decided will grow exponentially.

4   Model Compression Beyond Size Reduction

The objective of model compression is to reduce the models size. But the size reduction can alter the behaviour of the network that can have both positive and negative consequences. In the case where it benefits, it will be an extra advantage. In fact, in some cases, like [48], the compression can even be done for the by-product. But in the cases where it is disadvantageous there is a trade-off to be addressed appropriately. This section highlights these issues.

4.1   Reducing Overfitting

Ideally, a model is expected to generalize, and not overfit. Overfitting is when a model is trained on a training data to the extent that it negatively impacts its accuracy on data beyond the training set. Dramatic size reduction of any kind of compression impacts generalization negatively [33,71]. But a certain level of compression can help reduce overfiting. In general, compression methods can be used as noise injection mechanisms which has a regularizing effect [37] for the network by forcing parameters to learn representations independently. In fact, in the beginning days of Artificial Intelligence, one objective of NN Pruning was to reduce overfitting [48]. Recently, dropouts, randomly dropping out weights from the network with a certain probability, [47] enabled for models to go deeper than usual and reignited the consideration of compression as a cure for overfitting.

4.2 Explainability

Model Compression is also tied with Explainability or Interpretability, an effort to try to understand the decisions of models which is getting more and more attention due to their applications in high stake areas. The problem of Explainability can be solved by KD, sometimes at a cost of a slight accuracy, by transferring the knowledge of a high performing neural network into a Decision Tree model which is explainable inherently [23,51]. But this is a double-edged phenomenon because compressing a trained model impacts explanations as can be seen [42] and [63] where the authors suggested explanation preserving methods. There is a lack of detailed work between compression procedures and explainability. For example, what model compression does to Mechanstic Interpretability, an effort trying to understand what happens inside Neural Networks, remained a mystery [61].

4.3 Neural Architecture Search

Neural Architecture Search is an attempt to find a an optimal architecture in an educated way. This is because most novel architectures are purely results of the choice of the designer rather than. The relationship of Neural Architecture Search with model compression is also intuitive and well recognised in literature [16]. The task of optimal compression can be seen as a search in the space of sub-architectures. For example the task of Pruning can be taken as a search in the space of NN architectures that are sub networks of the original network using a certain algorithm [3,86].

4.4 Algorithmic Fairness

Algorithmic fairness has become increasingly vital due to the increasing impact of AI in society. Particularly, as AI solutions are being adopted in various fields of high social importance or automate decision-making, the question of how fair the algorithm is critical now more than ever. Since Model Compression is becoming a default component of ML deployment, its impact on fairness have to be examined. A recent work aimed at this problem reported that model compression, Pruning and Weight Decomposition, exacerbate the bias in a network [74].

4.5 Security

Security issues regarding Neural Networks include Gradient Leakage Attacks, where an attacker can gain access to private training data from a model's gradient, Adversarial Samples, where an attacker misleads a trained classifier with carefully designed inputs [27], and Membership Inference Attacks, where an attacker learns about the training data by making repeated inferences [81].

In general, neither Quantization nor Pruning help mitigate Adversarial attacks without costing accuracy [94]. Knowledge Distillation is extensively used

Table 3. Summary of Model Compression and its consequences.

Network Behaviour	Relationship
Overfitting	Slight compression can help [37,48], but extreme compression of any kind damages it
Explainability	Both Pruning and Knowledge Distillation damage Explainability(Attribution) but Knowledge Distillation indirectly solves the problem of Explainability by transferring knowledge to an interptetable model [42,63]
Neural Architecture Search	It has a two way positive relationship with Pruning and Knowledge Distillation [3,16]
Algorithmic Bias	All compression methods exacerbate the existing bias [74]
Security	Against adversarial attacks, Quantization and Pruning do not help against without loss of accuracy [94], but Knowledge Distillation does [62]. Pruning can help against Membership Inference Attacks [81]

as a defense mechanism for Adversarial attacks [62]. Pruning can also be used to prevent Membership Inference Attack [81] (Table 3).

Basically, all decisions that were made about the network before compressing it can be questioned after the compression, but mentioned here are few of them for there is a lack of enough work in the area. In some cases, it might make sense to ask whether or not a particular behaviour observed on a network might affect the compression performance.

5   Findings

At core level, most Model Compression methods are somehow related with some kind of natural phenomena outside of AI. Quantization is related with the discrete way of information decoding and storage in the human brain [25]. The original KD paper discussed about its similarity between the development of insects. Pruning is related with how humans have less neuron connections when they are babies, than adults. This begs the question whether or not other ideas can also be considered or even if there is an even bigger mystery.

Another high-level observation is that the methods can be seen as micro level and macro level. KD and Weight Decomposition are macro-level compression methods, they work at network level. Quantization and Pruning are relatively micro compression methods, they have mechanisms to deal with specific parameters [33]. Those in the latter group have patterns across their techniques and trade-offs introduced by their generic paradigms. For example in both Pruning and Quantization, the conventional method is post-training compression, getting more surgical by applying them while training is possible but it has an additional cost of complexity, and have alternatives to deal with parameters individually or in groups. Particularly, Unstructured pruning and Uniform Quanitzation are analogous. But Quantization has more headaches to be surgical. For this reason, they are heavily applied in structured in Pruning (in uniform in Quantization) in practical settings. AutoML solutions such as RL and NAS can be utilized but the number of hyper-parameters increases exponentially.

In general, Model Compression techniques can be seen in two broad categories. The methods in the first category, such as Pruning, Quantization and Tensor Decomposition, transform a trained model into a smaller or optimized version of itself. The methods in the second category try to create a new but smaller model from scratch. Knowledge distillation can be seen as creating a model from scratch. Any other design choices that can reduce model size can be categorized in the second category.

Most compression methods are vision native, they are made for computer vision applications especially CNN based architectures. That is most likely because vision data is abundant, to make inference at edge devices where the camera resides, or to take advantage of compression methods that remove structures at a time. Its only recently, with the development of Large Language Models, that the methods are being adapted for language models.

5.1   Pruning

The most important gap common in all the Pruning methods is that it is hard to compare different variants due to lack of benchmark metric. The only benchmark effort is Shrinkbench [9], a comparison framework Pruning based compression procedures.

There is a critical difference between unstructured and structured Pruning. Unstructured pruning, is implemented by making individual parameters set to be zero. This makes unstructured pruning almost surgical and more accurate in identifying what to remove. But this implementation doesn't actually reduce the computation time since the GPU will do the operation anyway. On the other hand, structured pruning will remove a complete layer or a channel or a filter. And then the rest of the connections will be connected afterwards. This increases efficiency both pruning time and implementation time. But this too has its own consequences as it is not surgical. The layer or channel to be removed might still have important weights that are needed for inference.

Another common limitation, which can be caused by the lack of a common benchmark, is that they are architecture dependent. Almost all of them involve at least some amount of fine-tuning or retraining which requires having original data to train network is trained on which in some cases might not be available.

Considering randomly dropping weights or magnitude based pruning, it is justified to say that Pruning is the fastest.

5.2   Knowledge Distillation

Knowledge Distillation methods actually construct a brand new smaller model that tries to mimic the bigger model. This means training a new model from scratch which will take as much time as the training time for the teacher. The loss have to be a softmax loss function whose output is a probability distribution. They doesn't give a bigger size reduction. Some might even need a teacher assistant to catch up to the teacher [56].

In Knowledge Distillation (KD), the added term, the distillation loss which is seen above Fig. 4, does serve as a regularize [72], but the exact part of Dark Knowledge the student is taking advantage of is still being studied [89,92].

5.3   Quantization

Quantization methods make weights discrete. They might also damage the precision of important weights. There are ways to bypass that, dynamic, Asymmetric Quantization or Quantization Aware Training), but they come at the expense of computation which is what compression was needed for in the first place (Table 4).

Table 4. Summary of model compression methods.

Method	Description	Remark
Pruning	Removing parameters by setting them to zero	The oldest, fastest and one with the biggest compression rate
Knowledge Distillation	Train a new smaller model with the predictions the bigger model	Most versatile and model agnostic but works with only certain types of loss functions
Quantization	Reduce the amount of bits required to represent the parameters	Work well with pruning, effective to reduce memory size as well as computation
Other methods	Methods that reduce model size with techniques other than the above three.	Efficient architecture designs, inspired by file compression methods, or matrix decomposition based methods

6   Factors Affecting Choice of Methods

There is no size fits all method. One has to find the right one for the task at hand. These are the factors that can be cons

- **Trade-off:** the paradigms discussed above introduce trade-offs that can influence what the choice of a compression method.
- **Area of application.** How tolerant the task at hand is can affect the choice of a compression method in relation to alignment, accuracy, etc.
- **Type of data (Architecture)** Computer vision and natural language related tasks can require architectures that suite their purpose which in-turn affect the choice of compression strategy. For example structured Pruning can effectively remove channels and filters from CNNs on the other hand there are real world cases where large language models are effectively compressed with Knowledge Distillation. Classical methods can have comparable performance as Neural Networks.
- **Expertise.** Some of the compression methods require expertise to be implemented and require high level of sophistication to be carried out effectively.

7   Open Research Problems

There are numerous open issues in Model Compression that can be formulated as valid research questions. They are presented in this section according to the classification used in the paper.

7.1   Knowledge Distillation (KD)

Knowledge Distillation (KD) is one of the major compression methods. In its framework as can be seen in the Fig. 4, the added term in the loss part is the knowledge that is assumed to be being helpful for the teacher. It does serves as a regularizer [37]. But the performance and even the need of the teacher network itself, especially in response based KD, is being questioned repeatedly [4,10,72,89]. What part of the dark knowledge the student takes advantage of is still an open problem.

There are also understudied variants of KD. An example is Subclass distillation [58] that entail a powerful concept. Especially, its converse, extracting specialists from a bigger model, seems a fruitful direction. Zero shot knowledge distillation methods, as discussed before, use random inputs to the trained model to generate pseudo data to train the small network with. Studying how the result will turn out for a curated input is also a possible direction.

7.2   Hybrid Methods

As described in section three, combining compression methods can be beneficial if the added complexity is not an issue. In general, there could combinations in two ways: combining variants of the same method to take advantage of them and combinations between different compression methods as in [32]. Thus,a study on the combination of variants of the same compression method can be good direction. An example is trying to synchronize unstructured and structured pruning.

Such methods can be possible with Reinforcement Learning (RL) based approach pursue as the algorithms get more faster and advanced. There is also a lack of exploration combining other compression methods. Additionally, a comprehensive survey of this specific area can also be helpful for researchers.

7.3 Model Compression Beyond Size Reduction

Despite efforts to train smaller networks from scratch [22], most Model Compression methods are applied after a big model is trained. Thus, the compression ought to have an effect on other aspects of the model. For example, as pointed out in [16], there are still remaining works that can bridge the concept of a models size (compression) and its Explainability. Some applications of Explainability are mentioned in the pruning section of this writing. But, there are only few works, save for [13], that even acknowledge the existence of a bridge between them. Thus, a formalized future work in this direction can be fruitful.

Basically, one can raise many components of the network and ask how compression impacts it. Presented in section four are only a limited number of them because there is still much work to be done in the area. Again, a comprehensive survey on the effect of Model Compression beyond size reduction can be extremely helpful to build Model Compression without ramifications and beyond.

7.4 Miscellaneous

Some model compression methods are developed and are experimented for a specific types of architectures. These makes them limited in applications. In general RL based approaches will be suitable in the future to adapt compression techniques to the given model.

There is little innovation in methods other than pruning, quantization and knowledge distillation. Design choices can make a considerable change [39, 40, 75, 90]. Since the aim problem of model compression is simple and intuitive, any model size reduction method can be called a model compression technique as long as it performs well.

The idea of ensembles have been in use and in classical ML world. It is about using multiple machine learning models for a single task simultaneously. It increases accuracy by taking advantage of the performance of individual models. The concept have been far from being even mentioned in the context of neural networks as the complexity is overwhelming even to thing about. But with parallel advances in model compression and hardware, it seems it will be within the reach of industry leaders or whoever has the access and motive to try. Since that has most likely never been explored, it is worth the shot. Hardware issues, thought they are not discussed in this survey, are highly related with compression and optimization.

8 Conclusion

A brief review of Model Compression techniques in Deep Learning with their challenges, and opportunities has been presented. It started by defining Model

Compression and the challenges it will introduce. Then thirty years of work on Pruning, a number of works on Knowledge Distillation and Quantization are synthesized. How each methods is combined with another one is also discussed. It contained a dedicated section intended to magnify the relationship between model compression and the networks behavior. Findings and patterns from each section are presented in a separate section. Actionable future research directions have been put forward to assist interested researchers.

References

1. Aghli, N., Ribeiro, E.: Combining weight pruning and knowledge distillation for CNN compression. In: 2021 IEEE/CVF Conference on Computer Vision and Pattern Recognition Workshops (CVPRW), pp. 3185–3192 (2021)
2. Ashok, A., Rhinehart, N., Beainy, F.N., Kitani, K.M.: N2N learning: network to network compression via policy gradient reinforcement learning. ArXiv abs/1709.06030 (2017)
3. Ashok, A., Rhinehart, N., Beainy, F.N., Kitani, K.M.: N2N learning: network to network compression via policy gradient reinforcement learning. ArXiv abs/1709.06030 (2018)
4. Bang, D., Lee, J., Shim, H.: Distilling from professors: enhancing the knowledge distillation of teachers. Inf. Sci. **576**, 743–755 (2021). https://doi.org/10.1016/j.ins.2021.08.020, https://www.sciencedirect.com/science/article/pii/S0020025521008203
5. Banner, R., Nahshan, Y., Hoffer, E., Soudry, D.: ACIQ: analytical clipping for integer quantization of neural networks. ArXiv abs/1810.05723 (2018)
6. Bengio, Y., et al.: Learning deep architectures for AI. Found. Trends® Mach. Learn. **2**(1), 1–127 (2009)
7. Bernstein, L., Sludds, A., Hamerly, R., Sze, V., Emer, J.S., Englund, D.: Freely scalable and reconfigurable optical hardware for deep learning. Sci. Rep. **11**, 3144 (2020)
8. Bianco, S., Cadene, R., Celona, L., Napoletano, P.: Benchmark analysis of representative deep neural network architectures. IEEE Access **6**, 64270–64277 (2018). https://doi.org/10.1109/ACCESS.2018.2877890
9. Blalock, D.W., Ortiz, J.J.G., Frankle, J., Guttag, J.V.: What is the state of neural network pruning? ArXiv abs/2003.03033 (2020)
10. Boo, Y., Shin, S., Choi, J., Sung, W.: Stochastic precision ensemble: self-knowledge distillation for quantized deep neural networks. In: Proceedings of the AAAI Conference on Artificial Intelligence, vol. 35, pp. 6794–6802 (2021)
11. Bucila, C., Caruana, R., Niculescu-Mizil, A.: Model compression. In: KDD 2006 (2006)
12. Cai, Y., Yao, Z., Dong, Z., Gholami, A., Mahoney, M.W., Keutzer, K.: ZeroQ: a novel zero shot quantization framework. In: 2020 IEEE/CVF Conference on Computer Vision and Pattern Recognition (CVPR), pp. 13166–13175 (2020)
13. Calvi, G.G., Moniri, A., Mahfouz, M., Zhao, Q., Mandic, D.P.: Compression and interpretability of deep neural networks via tucker tensor layer: from first principles to tensor valued back-propagation. arXiv Learning (2019)
14. Chen, L., Chen, Y., Xi, J., Le, X.: Knowledge from the original network: restore a better pruned network with knowledge distillation. Complex Intell. Syst. (2021)

15. Chen, T., et al.: Only train once: a one-shot neural network training and pruning framework. In: Neural Information Processing Systems (2021)
16. Cheng, Y., Wang, D., Zhou, P., Zhang, T.: A survey of model compression and acceleration for deep neural networks. ArXiv abs/1710.09282 (2017)
17. Courbariaux, M., Bengio, Y.: BinaryNet: training deep neural networks with weights and activations constrained to +1 or −1. ArXiv abs/1602.02830 (2016)
18. Courbariaux, M., Bengio, Y., David, J.P.: BinaryConnect: training deep neural networks with binary weights during propagations. In: NIPS (2015)
19. Devlin, J., Chang, M.W., Lee, K., Toutanova, K.: BERT: pre-training of deep bidirectional transformers for language understanding. ArXiv abs/1810.04805 (2019)
20. Ding, X., Wang, Y., Xu, Z., Wang, Z.J., Welch, W.J.: Distilling and transferring knowledge via CGAN-generated samples for image classification and regression. Expert Syst. Appl. **213**, 119060 (2023). https://doi.org/10.1016/j.eswa.2022.119060, https://www.sciencedirect.com/science/article/pii/S0957417422020784
21. Dong, X., Yang, Y.: Network pruning via transformable architecture search. In: NeurIPS (2019)
22. Frankle, J., Carbin, M.: The lottery ticket hypothesis: finding sparse, trainable neural networks. arXiv Learning (2019)
23. Frosst, N., Hinton, G.E.: Distilling a neural network into a soft decision tree. ArXiv abs/1711.09784 (2017)
24. Furlanello, T., Lipton, Z.C., Tschannen, M., Itti, L., Anandkumar, A.: Born again neural networks. In: ICML (2018)
25. Gholami, A., Kim, S., Dong, Z., Yao, Z., Mahoney, M.W., Keutzer, K.: A survey of quantization methods for efficient neural network inference. ArXiv abs/2103.13630 (2022)
26. Gong, Y., Liu, L., Yang, M., Bourdev, L.D.: Compressing deep convolutional networks using vector quantization. ArXiv abs/1412.6115 (2014)
27. Goodfellow, I.J., Shlens, J., Szegedy, C.: Explaining and harnessing adversarial examples. CoRR abs/1412.6572 (2014)
28. Gou, J., Yu, B., Maybank, S.J., Tao, D.: Knowledge distillation: a survey. ArXiv abs/2006.05525 (2021)
29. Guan, Y., et al.: Differentiable feature aggregation search for knowledge distillation. ArXiv abs/2008.00506 (2020)
30. Gupta, M., Aravindan, S., Kalisz, A., Chandrasekhar, V.R., Jie, L.: Learning to prune deep neural networks via reinforcement learning. ArXiv abs/2007.04756 (2020)
31. Gupta, S., Agrawal, A., Gopalakrishnan, K., Narayanan, P.: Deep learning with limited numerical precision. In: International Conference on Machine Learning (2015)
32. Han, S., Mao, H., Dally, W.J.: Deep compression: compressing deep neural network with pruning, trained quantization and Huffman coding. arXiv Computer Vision and Pattern Recognition (2016)
33. Han, S., Pool, J., Tran, J., Dally, W.: Learning both weights and connections for efficient neural network. Adv. Neural Inf. Process. Syst. **28** (2015)
34. Haroush, M., Hubara, I., Hoffer, E., Soudry, D.: The knowledge within: methods for data-free model compression. In: 2020 IEEE/CVF Conference on Computer Vision and Pattern Recognition (CVPR), pp. 8491–8499 (2019)
35. Hassibi, B., Stork, D., Wolff, G.: Optimal brain surgeon and general network pruning. In: IEEE International Conference on Neural Networks, vol. 1, pp. 293–299 (1993). https://doi.org/10.1109/ICNN.1993.298572

36. He, Y., Lin, J., Liu, Z., Wang, H., Li, L.J., Han, S.: AMC: AutoML for model compression and acceleration on mobile devices. In: ECCV (2018)
37. Hinton, G.E., Vinyals, O., Dean, J.: Distilling the knowledge in a neural network. ArXiv abs/1503.02531 (2015)
38. Hornik, K., Stinchcombe, M., White, H.: Multilayer feedforward networks are universal approximators. Neural Netw. 2(5), 359–366 (1989)
39. Howard, A.G., et al.: MobileNets: efficient convolutional neural networks for mobile vision applications. ArXiv abs/1704.04861 (2017)
40. Iandola, F.N., Moskewicz, M.W., Ashraf, K., Han, S., Dally, W.J., Keutzer, K.: SqueezeNet: AlexNet-level accuracy with 50x fewer parameters and <1mb model size. ArXiv abs/1602.07360 (2016)
41. Jacob, B., et al.: Quantization and training of neural networks for efficient integer-arithmetic-only inference. In: 2018 IEEE/CVF Conference on Computer Vision and Pattern Recognition, pp. 2704–2713 (2018)
42. Joseph, V., et al.: Going beyond classification accuracy metrics in model compression (2020)
43. Kim, J., youn Park, C., Jung, H.J., Choe, Y.: Differentiable pruning method for neural networks. ArXiv abs/1904.10921 (2019)
44. Kim, J., Bhalgat, Y., Lee, J., Patel, C., Kwak, N.: QKD: quantization-aware knowledge distillation. arXiv preprint arXiv:1911.12491 (2019)
45. Kim, Y., Rush, A.M.: Sequence-level knowledge distillation. In: Conference on Empirical Methods in Natural Language Processing (2016)
46. Kossaifi, J., Lipton, Z.C., Khanna, A., Furlanello, T., Anandkumar, A.: Tensor regression networks. ArXiv abs/1707.08308 (2020)
47. Krizhevsky, A., Sutskever, I., Hinton, G.E.: ImageNet classification with deep convolutional neural networks. Commun. ACM 60, 84–90 (2012)
48. LeCun, Y., Denker, J.S., Solla, S.A.: Optimal brain damage. In: NIPS (1989)
49. Li, L., Lin, Y., Ren, S., Li, P., Zhou, J., Sun, X.: Dynamic knowledge distillation for pre-trained language models. ArXiv abs/2109.11295 (2021)
50. Li, Z., et al.: Train large, then compress: rethinking model size for efficient training and inference of transformers. ArXiv abs/2002.11794 (2020)
51. Liu, X., Wang, X., Matwin, S.: Improving the interpretability of deep neural networks with knowledge distillation. In: 2018 IEEE International Conference on Data Mining Workshops (ICDMW), pp. 905–912 (2018)
52. Liu, Y., Zhang, W., Wang, J., Wang, J.: Data-free knowledge transfer: a survey. ArXiv abs/2112.15278 (2021)
53. Lopes, R.G., Fenu, S., Starner, T.: Data-free knowledge distillation for deep neural networks. ArXiv abs/1710.07535 (2017)
54. Lopez-Paz, D., Bottou, L., Schölkopf, B., Vapnik, V.N.: Unifying distillation and privileged information. CoRR abs/1511.03643 (2015)
55. Malach, E., Yehudai, G., Shalev-Shwartz, S., Shamir, O.: Proving the lottery ticket hypothesis: pruning is all you need. In: ICML (2020)
56. Mirzadeh, S.I., Farajtabar, M., Li, A., Levine, N., Matsukawa, A., Ghasemzadeh, H.: Improved knowledge distillation via teacher assistant. In: AAAI (2020)
57. Mozer, M.C., Smolensky, P.: Skeletonization: a technique for trimming the fat from a network via relevance assessment. In: NIPS (1988)
58. Müller, R., Kornblith, S., Hinton, G.E.: Subclass distillation. ArXiv abs/2002.03936 (2020)
59. Nayak, G.K., Mopuri, K.R., Shaj, V., Babu, R.V., Chakraborty, A.: Zero-shot knowledge distillation in deep networks. ArXiv abs/1905.08114 (2019)

60. Novikov, A., Podoprikhin, D., Osokin, A., Vetrov, D.P.: Tensorizing neural networks. In: NIPS (2015)

61. Olah, C.: Mechanistic interpretability, variables, and the importance of interpretable bases (2022). https://transformer-circuits.pub/2022/mech-interp-essay/index.html. Accessed 14 Dec 2022

62. Papernot, N., Mcdaniel, P., Wu, X., Jha, S., Swami, A.: Distillation as a defense to adversarial perturbations against deep neural networks. In: 2016 IEEE Symposium on Security and Privacy (SP), pp. 582–597 (2015)

63. Park, G., Yang, J.Y., Hwang, S.J., Yang, E.: Attribution preservation in network compression for reliable network interpretation. Adv. Neural. Inf. Process. Syst. **33**, 5093–5104 (2020)

64. Park, J., No, A.: Prune your model before distill it. In: Avidan, S., Brostow, G., Cissé, M., Farinella, G.M., Hassner, T. (eds.) ECCV 2022. LNCS, vol. 13671, pp. 120–136. Springer, Cham (2021). https://doi.org/10.1007/978-3-031-20083-0_8

65. Park, W., Kim, D., Lu, Y., Cho, M.: Relational knowledge distillation. In: 2019 IEEE/CVF Conference on Computer Vision and Pattern Recognition (CVPR), pp. 3962–3971 (2019)

66. Patterson, D., et al.: Carbon emissions and large neural network training. ArXiv abs/2104.10350 (2021)

67. Polino, A., Pascanu, R., Alistarh, D.: Model compression via distillation and quantization. arXiv preprint arXiv:1802.05668 (2018)

68. Ramanujan, V., Wortsman, M., Kembhavi, A., Farhadi, A., Rastegari, M.: What's hidden in a randomly weighted neural network? In: 2020 IEEE/CVF Conference on Computer Vision and Pattern Recognition (CVPR), pp. 11890–11899 (2020)

69. Rastegari, M., Ordonez, V., Redmon, J., Farhadi, A.: XNOR-Net: ImageNet classification using binary convolutional neural networks. In: Leibe, B., Matas, J., Sebe, N., Welling, M. (eds.) ECCV 2016. LNCS, vol. 9908, pp. 525–542. Springer, Cham (2016). https://doi.org/10.1007/978-3-319-46493-0_32

70. Reed, R.: Pruning algorithms-a survey. IEEE Trans. Neural Netw. **4**(5), 740–747 (1993). https://doi.org/10.1109/72.248452

71. Romero, A., Ballas, N., Kahou, S.E., Chassang, A., Gatta, C., Bengio, Y.: FitNets: hints for thin deep nets. CoRR abs/1412.6550 (2015)

72. Sau, B.B., Balasubramanian, V.N.: Deep model compression: distilling knowledge from noisy teachers. arXiv preprint arXiv:1610.09650 (2016)

73. Simonyan, K., Zisserman, A.: Very deep convolutional networks for large-scale image recognition. CoRR abs/1409.1556 (2015)

74. Stoychev, S., Gunes, H.: The effect of model compression on fairness in facial expression recognition. ArXiv abs/2201.01709 (2022)

75. Szegedy, C., et al.: Going deeper with convolutions. In: 2015 IEEE Conference on Computer Vision and Pattern Recognition (CVPR), pp. 1–9 (2015)

76. Tang, J., Liu, M., Jiang, N., Cai, H., Yu, W., Zhou, J.: Data-free network pruning for model compression. In: 2021 IEEE International Symposium on Circuits and Systems (ISCAS), pp. 1–5 (2021). https://doi.org/10.1109/ISCAS51556.2021.9401109

77. Tian, Y., Krishnan, D., Isola, P.: Contrastive representation distillation. ArXiv abs/1910.10699 (2020)

78. Van Baalen, M., et al.: Bayesian bits: unifying quantization and pruning. Adv. Neural. Inf. Process. Syst. **33**, 5741–5752 (2020)

79. Vaswani, A., et al.: Attention is all you need. ArXiv abs/1706.03762 (2017)

80. Wang, K., Liu, Z., Lin, Y., Lin, J., Han, S.: HAQ: hardware-aware automated quantization with mixed precision. In: 2019 IEEE/CVF Conference on Computer Vision and Pattern Recognition (CVPR), pp. 8604–8612 (2018)

81. Wang, Y., et al.: Against membership inference attack: pruning is all you need. In: International Joint Conference on Artificial Intelligence (2020)

82. Wang, Y., Lu, Y., Blankevoort, T.: Differentiable joint pruning and quantization for hardware efficiency. ArXiv abs/2007.10463 (2020)

83. Wang, Y., Zhang, X., Hu, X., Zhang, B., Su, H.: Dynamic network pruning with interpretable layerwise channel selection. In: AAAI (2020)

84. Wang, Y., et al.: Pruning from scratch. In: AAAI (2020)

85. Wiedemann, S., et al.: DeepCABAC: a universal compression algorithm for deep neural networks. IEEE J. Sel. Top. Signal Process. **14**, 700–714 (2020)

86. Yang, Z., et al.: CARS: continuous evolution for efficient neural architecture search. In: 2020 IEEE/CVF Conference on Computer Vision and Pattern Recognition (CVPR), pp. 1826–1835 (2020)

87. Yeom, S.K., Seegerer, P., Lapuschkin, S., Wiedemann, S., Müller, K.R., Samek, W.: Pruning by explaining: a novel criterion for deep neural network pruning. ArXiv abs/1912.08881 (2021)

88. Yim, J., Joo, D., Bae, J.H., Kim, J.: A gift from knowledge distillation: fast optimization, network minimization and transfer learning. In: 2017 IEEE Conference on Computer Vision and Pattern Recognition (CVPR), pp. 7130–7138 (2017)

89. Yuan, L., Tay, F.E., Li, G., Wang, T., Feng, J.: Revisiting knowledge distillation via label smoothing regularization. In: Proceedings of the IEEE/CVF Conference on Computer Vision and Pattern Recognition, pp. 3903–3911 (2020)

90. Zhai, S., Cheng, Y., Zhang, Z., Lu, W.: Doubly convolutional neural networks. In: NIPS (2016)

91. Zhang, Z., Shao, W., Gu, J., Wang, X., Ping, L.: Differentiable dynamic quantization with mixed precision and adaptive resolution. ArXiv abs/2106.02295 (2021)

92. Zhao, B., Cui, Q., Song, R., Qiu, Y., Liang, J.: Decoupled knowledge distillation. In: 2022 IEEE/CVF Conference on Computer Vision and Pattern Recognition (CVPR), pp. 11943–11952 (2022)

93. Zhao, H., Sun, X., Dong, J., Chen, C., Dong, Z.: Highlight every step: knowledge distillation via collaborative teaching. IEEE Trans. Cybern. **52**, 2070–2081 (2019)

94. Zhao, Y., Shumailov, I., Mullins, R.D., Anderson, R.: To compress or not to compress: understanding the interactions between adversarial attacks and neural network compression. ArXiv abs/1810.00208 (2018)

Convolution Filter Equivariance/Invariance in Convolutional Neural Networks: A Survey

Sinshaw Bekele Habte[1]([⊠]) [iD], Achim Ibenthal[2] [iD], Ephrem Tehsale Bekele[1] [iD],
and Taye Girma Debelee[3,4] [iD]

[1] Addis Ababa University, Addis Ababa, Ethiopia
sinshawb@gmail.com
[2] HAWK University of Applied Sciences and Arts, Göttingen, Germany
achim.ibenthal@hawk.de
[3] Ethiopian Artificial Intelligence Institute, Addis Ababa, Ethiopia
[4] Addis Ababa Science and Technology University, Addis Ababa, Ethiopia

Abstract. Models parameterized by Convolutional Neural Networks (CNNs), reportedly, have garnered a commanding position in learning based multidimensional signal processing. This feat is achieved to a large extent through the translation equivariance property of the convolutional filters employed. While popular, the required optimum level of model parameters, the limited availability of signal datasets, robustness of the model to input signal transformations, and generalization to out of distribution signal sets are some of the challenges of CNN models. The incorporation of equivariance or consistency to symmetry transformations in which invariance is a special case, have been suggested to not only alleviate these challenges but also bring about model interpretability. This work presents a systematic survey of the equivariant convolutional filter design for convolutional neural networks in image processing applications with the aim of bringing forth design methods in terms of group theory, discrete Fourier transform, discrete cosine transform, and wavelet transform. The theoretical foundations for translation, rotation, scale and affine equivariance under nonlinear transform, their efficient implementations especially in natural image processing applications has been thoroughly discussed.

Keywords: CNN · convolutional filter · invariance · equivariance · symmetry transformation

1 Introduction

Neural network based modeling of the complex and often nonlinear internal structure of signals can be approached differently which includes Boltzmann

Supported by DAAD and HAWK.

machines (BMs) [19], Spiking Neural Networks (SNNs) [18], and Convolutional Neural Networks (CNNs). The use of convolutional filtering in CNNs which ensures weight sharing leading to sparsity of connectivity and shift equivariance coupled with continued development has made CNNs popular model of choice.

Convolutional Neural Networks are designed to be able to work specially with input signals having a grid-like sampling structure with spatial dependencies such as image signals. While image based applications are the main focus, CNNs can also be applied for processing different time-domain or spatio-temporal data. The earliest form of CNN was the neocognitron [16] inspired by the work done on cat's visual cortex [20]. It then obtained its modern structure with the development of the LeNet-5 [26] model. The use of CNNs was further popularized by the work of Alex Krizhevsky et al. AlexNet [25] coupled with further developments in the processing power of computers.

In its current form, each layer of a CNN model comprises convolutional, activation and downsampling layers forming its key parts. The input signal to the CNN is convolved with filters parameterized by adaptable weights in the convolutional layer. Features are extracted as filters are made to move across the signal according to a stride value. Considering the lth layer of a CNN model, the extracted features for the input signal samples $\mathbf{X} \in \mathbb{R}^{N \times N}$ and convolution filter weight $\mathbf{w} \in \mathbb{R}^{K \times K}$ will be

$$z_{u,v}^{(l)} = \sum_{i=-K/2}^{K/2} \sum_{j=-K/2}^{K/2} w_{i,j}^{(l)} x_{i+u,j+v}^{(l)} + b^{(l)}. \tag{1}$$

where b's are bias parameters. Additional different sized filters can be incorporated to obtain a varied set of features. The weight parameters are learnt through training by minimizing a loss function and updating the weights using back-propagation algorithm. Here, if the weight parameters are to converge to the value of $\mathbf{X}$, they will form a matched filter [41].

A representation of the signal is then obtained by nonlinear mapping by the activation layer. The activations are obtained as:

$$a_{i,j}^{(l)} = \sigma \left(z_{i,j}^{(l)} \right) \tag{2}$$

of which the Rectified Linear Unit (ReLU), Eq. 3, is the most commonly used nonlinear mapping [25]

$$\sigma(x) = \max(x, 0). \tag{3}$$

The dimensionality of the learned representation can then be reduced by the downsampling (pooling) layer. Pooling has been utilized for dimensionality reduction and construct hierarchy in representations since first suggested by Hubel and Wiesels' work [20]. It has also been part of classical object detection algorithms of which SIFT (Scale-Invariant Features) [29] and HOG (Histogram of Oriented Gradients) [13] are an example. Pooling can performed on the local region of the feature maps via operations such as max pooling [47] Eq. 4 and average pooling [26] Eq. 5:

$$r_{i,j} = \max_{(m,n) \in \mathbf{r}_{i,j}} a_{m,n} \quad \text{(Max Pooling)} \tag{4}$$

$$r_{i,j} = \frac{1}{|\mathbf{r}_{i,j}|} \sum_{(m,n) \in \mathbf{r}_{i,j}} a_{m,n} \quad \text{(Average Pooling)}. \tag{5}$$

On the other hand, stochastic pooling [48] introduces randomness into the pooling operation intended at preventing model overfitting:

$$r_{i,j} = \sum_{(m,n) \in \mathbf{r}_{i,j}} p_{m,n} a_{m,n} \quad \text{with} \quad p_{m,n} = \frac{a_{m,n}}{\sum_{(m,n) \in \mathbf{r}_{i,j}} a_{m,n}} \tag{6}$$

where $p_{m,n}$ is the probability assigned to each feature point. Here, beyond its dimensionality reduction property, pooling can help make the convolution filter receptive field expand and further in learning representations that are invariant under small local variations on input samples. Moreover, pooling can also be carried out over the whole feature map using global pooling and construct the ultimate feature vector representation of the input signal [22] in CNN based classifiers.

The filter weight sharing characteristics of the convolutional layer leads the CNN models being equivariant to shift transformation. That is any shift transformation on the input signal produces an equivalent shift in the learned representation. Furthermore, Chris Olah et al. [35] pointed out that a layer by layer observation of CNN learned features show some level of rotation, reflection and scale equivariance among others. This has been acknowledged as the contributing factor to the success of CNN models in applications such as object detection and classification. But in general, CNN models as a whole are not invariant or equivariant under geometric transformations including shift, rotation, reflection, and scaling in the input signal.

The incorporation of inductive biases in terms of equivariance to geometric transformations on the input signal by taking advantage of symmetry on the network design brings about the reduction of sample complexity [14]. This is specially important in applications where training signal datasets are limited. Furthermore higher level of weight sharing can be achieved in the convolutional layer. The equivariant design ensures that no loss of feature information occurs when the input sample is geometrically transformed leading to an increased expressivity of the learned representation and thereby improving generalization on unseen signal samples.

The remaining part of the paper is arranged as follows, review and survey works related to this survey are summarized in Sect. 2 illustrating the merits and limitations of their approach. In Sect. 3, the strategy followed for the literature survey is outlined. In Sect. 4, a theoretical background on symmetry transformation groups, invariance and equivariance is covered. In Sect. 5, equivariant

CNN designs for different geometric transforms are discussed. The application in Sect. 6, summary of the work in Sect. 7 and finally Sect. 8 presenting concluding remarks.

2   Related Work

A general survey of CNNs was done by Li et al. [28] focusing on different CNN model designs their analysis. While comprehensive, the significance of symmetric structures on the design of CNNs was not elaborated. In contrast, Patrick et al. [36] surveyed capsule network designs which take the feature vectors at the output of CNNs. The likelihood that the feature encoded by the capsule is present and a group of vector values known as instantiation parameters make up the output of the capsule network. It is an alternative design to CNNs targeting equivariance but the survey focuses on only one design direction. Table 1 presents recent survey work with their merit and limitations.

Table 1. Survey Work on Equivariant CNNs.

Publication	Merit	Limitation
Li et al. 2021 [28]	- Coverage of different convolutional designs and their application	- Limited discussion on equivariant designs or their application - survey strategy not clearly presented
Patrick et al. 2019 [36]	- Capsule network design which provides affine equivariance is discussed - design structure, implementation and application are throughly discussed	- Only one design method was surveyed - Survey strategy not clearly presented

In this work we attempt to present a survey of equivariant CNN designs going through each geometric transform how it can be handled. It is an attempt at setting the ground work for a developing interpretable models based on CNNs.

3   Method

This survey is targeted at answering a) Are the equivariant CNN design methods rooted with strong theoretical foundation? b) Can they be implemented with reasonable level of complexity? and c) Do they also have utility on segmentation, object detection and classification tasks?

The following **databases** were used as literature source: (i) ScienceDirect, (ii) IEEE Xplore, (iii) Google Scholar, (iv) MDPI, and (v) PubMed. The search was carried out using these **keywords** including ("Convolution Filter") AND ("Symmetry transform") AND ("Equivariance") AND ("Invariance") AND ("Convolutional Neural Network"). Then, the search results were refined based on suitability criteria listed under Table 2 to select the final paper list for the survey. All of which is combined and carried out according to the steps outlined in Algorithm 1.

Table 2. Criteria for Literature selection.

Inclusion Criteria (InCr)	Exclusion Criteria (ExCr)
InCr1: Paper published within the last five years.	ExCr1: Publication on neural networks other than CNNs.
InCr2: Study on Invariant/Equivariant CNNs.	ExCr2: Duplicate publication on other different databases.
InCr3: Study on image based applications.	ExCr3: Publication with low level of citation by other publications.
InCr4: Study on Invariant/Equivariant deep generative models.	ExCr4: Thesis and Dissertation Papers.
	ExCr5: Studies published earlier than 2017

Algorithm 1. Paper selection searched from publication databases.

---

procedure TOPIC: CONVOLUTION FILTER EQUIVARIANCE/INVARIANCE IN CNNS( )
    $SearchDatabases \leftarrow databases$
    $SearchYear \leftarrow 2017 - 2022$ ▷ Selected older papers to establish background
    $i \leftarrow 1$ ▷ Initialize Count
    $N \leftarrow 5$ ▷ N No. Databases used
    while $N \neq 0$ **do**
        $Keyword \leftarrow keywords$
        if $SearchLink \in SearchDatabases$ And $Year \in SearchYear$ **then**
            $Search \leftarrow Keyword$
        end if
    end while
    if $NumberofPapers \geq 0$ **then**
        $TryInclusionCriteria \leftarrow InCr1, InCr2, InCr3, InCr4$
        $TryExclusionCriteria \leftarrow ExCr1, ExCr2, ExCr3, ExCr4, ExCr5$
    end if
end procedure

---

4   Symmetry Transformations and Equivariance

Symmetry transformation implies the geometric properties of the object under the transform remain unchanged, Fig. 1 showing an example. The modes of transformation might be isometrics such as translation, rotation, and reflection or scaling etc. Hence, if the object of interest is unchanged under rotation it is said to have rotational symmetry. This desirable characteristics can be incorporated into the representation learning of the input signal samples with CNNs via symmetric constrained design of the network. This can be accomplished leveraging group and representation theory as a framework.

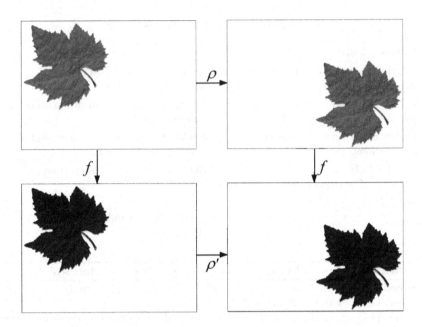

Fig. 1. Shift-Equivariance in CNNs [21].

4.1   Group Theory

Group theory provides us with a mathematical formalism which enables us to work with symmetries. Here, the object of interest is how to integrate symmetry in to the design of CNNs fostering a capability to deal with geometric transformations on the input signal.

Definition 1. *Group: a set consisting of transformations* $\mathcal{T}$ *along with a binary operation (group product ·)from* $\mathcal{T} \times \mathcal{T} \rightarrow \mathcal{T}$ *) satisfying associativity and closure and having identity and inverse elements. Hence for all* $t_1, t_2, t_3 \in \mathcal{T}$:

- **Closure:** $\forall t_1, t_2 \in \mathcal{T}$ we have $t_1 \cdot t_2 \in \mathcal{T}$ - a symmetry transformation carried out after another symmetry transformation results in a symmetry transformation, in other words, the binary operation is performed without leaving the group.
- **Associativity:** for transforms $r, s, t \in \mathcal{T}$

$$r \cdot (s \cdot t) = (r \cdot s) \cdot t. \tag{7}$$

- **Identity:** the existence of an identity element e for which

$$t \cdot e = t = e \cdot t. \tag{8}$$

- **Inverse:** for transform $t \in \mathcal{T}$, an inverse transform $t^{-1} \in \mathcal{T}$ exists such that

$$t \cdot t^{-1} = t^{-1} \cdot t = e. \tag{9}$$

A group is not generally commutative but commutative groups are called Abelian group. Moreover, the group elements are capable of acting on elements of our input sample space $\mathcal{X}$ and geometrically transform them $(\mathcal{T} \times \mathcal{X} \rightarrow \mathcal{X})$ which is a mapping of them back to the space $\mathcal{X}$.

Definition 2. Group Representation: *is the representation ρ of a group* **G** *through the use of invertible matrices and thereby realizing group actions by matrix multiplication. Hence, $\rho(x)$ is a linear transformation of some vector* $\mathbf{x} \in \mathcal{X}$ *parameterized by the group elements and an $n \times n$ matrix under which the group structure is respected:*

$$\rho(t_1 \cdot t_2)[\mathbf{x}] = \rho(t_1) \circ \rho(t_2)[\mathbf{x}] \tag{10}$$

Here, the representation is not considered to be unique, meaning the same symmetry group may have different representations. Furthermore, through left regular representation, the symmetry transformation of functions can be realized via the transformation of their domain through the action of the group elements:

$$[\mathcal{T}_g f][x] = [f \circ g^{-1}][x] = f(g^{-1}x) \tag{11}$$

In this work, we will consider the following major transform groups:

– Translation Group $(\mathbb{R}^2, +)$ is a group of all the possible translations in $\mathbb{R}^2$ as illustrated in Fig. 2. The translation group action represented as vector addition that is $\forall \mathbf{x}, \mathbf{x}' \in \mathbb{R}^2$ for translations $t, t^{-1}, t' \in \mathcal{T}$

$$t' \cdot t = (\mathbf{x}' + \mathbf{x}) \qquad t^{-1} = (-\mathbf{x}). \tag{12}$$

– Rotation Group SO(2) (2D Special Orthogonal group) and translation group form a roto-translation group SE(2) the 2D Special Euclidean motion group. This group is represented as vector addition and multiplication by rotation matrix $\mathbf{R}_\theta$:

$$g = (\mathbf{x}, \mathbf{R}) \qquad \mathbf{G} = \begin{bmatrix} \cos\theta & -\sin\theta & x \\ \sin\theta & \cos\theta & y \\ 0 & 0 & 1 \end{bmatrix} = \begin{pmatrix} \mathbf{R}_\theta & \mathbf{x} \\ \mathbf{0}^T & 1 \end{pmatrix}. \tag{13}$$

The group **p4m** which includes discrete shifts, 90^0 rotations and horizontal/vertical mirroring forming a special case.

– Scale-translation Group consists of translation by $\mathbf{x}$ in $\mathbb{R}^2$ and scale factors s in $\mathbb{R}^+$ and represented as:

$$g = (\mathbf{x}, s) \qquad \mathbf{G} = \begin{bmatrix} \mathbf{I}_s & \mathbf{x} \\ \mathbf{0}^T & 1 \end{bmatrix}. \tag{14}$$

– Affine Groups $(\mathbf{G} = \mathbb{R}^2 \rtimes \mathbf{H})$: transformation groups composed of translation in $\mathbb{R}^2$ and transformation, such as rotation, $\mathbf{H}$ with action on $\mathbb{R}^2$.
All the symmetry transformation groups mentioned above, translation, roto-translation, reflection, scale-translation groups are examples of affine transformation groups.

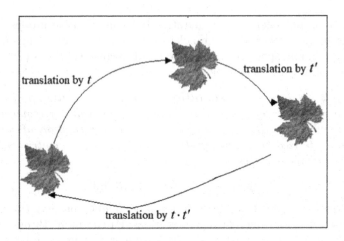

Fig. 2. Translation group action.

4.2 Equivariance

The insensitivity to geometric transformation in general is termed as equivariance. Mathematically for a feature extractor f from an input x and transforms $\mathcal{T}, \mathcal{T}'$ if

$$f[\mathcal{T}(x)] = \mathcal{T}'[f(x)], \tag{15}$$

then, the feature extraction is equivariant to the geometric transform $\mathcal{T}$. This means if the network is equivariant, then for a geometric transformation of the input the output transforms predictably. A more strict condition for which a symmetry transform of the input will not produce any change on the extracted feature

$$f[\mathcal{T}(x)] = [f(x)], \tag{16}$$

normally known as invariance as seen in Fig. 3. Equivariance can also be defined in terms of group action. That is for a symmetry group G whose actions are ρ on $\mathbb{R}^n$ and ρ' on $\mathbb{R}^m$, then

$$f[\rho(g)(x)] = \rho'(g)f(x), \tag{17}$$

implying that equivariant representation commutes with group action. Furthermore, since compositions of a group action are also a group, compositions of equivariant functions are also equivariant. Considering that neural networks are compositions of linear and nonlinear functions, if the linear and also activation layers are equivariant, in consequence, the neural network model will be equivariant to transformations.

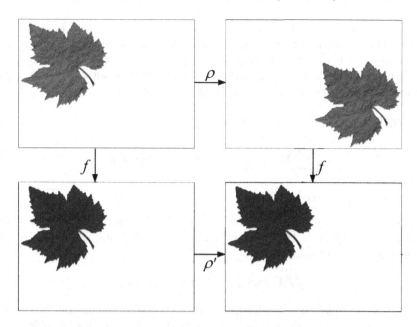

Fig. 3. Shift-Invariance in CNNs.

5   Equivariant Convolutional Neural Networks

Based on what is reported by Cohen and Welling [12], a generalized framework and design of equivariant CNNs based on group theory was reported [11,15, 24]. This has opened up the avenue for the utility of incorporating symmetric structure in CNN design. The equivariance design can be done through group transformation [4] or transform domain actions [45]. In this section we present such CNN designs aimed at overcoming various geometric transform variances.

Equivariance in CNNs can be achieved through:

1. Data augmentation: involves providing enough transformed copies of the input signal samples to the network to learn the desired transformation equivariance. While useful in capturing equivariance to global transformations, results in redundant feature maps in which most of the convolution filters are rotated copies each other and hence inefficient [25]. The invariant representation learning through this method is inefficient in computation resource utilization with no guarantee of transformation invariance and geometric consistency [3].
2. Loss function equivariant constraint: similar to data augmentation method equivariance representation learning through loss function constraint can not guarantee invariance [30].
3. Equivariant architecture: integrating symmetry structure in the network design brings guaranteed equivariance to both local and global transformation of the input sample and hence ensuring geometric information is preserved. What is more, it results in sample and parameter efficiency [12].

In CNNs both correlation and convolution operations are used in the forward path and back-propagation step both generically termed convolution operations. Here, starting with Eq. 1 modifying it with parameter change for convenience in which an image input $\mathbf{I} \in \mathcal{I}$ is convolved with convolution filter $\mathbf{w}$ and dropping the bias term, we can show that a shift in the input image

$$
\begin{aligned}
[[\mathcal{T}_t \mathbf{I}] * \mathbf{w}](\mathbf{x}) &= \sum_{\mathbf{x} \in \mathbb{R}^2} \mathbf{I}(\mathbf{x} - t)\mathbf{w}(\mathbf{x} - \beta) \\
&= \sum_{\mathbf{x} \in \mathbb{R}^2} \mathbf{I}(\mathbf{x})\mathbf{w}(\mathbf{x} - (\beta + t)) \quad \text{by replacing} \quad \mathbf{x} \to \mathbf{x} + t \quad (18) \\
&= \mathcal{T}_t[\mathbf{I} * \mathbf{w}](\mathbf{x})
\end{aligned}
$$

produces a corresponding shift in the output. This brings forth the implicit shift equivariant property of the convolutional layer. Going through with the same thought process and using Eq. 11, we can show that

$$
[[\mathcal{T}_g \mathbf{I}] * \mathbf{w}](\mathbf{x}) = \mathcal{T}_g[\mathbf{I} * \mathcal{T}_{g^{-1}} \mathbf{w}](\mathbf{x}). \quad (19)
$$

Hence, CNNs while not equivariant to other groups of symmetries but can be made to exploit those symmetries. As can be deduced from Eq. 19, if furnished with transformed copies of the same filter, CNNs can be made equivariant to other groups of symmetries on the sampling grid of the input signal.

5.1   Translation Equivariance

CNNs are made up of convolutional layers which are shift equivariant due to weight sharing as is verified in Eq. 18. However, convolutional layers are not necessarily translation equivariant rather shift equivariant because shift equivariance is a discrete symmetry while translation equivariance is a continuous symmetry [31].

Shift variance problem in CNNs arises from the use of strided convolutions and downsampling layers such as maxpooling. This is because the downsampling is done without due consideration for Nyquist theorem. The shift variance problem has been investigated by providing a shifted version of a sample signal and measuring the cosine similarity [3,9].

An initial concept put forward is to make the convolutional filter full, F-conv [23], that is every filter element will come in contact with every pixel by the way of increased padding. This design reduces the sensitivity of the network to image pixel location information. Then, different solutions have been suggested for the shift variance issue mostly based on anti-aliasing filter mechanisms. One of the suggested methods involves applying lowpass filtering before downsampling and termed as blurpooling [49]. Similarly, in pyramidal blurpooling [40] the filter size can be made to be larger at the first downsampling layer and will be decreased gradually toward the latter layers, aimed at enhancing the feature consistency without compromising the performance. This is due to the fact that severe filtering will result in the loss of feature information. Another method reported is the use of adaptive polyphase downsampling which while based on the same direction it has increased implementation complexity [6]. Transform methods are also suggested to provide anti-aliased downsampling using wavelet methods [27]. This method has been reported to also provide noise robustness in addition to performance improvement.

All the proposed methods are shown to consistently provide improved performance regardless of the associated complexity level at a reduced training sample set compared to conventional CNN designs. This has been especially shown in [5] by providing equivariant global pooling layer and no downsampling layers, a translation equivariant CNN was designed and that its test error performance, as number of training dataset increases, has been shown to improve as opposed to conventional designs.

5.2 Rotation, Reflection and Scale Equivariance

The convolutional layer while providing shift-equivariant implicitly, CNN designs are not done with rotation, reflection or scale symmetry in mind. The suggested rotation and scale variance problem while varying the most efficient design is provided by decomposed filter designs [17]. Decomposed filter design, for discrete rotation symmetry [8] provides the least complex design with competitive performance. This design can be also obtained in the transform domain (Fourier and wavelet). It is also reported to present an increased level of weight sharing thereby improving model parameter efficiency. In similar decomposed design concept, scale symmetry can be included in CNN networks [50]. Harmonic structures can also be used to provide rotational symmetry in addition to translation equivariance [44].

Rotation equivariance can be integrated into the convolution filter design based on circular harmonics by using steerable filters [1] of the form

$$W = \sum_j \sum_k w_{ik} \psi_{ii}(x) \tag{20}$$

where $\psi_{jk}(r, \phi) = \tau_j(r)e^{jk\phi}$ is the steerable basis function with τ a radial function and (r, ϕ) denoting polar coordinates of x. The basis function and thereby the convolutional filter can be rotated(steered) by any angle $\theta \in [-\pi, \pi]$ through multiplication with a complex exponential

$$\rho_\theta \psi_{ik} = e^{jk\theta} \psi_{ik}. \tag{21}$$

Then, the use of orientation pooling that is the maximum activation in each orientation at the final stage ensures rotation and cyclic shift equivariance of the overall network.

A similar strategy has been also reported that is based on using steerable filter for scale equivariance [34]. Yet another direction reported to incorporate rotation and scale equivariance is the use of Discrete Cosine transform [42] and Wavelet transform [39].

6   Application

CNN models with symmetry structure are reported to be used in different applications specially in image segmentation and classification tasks. In object detection [7], segmentation [32], microscopy image analysis [10], digital pathology [43], Electrical Impedance Tomography (EIT) imaging [38] which exhibits circular symmetry. Similarly, scale symmetry for land-use classification task [33].

Deep generative models also take advantage of symmetry for better design of autoencoder [37] and generative adversarial network [46] design. Equivariance designs in generative models have shown to aid in model stability, intepretability, and improved generalization over out of distribution samples.

7   Summary

This work has attempted to present a survey of Equivariant convolutional neural network designs as a way of interpretable model development. It has been recently pointed out [2] that a representation z learnt from input signal samples x about a predictive task y should be

- Sufficient: should encode enough information about the predictive task as expressed equivalently in information theoretic term as $I(X;Y) = I(Z;Y)$.
- Minimal: avoid redundancy by arriving at a minimum representation of the input $\arg \min I(X;Z)$.
- Invariant under variations in the input samples, and
- Maximally disentangled such that every dimension of the encoding represents on mode of variation in the input samples or probabilistically $p(z) = \prod_i p(z_i)$.

Hence, equivariant CNN design leads to better disentangled representation learning and thereby to improved predictive task performance and improved generalization.

In this regards, the necessity of anti-aliasing filtering directly or using wavelet based downsampling to ensure shift-equivariance was pointed out. The multiresolution analysis property of wavelets coupled with their noise robustness stands out when applied in downsampling layers for shift-equivariant design.

The rotation, reflection and scale symmetry can be incorporated best by using decomposed filter design which is also Fourier and wavelet transform friendly. Specially Fourier based equivariance design of convolution filters can also be able to best address implementation efficiency.

8   Conclusion

The theoretical background on symmetry transforms and group theory and then the incorporation of equivariance to various geometric transformation in CNN design has been presented in this work. It is observed that while the equivariant convolutional filter design has an associated implementation complexity, the gain in terms of sample complexity reduction and model parameter efficiency makes it worthwhile. Hence the inclusion of symmetry structure specially in deep generative modeling based image processing will be one of the way forward in developing stable, disentangled and interpretable models.

References

1. Learning Steerable Filters for Rotation Equivariant CNNs (2018). https://doi.org/10.1109/CVPR.2018.00095
2. Achille, A., Soatto, S.: Emergence of invariance and disentanglement in deep representations. J. Mach. Learn. Res. **19**(1), 1947–1980 (2018)
3. Azulay, A., Weiss, Y.: Why do deep convolutional networks generalize so poorly to small image transformations? J. Mach. Learn. Res. **20**(184), 1–25 (2019)
4. Bietti, A., Mairal, J.: Group invariance, stability to deformations, and complexity of deep convolutional representations. J. Mach. Learn. Res. **20**(1), 876–924 (2019). https://doi.org/10.5555/3322706.3322731
5. Bulusu, S., Favoni, M., Ipp, A., Müller, D.I., Schuh, D.: Generalization capabilities of translationally equivariant neural networks. Phys. Rev. D **104**, 074504 (2021). https://doi.org/10.1103/PhysRevD.104.074504
6. Chaman, A., Dokmanić, I.: Truly shift-invariant convolutional neural networks. In: 2021 IEEE/CVF Conference on Computer Vision and Pattern Recognition (CVPR), pp. 3772–3782 (2021) ·
7. Cheng, G., Han, J., Zhou, P., Xu, D.: Learning rotation-invariant and fisher discriminative convolutional neural networks for object detection. IEEE Trans. Image Process. **28**, 265–278 (2019)
8. Cheng, X., Qiu, Q., Calderbank, R., Sapiro, G.: RotDCF: decomposition of convolutional filters for rotation-equivariant deep networks. In: International Conference on Learning Representations (ICLR 2019) (2019)
9. Cheoi, K.J., Choi, H., Ko, J.: Empirical remarks on the translational equivariance of convolutional layers. Appl. Sci. (2020)
10. Chidester, B., Zhou, T., Do, M.N., Ma, J.: Rotation equivariant and invariant neural networks for microscopy image analysis. Bioinformatics **35**, i530–i537 (2019)
11. Cohen, T., Geiger, M., Weiler, M.: A general theory of equivariant CNNs on homogeneous spaces. arXiv abs/1811.02017 (2019)
12. Cohen, T., Welling, M.: Group equivariant convolutional networks. In: ICML (2016)
13. Dalal, N., Triggs, B.: Histograms of oriented gradients for human detection. In: IEEE Computer Society Conference on Computer Vision and Pattern Recognition, CVPR 2005, vol. 1, pp. 886–893 (2005). https://doi.org/10.1109/CVPR.2005.177
14. Elesedy, B., Zaidi, S.: Provably strict generalisation benefit for equivariant models. In: Meila, M., Zhang, T. (eds.) Proceedings of the 38th International Conference on Machine Learning, ICML 2021, 18–24 July 2021, Virtual Event. Proceedings of Machine Learning Research, vol. 139, pp. 2959–2969. PMLR (2021)
15. Finzi, M., Stanton, S., Izmailov, P., Wilson, A.G.: Generalizing convolutional neural networks for equivariance to lie groups on arbitrary continuous data. In: ICML (2020)
16. Fukushima, K.: Neocognitron: a self-organizing neural network model for a mechanism of pattern recognition unaffected by shift in position. Biol. Cybern. **36**, 193–202 (1980)

17. Gao, L.M., Lin, G., Zhu, W.: Deformation robust roto-scale-translation equivariant CNNs. arXiv abs/2111.10978 (2021)
18. Ghosh-Dastidar, S., Adeli, H.: Spiking neural networks. Int. J. Neural Syst. **19**(04), 295–308 (2009)
19. Hinton, G.E., Osindero, S., Teh, Y.W.: A fast learning algorithm for deep belief nets. Neural Comput. **18**, 1527–1554 (2006)
20. Hubel, D.H., Wiesel, T.N.: Receptive fields of single neurons in the cat's striate cortex. J. Physiol. **148**, 574–591 (1959)
21. Ibenthal, A., et al.: AI algorithms for crop disease management under small database training conditions. In: International Conference on Climate Resilient Agriculture for Food Security and Sustainability, Hisar, India (2023)
22. Islam, M.A., Kowal, M., Jia, S., Derpanis, K.G., Bruce, N.B.: Global pooling, more than meets the eye: position information is encoded channel-wise in CNNs. In: 2021 IEEE/CVF International Conference on Computer Vision (ICCV), Los Alamitos, CA, USA, pp. 773–781. IEEE Computer Society (2021). https://doi.org/10.1109/ICCV48922.2021.00083
23. Kayhan, O.S., van Gemert, J.C.: On translation invariance in CNNs: convolutional layers can exploit absolute spatial location. In: CVPR (2020)
24. Kondor, R., Trivedi, S.: On the generalization of equivariance and convolution in neural networks to the action of compact groups. arXiv abs/1802.03690 (2018)
25. Krizhevsky, A., Sutskever, I., Hinton, G.E.: ImageNet classification with deep convolutional neural networks. In: Pereira, F., Burges, C.J.C., Bottou, L., Weinberger, K.Q. (eds.) Advances in Neural Information Processing Systems, vol. 25, pp. 1097–1105. Curran Associates, Inc. (2012)
26. LeCun, Y., Bottou, L., Bengio, Y., Haffner, P.: Gradient-based learning applied to document recognition. In: Proceedings of the IEEE, vol. 86, pp. 2278–2324 (1998)
27. Li, Q., Shen, L., Guo, S., Lai, Z.: WaveCNet: wavelet integrated CNNs to suppress aliasing effect for noise-robust image classification. IEEE Trans. Image Process. **30**, 7074–7089 (2021)
28. Li, Z., Yang, W., Peng, S., Liu, F.: A survey of convolutional neural networks: analysis, applications, and prospects. IEEE Trans. Neural Netw. Learn. Syst. (2021)
29. Lowe, D.G.: Distinctive image features from scale-invariant keypoints. Int. J. Comput. Vis. **60**(2), 91–110 (2004). https://doi.org/10.1023/B:VISI.0000029664.99615.94
30. Lyle, C., Wilk, M., Kwiatkowska, M., Gal, Y., Bloem-Reddy, B.: On the benefits of invariance in neural networks (2020). https://arxiv.org/abs/2005.00178
31. McGreivy, N., Hakim, A.: Convolutional layers are not translation equivariant. arXiv abs/2206.04979 (2022)
32. Murase, R., Suganuma, M., Okatani, T.: How can CNNs use image position for segmentation? arXiv abs/2005.03463 (2020)
33. Murray, J.J., Marcos, D., Tuia, D.: Zoom in, zoom out: injecting scale invariance into landuse classification CNNs. In: 2019 IEEE International Geoscience and Remote Sensing Symposium, IGARSS 2019, pp. 5240–5243 (2019)
34. Naderi, H., Goli, L., Kasaei, S.: Scale equivariant CNNs with scale steerable filters. In: 2020 International Conference on Machine Vision and Image Processing (MVIP), pp. 1–5 (2020). https://doi.org/10.1109/MVIP49855.2020.9116889
35. Olah, C., Cammarata, N., Voss, C., Schubert, L., Goh, G.: Naturally occurring equivariance in neural networks. Distill (2020). https://doi.org/10.23915/distill.00024.004
36. Patrick, M.K., Adekoya, A.F., Mighty, A.A., Edward, B.Y.: Capsule networks - a survey. J. King Saud Univ. Comput. Inf. Sci. **34**, 1295–1310 (2022)

37. Qi, G.J., Wang, X.: Learning generalized transformation equivariant representations via autoencoding transformations. IEEE Trans. Pattern Anal. Mach. Intell. **44**, 2045–2057 (2022)

38. Rixen, J., et al.: A rotational invariant neural network for electrical impedance tomography imaging without reference voltage: RF-REIM-NET. Diagnostics **12** (2022)

39. Romero, D.W., Bekkers, E.J., Tomczak, J.M., Hoogendoorn, M.: Wavelet networks: scale equivariant learning from raw waveforms. arXiv abs/2006.05259 (2020)

40. Sharifzadeh, M., Benali, H., Rivaz, H.: Shift-invariant segmentation in breast ultrasound images. In: 2021 IEEE International Ultrasonics Symposium (IUS), pp. 1–4 (2021)

41. Sun, Z., Li, J., Fan, J.: Convolutional neural filtering for intelligent communications signal processing in harsh environments. IEEE Access **9**, 8212–8219 (2021). https://doi.org/10.1109/ACCESS.2021.3049950

42. Ulicny, M., Krylov, V.A., Dahyot, R.: Harmonic convolutional networks based on discrete cosine transform. Pattern Recogn. **129**, 108707 (2022)

43. Veeling, B.S., Linmans, J., Winkens, J., Cohen, T., Welling, M.: Rotation equivariant CNNs for digital pathology. In: Frangi, A.F., Schnabel, J.A., Davatzikos, C., Alberola-López, C., Fichtinger, G. (eds.) MICCAI 2018. LNCS, vol. 11071, pp. 210–218. Springer, Cham (2018). https://doi.org/10.1007/978-3-030-00934-2_24

44. Worrall, D.E., Garbin, S.J., Turmukhambetov, D., Brostow, G.J.: Harmonic networks: deep translation and rotation equivariance. In: 2017 IEEE Conference on Computer Vision and Pattern Recognition (CVPR), pp. 7168–7177 (2017)

45. Xie, Q., Zhao, Q., Xu, Z., Meng, D.: Fourier series expansion based filter parametrization for equivariant convolutions. IEEE Trans. Pattern Anal. Mach. Intell. (2022)

46. Xu, R., Wang, X., Chen, K., Zhou, B., Loy, C.C.: Positional encoding as spatial inductive bias in GANs. In: 2021 IEEE/CVF Conference on Computer Vision and Pattern Recognition (CVPR), pp. 13564–13573 (2021)

47. Zafar, A., et al.: A comparison of pooling methods for convolutional neural networks. Appl. Sci. (2022)

48. Zeiler, M.D., Fergus, R.: Stochastic pooling for regularization of deep convolutional neural networks. In: Bengio, Y., LeCun, Y. (eds.) 1st International Conference on Learning Representations, ICLR 2013, Scottsdale, Arizona, USA, 2–4 May 2013, Conference Track Proceedings (2013)

49. Zhang, R.: Making convolutional networks shift-invariant again. In: Chaudhuri, K., Salakhutdinov, R. (eds.) Proceedings of the 36th International Conference on Machine Learning. Proceedings of Machine Learning Research, vol. 97, pp. 7324–7334. PMLR (2019)

50. Zhu, W., Qiu, Q., Calderbank, A.R., Sapiro, G., Cheng, X.: Scale-equivariant neural networks with decomposed convolutional filters. arXiv abs/1909.11193 (2019)

Human-Machine Interaction

Deep Learning Models for Audio Processing Applications Under Resource-Constrained Devices: A Survey

Taye Girma Debelee[1,2] and Yehualashet Megersa Ayano[1(✉)]

[1] Artificial Intelligence Institute, 40782 Addis Ababa, Ethiopia
yehualeuven@gmail.com
[2] College of Electrical and Computer Engineering, Addis Ababa Science and Technology University, 16417 Addis Ababa, Ethiopia

Abstract. In the recent few years, integrating deep learning models into resource-constrained consumer electronic devices for use in applications ranging from simple personal assistants to clinical decision-making has gained more attention both in industry and academia. This is partially due to the advent of consumer electronic devices such as smartphones and the impressive capability of deep learning (DL) models in learning highly complex problems. However, the processing and memory capacity of consumer devices such as smartphones, smartwatches, and other lightweight embedded systems fall short in handling a computation involving millions of parameters of the DL models. As a result, devising techniques for squeezing DL models to reduce the computational complexity and fit into the capacity of resource-constrained devices (RCDs) has been a topic of active research. This work presented DL architectures commonly used for audio processing tasks on RCDs. Also, the model compression techniques proposed in the literature to squeeze the baseline models have been investigated. The reported results from the proposed architectures and model squeezing techniques indicate that a compressed model with fewer parameters can be achieved without or with minimal loss of accuracy compared to the baseline deep learning model. This survey work also investigated challenges in deploying DL models in RCDs. These challenges include the limitation for performing on-device model training, lack of sufficient datasets for model training, difficulty in model interpretability, and lack of robustness.

Keywords: Deep Learning · Models' architecture · Resource-constrained devices · Model squeezing · Audio processing

1 Introduction

In shallow-structured machine learning architectures, which typically contain at most a single or couple of nonlinear feature transformation, well-constrained problems have been effectively solved. Examples of these shallow architectures

T. Girma Debelee et al. (Eds.): PanAfriCon AI 2022, CCIS 1800, pp. 209–232, 2023.
https://doi.org/10.1007/978-3-031-31327-1_12

include logistic regression, neural networks with one hidden layer, support vector machines (SVMs), and Gaussian mixture models (GMMs). These architectures have a convex loss function, which makes it efficient to achieve the global optimum at the expense of sacrificing modeling power. Having reduced modeling power, these shallow architectures face difficulties in representing complex problems containing signals such as human speech, and other natural sounds [1]. However, these signals can be modeled through efficient and robust deep learning algorithms [1].

Different deep-learning model architectures have been proposed in the literature to process audio signals. These include deep neural networks (DNN) [11], convolutional neural networks (CNN) [31], recurrent neural networks (RNN) [42], and long short-term memory (LSTM) [16]. These deep learning techniques have grown in popularity because they commonly outperform shallow-structured machine learning techniques in automatically extracting features from unprocessed raw data. This ability makes deep learning techniques a better alternative in the abstraction of the raw data for subsequent learning-based tasks such as detection, retrieval, classification, and prediction [2]. However, the size of trainable parameters, the need for a large amount of data in model building, and the non-convexity of the network are some of the difficulties posed in exploiting the potential deep learning techniques [3,4].

In this work, the nomenclature resource-constrained is used to refer to embedded computing boards such as Raspberry Pi and NVIDIA Jetson, end-user, and wearable devices like smartphones, smartwatches, and smart glasses. Here it is important to remember that processing, memory, and energy consumption efficiency of these resource-constrained devices has been improving dramatically. Nowadays, the processing, memory, and efficient energy consumption capability of resource-constrained devices has been improving with a combination of hardware accelerators and multi-core architectures. And, it is believed that there will be more improvement in the future [5].

2   Deep Learning Architectures

DL is a rapidly evolving discipline and there are several architectures available in the literature. Some of the most commonly used deep learning architectures for audio processing tasks are presented as follows.

2.1   Deep Feed-Forward Neural Network (DFFNN)

A DFFNN is a multi-layer perceptron with more than one hidden layer between the input and output layers is referred to as a deep feed-forward neural network. The process of deciding exact number of hidden layers and neurons on each hidden layer that yields the best model, however, has no theoretical basis [6].

The neurons on the hidden and output layer use activation functions to compute their output value. Different activation functions have been used in practice and perform comparably. These include linear, logistic sigmoid, hyperbolic tangent, rectified linear units, softmax, and exponential linear units [10]. Each activation function has advantages and limitations, and there are no rich definitive theoretical guiding principles to choose one from the other. Empirically, the activation functions can be preferred based on ease of optimizing, generalization capability, learning time requirement, simplicity, and computational requirement [2,7]. To this end, rectified linear units (ReLUs) are commonly used in hidden units, and a softmax is used in output units of deep neural networks [7,8,10]. Besides, learning in DFFNN is carried out by optimizing the objective function by back-propagating the error between the ground truth outputs and the model outputs produced on every iteration of the training. The objective function is decided based on the task to be performed and the activation function used on the output layer. For instance, if the activation function on the output layer is a softmax, then the most suitable objective function is the cross-entropy between the class probabilities and the softmax output [9].

Some of the problems that exist in training deep feedforward neural networks include overfitting, vanishing and exploding gradients, and being trapped in local minima. To alleviate these issues, different techniques have been implemented including regularization, batch normalization, and a good set of weight initialization [10]. In addition to this, the training and deployment of the regular deep feedforward network on resource-constrained devices are almost impractical. As a result, in the last few years, techniques have been proposed to make deep feedforward neural networks fit on the processing and memory capability resource-constrained devices [11–13].

Among the techniques used to squeeze the DNN network, singular value decomposition (SVD) is the one that reduces the number of parameters with minimal or no loss of accuracy [12,13]. Jian Xue et al. [12] applied SVD to decompose the weight matrices on the trained DNN model. Then, by keeping only k biggest singular values and discarding the rest the trained deep feedforward neural network is restructured. To make clear this technique, let the weight matrix be $\mathbf{W}_{m \times n}$, then by applying the SVD method it can be decomposed to three matrices $\mathbf{U}_{m \times n}$, $\sum_{m \times n}$ and $\mathbf{V}^T_{n \times n}$, that is,

$$\mathbf{W}_{m \times n} = \mathbf{U}_{m \times n} \cdot \sum_{m \times n} \cdot \mathbf{V}^T_{n \times n} \tag{1}$$

where the columns of $\mathbf{U}$ and $\mathbf{V}$ are called left-singular eigen vectors and right-singular eigen vector of $\mathbf{W}$, respectively. $\sum$ denotes a diagonal matrix with values in decreasing order and represents the singular values of $\mathbf{W}$.

Then by keeping only k biggest singular values of $\mathbf{W}$ Eq. (1) can be rewritten as:

$$\mathbf{W}_{m \times n} = \mathbf{U}_{m \times k} \cdot \left(\sum_{k \times k} \cdot \mathbf{V}^T_{k \times k} \right) = \mathbf{U}_{m \times k} \cdot \mathbf{N}_{k \times k} \tag{2}$$

These two weight matrices, $\mathbf{U}$ and $\mathbf{N}$, are smaller in their size compared to the original weight matrix $\mathbf{W}$. As a result, if $k \ll n$ the model size can significantly be squeezed from mn to $(m + n)k$ [12].

Another DFNN compression techniques is a sparse-coding [4,13], shown in Fig. 1 [4]. The technique does not require retraining and major changes in the original DNN model [4]. Sourav Bhattacharya et al. [13], developed an optimized deep neural network framework by using a sparse dictionary learning concept. The main idea of their concept is to squeeze the original complex synaptic weight matrix, $\mathbf{W}_{m \times n}$, as a sparse dictionary. In this technique a dictionary $\mathbf{B} = \{\beta\}_{i=1}^{k} \ \forall \beta_i \in \mathbb{R}^m$ is learned from the weights $\mathbf{W}_{m \times n}$ using unsupervised learning. The sparse coding approximates each input vector $w_i = \mathbb{R}^m$ of $\mathbf{W}_{m \times n}$ as a linear combination of basis vectors β from the dictionary and a sparse vector of coefficients a^i, that is,

$$w_i = \sum_{j=1}^{k} a_j^i \cdot \beta_j \tag{3}$$

$$\min_{B,A} \| \mathbf{W}_{m \times n} - \mathbf{B} \cdot \mathbf{A} \|_2^2$$
$$\textit{subject to: } \forall i \| a^i \|_0 \leq K \tag{4}$$

After $\mathbf{A}$ and $\mathbf{B}$ are learned, the sparse factorization of the original weight matrix, $\mathbf{W}_{m \times n}$ is given as [13]:

$$\mathbf{W}_{m \times n} \approx \mathbf{B} \cdot \mathbf{A} \tag{5}$$

where $\mathbf{A} \in \mathbb{R}^{k \times n}$, $\mathbf{B} \in \mathbb{R}^{m \times k}$, and K is the sparsity constant factor.

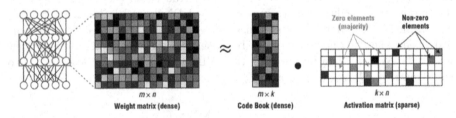

Fig. 1. Illustration of Sparse-coding base weight matrix factorization [4].

Deep restricted Boltzmann networks are made-up by stacking a restricted Boltzmann machines (RBM). An RBM is a shallow and stochastic network containing a visible layer ($\mathbf{v}$) units and a hidden layer ($\mathbf{h}$) units [1,10,14]. As shown in Fig. 2 [14], the RBM model has two groups, that are, $\mathbf{h}$ and $\mathbf{v}$, and their interconnection is described by the weight matrix, $\mathbf{W}$. The joint probability distribution, $p(\mathbf{v}, \mathbf{h}; \theta)$ on $\mathbf{v}$ and $\mathbf{h}$, given $\theta = \{\mathbf{W}, \mathbf{b}, \mathbf{c}\}$, where $\mathbf{b}$ is $\mathbf{v}$ units' biases and $\mathbf{c}$ $\mathbf{h}$ units' biases that is defined as,

$$p(\mathbf{v}, \mathbf{h}; \theta) = \frac{1}{Z} e^{-E(\mathbf{v}, \mathbf{h}; \theta)} \tag{6}$$

and the marginal probability the model assigns to $\mathbf{v}$ units is:

$$p(\mathbf{v}; \theta) = \frac{1}{Z} \sum_h e^{-E(\mathbf{v}, \mathbf{h}; \theta)} \tag{7}$$

where $E(\mathbf{v}, \mathbf{h}; \theta)$ is the energy function given by,

$$E(\mathbf{v}, \mathbf{h}) = -\mathbf{b}^T\mathbf{v} - \mathbf{c}^T\mathbf{h} - \mathbf{v}^T\mathbf{W}\mathbf{h} \tag{8}$$

and $\mathbf{Z}$ is a partition function given by,

$$\mathbf{Z} = \sum_{\mathbf{v}} \sum_{\mathbf{h}} e^{-E(\mathbf{v}, \mathbf{h})} \tag{9}$$

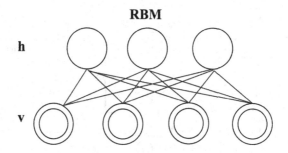

Fig. 2. Restricted Boltzmann Machines [14].

In RBM inference, the conditional probability of $\mathbf{h}$ given $\mathbf{v}$ and vise versa over the individual binary units h_j and v_k are given by Eq. (10) and Eq. (11), respectively [1],

$$P(h_j = 1|\mathbf{v}; \theta) = \sigma(c_j + \sum_{i=1}^{I} v_i w_{ij}) \tag{10}$$

$$P(v_i = 1|\mathbf{h}; \theta) = \sigma(b_i + \sum_{j=1}^{J} h_j w_{ij}) \tag{11}$$

where $\sigma(x) = \frac{1}{(1+e^{-x})}$

In the process of training an RBM, a stochastic gradient descent (SGD) for maximizing the probability of a particular configuration of visible states, $p(\mathbf{v}; \theta)$ is performed by computing the derivative of the negative log-likelihood, $p(\mathbf{v}; \theta)$, as given in Eq. (12). Then, RBM weights are updated according to Eq. (13) [1],

$$\frac{\partial - \log p(\mathbf{v}; \theta)}{\partial w_{ij}} = \mathbb{E}_{data}(v_i h_j) - \mathbb{E}_{model}(v_i h_j) \tag{12}$$

$$\Delta w_{ij} = \epsilon(\mathbb{E}_{data}(v_i h_j) - \mathbb{E}_{model}(v_i h_j)) \tag{13}$$

where ϵ is the learning rate, w_{ij} representing the weight between the visible unit i and the hidden unit j, and $\mathbb{E}_{data}(v_i h_j)$ and $\mathbb{E}_{model}(v_i h_j)$, respectively, are the observed expectation in the training data and expectation defined by the model.

For resource-constrained devices, Nicholas D. Lane *et al.* [6] proposed an architecture called "DeepEar" which is built by stacking an RBM. The architecture uses RBM as a building block in which the **h** units from one set of RBMs act as the **v** for the next units. The architecture of the DNN model used in DeepEar is shown in Fig. 3.

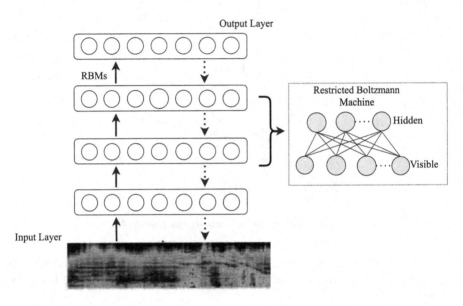

Fig. 3. Stacked RBM architecture used in 'DeepEar' [6].

In the above architecture, a hidden unit $(h^{(k)})$ computes its state (y_k), which is to be passed to subsequent layers, using rectified linear units (ReLus) activation function, as given in Eq. (14)

$$y_{max} = max(0, x_k) \tag{14}$$

where x_k is an intermediate state computed, as given in Eq. (15), from the hidden unit's-specific bias term b_k, each unit's state in the prior layer y_i, and the weight between the hidden unit k and each unit in the prior layer, w_{ik},

$$x_k = b_k + \sum_i y_i w_{ik} \tag{15}$$

In the DeepEar architecture, softmax, ReLu, and Gaussian activation functions are used in output, hidden, and visible units, respectively. To address overfitting, the DeepEar used a dropout regularization technique. Generally, the model is efficient in energy consumption and executes within the run-time memory requirement of 8 MB having 3 hidden layers [6].

In another scenario, Petko Georgiev *et al.* [41] proposed a multi-tasking learning approach to reduce the computational complexity while improving model robustness and accuracy through knowledge transferring between related tasks. As shown in Fig. 4 [41], the multi-task model shares hidden layers of the learning model between selected audio processing tasks. The building block of the multi-tasking architecture is a deep belief network (DBN), built from stacked RBMs [41].

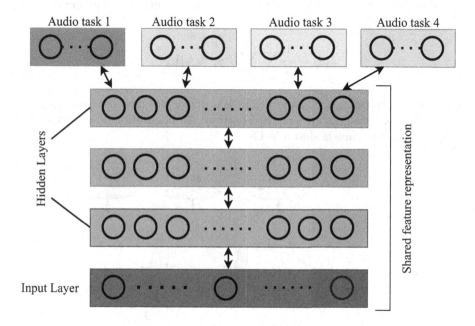

Fig. 4. DBN architecture for multi-task audio processing [41].

In the above architecture, the input layer and hidden layers are shared across audio analysis tasks. This is mainly used as a front end in the universal feature transformation to capture multiple acoustic observations. On the other hand, each audio sensing task has its output layer which acts as a classifier. During model training, the shared hidden layers and the task-specific output layer are updated while the remaining output layers are kept intact. The backpropagation algorithm is used to fine-tune the parameters of the model [41].

2.2 Deep Recurrent Neural Networks

An RNN is a family of neural networks commonly used for processing time-series data having a set of N training sequence $D = \{(x_1^{(n)}, y_1^{(n)}), ..., (x_{T_n}^{(n)}, y_{T_n}^{(n)})\}_{n=1}^{N}$

[10,15]. Besides, an RNN simulates a discrete-time dynamical system that has an input ($\mathbf{x}_t$), a hidden state ($\mathbf{h}_t$) and an output ($\mathbf{y}_t$) defined as [15]

$$\mathbf{h}_t = f_h(\mathbf{x}_t, \mathbf{h}_{t-1}; \theta_{\mathbf{h}}) = f_h(\mathbf{W}_h, \mathbf{h}_{t-1} + \mathbf{W}_x \mathbf{x}_t) \tag{16}$$

$$\mathbf{y}_t = f_0(\mathbf{h}_t; \theta_{\mathbf{0}}) = f_0(\mathbf{W}_0 \mathbf{h}_t) \tag{17}$$

where f_h denotes a state transition activation function parameterized by $\theta_{\mathbf{h}} = \{\mathbf{W}_h, \mathbf{W}_x\}$, $\mathbf{W}_h$ is a transition weight matrix, $\mathbf{W}_x$ is an input weight matrix, and f_o denotes an output activation function parameterized by $\theta_0 = \{\mathbf{W}_0\}$, $\mathbf{W}_0$ is an output weight matrix. The parameters are optimized by minimizing the cost function, $J(\theta)$:

$$J(\theta) = \frac{1}{N} \sum_{n=1}^{N} \sum_{t=1}^{T_n} d(\mathbf{y}_t^{(n)}, f_0(\mathbf{h}_t^{(n)})) \tag{18}$$

where $\mathbf{h}_t^{(n)} = f_h(\mathbf{x}_t^{(n)}, \mathbf{h}_{t-1}^{(n)})$, and $d(\mathbf{j}, \mathbf{k})$ is a divergence measure between $\mathbf{j}$ and $\mathbf{k}$, such as Euclidean distance or cross-entropy. An illustration of a conventional RNN unfolded in time is shown in Fig. 5 [15].

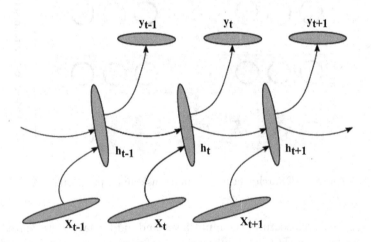

Fig. 5. A conventional recurrent neural network unfolded in time [15].

To construct deep RNN from the conventional shallow RNN, Pascanu *et al.* [15] identified three approaches, that are, input to a hidden function, hidden to output function, and hidden to hidden transition. Those representations are more efficient in representing complex functions than shallow networks. But, the computational complexity increases and suffers from vanishing and exploding gradient problems when trained with backpropagation. The vanishing and exploding gradient problems can be alleviated by replacing the hidden units with Long Short Term Memory (LSTM) cell units [16].

Jie Zhang *et al.* [16] proposed an architecture, called DirNet, where the recurrent and inter-layer weight matrices of an RNN are to be compressed simultaneously with minimal loss of accuracy. The architecture, as shown in Fig. 6, is based on sparse coding and contains two steps. In the first step, the dimension of the shared dictionary matrix among inter-layer and recurrent layer ($\mathbf{D}^l$) is adjusted dynamically. In the second step, by taking into consideration different usages between hidden layers in the hierarchy, the method dynamically changes the hidden layers' sparsity. The DirNet, on the LibriSpeech dataset, compresses the original architecture with the number of neurons at each layer (500, 500, 500, 500, 500) having a total number of 10.3 million (M) parameters to (25, 35, 45, 50, 55) neurons at each layer having 1.3M parameters with only 0.2% of accuracy loss.

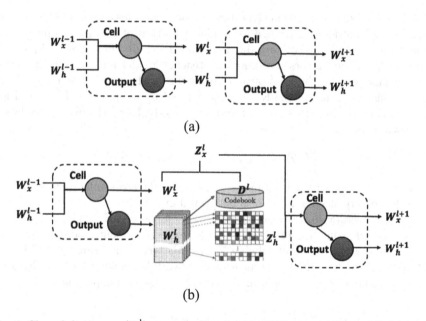

Fig. 6. Shared dictionary ($\mathbf{D}^l$) sparse coding based RNN's compression, (a) the initial model (b) the model compressed by jointly dynamically adjust sparsity of recurrent $\mathbf{W}_h^l$ and inter-layer $\mathbf{W}_x^l$ weight matrices [16].

The other approach used for RNN compression is network pruning [17,18] and quantization [17,19]. Pruning describes the process of masking out certain weights in an RNN. In pruning, the first step is training a model to learn important weights. Then, the second step is to mask out weights that contributes less for the prediction accuracy. After masking out less important weights, the final step is retraining the model given the sparsity constraint [17]. The pruning approach can also be classified into non-structured and structured pruning. In non-structured pruning, certain weights are masked based on some criteria, for instance, based on the magnitude value of weights. But, this non-structured removal of weights results in non-structured sparse weight matrices which in turn make it difficult to effectively accelerate the computation because of the irregularity in accessing memory [18]. The structured pruning techniques have been introduced for alleviating the problem in an irregular sparse weight matrices, for instance, by deleting the columns and rows of weight matrices [21], pruning blocks of weights in a layer [22], and integrating neuron selection mechanism in the design [17].

On the other hand, quantization is a technique to reduce the number of bits used to represent parameters by reducing the precision of the operands. The parameters which can be quantized include the network weights, biases, activations, and inputs. And there exist different methods of quantization such as fixed-point quantization, binary code quantization, and exponential quantization [17].

In a knowledge distillation (KD) based model compression, a smaller network model called a student is trained to mimic the output of a larger complex model called a teacher [20]. There are different knowledge distillation techniques, the common technique is first training the teacher model and then training the student model using the logit outputs from the teacher model (soft labels) [20, 23]. For instance, in [20] the KD was performed by minimizing the overall loss function composed of cross-entropy and Kullback-Leibler (KL) divergence losses, as shown in Eq. (19)

$$L(\theta) = \alpha L_{CE}(\theta) + (1 - \alpha)L_{KL}(\theta) \tag{19}$$

where θ is student's model parameter, $L_{CE}(\theta)$ is the cross-entropy loss, $L_{KL}(\theta)$ is the KL divergence loss, and α is between 0 and 1.

A cross-entropy loss is from training data labels (hard labels) and student model outputs, while KL divergence loss is from the student model outputs and teacher model outputs (soft labels). Using this technique, Yangyang Shi *et al.* [20] reduced the baseline recurrent neural network language model size by up to 18.5% without loss of accuracy in the speech recognition experiment.

2.3   Convolutional Neural Networks (CNN)

A CNN is a neural network that uses convolutional operation instead of general matrix multiplication in an at least one of its layers. Compared to the classical deep neural networks, the convolution introduces the sparse interaction, parameter sharing, and equivariant representations concepts to improve the learning system through optimizing the time and space complexity [10].

A variety of CNN-based audio processing deep learning architecture has been proposed in the literature [24–28]. There exist different architectures of the CNN model, however, a classic CNN consists of an input layer, a group of convolutional and pooling layers, a limited number of fully connected layers, and an output layer stacked together to form a deep architecture. CNN's actual difference from the deep forward neural network is the introduction of a combination of convolution and pooling operations. The convolution layer contains a set of kernels whose parameters are trainable. The dimension of the kernel is small compared to the size of the input vector, and it slides across on the input to perform the dot product at every input location. After the product in the convolution layer passed through an activation function, the pooling layer replaces the output with summary statistics of neighbor outputs. The most common pooling functions include max pooling, L^2-norm of neighbors, and a weighted average [10]. These multiple convolutional and pooling layers extract features, and the inference is made using the fully-connected layers.

CNN was initially designed for image processing applications with 2-dimensional input. In most audio processing tasks, the convolution and pooling layers are 2-dimensional, and the inputs are audio features such as log-Mel spectrogram and Mel frequency cepstral coefficients (MFCC) [24,26,27]. However, the 1D CNN model that uses raw audio data as its input has also been used in audio processing applications as shown in Fig. 7 [25].

The high memory and computational resource requirement pose a challenge for deploying the convolutional neural network models on resource-constrained devices. The existing solution to accelerate the deep CNN models is to reduce the number of trainable parameters while preserving the accuracy to an acceptable level. The reduction of parameters in CNN can be achieved by squeezing the convolutional layers since they constitute the bulk of all computations in convolutional neural networks [13,29,30].

Cheng Tai *et al.* [29] proposed a low-rank tensor decomposition-based technique to remove the redundancy in the convolutional kernels that can reduce the computational complexity. The idea is to replace the 4D convolutional kernel with two consecutive kernels having a lower rank. The technique is described as follows, given $\mathbf{W} \in \mathbb{R}^{N \times d \times d \times C}$ be a set of convolutional kernels, where N, C are the number of the output and input feature maps respectively, and d is the spatial kernel size, the goal is to find an approximation $\widetilde{\mathbf{W}}$ of $\mathbf{W}$ which can be decomposed as given in Eq. (20) [29],

$$\widetilde{\mathbf{W}}_n^c = \sum_{k=1}^{K} \mathbf{H}_n^k (\mathbf{V}_k^c)^T \tag{20}$$

where $\mathbf{K}$ is a hyper-parameter controlling the rank of the horizontal filter $\mathbf{H} \in \mathbb{R}^{N \times 1 \times d \times K}$ and a vertical filter $v\mathbf{V} \in \mathbb{R}^{K \times d \times 1 \times C}$.

Then, $\mathbf{Z} \in \mathbb{R}^{X \times Y \times C}$ be the input feature map, the original convolution becomes [29]:

$$\mathbf{W}_n * \mathbf{Z} \approx \widetilde{\mathbf{W}}_n * \mathbf{Z} = \sum_{k=1}^{K} \mathbf{H}_n^k * \left(\sum_{c=1}^{C} \mathbf{V}_k^c * Z^c \right) \tag{21}$$

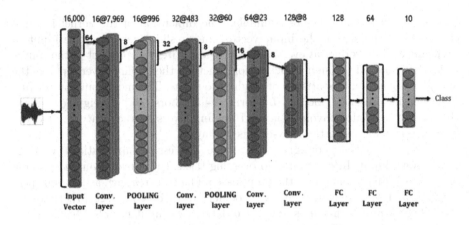

Fig. 7. One-dimensional CNN architecture [25].

Both **H** and **V** are learnable parameters that are approximated by minimizing the objective function given in Eq. (22) [29]:

$$\mathbf{E}_1(\mathbf{H}, \mathbf{V}) = \sum_{n,c} \|\mathbf{W}_n^c - \sum_{k=1}^{K} \mathbf{H}_n^k (\mathbf{V}_k^c)^T\|_F^2 \tag{22}$$

The above decomposition technique reduces the computational complexity to $\mathcal{O}(\mathbf{dK(N+C)XY})$ from the high computational cost associated with a classic convolution, that is, $\mathcal{O}(\mathbf{d^{2NCXY}})$ [29]. Apart from the decomposition technique, different filter pruning-based convolution layer squeezing methods have also been proposed in literature [31–33].

2.4   Autoencoders

Autoencoders are simple neural network architectures having an encoder, a hidden (latent), and a decoder unit, as shown in Fig. 8 [34]. An input to the encoder is raw data, and an output is a reconstructed approximation of the original input. An encoder transforms the original input (x_i) into a hidden representation $h(x_i)$, while the decoder reconstructs the encoded version of the original input $(\widetilde{x}_i)$ from the hidden representation. The hidden layer dimension is either smaller or larger than the dimension of the input, and its task is to extract essential information from the input (x_i) [1,34].

Given the input data vector **x**, an encoder maps it into the hidden layer with a weight matrix (**W**) and a bias (**b**) that can be expressed using Eq. (23)

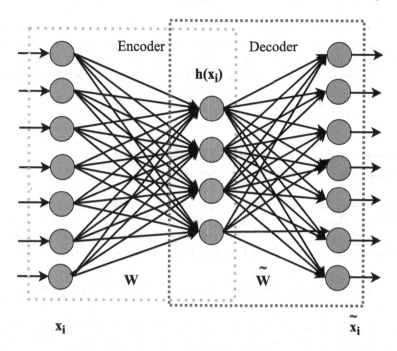

Fig. 8. Autoencoder architecture [34].

$$\mathbf{h} = g(\mathbf{W}\mathbf{x} + b) \tag{23}$$

where $g(\cdot)$ is an activation function of the hidden unit. Then, using hidden units output (**h**), the weight matrix ($\widetilde{\mathbf{W}}$) and the bias ($\mathbf{b}_h$) the decoder unit reconstructs the input using Eq. (24)

$$\widetilde{\mathbf{x}} = f(\widetilde{\mathbf{W}}\mathbf{h} + \mathbf{b}_h) \tag{24}$$

where $f(\cdot)$ is an activation function of the decoder unit.

An autoencoder is employs an unsupervised learning technique and applies backpropagation in approximating the input through reducing the reconstruction error. The error evaluates the discrepancy among $\mathbf{x}$ and $\widetilde{\mathbf{x}}$, and is defined as a mean square error or cross-entropy. Several variants of autoencoders exist, including sparse, denoising, variational, and convolutional autoencoders. In most cases, an autoencoder is used as a preprocessing module in modeling the state-of-the-art audio processing algorithms that are used in different applications, such as denoising an audio signal [35], audio feature extraction [36,37], and dimensionality reduction (compression) [38].

The implementation of deep learning algorithms, including deep autoencoders, on resource-constrained computing devices, has to take into consideration the computing power and memory spaces of these devices. To this end, Akihiro Suzuki *et al.* [39] proposed tied weight techniques to reduce the number of parameters while implementing autoencoder in FPGA. In this technique, the weight matrix is shared between the input and hidden layer, and between the hidden and output layers. Accordingly, the weight matrix of the hidden and output layers are denoted as a transposed matrix of each other as given in Eq. (25) [39]. A detailed asymptotic analysis of tied weight deep autoencoders is provided in [40].

$$\widetilde{\mathbf{W}} = \mathbf{W}^T \tag{25}$$

3   Performance of Squeezed DL Models in Resource-Constrained Devices

In this section, the performance improvement achieved by implementing the compressed DL models on RCDs is presented. In literature, the performance improvement is reported merely in terms of computational requirement, memory space requirement, and overall task accuracy.

3.1   Comparison of Classical Versus Squeezed Deep Feedforward Models

As discussed in Subsect. 2.1, decomposing the weight matrix [12], sparse dictionary learning [12,13], and using gated units to regulate information flow [11] have proposed for reducing the computational complexity and memory space requirement of classical deep feedforward models without significantly reducing the models' accuracy. Table 1 renders the comparison between baseline DFNN models and their squeezed counterparts.

Table 1. Comparison of base line DFNN and its squeezed counterpart.

Method	Model	#layer	#dim	#param. (M)	WER (%)	Dataset
L. Lu et al. [11]	Baseline	6	2048	30.3	26.8	AMI meeting speech transcription corpus
		10	512	4.7	28.8	
		15	256	2.1	31.5	
	HDNN	10	1024	16.2	26.8	
		10	256	1.9	28.8	
		15	128	0.85	31.4	
Jian Xue et al. [12]	Baseline	6	2048	5.6	25.6 [a]	large vocabulary continuous speech recognition
					21.0 [2]	
	SVD on all hidden and output layers	6	192	5.6	26.2 [1]	
					21.5 [b]	

[a] The test was performed on a 750 h long audio recording having 31829 words and 9562 utterances. [b] The test was performed on a 300 h long audio recording having 16028 words and 2286 utterances.

As indicated in Table 1, the HDNN models have a comparable, and even slightly better, accuracy in terms of word error rate (WER) compared to plain

DNNs at a smaller number of parameters for speech recognition experiment on AMI meeting speech transcription corpus dataset. Jian Xue et al. [12] reported that by retaining only 192 neurons from each hidden layer and an output layer the number of parameters is reduced to 5.6M with a small loss in accuracy.

3.2 Comparison of Classical Versus Squeezed Deep Restricted Boltzmann Models

As discussed in Subsect. 2.1, an RBM is one of the DL models that are used in the field of ML-based audio processing.

Nicholas D. Lane et al. [6], experimentally squeezed the baseline model into 3 hidden layers each with 256 units for ambient scene analysis, and 3 hidden layers each with 512 units for emotion recognition and speaker identification with <3% loss in accuracy. Initially, the baseline model contains four internal deep learning models each with 3 hidden layers and 1024 units per hidden layer. In terms of memory requirement, the squeezed model requires 8 MB runtime memory compared to the baseline model which requires 30 MB.

Petko Georgiev et al. [41] compared the performance of deep architectures with the shared hidden layers for audio analysis in resource-constrained devices against standalone models for each audio analysis task. Their squeezed model with shared hidden layers requires only 2.7 MB of runtime memory, with four-fold less than the baseline model.

3.3 Comparison of Classical Versus Compressed RNN Models

Recurrent neural networks, with their variants LSTM and GRU, are one of the most commonly used DL models for applications using time series and sequential data, such as audio signals. But, they require computing devices to have a high computational capability and a large memory space [17,19], which are scarce resources in many embedded and smart mobile devices. So, as discussed in Subsect. 2.2, techniques have been proposed to compress the RNN models and make them fit for resource-constrained devices.

Jie Zhang et al. [16], proposed an RNN model called DirNet that dynamically adjusts the sparsity within the layer, and adaptively changes the hierarchical structures of the network through adaptive sparsity learning. The baseline model of DirNet for speech recognition application learned using the LibriSpeech dataset composed of 5 hidden layers and each layer contains 500 LSTM units. The DirNet model was compared against an LSTM model compressed using singular value decomposition (LSTM-SVD) and online dictionary learning (LSTM-ODL).

As indicated in Table 2, the DirNet is the squeezed counterpart of the baseline LSTM model with a reduced number of parameters, that is, from 10.3M to 2.4M with a compression ratio of 4.3, while maintaining the accuracy at 12.7% (WER). Also, the 4.2 times speedup achieved by DirNet is well above the other two compression techniques. Furthermore, when the models are compressed by

7.9 times from the baseline model, the LSTM-ODL and LSTM-SVD experienced higher losses of accuracy at 1.6% (WER) and 3.4%(WER), respectively. Whereas, the DirNet maintains the accuracy loss to 0.2% (WER) from the baseline model and in the meantime achieves a compression ratio of 7.9 times and speeds up the inference by 7.6 times [16].

Table 2. The comparison between the base line and squeezed models in terms of: parameters (#param), compression rate (R), speedup (T), and word error rate (WER).

Network	#param. (M)	R(x)	T(x)	WER (%)
Baseline LSTM	10.3M	1	1	12.7
LSTM- SVD	6.9M	1.5	1.4	12.7
LSTM- ODL	3.7M	2.8	2.6	12.7
DirNet	2.4M	4.3	4.2	12.7
LSTM- SVD	1.3M	7.9	7.6	16.1
LSTM- ODL	1.3M	7.9	7.6	14.3
DirNet	1.3M	7.9	7.6	12.9

Liangjian Wen *et al.* [18] proposed structured pruning techniques for compressing an RNN by introducing binary gates on the recurrent and input units. These binary gates allow an effective neuron selection under sparsity constraints. The proposed pruning technique was compared with the intrinsic sparse structure technique proposed by Wei Wen *et al.* [21], using Penn Treebank (PTB) datasets. The technique was evaluated using perplexity metrics where vanilla LSTM is a baseline model.

The reported results are shown in Table 3. As indicated in Table 3, the structured pruning technique proposed in [18] resulted in the most compact structure with the number of the first (L1) and the second hidden (L2) units reduced to 296 and 247 respectively from 1500. That decreased the number of weight parameters from 66.0M in the baseline model to 6.16M, which is greater than a 10× reduction. The overall speedup is also 19.39× the baseline vanilla LSTM models with a very small accuracy loss.

Table 3. Comparison of baseline vanilla stacked LSTM, and compact versions compressed by structured pruning techniques.

Method	#param. (M)	LSTMs layers (input, L1, L2)	Perplexity (validate, test)	speedup	Dataset
Baseline: Vanilla stacked LSTM	66.0	(1500, 1500, 1500)	(82.57, 78.57)	1.00×	Penn Treeban
Wei Wen *et al.* [21]	21.8	(1500, 373, 315)	(82.59, 78.65)	9.17×	
Wen *et al.* [18]	6.16	(251, 296, 247)	(81.62, 78.08)	19.39×	

In a related experiment, Chauhan *et al.* [42] evaluated a baseline RNN having two hidden layers and 120 LSTM cells on each hidden layer with its quantization-based compressed version. The models are compared using a breath acoustic dataset for breathing-based end-to-end authentication applications. The user authentication accuracy was maintained at more than 90% in both cases, and the model memory footprint size for quantized RNN is 4 to 6 times lower than the baseline model, as shown in Table 4 [42].

Table 4. Comparison of baseline RNN with its quantization based compressed counterpart.

Method	Model	#hidden layer	# LSTM cells per layer	Memory footprint	Dataset
Chauhan *et al.* [42]	Baseline RNN	2	120	1.1 MB	deep breathing
				1.1 MB	sniffing
	Quantized RNN	2	120	264 KB	deep breathing
				175 KB	sniffing

3.4   Comparison of Classical Versus Squeezed CNN Models

Though initially designed for computer vision applications, squeezed CNN models have been proposed in the literature for audio analysis applications on resource-constrained devices.

Sajjad Abdoli *et al.* [25] have evaluated the performance and number of parameters of CNN models using the UrbanSound8k dataset. Their proposed model is shown in Fig. 7, and it has outperformed the other CNN models in terms of accuracy and has a minimum number of parameters. These small number of parameters enable the model to be implemented on resource-constrained devices and trained with a small-size dataset. The proposed model achieved a mean accuracy of 89% with a total of 550k parameters when the first convolutional layer is initialized by a Gamma tone filter bank and a mean accuracy of 87% with a total of 256k parameters when the first convolutional layer is randomly initialized.

Jyun-Yi Wu *et al.* [31] proposed a model compression technique that integrates parameter pruning (PP), parameter quantization (PQ), and feature quantization to compress the original fully convolutional neural network having 7 hidden layers and 300.3k parameters. The paper used parameter pruning with sparsity threshold (θ) of 0.65 and clustering-based weight quantization with cluster number of ($k = 16$). The squeezing techniques brought down the total number of the parameter to 29,309 with a small loss of accuracy as shown in Table 5.

The hybrid of parameter pruning and quantization-based model compression is also used in [43]. Md Mohaimenuzzaman *et al.* [43] proposed a baseline CNN model called ACDNet for state-of-the-art classification performance in classifying environmental sounds. Then, squeezed the model by using a hybrid technique consisting of pruning and quantization. As shown in Table 6, the ACDNet contains convolutional layers with a total of 2074 filters and a total trainable parameter of 4.74M. The compression technique squeezed the ACDNet model to

Table 5. The reduction in model parameter and the corresponding accuracy of the FCN model.

Method	Model	#Param.	PESQ [a]	STOI [b]	Dataset
Jyun-Yi Wu et al. [31]	Baseline	300,300	2.55	0.85	TIMIT corpus
	$PP(\theta = 0.65)$	234,800	≈2.55	≈0.85	
	$PP + PQ$	29,309	2.52	0.84	

[a] Perceptual Evaluation Speech Quality. [b] Short-time Objective Intelligibility.

the level that the size in MB is reduced by 97.22% and the Floating-point operations per second (FLOPs) by 97.28% while maintaining close to state-of-the-art accuracy by 83.65% on Environmental Sound Classification dataset (ESC-50).

Table 6. The reduction in model parameter (in million), size (in MB) and the corresponding accuracy (in %) of the ACDNet model.

Method	Model	#Filters	#Param.	Size	FLOPs	Acc.	Dataset
Mohaimenuzzaman et al. [43]	ACDNet	2074	4.74	18.06	0.544	87.05	ESC
	ACDNet-20	415	0.131	0.5	0.0148	83.65	

4   Challenges in Deploying DL Models on Resource-Constrained Devices

Squeezed deep learning models are more suitable for deployment on computationally constrained platforms. This is because the compressed models require less memory and computation compared to the uncompressed baseline models. Also, compression can be achieved with little or no significant loss of accuracy. However, beyond the reported results on deep learning model optimization, there are still challenges in using deep learning for machine learning applications in resource-constrained devices. These challenges include difficulties for performing on-device model training, lack of sufficient audio datasets, issues with model interpretability, and adaptability issues for unknown acoustic conditions and recording devices.

4.1   On-Device Learning

There are different possibilities for using DL models on low-resource mobile and embedded devices. One of the possibilities is to perform the entire learning and the inference in the cloud and push back the result to the device [44]. The other possibility is to perform the training using on-premises devices with higher computational power so that training is completed in a reasonable short time frame. Then, the trained model is ported to the resource-constrained device using application program interfaces (APIs) such as NNAPI [45] or third-party libraries such as Mobile AI Compute Engine (MACE) [46] to carry out on-device inference. This technique reduces latency, improves reliability, and protects privacy compared to Cloud-based DL model training. However, the variation in computational resource capabilities among devices exhibits different runtime behaviors for DL models trained ex-situ and their associated inference tasks [47]. These limitations necessitate the DL models to be trained on the device in which the inference is performed. The on-device training makes the DL models tailored to each user's need, and as user data never leaves the device it helps to protect the user's privacy. Also, it avoids sending user data across the internet and using expensive computing devices to train the model.

According to the experiment carried out in [44] on-device training of deep learning models from scratch results in a loss of accuracy compared to models trained on Clouds. To this end, the existing on-device model training techniques focus on fine-tuning and optimizing the baseline models shipped with APIs using the data collected from the device. For example, a Core ML [48] API supports on-device training to a certain extent. But, most APIs support only limited types of DL models, and the task of performing on-device learning for many DL models remains a challenge that needs to be addressed.

4.2   Limited Dataset Availability

A large dataset that meets the basic quality standards is specifically essential in the supervised learning approach to avoid overfitting and increase the generalization ability of a DL model. However, compared to image dataset repositories, there are a limited number of well-labeled audio datasets repositories. Besides, most of the audio datasets on repositories are recorded using high-quality electric microphones. This result in inference accuracy degradation when a model trained using a high-quality audio dataset is deployed on resource-constrained devices with low-quality microphones, such as MEMS microphones [49]. Also, collecting a large volume of audio data using resource-constrained devices is an expensive and laborious process. To minimize these challenges, techniques such as data augmentation [50] and feature embedding [51] have been proposed in the literature. However, increasing the dataset size by data augmentation may not always improve the model's generalization capability [52].

4.3   Robustness

Robustness is a property that characterizes the effectiveness of the DL algorithm when being tested on the new audio dataset recorded with an unknown microphone and acoustic environment. Even though there are several factors, such as environmental noise and room reverberation that affect the robustness, microphone variability is the one that severely challenges the robustness of audio processing deep learning models on resource-constrained devices [6,53,54]. According to Akhil Mathur *et al.* [54], the microphone variability can degrade up to 15% of the performance accuracy of DL models. This is mainly due to the variability in the transfer function of microphones. Parameters such as frequency response, impedance rating, and output levels determine the transfer function of the microphone.

To improve the reduced performance due to the variability between training and target data, different techniques have been proposed in the literature, including, adapting the trained model for the target data [53] and mapping (translation) between source and target microphones [54]. Techniques employed in [53] require the target model to be retrained through adversarial domain adaptation after the source model was trained and optimized on the source data. This process is computationally intensive, and the model accuracy on the target domain is far less than on the source domain. The technique proposed in [54], aims to reduce the effect of microphone variability in the performance of the target domain through audio mapping (translation) between the two domains through cyclical generative adversarial network technique. The reported result indicates a performance improvement in the target domain. However, the front-end mapping module brings additional computational complexity that consecutively increases the latency and energy consumption of the inference task. So, building robust device-independent deep learning-based audio processing applications on a resource-constrained device is a challenge that needs to be addressed.

4.4   Interpretability

According to S. Chakraborty et al., [56], a DNN model should provide justifications for its output to provide an insight into its inner workings so that human experts have a better understanding of how the model performs. However, deep learning models' decision-making process is not explainable because of the inherent high complexity and a high number of trainable parameters. As a result, DL models are often considered as a black-box. This lack of model interpretability has brought concerns, and a lack of confidence in deploying deep learning models in a high-level application such as in clinical decision-making [55–57].

Recently interpretable deep learning models have been proposed in several application areas. These models use methods such as a layer-wise relevance propagation (LRP) [58,59], activation regularisation [60], and an adversarial explanation [61], to better understand how the models perform on a particular task. However, the issue of model interpretability is not confined to DL models on RCDs but it is a challenge that hinders deep learning models' deployment irrespective of devices' computational capability, and it is a topic of active research.

5   Conclusion

The advent of consumer devices such as smartphones, smartwatches, and other lightweight and mobile embedded systems has brought enormous benefits to human life through machine learning-based monitoring and decision-making. DL models are build by stacking multiple neural layers on top of each other and contain millions of parameters that can learn more complex functions compared to shallow machine learning algorithms. However, computations involving such millions of parameters undoubtedly overpower the capacity of devices with a low-computational resource. Therefore, to harness the potential of DL algorithms applications on RCDs, several model squeezing methods have been proposed in the literature.

In this work, we have presented a survey of DL model architectures in audio processing applications and their compression techniques. In addition, the performance of compressed DL models reported in the literature and the challenges in deploying the models on resource-constrained devices have been presented. The reported results indicate that the squeezed DL models are less complex with fewer parameters. As a result, they require less runtime memory, reduced power consumption, and perform the inference task with lower latency. Besides, these improvements are obtained without significant loss of accuracy when compared to the uncompressed baseline DL models.

Furthermore, challenges that cannot be addressed by only modifying DL architectures and model optimizations have also been discussed. These include limitations in on-device training, in maintaining model robustness in the varying acoustic environment and audio recording devices, scarcity of training datasets, and the difficulty in DL models' output interpretability. Also, the solutions proposed in the literature to mitigate these limitations are presented.

In conclusion, despite all the promising results, there exist challenges that need to be addressed to make robust deep learning-based applications on computationally constrained devices. The solutions to these challenges may span from model optimization to upgrading device hardware.

References

1. Deng, L.: Deep learning: methods and applications. Found. Trends® Sig. Process. **7**, 197–387 (2014)
2. LeCun, Y., Bengio, Y., Hinton, G.: Deep learning. Nature **521**, 436–444 (2015)
3. Lane, N., Georgiev, P.: Can deep learning revolutionize mobile sensing? In: Proceedings of the 16th International Workshop on Mobile Computing Systems and Applications (2015)
4. Lane, N., Bhattacharya, S., Mathur, A., Georgiev, P., Forlivesi, C., Kawsar, F.: Squeezing deep learning into mobile and embedded devices. IEEE Pervasive Comput. **16**, 82–88 (2017)
5. Cardoso, J., Figueiredo Coutinho, J., Diniz, P.: Embedded Computing for High Performance. Elsevier, Amsterdam (2017)
6. Lane, N., Georgiev, P., Qendro, L.: DeepEar: robust smartphone audio sensing in unconstrained acoustic environments using deep learning. In: Proceedings of the 2015 ACM International Joint Conference on Pervasive and Ubiquitous Computing - UbiComp 2015 (2015)
7. Zeiler, M., et al.: On rectified linear units for speech processing. In: 2013 IEEE International Conference on Acoustics, Speech and Signal Processing (2013)
8. Lopez-Moreno, I., Gonzalez-Dominguez, J., Martinez, D., Plchot, O., Gonzalez-Rodriguez, J., Moreno, P.: On the use of deep feedforward neural networks for automatic language identification. Comput. Speech Lang. **40**, 46–59 (2016)

9. Hinton, G., et al.: Deep neural networks for acoustic modeling in speech recognition: the shared views of four research groups. IEEE Sig. Process. Mag. **29**, 82–97 (2012)

10. Goodfellow, I., Bengio, J., Courville, A.: Deep Learning. MIT Press Ltd., Cambridge (2016)

11. Lu, L., Renals, S.: Small-footprint highway deep neural networks for speech recognition. IEEE/ACM Trans. Audio Speech Lang. Process. **25**, 1502–1511 (2017)

12. Xue, J., Li, J., Gong, Y.: Restructuring of deep neural network acoustic models with singular value decomposition. In: Interspeech, pp. 2365–2369 (2013)

13. Bhattacharya, S., Lane, N.: Sparsification and separation of deep learning layers for constrained resource inference on wearables. In: Proceedings of the 14th ACM Conference on Embedded Network Sensor Systems CD-ROM (2016)

14. Hu, H., Gao, L., Ma, Q.: Deep restricted boltzmann networks. arXiv:1611.07917v1 (2016)

15. Pascanu, R., Gulcehre, C., Cho, K., Bengio, Y.: How to construct deep recurrent neural networks. arXiv:1312.6026v5 (2013)

16. Zhang, J., Wang, X., Li, D., Wang, Y.: Dynamically hierarchy revolution: DirNet for compressing recurrent neural network on mobile devices. In: Proceedings of the 27th International Joint Conference on Artificial Intelligence, pp. 3089–3096 (2018)

17. Han, S., et al.: ESE: efficient speech recognition engine with sparse LSTM on FPGA. In: Proceedings of the 2017 ACM/SIGDA International Symposium on Field-Programmable Gate Arrays (2017)

18. Wen, L., Zhang, X., Bai, H., Xu, Z.: Structured pruning of recurrent neural networks through neuron selection. Neural Netw. **123**, 134–141 (2020)

19. Rezk, N., Purnaprajna, M., Nordstrom, T., Ul-Abdin, Z.: Recurrent neural networks: an embedded computing perspective. IEEE Access. **8**, 57967–57996 (2020)

20. Shi, Y., Hwang, M., Lei, X., Sheng, H.: knowledge distillation for recurrent neural network language modeling with trust regularization. In: ICASSP 2019–2019 IEEE International Conference on Acoustics, Speech and Signal Processing (ICASSP) (2019)

21. Wen, W., et al.: Learning intrinsic sparse structures within long short-term memory. ArXiv:1709.05027 (2018)

22. Narang, S., Undersander, E., Diamos, G.: Block-sparse recurrent neural networks. arXiv:1711.02782v1 (2017)

23. Phuong, M., Lampert, C.: Towards understanding knowledge distillation. In: Proceedings of the 36th International Conference on Machine Learning, ICML 2019, 9–15 June 2019, Long Beach, California, USA, vol. 97, pp. 5142–5151 (2019)

24. Su, Y., Zhang, K., Wang, J., Madani, K.: Environment sound classification using a two-stream CNN based on decision-level fusion. Sensors **19**, 1733 (2019)

25. Abdoli, S., Cardinal, P., Koerich, A.: End-to-end environmental sound classification using a 1D convolutional neural network. ArXiv (2019)

26. Sehgal, A., Kehtarnavaz, N.: A convolutional neural network smartphone app for real-time voice activity detection. IEEE Access **6**, 9017–9026 (2018)

27. Dorfler, M., Bammer, R., Grill, T.: Inside the spectrogram: convolutional neural networks in audio processing. In: 2017 International Conference on Sampling Theory and Applications (SampTA) (2017)

28. Piczak, K.: Environmental sound classification with convolutional neural networks. In: 2015 IEEE 25th International Workshop on Machine Learning for Signal Processing (MLSP) (2015)

29. Tai, C., Xiao, T., Zhang, Y., Wang, X.: Convolutional neural networks with low-rank regularization. arXiv:1511.06067v3 (2015)
30. Lin, S., Ji, R., Li, Y., Deng, C., Li, X.: Toward compact ConvNets via structure-sparsity regularized filter pruning. IEEE Trans. Neural Netw. Learn. Syst. **31**, 574–588 (2020)
31. Wu, J., Yu, C., Fu, S., Liu, C., Chien, S., Tsao, Y.: Increasing compactness of deep learning based speech enhancement models with parameter pruning and quantization techniques. IEEE Sig. Process. Lett. **26**, 1887–1891 (2019)
32. Li, H., Kadav, A., Durdanovic, I., Samet, H., Graf, H.: Pruning filters for efficient ConvNets. In: 5th International Conference on Learning Representations, ICLR 2017, Toulon, France, April 24–26, 2017, Conference Track Proceedings (2017)
33. Molchanov, P., Tyree, S., Karras, T., Aila, T., Kautz, J.: Pruning convolutional neural networks for resource efficient inference. In: 5th International Conference On Learning Representations, ICLR 2017, Toulon, France, April 24–26, 2017, Conference Track Proceedings (2017)
34. Ahmed, H., Wong, M., Nandi, A.: Intelligent condition monitoring method for bearing faults from highly compressed measurements using sparse over-complete features. Mech. Syst. Sig. Process. **99**, 459–477 (2018)
35. Lu, X., Tsao, Y., Matsuda, S., Hori, C.: Speech enhancement based on deep denoising autoencoder. In: Interspeech 2013 (2013)
36. Xu, Y., et al.: Unsupervised feature learning based on deep models for environmental audio tagging. IEEE/ACM Trans. Audio Speech Lang. Process. **25**, 1230–1241 (2017)
37. Luo, D., Yang, R., Li, B., Huang, J.: Detection of double compressed AMR audio using stacked autoencoder. IEEE Trans. Inf. Forensics Secur **12**, 432–444 (2017)
38. Abeßer, J., Mimilakis, S., Gräfe, R., Lukashevich, H., Fraunhofer, I.: Acoustic scene classification by combining autoencoder-based dimensionality reduction and convolutional neural networks. In: DCASE, pp. 7–11 (2017)
39. Suzuki, A., Morie, T., Tamukoh, H.: A shared synapse architecture for efficient FPGA implementation of autoencoders. PLoS ONE **13**, e0194049 (2018)
40. Li, P., Nguyen, P.: On random deep weight-tied autoencoders: exact asymptotic analysis, phase transitions, and implications to training. In: International Conference On Learning Representations (2019)
41. Georgiev, P., Bhattacharya, S., Lane, N., Mascolo, C.: Low-resource multi-task audio sensing for mobile and embedded devices via shared deep neural network representations. Proc. ACM Interact. Mob. Wearable Ubiquit. Technol. **1**, 1–19 (2017)
42. Chauhan, J., Seneviratne, S., Hu, Y., Misra, A., Seneviratne, A., Lee, Y.: Breathing-based authentication on resource-constrained IoT devices using recurrent neural networks. Computer **51**, 60–67 (2018)
43. Mohaimenuzzaman, M., Bergmeir, C., West, I., Meyer, B.: Environmental sound classification on the edge: a pipeline for deep acoustic networks on extremely resource-constrained devices. arXiv:2103.03483v4 (2021)
44. Song, M., et al.: In-situ AI: towards autonomous and incremental deep learning for IoT systems. In: 2018 IEEE International Symposium on High Performance Computer Architecture (HPCA) (2018)
45. Ignatov, A., et al.: AI benchmark: running deep neural networks on android smartphones. arXiv:1810.01109v2 (2018)
46. Deng, Y.: Deep learning on mobile devices: a review. In: Mobile Multimedia/Image Processing, Security, and Applications (2019)

47. Dalgaty, T., Esmanhotto, E., Castellani, N., Querlioz, D., Vianello, E.: Ex situ transfer of Bayesian neural networks to resistive memory-based inference hardware. Adv. Intell. Syst. **3**, 2000103 (2021)

48. Sehgal, A., Kehtarnavaz, N.: Guidelines and benchmarks for deployment of deep learning models on smartphones as real-time apps. Mach. Learn. Knowl. Extr. **1**, 450–465 (2019)

49. Abeßer, J.: A review of deep learning based methods for acoustic scene classification. Appl. Sci. **10** (2020)

50. Mathur, A., et al.: Using deep data augmentation training to address software and hardware heterogeneities in wearable and smartphone sensing devices. In: 2018 17th ACM/IEEE International Conference on Information Processing in Sensor Networks (IPSN) (2018)

51. Liang, D., Thomaz, E.: Audio-based activities of daily living (ADL) recognition with large-scale acoustic embeddings from online videos. Proc. ACM Interact. Mob. Wearable Ubiquit. Technol. **3**, 1–18 (2019)

52. Mignot, R., Peeters, G.: An analysis of the effect of data augmentation methods: experiments for a musical genre classification task. Trans. Int. Soc. Music Inf. Retrieval **2**, 97–110 (2019)

53. Drossos, K., Magron, P., Virtanen, T.: Unsupervised adversarial domain adaptation based on the wasserstein distance for acoustic scene classification. In: 2019 IEEE Workshop on Applications of Signal Processing to Audio and Acoustics (WASPAA) (2019)

54. Mathur, A., Isopoussu, A., Kawsar, F., Berthouze, N., Lane, N.: Mic2Mic. proceedings of the 18th International Conference on Information Processing in Sensor Networks (2019)

55. Ayano, Y.M., Friedhelm, S., Dufera, B.D., Debelee, T.G.: Interpretable machine learning techniques in ECG-based heart disease classification: a systematic review. Diagnostics **13**, 111 (2022)

56. Chakraborty, S., et al.: Interpretability of deep learning models: a survey of results. In: 2017 IEEE SmartWorld, Ubiquitous Intelligence & Computing, Advanced & Trusted Computed, Scalable Computing & Communications, Cloud & Big Data Computing, Internet of People and Smart City Innovation (SmartWorld/SCALCOM/UIC/ATC/CBDCom/IOP/SCI), pp. 1–6 (2017)

57. Lipton, Z.: The mythos of model interpretability. Queue **16**, 31–57 (2018)

58. Montavon, G., Samek, W., Müller, K.: Methods for interpreting and understanding deep neural networks. Digit. Sig. Process. **73**, 1–15 (2018)

59. Arras, L., et al.: Explaining and interpreting LSTMs. In: Samek, W., Montavon, G., Vedaldi, A., Hansen, L.K., Müller, K.-R. (eds.) Explainable AI: Interpreting, Explaining and Visualizing Deep Learning. LNCS (LNAI), vol. 11700, pp. 211–238. Springer, Cham (2019). https://doi.org/10.1007/978-3-030-28954-6_11

60. Wu, C., Gales, M., Ragni, A., Karanasou, P., Sim, K.: Improving interpretability and regularization in deep learning. IEEE/ACM Trans. Audio Speech Lang. Process. **26**, 256–265 (2018)

61. Rahnama, A., Tseng, A.: An adversarial approach for explaining the predictions of deep neural networks. arXiv:2005.10284v4 (2020)

Offline Handwritten Amharic Character Recognition Using Few-Shot Learning

Mesay Samuel[1]([✉]), Lars Schmidt-Thieme[2], D. P. Sharma[3], Abiot Sinamo[4], and Abey Bruck[1]

[1] Faculty of Computing and Software Engineering, Arba Minch University, Arba Minch, Ethiopia
{mesay.samuel,abey.bruck}@amu.edu.et
[2] Information Systems and Machine Learning Lab, 31141 Hildesheim, Germany
schmidt-thieme@ismll.uni-hildesheim.de
[3] AMUIT MOEFDRE under UNDP, Addis Ababa, Ethiopia
[4] Ministry of Innovation and Technology, Federal Democratic Republic of Ethiopia, Addis Ababa, Ethiopia

Abstract. Few-shot learning is a demanding and challenging problem in machine learning aimed at learning from only fewer labeled training examples. It has become an active area of research due to deep learning requiring huge amounts of labeled dataset, which is not easy practically. Learning from fewer examples is also an important attempt towards learning like humans. Few-shot learning has proven a very good promise in different areas of machine learning applications, particularly in image classification. As it is a recent technique, most researchers focus on understanding and solving the issues related to its concept by focusing only on common image datasets like Mini-ImageNet and Omniglot. Few-shot learning also opens an opportunity to address low resource languages like Amharic. Hence in the current study, it is used to address offline handwritten character recognition for Amharic language. Particularly, prototypical networks, the popular and simpler type of few-shot learning, is implemented as a baseline. Using the opportunities explored in the nature of Amharic alphabet having columnwise and rowwise characters' similarities, a novel way of augmenting the training episodes is proposed. According to the study's experimental result, it was observed that the proposed method outperformed the baseline method in 1-shot setting. This study has implemented few-shot learning for Amharic characters for the first time. More importantly, the findings of the study open new ways of examining the influence of training episodes in few-shot learning, which is one of the critical issues requiring further exploration. The datasets used for this study are collected from native Amharic language writers using an Android App developed as a part of this study.

Keywords: Amharic · Character Recognition · Deep Learning · Handwritten · Few-shot Learning · Prototypical Networks · Training Episode

T. Girma Debelee et al. (Eds.): PanAfriCon AI 2022, CCIS 1800, pp. 233–244, 2023.
https://doi.org/10.1007/978-3-031-31327-1_13

1   Introduction

Few-shot learning can be defined as a type of machine learning which aims at gaining good learning performance with few (usually 20 or less) supervised training examples [1]. It is an important area of machine learning which contributes to the advancement in AI in the aspect of learning humanly as humans easily learn from fewer examples. It also helps in learning rare cases which can be applied to fraud detection in electronic transactions. The applications of few-shot learning encompasses different domains including robotics, computer vision, natural language processing, acoustic signal processing, drug discovery, and the like. Few-shot learning also reduces the data gathering effort and computational cost associated with big datasets which are very common issues in deep learning.

The problem of few-shot learning can be addressed using various techniques. In all cases however, there is a way to exploit prior knowledge accumulated in the data, model or algorithm of any related machine learning task. The most common and effective way is through algorithm approach particularly meta-learning. Meta-learning is an attempt to improve performance of a new task using the meta-knowledge extracted from related tasks through a meta-learner [1]. Hence, the formulation of tasks plays a crucial role in such problems. These tasks are also known as episodes having their own training and test sets. Support and query sets are also commonly used terminologies in few-shot learning to refer to the training and test sets respectively. Each task has an equal number of classes (referred as ways) for the support and query sets. However, the number of examples per class in the support set only defines the shot. Hence, a 3 way 5 shot few-shot learning problem describes a task formulation with 3 classes and 5 examples per class in the support set.

Meta-learning (learning to learn) is any type of learning based on prior experience in learning with other tasks. Even though defining task similarity remains as the main challenge, it plays a major role in meta-learning. That is, more similar tasks help in extracting more meta-data. Other types of learning including transfer learning, multi-task learning, and ensemble learning can also be meaningfully integrated with meta-learning systems. Hence, the scientific contributions in meta-learning facilitates the innovation of machine learning pipelines and also allow us to produce novel algorithms which can be developed through learning in a data-driven way [2]. Likewise this study explores and opens a wide range of perspectives into examining task similarities and their related effects on specific applications of deep learning and few-shot learning.

Amharic optical character recognition in general and the handwritten character recognition in particular is not a well studied area of research. The unavailability of standard public datasets make Amharic as one of the low resource languages. Even though there are limited attempts, most of these works focus on implementation of off-the-shelf inventions which are particularly designed for Latin scripts. This trend has created two interconnected problems. The first one is associated with the limitations to fit the real problem and proposed solution. Another problem arises from overlooking the opportunities that might have emerged with any possible innovations from the exploration of specific contexts which can then be scaled up to generalized solutions [3–6].

In this study, offline handwritten Amharic character recognition is addressed by using few-shot learning technique for the first time. Few-shot learning is a recent and promising area of study resolving the limitations of deep learning which requires huge amounts of labeled data. Accordingly, such techniques open a way to address low resource languages like Amharic. It is also suitable to address the issue of rarely occurring characters in real life documents. More importantly in this study, training episodes are examined from the context and nature of Amharic characters, which are the core issues in few-shot learning problems. Most of the studies in few-shot learning focus on understanding the problem itself and hence are based on common image datasets like Mini-ImageNet and Omniglot. However, in this study a more realistic application of few-shot learning is presented using prototypical networks which is a popular and simpler type of few-shot learning.

The challenges facing deep learning studies when it comes to low resource languages is not only unavailability of huge standard datasets but also the difficulty of training deep learning models. That is, the architecture of a deep learning model may have by far more parameters than its training sets [7]. In regard to few-shot learning also, the datasets used to assess are not challenging and realistic as compared to the progress made in the techniques and models [8]. Hence in this study, a suitable few-shot learning dataset is organized for Amharic characters using an Android App developed as a part of this study. Generally, the contributions of this paper can be summarized as follows:

i. Organized a new few-shot learning dataset for Amharic handwritten characters with the appropriate split of train, validation, and test sets.
ii. Implemented few-shot learning for Amharic handwritten characters recognition for the first time as a benchmark.
iii. Empirically explored how training episodes affect the performance in few-shot learning with a novel contribution in the context of Amharic handwritten characters recognition.

2   Related Work

Different recent papers have emerged to clarify the progress in few-shot learning [8–11]. These studies mainly address the problems associated with few-shot learning datasets and performance measures. Triantafillou et al. [8] proposed META-DATASET: a large-scale dataset containing authentic and various types of tasks which also serve as a strong baseline for few-shot learning. Dhillon et al. [9] performed a rigorous experiment and proposed a new metric which is used to measure the hardness associated with few-shot episodes. This is particularly important in reporting the results of few-shot techniques in a better and principled manner.

Wang et al. [1] have made a rigorous review on few-shot learning problems to formally define and construct a good taxonomy of few-shot learning problems.

Authors gave a formal definition of few-shot learning which connects to the general problem of machine learning by illustrating the unreliable empirical risk minimizer. That is the core issue in few-shot learning that arises due to fewer examples. This can be easily identified when the loss is decomposed as a supervised machine learning problem. Therefore, few-shot learning techniques should find a way to use prior knowledge accumulated in data, model, and algorithm of other related tasks. Accordingly, Wang et al. [1] classified few-shot learning methods by their focus on these three constituents into data (augment training dataset using prior knowledge), model (constrain hypothesis space by prior knowledge), and algorithm (alter search strategy in hypothesis space by prior knowledge).

Typical examples of algorithm few-shot learning are Model-Agnostic Meta-Learning (MAML) [12] and its variants like Reptile [13]. These methods learn parameter initialization which can easily be adjusted for a new task. MAML learns initialization through effective gradient steps for a new task with a few training data to reach at better generalization. Reptile performs this to move the initialization to the trained weights on a new task through repeated task sampling and training [1,12,13]. Another set of Model few-shot learning methods include siamese neural networks, matching networks, and prototypical networks which are task-invariant embedding learning models [1]. These methods are also known as metric learning as they learn to classify new images based on their similarity to support images unlike gradient-based meta-learning which leverages gradient descent to learn commonalities among various tasks [14–16]. Simple Neural Attentive Learner (SNAIL) is another embedding network which integrates temporal convolution layers and attention layers. This provides the opportunity for generic architectures to harness specific tasks [1,17]. In this study, both model and algorithm few-shot methods are exhibited due to the implementation of prototypical networks and incorporation of auxiliary task episodic training.

More related papers address few-shot learning from two main perspectives which are interrelated by nature. The first one is focusing on extraction of highly discriminative features which can easily generalize classes so that very few samples would be sufficient. Another direction is looking for different possible auxiliary or related tasks that can be used to complement the main few-shot classification task. This can be done by proposing creative classification tasks that can be trained in a multi-task learning fashion [18]. Mazumder et al. [18] proposed an approach which uses self-supervised auxiliary tasks to produce highly discriminative generic features from image datasets. The auxiliary task here is a two stage rotation of patches including within the image rotation and the whole image rotation which creates another classification problem for the multiple rotation classes. When these tasks are trained simultaneously, the model learns generic and relevant features which increase the performance of the main few-shot classification task. Such methods actually utilize the concept of gradient/ optimization-based meta-learning approach of few-shot learning. Accordingly, a related work by Tripathi et al. [19] further integrated both induction and transduction learning into the base learner in the framework of an optimization-based meta-learning. On the other hand Ravi and Larochelle [20], rather than training an individual model over multiple episodes, introduced an LSTM based meta-learner which trains a custom model for each few-shot episode.

A simpler and more efficient approach to few-shot learning is prototypical networks which is a metric learning. The main idea is to find a representative prototype for each class through the average embedding of the data points. Classification in prototypical networks is performed for an embedded query set point by easily assigning it to the closest class prototype. "Prototypical networks learn a non-linear mapping of the input into an embedding space using neural networks and take a class's prototype to be the mean of its support set in the embedding space" [16]. Building on prototypical networks, Fort [21] extended to Gaussian prototypical networks incorporating a Gaussian covariance matrix, where the network constructs a direction and class dependent distance metric on the embedding space, using uncertainties of individual data points as weights.

3 Methodology

3.1 Dataset Preparation

The dataset used for this study is collected using an Android app developed as part of this study. Screenshots of the app are shown in Fig. 1. The link to the app with a brief notice was distributed using different platforms including email, Facebook messenger, Telegram and WhatsApp to different groups of individuals who can write Amharic. For this few-shot learning study, a total of 1,325 hand-written character images were organized. That is, five images per character for 265 Amharic characters in the Amharic alphabet. The five character images are randomly selected from those written by more than 35 individuals. The images are resized to 32 × 32 pixels and are grouped into 120, 61, and 84 unique sets of characters for train, validation, and test splits respectively. A table showing the specific characters used for these splits is available in Appendix A. The dataset of this study is publicly available[1]

3.2 Prototypical Networks

This study implemented Prototypical Networks as a baseline. By exploiting the opportunities from the Amharic alphabet having row-wise and column-wise characters' similarities, meaningful alterations are made in the training episodes for the proposed methods. Prototypical Networks is one of the popular metric based few-shot learning methods which classify new classes based on their similarity to a small number of examples per class. This small number of classes is the support set which is the only information used by a few-shot classification model in order to classify query images. During training, Prototypical Networks produce a prototype for each class, which is the average of all embeddings of support

---

[1] https://github.com/mesaysama/amharic-handwritten-character-dataset.

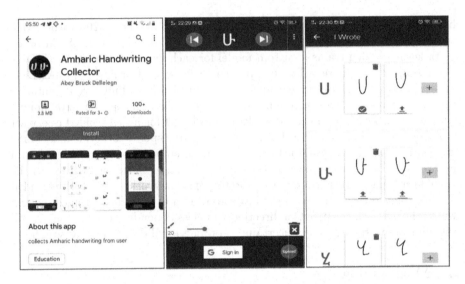

Fig. 1. Screenshots of the data collection app.

set data points from this class. For evaluation, each query point is simply pre-dicted based on the closest euclidean distance from the prototypes in the feature vector. Whereas the support sets have labels both during training and testing time, the query sets have labels only during training time. Hence, for each image in the query set, the aim is to classify to a label from the support set during testing time. This study used a pretrained ResNet18 as a backbone to produce the embedding of both support and query sets.

4   Results and Discussion

All the experiments in this study are implemented using Pytorch machine learn-ing library on the Google Colab and the computing cluster of Information Sys-tems and Machine Learning Lab (ISMLL) from the University of Hildesheim. More importantly, the implementations are based on easy few-shot learning code by Bennequin [22]. During this study, many few-shot learning experiments were performed to explore the possible ways one can make episodic training for the case of Amharic handwritten character recognition. For instance, one can train a model with *label A* and test the model with *label B* which is not the case in regular machine learning practice. *Label A* could be the Amharic character row label and *label B* may refer to the specific character label in the Amharic Alpha-bet. This is possible since a few-shot learning method allows testing a new class with its own few supervised samples. Particularly, this is due to the possibility of assigning an Amharic character to multiple labels from its tabular alphabet chart as shown in Appendix A.

Even though there are many ways one can implement few-shot learning using episodic training, this study is limited to focus on exploring meaningful insights with the most common Few-shot settings in the literature [8,23,24]. Accordingly, this study implemented a few-shot learning for 1,2 and 3 shots with 5 way settings only. In all the settings, the query sets are kept to hold only two samples per class. A custom data loader is used to organize and feed the model with the appropriate combination of support and query set in each task. Training episodes are set to 20,000 tasks which are randomly generated few-shot classification tasks. The model iterates over these tasks to fit and update after each task which is called episodic training. The model classifies the query set based on what is learned from the support set. Then, the loss is obtained when the ground truth values and the predicted labels of the query set are compared. To give more emphasis on the episodic task formulation, in this study the common standard cross entropy loss and Adam optimizer are used like several related studies [8,23,24].

For validation and testing experiments, a separate set of previously unseen classes are used with 1000 tasks each. For the case of proposed methods, half of the training episodes are replaced with row label and column label based task formulations for the proposed method 1 and 2 respectively. This is a novel way of task formulation which is used to augment the training episodes using the advantages of rowwise and columnwise relationships in the Amharic alphabet. Sample datasets showing the task formulations for the baseline and proposed methods are presented in Fig. 2.

Baseline Method using character label, 1-shot		Proposed Method 1 using character row label, 3-shot		Proposed Method 2 using character column label, 2-shot	
Support set	*Query set*	*Support set*	*Query set*	*Support set*	*Query set*

Fig. 2. Sample dataset from episodes/ task formulation in the baseline and proposed methods.

As shown in Table 1, a total of nine models are experimented to compare the results between the baseline and proposed methods for the three few-shot settings. Each experiment is run three times and the average result of the accuracy scores on a test set for 1000 character label classification task is also presented in Table 1. As can be seen from this table, the baseline method scored 38.10%, 91.10%, and 93.70% accuracy for 1, 2, and 3 shot settings respectively. The

Table 1. Accuracy scores of the competing models on a test set under different few-shot settings.

Methods	1-shot	2-shot	3-shot
Baseline	38.10%	**91.10%**	**93.70%**
Proposed Method 1	**75.90%**	90.10%	88.40%
Proposed Method 2	38.30%	87.00%	92.90%

proposed method 1 scored 75.90%, 90.10%, and 88.40% for 1, 2, and 3 shot settings respectively. Likewise, the proposed method 2 scored 38.30%, 87.00%, and 92.90% for 1, 2, and 3 shot settings respectively.

An important finding of this study revealed the superior performance of the proposed method 1 which uses row based episodic training. That is, 75.90% accuracy which outperformed other methods by a significant margin in a 1-shot setting. Even though the baseline method has a better performance for the 2 and 3-shot settings, still the proposed methods showed comparable results. That is, the results of the baseline and proposed method 1 are relatively closer to each other in a 2-shot setting. Similarly, the results of the baseline and proposed method 2 are close to each other in the 3-shot setting.

Another important finding from this study is that both proposed methods have their own relevance in the different few-shot settings. That is, the proposed method 1 which uses row based episodic training helps when it is very few-shot. In contrast, proposed method 2 which uses column based episodic training appears to help when the shots are increasing. This is an interesting behavior which needs further investigation to help Amharic handwritten character recognition using few-shot learning. In line with this, both the baseline and proposed method 2 have shown an increase in performance along with the increase in shots. This is an expected empirical result in few-shot learning as studied by Triantafillou et al. [8] on the effects varying the number of shots and ways in different few-shot methods including prototypical networks. Another study by Dhillon et al. [9] identified that to get higher performance when there are large number of few-shot ways, it is helpful to employ a large number of meta-training classes. Hence, even though the effect of varying ways is not investigated in this study, the large number of Amharic characters in the alphabet and the experiments explored in this study open an interesting area of further study.

The results of the proposed methods in this study have shown how episodic task formulation affects the performance of few-shot learning. This supports the emphasis given to meta-training distribution of episodes by different studies [1,18–20,25]. However, as attempted to explore in this study, the proportion and the pattern of formulating the tasks from character label, row label, and col label will remain an open area of research. This is particularly relevant during the training phase for few-shot learning since the test sets contain previously unseen classes with their own labels in the support set.

Finally, this study has benefited from both types of few-shot learning approaches including the metric learning and optimization-based learning. The use of prototypical networks helps to learn an embedding space which signifies metric learning [19]. On the other hand, the study exploited the advantage of transfer learning and multi-task learning through episode design in meta-learning [25] which also improves generalization by enabling the extraction of discriminative generic features [16, 18].

5   Conclusion

This study addressed offline handwritten Amharic character recognition using few-shot learning for the first time. As a baseline method, this study implemented prototypical networks which is an embedding and metric based few-shot learning method. From the opportunities of Amharic alphabet having row-wise and column-wise characters' similarities, a novel way of augmenting the training episodes is explored as a proposed method. The results of the study revealed that the proposed method outperformed the baseline method by a significant margin in a 5-way 1-shot few-shot learning setting. This study has also proven how formulation of training episodes using related auxiliary tasks could affect the performance of few-shot learning methods. The dataset prepared by this study is another important contribution for Amharic few-shot learning research by bringing a more suitable and realistic dataset which can be used by other researchers.

Even though this study experimented with few-shot learning in different settings by varying the shots, the effects of varying ways remain unexplored. Hence, future studies can focus on extending the experiments to find the most optimum few-shot learning setting. Studying the formulation of training episodes from the combination of character, row, and column labels is also an important area of research to progress in few-shot learning for Amharic handwritten character recognition.

Appendix A. The Amharic Characters

The table below shows how the Amharic characters are selected for the train, validation, and test splits from the Amharic alphabet. This is particularly organized to be suitable for few-shot learning research. Accordingly, 120, 61, and 84 unique characters are identified for train, validation, and test sets respectively. The inclusion and exclusion of characters and their families to the specific set is done carefully so that the balance between training and evaluation challenges could not be affected. The numbers (1–9) above the table show the column labels and the numbers (1–34) to the left show the row labels of the characters. However, the individual character label is given sequentially in the Amharic alphabet from 1 to 265. Hence, the first Amharic character for instance, has label 1 for its character, row, and column labels. Likewise, the last character has labels 265, 34, and 7 for its character, row, and column labels respectively.

Characters for train set: #120

	1	2	3	4	5	6	7	8	9
1	ሀ	ሁ	ሂ	ሃ	ሄ	ህ	ሆ		
2	ለ	ሉ	ሊ	ላ	ሌ	ል	ሎ	ሏ	
3	ሐ	ሑ	ሒ	ሓ	ሔ	ሕ	ሖ		
4	መ	ሙ	ሚ	ማ	ሜ	ም	ሞ	ሟ	
6	ረ	ሩ		ራ		ር	ሮ	ሯ	
7	ሰ		ሲ	ሳ	ሴ	ስ	ሶ	ሷ	
8	ሸ	ሹ	ሺ	ሻ	ሼ	ሽ	ሾ	ሿ	
9	ቀ	ቁ	ቂ	ቃ	ቄ	ቅ	ቆ	ቈ	
11	ተ	ቱ	ቲ	ታ	ቴ	ት	ቶ		
12			ቺ	ቻ	ቼ	ች	ቾ		
13		ኁ	ኂ	ኃ	ኄ	ኅ	ኆ		
15	ኘ	ኙ	ኚ	ኛ	ኜ	ኝ	ኞ	ኟ	
16		ኡ	ኢ	ኣ	ኤ		ኦ	ኧ	
18	ዐ	ዑ	ዒ	ዓ	ዔ	ዕ	ዖ		
20	ኸ	ኹ	ኺ	ኻ	ኼ	ኽ	ኾ		
21		ዙ	ዚ	ዛ		ዝ	ዞ		
22	ዠ				ዤ				
24	ገ	ጉ	ጊ	ጋ					
25	ደ	ዱ	ዲ	ዳ					

Characters for validation set: #61

	1	2	3	4	5	6	7	8	9
5	ሠ	ሡ	ሢ	ሣ	ሤ	ሥ	ሦ		
6			ሪ		ሬ				
7		ሱ							
10	በ	ቡ	ቢ	ባ	ቤ	ብ	ቦ	ቧ	
11								ቷ	
12	ቸ	ቹ						ቿ	
13	ኀ							ኈ	
14	ነ	ኑ	ኒ	ና	ኔ	ን	ኖ	ኗ	
16	አ					እ			
17	ወ	ዉ	ዊ	ዋ	ዌ	ው	ዎ		
19	ከ	ኩ	ኪ	ካ	ኬ	ክ	ኮ	ኰ	
21	ዘ				ዜ				
22		ዡ	ዢ	ዣ					
23	የ	ዩ	ዪ	ያ					
27	ጠ	ጡ	ጢ						

Characters for test set: #84

	1	2	3	4	5	6	7	8	9
9									ቋ
13									ኋ
19									ኳ
21								ዟ	
22						ዥ	ዦ	ዧ	
23					ዬ	ይ	ዮ		
24						ግ	ጎ	ጐ	ጓ
25					ዴ	ድ	ዶ	ዷ	
26	ጀ	ጁ	ጂ	ጃ	ጄ	ጅ	ጆ	ጇ	
27				ጣ	ጤ	ጥ	ጦ	ጧ	
28	ጨ	ጩ	ጪ	ጫ	ጬ	ጭ	ጮ	ጯ	
29	ጰ	ጱ	ጲ	ጳ	ጴ	ጵ	ጶ	ጷ	
30	ፀ	ፁ	ፂ	ፃ	ፄ	ፅ	ፆ		
31	ጸ	ጹ	ጺ	ጻ	ጼ	ጽ	ጾ		
32	ፈ	ፉ	ፊ	ፋ	ፌ	ፍ	ፎ	ፏ	
33	ፐ	ፑ	ፒ	ፓ	ፔ	ፕ	ፖ		
34	ቨ	ቩ	ቪ	ቫ	ቬ	ቭ	ቮ		

References

1. Wang, Y., Yao, Q., Kwok, J.T., Ni, L.M.: Generalizing from a few examples: a survey on few-shot learning. ACM Comput. Surv. (CSUR) **53**(3), 1–34 (2020)
2. Vanschoren, J.: Meta-learning: a survey. arXiv preprint arXiv:1810.03548 (2018)
3. Obsie, E.Y., Qu, H., Huang, Q.: Amharic character recognition based on features extracted by CNN and auto-encoder models. In: 2021 The 13th International Conference on Computer Modeling and Simulation, pp. 58–66 (2021)
4. Belay, B.H., Habtegebrial, T., Liwicki, M., Belay, G., Stricker, D.: A blended attention-CTC network architecture for Amharic text-image recognition. In: ICPRAM, pp. 435–441 (2021)
5. Gondere, M.S., Schmidt-Thieme, L., Sharma, D.P., Scholz, R.: Multi-script handwritten digit recognition using multitask learning. J. Intell. Fuzzy Syst. **43**(1), 355–364 (2022)
6. Gondere, M.S., Schmidt-Thieme, L., Sharma, D.P., Boltena, A.S.: Improving Amharic Handwritten Word Recognition Using Auxiliary Task. arXiv preprint arXiv:2202.12687 (2022)
7. Hu, Y., Gripon, V., Pateux, S.: Leveraging the feature distribution in transfer-based few-shot learning. In: Farkaš, I., Masulli, P., Otte, S., Wermter, S. (eds.) ICANN 2021. LNCS, vol. 12892, pp. 487–499. Springer, Cham (2021). https://doi.org/10.1007/978-3-030-86340-1_39
8. Triantafillou, E., et al.: Meta-dataset: A dataset of datasets for learning to learn from few examples. arXiv preprint arXiv:1903.03096 (2019)
9. Dhillon, G.S., Chaudhari, P., Ravichandran, A., Soatto, S.: A baseline for few-shot image classification. arXiv preprint arXiv:1909.02729 (2019)
10. Chen, W.Y., Liu, Y.C., Kira, Z., Wang, Y.F., Huang, J.B.: A closer look at few-shot classification. arXiv preprint arXiv:1904.04232 (2019)
11. Lake, B.M., Salakhutdinov, R., Tenenbaum, J.B.: The omniglot challenge: a 3-year progress report. Curr. Opin. Behav. Sci. **29**, 97–104 (2019)
12. Finn, C., Abbeel, P., Levine, S.: Model-agnostic meta-learning for fast adaptation of deep networks. In: International Conference on Machine Learning. PMLR, pp. 1126–1135 (2017)
13. Nichol, A., Achiam, J., Schulman, J.: On first-order meta-learning algorithms. arXiv preprint arXiv:1803.02999 (2018)
14. Koch, G., Zemel, R., Salakhutdinov, R.: Siamese neural networks for one-shot image recognition. In: ICML Deep Learning Workshop, vol. 2. Lille (2015)
15. Vinyals, O., Blundell, C., Lillicrap, T., Kavukcuoglu, K., Wierstra, D.: Matching networks for one shot learning. In: Advances in Neural Information Processing Systems, vol. 29 (2016)
16. Snell, J., Swersky, K., Zemel, R.: . Prototypical networks for few-shot learning. In: Advances in Neural Information Processing Systems, vol. 30 (2017)
17. Mishra, N., Rohaninejad, M., Chen, X., Abbeel, P.: A simple neural attentive metalearner. arXiv preprint arXiv:1707.03141 (2017)
18. Mazumder, P., Singh, P., Namboodiri, V.P.: Improving few-shot learning using composite rotation based auxiliary task. In: Proceedings of the IEEE/CVF Winter Conference on Applications of Computer Vision, pp. 2654–2663 (2021)
19. Tripathi, A.S., Danelljan, M., Gool, L.V., Timofte, R.: Few-Shot Classification By Few-Iteration Meta-Learning. arXiv preprint arXiv:2010.00511 (2020)
20. Ravi, S., Larochelle, H.: Optimization as a model for few-shot learning (2016)

21. Fort, S.: Gaussian prototypical networks for few-shot learning on omniglot. arXiv preprint arXiv:1708.02735 (2017)
22. Bennequin, E.: easyfsl (n.d.). https://github.com/sicara/easy-few-shot-learning
23. Cao, T., Law, M., Fidler, S.: A theoretical analysis of the number of shots in few-shot learning. arXiv preprint arXiv:1909.11722 (2019)
24. Ye, H.J., Ming, L., Zhan, D.C., Chao, W.L.: Few-shot learning with a strong teacher. IEEE Trans. Pattern Anal. Mach. Intell. (2022)
25. Hospedales, T.M., Antoniou, A., Micaelli, P., Storkey, A.J.: Meta-learning in neural networks: a survey. IEEE Trans. Pattern Anal. Mach. Intell. **44**(9), 5149–5169 (2021)

Morpheme Based Amharic-Kistanigna Bi-directional Machine Translation Using Deep Learning

Mengistu Kinfe Negia[1]([envelope]), Rahel Mekonen Tamiru[1], and Million Meshesha[2]

[1] Bahir Dar Institute of Technology, Bahir Dar University, Bahir Dar, Ethiopia
mengistuk920@gmail.com
[2] Addis Ababa University, Addis Ababa, Ethiopia

Abstract. Machine translation is a natural language processing application that can be used to translate text from one natural language to other natural language. This study attempted to create bidirectional machine translation for Amharic-Kistanigna language. It is critical to develop machine translation between Kistanigna and Amharic languages in order to increase the number of language users, address issues concerning the endangered Kistanigna language, and expand the language's web contentNeural Machine Translation is a new approach to machine translation that has achieved a translation quality. The experiments are carried out using LSTM, Bi-LSTM, LSTM + attention, CNN + attention, and Transformer models. We have used 9,225 parallel sentences with morpheme based translation unit. To segment our morpheme data we used the morfessor tool. We considered training time, memory usage, and BLEU score when proposing an optimal model. Finally, we proposed morpheme-based bi-directional machine translation using Transformer with BLEU scores of 21.31 and 22.40 for Amharic-Kistanigna and Kistanigna-Amharic translation respectively. The study's main weakness is the lack of sufficient datasets to conduct a comprehensive experiment. As a result, parallel corpora are required for conducting similar research.

Keywords: Amharic and Kistanigna language · Neural Machine Translation · Deep Learning · LSTM · Bi-LSTM · LSTM + attention · CNN + attention · Transformer

1 Introduction

Machine translation is a branch of computational linguistics that investigates how software can be used to convert text or speech from one natural language to another [1,2]. Machine translation approaches that are commonly used are rule-based, example-based, statistical, hybrid, and neural [3–5]. Rule Based Machine Translation (RBMT) is based on linguistic rules that have been manually

T. Girma Debelee et al. (Eds.): PanAfriCon AI 2022, CCIS 1800, pp. 245–257, 2023.
https://doi.org/10.1007/978-3-031-31327-1_14

prepared. The analogy principle is used in example-based MT; sentences are deconstructed into fragments and then translated using an analogy. The statistical machine translation method makes use of parallel corpora that have been hand-crafted by humans. Every target sentence has the potential to become a translation of a source sentence during statistical machine translation (SMT). Statistical, rule-based, and example-based approaches are combined in a hybrid approach [6]. NMT is built on a neural network model that, like SMT, employs parallel corpus learning [7]. Machine translation can be performed in either a unidirectional or bidirectional fashion [6]. Unidirectional translation is only possible from one source natural language to another. Bidirectional translation allows both languages to serve as the source and target languages. There has been no attempt at machine translation research on Kistanigna among Ethiopian languages. This study looks at bidirectional machine translation of the Amharic-Kistanigna language.

2   The Nature of the Languages

Ethiopic is a writing system used by both Amharic and Kistanigna. These languages have left-to-right writing systems and alphabets, namely, Fidel. They both use subject-object-verb (SOV) sentence structure. The numbers and symbols in these languages are similar. However, their alphabetic characters differ slightly [8]. The Kistanigna language is a Guragigna dialect. According to Ethnologue, there were 260,000 native speakers in 2015 [9]. Amharic, on the other hand, is spoken by over 27 million people, making it the world's second most widely spoken Semitic language [10]. Morphologically, both Amhairc and Kistanigna are rich. Languages may have multiple morphemes per word. A word in either language can be a single morpheme or it can contain multiple morphemes formed from a collection of phonemes or sounds. By inflection or derivation, words can be formed from morphemes. Below Fig. 1 and Fig. 2 we have shown both Amahric and Kistanigna scripts respectively.

	Ge'ez ä	Ka'eb u	Salis i	Rab'e a	Hamis ē	Sadis ï	Sab'e o
h	ሀ	ሁ	ሂ	ሃ	ሄ	ህ	ሆ
l	ለ	ሉ	ሊ	ላ	ሌ	ል	ሎ
ḥ	ሐ	ሑ	ሒ	ሓ	ሔ	ሕ	ሖ
m	መ	ሙ	ሚ	ማ	ሜ	ም	ሞ
ś	ሠ	ሡ	ሢ	ሣ	ሤ	ሥ	ሦ
r	ረ	ሩ	ሪ	ራ	ሬ	ር	ሮ
s	ሰ	ሱ	ሲ	ሳ	ሴ	ስ	ሶ
š	ሸ	ሹ	ሺ	ሻ	ሼ	ሽ	ሾ
q	ቀ	ቁ	ቂ	ቃ	ቄ	ቅ	ቆ
b	በ	ቡ	ቢ	ባ	ቤ	ብ	ቦ
v	ቨ	ቩ	ቪ	ቫ	ቬ	ቭ	ቮ
t	ተ	ቱ	ቲ	ታ	ቴ	ት	ቶ
č	ቸ	ቹ	ቺ	ቻ	ቼ	ች	ቾ
ḫ	ኀ	ኁ	ኂ	ኃ	ኄ	ኅ	ኆ
n	ነ	ኑ	ኒ	ና	ኔ	ን	ኖ
ň	ኘ	ኙ	ኚ	ኛ	ኜ	ኝ	ኞ
a	አ	ኡ	ኢ	ኣ	ኤ	እ	ኦ
k	ከ	ኩ	ኪ	ካ	ኬ	ክ	ኮ
x	ኸ	ኹ	ኺ	ኻ	ኼ	ኽ	ኾ
w	ወ	ዉ	ዊ	ዋ	ዌ	ው	ዎ
a	ዐ	ዑ	ዒ	ዓ	ዔ	ዕ	ዖ
z	ዘ	ዙ	ዚ	ዛ	ዜ	ዝ	ዞ
ž	ዠ	ዡ	ዢ	ዣ	ዤ	ዥ	ዦ
y	የ	ዩ	ዪ	ያ	ዬ	ይ	ዮ
d	ደ	ዱ	ዲ	ዳ	ዴ	ድ	ዶ
ǧ	ጀ	ጁ	ጂ	ጃ	ጄ	ጅ	ጆ
g	ገ	ጉ	ጊ	ጋ	ጌ	ግ	ጎ
t'	ጠ	ጡ	ጢ	ጣ	ጤ	ጥ	ጦ
č'	ጨ	ጩ	ጪ	ጫ	ጬ	ጭ	ጮ
p'	ጰ	ጱ	ጲ	ጳ	ጴ	ጵ	ጶ
ṣ	ጸ	ጹ	ጺ	ጻ	ጼ	ጽ	ጾ
ṥ	ፀ	ፁ	ፂ	ፃ	ፄ	ፅ	ፆ
f	ፈ	ፉ	ፊ	ፋ	ፌ	ፍ	ፎ
p	ፐ	ፑ	ፒ	ፓ	ፔ	ፕ	ፖ

Fig. 1. List of Amharic scripts.

	ሀ ha	ሁ hu	ሂ Hi	ሃ Ha	ሄ he	ህ Hë	ሆ ho
	ä	u	i	a	e	ë	o
l	ለ	ሉ	ሊ	ላ	ሌ	ል	ሎ
m	መ	ሙ	ሚ	ማ	ሜ	ም	ሞ
r	ረ	ሩ	ሪ	ራ	ሬ	ር	ሮ
s	ሰ	ሱ	ሲ	ሳ	ሴ	ስ	ሶ
š	ሸ	ሹ	ሺ	ሻ	ሼ	ሽ	ሾ
k'	ቀ	ቁ	ቂ	ቃ	ቄ	ቅ	ቆ
b	በ	ቡ	ቢ	ባ	ቤ	ብ	ቦ
t	ተ	ቱ	ቲ	ታ	ቴ	ት	ቶ
č	ቸ	ቹ	ቺ	ቻ	ቼ	ች	ቾ
n	ነ	ኑ	ኒ	ና	ኔ	ን	ኖ
ň	ኘ	ኙ	ኚ	ኛ	ኜ	ኝ	ኞ
	አ	ኡ	ኢ	ኣ	ኤ	እ	ኦ
k	ከ	ኩ	ኪ	ካ	ኬ	ክ	ኮ
w	ወ	ዉ	ዊ	ዋ	ዌ	ው	ዎ
z	ዘ	ዙ	ዚ	ዛ	ዜ	ዝ	ዞ
ž	ዠ	ዡ	ዢ	ዣ	ዤ	ዥ	ዦ
y	የ	ዩ	ዪ	ያ	ዬ	ይ	ዮ
d	ደ	ዱ	ዲ	ዳ	ዴ	ድ	ዶ
ğ	ጀ	ጁ	ጂ	ጃ	ጄ	ጅ	ጆ
g	ገ	ጉ	ጊ	ጋ	ጌ	ግ	ጎ
t'	ጠ	ጡ	ጢ	ጣ	ጤ	ጥ	ጦ
č'	ጨ	ጩ	ጪ	ጫ	ጬ	ጭ	ጮ
p'	ጰ	ጱ	ጲ	ጳ	ጴ	ጵ	ጶ
S'	ጸ	ጹ	ጺ	ጻ	ጼ	ጽ	ጾ
f	ፈ	ፉ	ፊ	ፋ	ፌ	ፍ	ፎ
p	ፐ	ፑ	ፒ	ፓ	ፔ	ፕ	ፖ
v	ቨ	ቩ	ቪ	ቫ	ቬ	ቭ	ቮ
h	ኸ						

Fig. 2. List of Kistanigna scripts.

3   Related Works

There have been several attempts to conduct bidirectional Amharic-Kistanigna MT. The studies that are most relevant to our research are summarized below.

Chen et al. [11] A Neural Machine Translation model was developed for the languages English to French and English to Germany using RNN and Transformer models. They received BLEU scores of 25.6 and 35.1 during RNN from English to Germany and English to French, respectively. When they used the Transformers model, they got 27.6 and 38.1 BLEU scores from English to German and English to French, respectively. Their total dataset for their experiments was 4.5 million for English to German and 35.5 million for English to French.

Nouhaila et al. [12] For the task of machine translation between English and Arabic texts, a BiLSTM encoder and LSTM decoder model was developed. Their study focused on deep learning-based machine translation between English and Arabic. They developed a model that uses Bidirectional Long Short-Term Memory (BiLSTM) to map the input sequence to a vector and then decode the target sequence from the obtained vector. They received BLEU scores of 18% and 27% for English-to-Arabic and Arabic-to-English translations, respectively.

Arfaso [13] Machine translation from English to Afan Oromo was performed in both directions. To achieve their goal, they collected 5,550 parallel corpus data from various sources. They used 80% of the total dataset for training and 20% for testing. Three experiments were carried out to perform bidirectional Afan Oromo - English machine translation. The first experiment established a baseline using a word-based statistical approach, with BLEU scores of 20.51 for English to Afan Oromo and 19.86 for Afan Oromo to English, respectively. The second experiment used a recurrent neural network approach, specifically GRU with attention, with a BLEU score of 22.79 for English to Afan Oromo and 21.67 for Afan Oromo to English, whereas the third experiment used CNN with attention for both English to Afan Oromo and Afan Oromo to English, with BLEU scores of 24.37 and 23.18.

Workinhe [14] Attention-based Amharic to Wolaita neural machine translation was performed. With a total of 9,250 parallel corpus, the experiments included Amharic-wolaita with BLEU scores of 59.60% and 62.58% using GRU without and with attention, respectively.

Tadesse [10] Morpheme-Based Bidirectional Ge'ez-Amharic Machine Translation was carried out using a statistical approach. They demonstrated experimental results of 15.14% and 16.15% of BLEU score using Morpheme-Based for Ge'ez to Amharic and Amharic to Ge'ez, respectively. The other experiments used word-based translation, with BLEU scores of 6.77% and 7.73% for Ge'ez-Amharic and Amharic-Ge'ez, respectively. The researchers also used rule-based approach to calculate an average BLEU score of 0.6% for Ge'ez to Amharic and 1.27% for Amharic to Ge'ez. For their experiments, the researchers used a total of 13,833 simple and complex parallel sentences in Ge'ez and Amharic. Ninety percent are used for training and ten percent are used for testing.

S. T. Abate et al. [10] performed morpheme-based bidirectional statistical machine translation for seven Ethiopian language pairs. They studied Amharic-Tigrigna, Amharic to Afan-Oromo, Amhairc to Ge'ez, Amahric to Wolaytta, Tigrigna to Wolaytta, Tigrigna to Afan-Oromo, and Afan-Oromo to Wolaytta. All of these studies were conducted in both direction. They only gathered corpora from the religious domain, which includes the Holy Bible and various documents written on spiritual themes. The corpora they prepared are different among the language pairs. 34,349 sentences for Amahric and Tigrigna language pairs, 11,546 sentences for Amahric and Ge'ez language pairs, 11,546 sentences for Amahric and Afan-Oromo language pairs,10,987 sentences for Tigrigna and AfanOromo language pairs, 9,400 sentences for Amharic and Wolaytta language pairs, 2,923 sentences for Afan-Oromo and Wolaytta language pairs and 2,504 sentences for Tigrigna and Wolaytta language pairs.

4   Methods

The preprocessing of the morpheme input corpus, which includes tokenization and normalization, is done. After preprocessing the input corpus, the preprocessed corpus is converted to one-hot vectorization. The dimension of one-hot vectorization is larger. As a result, we used Keras embedding layer to convert it to a lower dimension vector. Finally, we fed embedded corpus into our encoder-decoder model. Below Fig. 3 is the proposed architecture diagram.

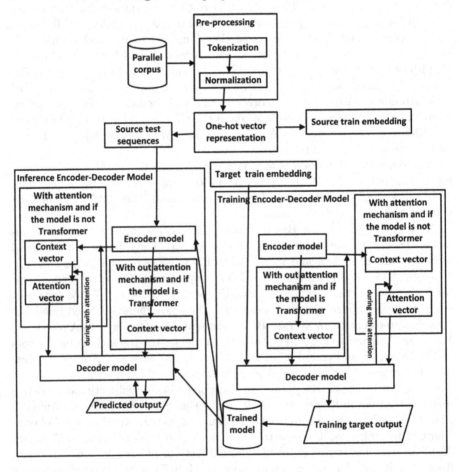

Fig. 3. Proposed architecture diagram.

4.1   Preparing Parallel Corpus

To begin our translation process, we created 9,225 morpheme-based parallel corpus. We used unsupervised segmentation tool called morfessor to prepare the morpheme data. To segment the word into morphemes, we created two different models for both the Amharic and Kistanigna corpus separately using morfessor script. Then we used these created models to segment an input corpus. The commands that we used are morfessortrain and morfessor-segment. The morfessor-train command is used to make training for morfessor models. Morfessor-segment commands are used to make segmentation of data with the morefessor model. Figure 4 below showS sample morpheme generated for Amharic and Kistanigna languages.

Amharic	ሰዎች ስለ ሰው ልጅ ሲጠሉ አትሁ ሲለዩ አትሁ ም ሲነቅፉ አትሁ ም ስማ ቸሁን ም እንደ ከፉ ሲያ ወጡ ብዓን ና ቸሁ is the Amharic segmentation of ሰዎች ስለ ሰው ልጅ ሲጠሉአትሁ ሲለዩአትሁም ሲነቅፉአትሁም ስማቸሁንም እንደ ከፉ ሲያወጡ ብዓን ናቸሁ
Kistanigna	ሰቦች ስለ ሰብ ባይ ዷጠለ መኸም ጐይ ዷሊይ መኸም ነይም ዷ ማኝ መኸም ጐይዎ ስም ደህመም ዎ ኽቡር ኮም ዷነስ ምጐይ ዎትባሪክ ም ነህም is Kistanigna segmentiaon of ሰቦች ስለ ሰብ ባይ ዷጠለመኸምጐይ ዷሊይመኸምነይም ዷማኝመኸምጐይም ስምደህመም ዎኽቡርኮም ዷነስምጐይ ዎትባሪክም ነህም

Fig. 4. Sample morpheme generated for Amharic and Kistanigna.

The limitation of morfessor's is it segments words based on corpus size. It may have some limitations if the corpus size is small. When there is a large corpus, the accuracy level rises.

4.2   Preprocessing

To make training easier, we preprocessed our corpus into a suitable format before feeding it to our model. Our data pre-processing tasks are tokenization and normalization.

Tokenization. Tokenization is a type of lexical analysis that divides sentences into tokens. When we tokenized, we determined the size of the vocabulary, the maximum length of sequences, and the representation of words with unique numbers. To assign a unique number to each word, we opened and visited all the parallel corpus data. As a result, once a word is seen, the process of assigning a unique number to the word begins, and the word is represented by a unique number. Depending on the length of each language's vocabulary, the last number is assigned to the most recently visited word. These activities make data preparation for training easier by converting the original dataset to an integer number representation form. The data that is converted to integer representation is the tokenized data. As a result, the row data is tokenized, and the vocabulary size for data pre-processing is specified. Each vocabulary is represented by an integer based on its size. The first vocabulary is represented by index 0 and the last vocabulary is represented by a vocabulary size-1 index. Our morpheme-based corpus has a total of 7,384 and 9,344 vocabularies for both Amharic and Kistanigna languages, respectively. In order to know the boundary of end sentences we have used sos to indicate the beginning of a new sentence and eos to indicate the end of the sentences.

Normalization. Text normalization is the next step in our data preprocessing process. We used three different normalization methods for Amharic sentences according to [14,15]. The first method is character replacement to normalize words. The second step is to normalize the labialized Amharic character. The third normalization involves replacing words written in short form with a forward slash (/) or a period (.) with words written in expanded form.

4.3 One Hot Vector Representation

The neural network does not directly operate on the vocabulary represented by integers. After converting the data to integer representation, each word of the sentences must be converted to two-dimensional longer vector representation, also known as one-hot vector representation, in order to perform suitable machine translation. We used zero values to the right during one hot vector representation to set the length of the sentences fixed, which is known as zero padding. The maximum length of the sequence in our case is 40. As a result, the remaining index on the right was set to zero. Once the padding was completed and the vector size was standardized, we fed such vectors into the neural network via embedding.

4.4 Embedding

When we feed a single hot vector to a neural network directly, we may encounter training waste rather than learning when we encounter zero values. We used Keras embedding layer for word embedding to solve this problem, which converts a higher dimensional one-hot vector to a lower dimensional one-hot vector. Word embedding is a process of converting words into numeric representations ranging from -1 to 1. To represent the embedding vector space, we used 128 embedding dimensions.

4.5   Encoder-Decoder Model

Finally, we fed our embedded corpus to a model of encoder-decoder. To accept and process the embedded token, the encoder model is used. The final context vector of the encoder is passed to the decoder model. The decoder model performs slightly differently during training and inference. To predict the target output, the decoder model accepts the context vector from the final encoder hidden layer as well as the sequence of target embedding during training. However, we did not feed the target token to the decoder model during inference. As a result, the decoder model predicts the output based on the previous predicted output and the context vector of the encoder hidden layer. Depending on the models, the previous predicted output could be all previous or the current predicted output. RNN (LSTM, BiLSTM, LSTM + Attention), CNN + Attention, and Transformer models were used. RNN and CNN use the current predicted output, whereas transformer uses all previous predicted output. For the first time, no previous predictions were made; in this case, we used sos. The model that we used is described in detail below.

LSTM. The encoder LSTM model sequentially accepts the source embedding by each internal state of the model, and we finally used only the final internal state as a context vector. We did not use individual hidden states for prediction during LSTM. In the decoder LSTM model, the context vector and current predicted output are accepted in order to predict the next output. We have no predicted output for the first time. As a result, we've used the beginning of the sentence, in this case sos. Until the end of the sequence, the decoder model predicts the next output. We used eos at the end of each sentence in our case.

Bi-LSTM. The workflow of the Bi-LSTM model is identical to that of the LSTM model. We only add a backward internal state (backward hidden state and backward cell state) to check and emphasize lost information, when the length of the input sequence is long.

LSTM+ Attention. In the LSTM and Bi-LSTM models, we only used the last encoder's internal state. Individual encoder output serves no purpose. The context vector may not hold all of the input's basic information. The final output is incorrect if the processed input is incorrect. So, we used an attention vector to test this type of problem. The attention mechanism's input here is the encoder's entire hidden state as well as the decoder's current output.

CNN+ Attention. The CNN model accepts all sequences in parallel. This is one of the main differences between RNN models, so we used two distinct embedding methods, token embedding, and target embedding. To pass the output, we used the GLU activation function between the encoder and the decoder.

Transformer. There is no additional attention mechanism in our transformer model. We have fed our transformer model both the token embedding and the position embedding vectors. Because the transformer model accepts all input in parallel time. Like the LSTM and Bi-LSTM model our transformer models, used only the last encoder context vector pass to the decoder directly, with no additional attention mechanism, because the transformer model has self-owned attention. The encoder transformer model includes a feedforward neural network and self-multi-head attention. Masked multi-head attention, multi-head attention, and a feedforward neural network were used in the decoder model.

5   Experiments and Results

We collected a total of 9,225 parallel corpora for the experiments, as shown in Table 1.

Table 1. Data collection source and size for experiment tables.

The source of the data	Number of parallel sentences
Saint Marikos Gospel	1,347
Saint Lukas Gospel	1,947
Saint Matiwos Gospel	2,501
Kistanigna-Amharic-English dictionary	3,430

To prepare morpheme based parallel corpus we have created a model. To create a model, we have used the following syntax for both Amharic and Kistanigna corpus

morfessor-train inputdata.txt -S model.segm

For example, to segment the Amharic input corpus:

morfessor-train am.txt -S am_model.segm

For Kistanigna: morfessor-train gr.txt -S gr_model.segm

After creating the model, we segmented the corpus using our training model by using the following syntax for both Amharic and Kistanigna respectively.

morfessor-segment -L am_model.segm am.txt>am.txt-segmented

morfessor-segment -L gr_model.segm gr.txt>gr.txt-segmented

5.1   Experimental Setup

We divided our parallel corpus into two sets for NMT experiments: 80% for training and 20% for testing [10,13,14,16]. We used a Paperspace with 30 GB of RAM and a GPU RTX5000 with a short training time for our experiments. We used Python programming language, as well as libraries such as Keras, TensorFlow, NumPy, and PyTorch, to create our model. The LSTM, BiLSTM, LSTM+ attention, CNN+ attention, and Transformer models are used in the experiments. For automatic scoring, Bilingual Evaluation under Study (BLEU) is used. Table 2 contains the model's detailed parameters and values.

Table 2. The model's parameters and values.

The parameters	value
Dimensional Embedding	128
Latent dimension	1024
dropout rate	0.2
learning rate	0.001
Epochs	50
Batch size	64

5.2   Results of the Experiment

We examined the impact of normalization on our study prior to conducting the final experiments. We obtained a BLEU score of 21.31 after normalization and a BLEU score of 20.48 without normalization from Amharic-Kistanigna using Transformer model. As a result, the impact of normalization in our study improves translation results. We presented the experimental result for morpheme-based bidirectional Amharic-Kistanigna machine translation in Table 3.

Table 3. Results of bidirectional experiments.

Model	Amharic to Kistanigna	Kistanigna to Amharic
LSTM	15.37%	16.43%
Bi-LSTM	16.55%	18.27%
LSTM +attention	17.01%	18.71%
CNN + attention	19.37%	20.06%
Transformer	21.3%	22.40%

5.3   Discussions

According to the BLEU results, the Transformer model is interesting. In terms of training time and memory utilization, Transformer models are also interesting. When compared to other models, the model is effective for long sentences because, the interdependence of words at the beginning and at the end of the sentence increases, and context within a sentence is defined in the transformer model based on the interdependence of all preceding words in a given sentence sequence. Despite being more context dependent, our Transformer model performs better with short sentences than long sentences. A comparison can also made with our other work on word based bidirectional Amharic-Kistanigna machine translation with the same datasets and models [17]. This demonstrates that morpheme-level translation outperforms word-level translation.

6 Conclusion

This paper presents an attempt to solve the problem of relying solely on human translation by using a Transformer model to perform bidirectional machine translation between the Amharic and Kistanigna language pairs. As a result, this study focuses on a scarce resource language pair, with a data set of 9,225 parallel corpuses gathered from data sources such as religion books (Saint Marikos, Saint Matiwos, and Saint Lukas gospels) and sentences from the Kistanigna-Amharic-English dictionary. To improve machine translation between the language pair, we ran experiments with LSTM, Bi-LSTM, LSTM + attention, CNN + attention, and Transformer models. In terms of time, memory, and BLEU score, our Transformer model is proposed as the best model. Our study's limitation is a lack of dataset. Due to the lack of available parallel corpora, we trained our model using small corpus, despite the fact that NMT requires a large amount of data to train and create an optimal model that learns the features between the two languages.

References

1. Rishita, M.V.S., Raju, M.A., Harris, T.A.: Machine translation using natural language processing. In: MATEC Web Conference, vol. 277, p. 02004 (2019). https://doi.org/10.1051/matecconf/201927702004
2. B. Abel, "Geez to Amharic Machine Translation," MSc Thesis, Addis Ababa University, AddisAbaba, Ethiopia (2018)
3. Okpor, M.D.: Machine translation approaches: issues and challenges. Int. J. Comput. Sci. Issues, **11**(5), 159–165 (2014). https://www.IJCSI.org
4. Tripathi, S., Sarkhel, J.: Approaches to machine translation. Ann. Libr. Inf. Stud. **57**(4), 388–393 (2010)
5. Genet, W.: "Ge ez-amharic machine translation using deep learning," MSc Thesis, Bahir Dar University, Bahir Dar, Ethiopia (2021)
6. Daba, J., Assabie, Y.: A hybrid approach to the development of bidirectional English-Oromiffa machine translation. In: Przepiórkowski, A., Ogrodniczuk, M. (eds.) NLP 2014. LNCS (LNAI), vol. 8686, pp. 228–235. Springer, Cham (2014). https://doi.org/10.1007/978-3-319-10888-9_24
7. Abate, S.T., et al.: "Parallel Corpora for bi Directional Statistical Machine Translation for Seven Ethiopian Language Pairs," October, vol. 1, pp. 153–156 (2018)
8. Gurmu, A.Y., et al.: The, "Word formation in K + stantfifia," MSc Thesis, Addis Ababa University, Addis Ababa, Ethiopia. No. January (2000)
9. Deriba, F,G.: "Developing part of speech tagger for guragigna language", MSc Thesis, Bahir Dar University, Bahir Dar, Ethiopia (2017)
10. Tadesse, K.: "Morpheme-Based Bi directional Ge'ez-Amharic Machine Translation", MSc Thesis, Addis Ababa University, Addis Ababa, Ethiopia (2018)
11. Chen, M., Li, Y., Li, R.: Research on neural machine translation model. In: Journal of Physics: Conference Series, vol. 1237, no. 5 (2019). https://doi.org/10.1088/1742-6596/1237/5/052020
12. Nouhaila, B., Habib, A., Abdellah, A., Abdelhamid, I. E. F.: Arabic machine translation using Bidirectional LSTM Encoder-Decoder (2017). https://indabaxmorocco.github.io/materials/posters/Bensalah.pdf

13. Arfaso, B.: "Bi-Directional English-Afan Oromo Machine Translation Using Convolutional Neural Network," MSc Thesis, Addis Ababa University, Addis Ababa, Ethiopia (2019)
14. Workinhe, W.: "Attention-based Amharic-to Wolaita Neural Machine Translation", MSc Thesis, Addis Ababa University, Addis Ababa, Ethiopia (2020)
15. Mindaye, T.: "Design and Implementation of Amharic search engine," MSc Thesis, Addis Ababa University, Addis Ababa, Ethiopia (2007)
16. Adamkew, K.: "Ge ez-Amharic machine translation using RNN," MSc Thesis, Bahir Dar University, Bahir Dar, Ethiopia (2021)
17. Negia, M.K., Tamiru, R.M., Meshesha, M.: "Amharic-Kistanigna bi-directional machine translation using deep learning. In: 2022 International Conference on Information and Communication Technology for Development for Africa (ICT4DA), Bahir Dar, Ethiopia, pp. 61–65 (2022). https://doi.org/10.1109/ICT4DA56482.2022.9971194

Economy and Security

Benefits and Challenges of Industry 4.0 in African Emerging Economies

Mesfin Kebede Kassa[1](✉) ⬤ and Hana Demma Wube[2] ⬤

[1] Department of Mechanical Engineering, Kombolcha Institute of Technology,
Wollo University, Kombolcha, Ethiopia
livemesfin@gmail.com
[2] Ethiopian Artificial Intelligence Institute, 40782 Addis Ababa, Ethiopia

Abstract. The fourth industrial revolution (Industry 4.0 or I4.0) originated in Germany and represents the next phase in the digitization of the manufacturing sector, driven by the Internet of Things (IoT), Cyber Physical System (CPS), computing, additive manufacturing, and smart factories. I4.0 offer an exciting opportunity for manufacturers, and small and medium enterprises of developed and developing nations to develop a novel business models and integrate into global value chains. However, implementing I4.0 will present many challenges. Much has been done in developed countries regarding the benefits and challenges of I4.0 compared to developing countries. Thus, it is important to study the challenges and benefits of I4.0 in the context of African emerging economies. In this vein, the purpose of this study is to explore the concept, key factors, national preparedness, benefits, and challenges of I4.0 using existing literature. A case study, challenge, and benefits analysis were then conducted to test the potential for I4.0 implementation in African emerging economies using various data sources. Finally, future study directions on the I4.0 phenomenon were presented. The implementation of I4.0 in African countries was discussed in terms of manufacturing capacity, R&D, human capital, and IT infrastructure. From the study, it was found that promoting innovative new technologies through spending on research and development, increasing the accumulation of intellectual property, and the necessary human capital, and developing the "Internet plus" industry are the main challenges to implement I4.0 in African countries with emerging economies.

Keywords: Industry 4.0 · Benefits · Challenges · African emerging economies

1 Introduction

The fourth industrial revolution (I4.0) was first introduced in 2011 and refers to the strategic plan developed by the German federal government for the high-tech manufacturing industry of tomorrow, describing a joint national strategy to improve the industry and a fundamental paradigm shift from centralized

T. Girma Debelee et al. (Eds.): PanAfriCon AI 2022, CCIS 1800, pp. 261–276, 2023.
https://doi.org/10.1007/978-3-031-31327-1_15

production to decentralized production and control [16]. I4.0 has the potential to transform optimized and cell production into a completely integrated, optimized, and automated workflow, leading to increased efficiency and reshaping traditional manufacturing relationships between customers, manufacturers, and suppliers, as well as between human and machine [40]. In general, I4.0 is mainly focused on automation, machine learning, and real-time interconnection. The concept of I4.0 is currently under research and will be the main strategic manufacturing plan for the development of the manufacturing sector in different parts of the world under various names such as "Smart Manufacturing" in the US and Korea and "Made in China 2025" in China. "Towards Industry 4.0" (Rumo à Indústria 4.0) and "La Nouvelle France Industrielle" in France and Brazil, respectively [11,27]. "Make in India" in India, "Society 5.0 or super smart society" in Japan, "Crafting the Future" in Mexico. I4.0 is also demonstrated in the digitization of production and service processes in Netherlands, Denmark, Finland, and Sweden with the most established digital economy in the EU, followed by Luxembourg, Belgium, the UK, Ireland, and Italy [21]. It can be seen from the above literature that the concepts and implementation status of I4.0 differ in each country and have an impact on the global economy and market competition. It is important to mention that the goal of all these programs, both in developed and developing nations, is to introduce I4.0 concepts and technologies to local businesses. However, as Hall et al. and Kumar et al. noted, the advent of cutting-edge technologies can present greater difficulties emerging economies [15,24]. In particular, companies in African emerging economies often lag behind compared to their counterparts in developed countries in terms of technology adoption, as developing countries' economies have traditionally been more focused on commercialization and resource extraction. In addition, since I4.0 is a new subject, there isn't much information accessible about it in the context of African emerging economies. Therefore, the objective of the current work is to explore the concept, key technologies, key factors for the realization, national preparedness, benefits, and challenges of implementing I4.0 using existing literature. Exploring the potential for I4.0 implementation using a challenges and benefits analysis in selected African countries with emerging economies using indicators.

2   Background

In this section, the key technologies, concepts, key enablers, national preparedness, benefits, and challenges of I4.0 have been explored and presented from existing literature. For this purpose, text mining was used to download papers from the Google Scholar database. The search for published articles is carried out using queries containing the keywords "Challenges", "Benefits", "Advantages", "Africa", and "Industry 4.0".

2.1   Industry 4.0 Key Technologies

The main driving forces behind the application of I4.0 are the Internet of Things (IoT) and Cyber-Physical Systems (CPS) in terms of interconnected smart grids, smart cities, logistics, and smart factories. It has been reported that IOT is the basis for building CPS by integrating the real world and digital world of CPS, and the smart factory is seen as a vision for I4.0 [28]. Cloud computing, big data, 3D printing, holograms, energy conservation, smart sensors, horizontal and vertical system integration, mobile computing, blockchain, cloud computing, and big data services for integrating industrial IoT networks are some of the key technologies needed for I4.0 implementation [19,34]. The main I4.0 pillars, which are commonly linked to the I4.0 concept, are depicted in Fig. 1.

Fig. 1. Pillars of Industry 4.0.

In terms of the application of I4.0 key technologies, Radio frequency identification (RFID) & cloud computing are the most frequently used essential technologies for the realization of I4.0. These technologies are used to detect abnormalities and introduce gold nano-rods into the input materials for the polymer-based biomedical device's [32]. I4.0 also finds application in intelligent manufacturing systems such as multi-agent technology, cloud-based solutions, and different manufacturing plants [5,23,47]. In addition, I4.0 is also being used in autonomous robots such as in the healthcare sector for elderly care and in surgery, surveillance systems used for monitoring, spying, and performing dangerous tasks, and used as assistants for guidance and control. In the agricultural sector, the IoT is being used to predict and improve the efficiency of farming by managing the breeding and cultivation process using intelligent agricultural tools [7, 42]. Further, blockchain technologies can transform the energy sector, supply chain management, distribution system, secure healthcare system, smart city development, business, manufacturing, and agricultural sector [8]. Furthermore, robot welding, workforce training, demand forecasting, physical layer authentication, predictive maintenance, and energy optimization are some of the industrial AI applications [35]. Other areas of application of the key technologies of I4.0 are summarized and presented in Table 1.

Table 1. Industry 4.0 key technologies with their applications.

Technologies	Applications	Source
Big Data and Analytics	Earlier industry threat detection in various production operations Predict new problems arise using data analysis previously recorded industry data	[4]
Autonomous Robots	To perform field work where are the human workers limited in work Use in the healthcare sector, emotional and social companionship, educational fields, surveillance, agriculture, and assistants for administration	[42]
Simulation	Use to mirror real processes and optimize decision making	[41]
System Integration: Horizontal and Vertical System Integration	Automation communication and cooperation especially along standardized processes	[13]
The Industrial IoT	Smart planning & machine control	[45]
Cyber security and CPS	Failure detection in machines and automatically prepare for troubleshooting actions on CPS	[22]
Cloud	Data Sharing	[40]
Additive Manufacturing	To manufacture small batches of customized products	[40]
Augmented Reality	For part selection in a warehouse and sending repair instructions over mobile devices	[40]

2.2 Key Factors for the Realization and National Preparedness of Industry 4.0

Following the above section, this section discusses the conceptual and technical studies related to I4.0. It primarily includes information on the key factors and national readiness for I4.0 to establish the study's key parameters. Li et al. explained that human resource development is a crucial human resource practice to create a suitable work environment and foster the innovation and creativity of human capital needed for I4.0 [25]. Kang et al. noted that infrastructure such as information and communication technology is a key technology to support smart manufacturing [19]. Strozzi et al. indicated that public policy, funding, and research in the field of I4.0 are key factors for the implementation of I4.0 [44]. Kim J. explained that machinery investment efficiency, total capital efficiency, research budgeting, research collaboration, IT security issues, and digital technologies are the main factors for I4.0 realization [21]. Li et al. indicated that manufacturing capability, R& D, and human capital are the main factors for the realization of I4.0 [25]. The key factors identified from the literature for the implementation of I4.0 are summarized and presented in Table 2. Further, in the literature, the realization of I4.0 in African countries is evidenced by the launch of I4.0 initiatives, including Smart Africa, the European Union-African Union Digital Task Force, and the African One Network [9]. However, it is also mentioned that the lack of electricity and internet infrastructure negatively affects the realization of I4.0. Despite the aforementioned negative effects of I4.0 realization, there are many benefits to be gained with its acceptance. For example, the productivity, profitability, and competitiveness of manufacturing sectors can be improved by adopting I4.0. In summary, it is clear from the aforementioned articles that the major variables listed above play a role in determining the national readiness of the African countries with emerging economies to implement I4.0.

Table 2. Key factors for the realization of Industry 4.0 identified from the literature.

No.	Key factors	Source
1	Human resource development	[26]
2	Government policy and funding	[44]
3	Infra system of manufacturing sites	[19]
4	Studies focusing on industry 4.0	[44]
5	IT security issues and Digital Technologies	[21]
6	Machinery investment efficiency and total capital efficiency, research budgeting and research collaboration	[21]

2.3   Benefits of Industry 4.0

Once the key factors for the realization of I4.0 have been identified, the benefits of implementing I4.0 need to be discussed. Kamble et al. indicated that I4.0 brought a new paradigm shift to the manufacturing sector by integrating new technologies to maximize productivity while using resources efficiently [18]. Erboz noted that the use of big data analytics in industries can lead to lower operating costs, faster decision making, and new product development. Further, big data analytics leads to a decisive advantage over competitors [12]. Alcacer and Cruz- Machado noted that the advantage of cloud computing is to lower cost of information, handle data effectively, and improve flexibility and efficiency [1]. According to Rghioui and Oumnad, the IoT can increase a company's level of efficiency by allowing data to be transferred between devices in real-time [39]. Anitah et al. reported that I4.0 is having a positive impact on operational performance such as product quality, flexibility, production lead times, delivery times, delivery reliability, and productivity levels of Kenyan fast-growing consumer goods manufacturers [2]. In summary, it can be concluded from the cited articles that companies can use I4.0 to increase efficiency and achieve significant cost savings. Based on this, I4.0 can be defined as the basis for the future competitiveness of manufacturing companies. The benefits of I4.0 identified from literature are summarized and depicted in Table 3.

Table 3. Benefits of Industry 4.0 identified from the literature.

Benefits	Source
Maximum performance with efficient use of resources	[1]
Lower operating costs, faster decision-making, and new product development	[39]
Real-time transmission of data between devices	[6]
Positive impact on operational performance	[31]
Lower cost of information	[2]

2.4   Challenges of Industry 4.0

The previous section highlights the benefits of implementing I4.0. However, to reap the benefits of I4.0, numerous hurdles must be overcome. This section outlines some of the challenges for successfully implementing I4.0. Many researchers report that the successful implementation of I4.0 at the micro and macro levels has been significantly influenced by the relevant skills and abilities of the country's technologically competent workforce. Moreover, the quality of the workforce's abilities and qualifications will be crucial in fostering innovation and competitiveness [6,31]. According to Pradhan and Agwa-Ejon, there is a severe lack of professionals with the I4.0 skill set in developing nations [37]. In addition, one of the biggest unresolved issues regardinf the implementation of I4.0

in developing nations is unemployment due to factors such as the mismatch between the available skills and the skills required by the industry, high rates of unskilled labor, and inadequate education [29]. Shvetsova and Kuzmina revealed that a fuzzy understanding of the skills that meet the requirements of I4.0 is also a serious problem in the implementation of I4.0 [43]. According to Raj et al., the introduction of new technologies will make it challenging to adopt I4.0 in the future because of worries about the secure handling of sensitive data and information [38]. Numerous sources also contend that a significant barrier to implementation of I4.0 is a lack of funding. The implementation of I4.0 may also be hampered by poor understanding of integration, lack of standardization, and concerns about secured infrastructure [3]. Further, socio-economic challenges such as non-inclusive economic growth are also factors hindering the implementation of I4.0 [30]. In summary, the aforementioned factors pose challenges for I4.0 implementation. In order to address them, national governments must place a high priority on the development of human resources, which includes improving the quality of education and acquiring the competencies needed to implement I4.0, which aims to combat poverty, inequality, and unemployment as well as create an inclusive economy. Table 4 provides an overview of I4.0 challenges identified in the cited literature.

Table 4. Challenges of Industry 4.0 identified from the literature.

Challenges	Source
Relevant skills and abilities of the country's workforce	[6, 29, 31, 37, 43]
Financial resources	[3]
Secured infrastructure	[38]
Socio-economic challenges	[30]

2.5   Industry 4.0 in Africa

Industry 4.0 is getting popular in various parts of the world, as discussed in the introductory part of this study. However, despite claims that I4.0 has the highest penetration rate in the world, I4.0 is gaining slow momentum in African countries. In these countries, the IoT, blockchain, 3D printing, big data, drones, and artificial intelligence (AI) are some of the breakthrough technologies of I4.0 in African countries [14]. The above technologies are used in industry, regional integration, energy, agriculture, education, and healthcare sectors. In this regard, the current research examined and presented the adoption of I4.0 in African nations with emerging economies.

3   Case Study - Analysis of the Challenges and Benefits of Implementing Industry 4.0

In the above sections, key technologies, key factors, challenges, and benefits of I4.0 were identified and highlighted. This section presents a case study to analyze the challenges and benefits of implementing I4.0 to check the potential of African emerging economies using a total of four key indicators: (i) Manufacturing capability, (ii) Research and development, (iii) Human capital, and (iv) ICT infrastructure. The indicators along with subcategories along with their data source are presented in Table 5. The case study begins by selecting the top five African countries with the high gross domestic product (GDP) (i.e. Ethiopia, Benin, Niger, Egypt, and Uganda) as depicted in Table 6, based on the data obtained from World bank for the end of 2021. In this regard, GDP was used to select the countries for the case study, since GDP is a widely considered indicator of the performance of a national economy. Subsequently, a numerical analysis is carried out for each indicator and presented in the following subsections.

Table 5. Industry 4.0 key indicators with data sources.

Indicator	Indicators	Data source
Manufacturing Capability	High Technology Exports as percentage of Manufacturing Exports	The World Bank Data (2020)
Research and Development	Expenditure On R&D Number of patent application	UNESCO Institute for Statistics (2018) The World Bank Data (2020)
Human Capital	Human capital in R& D	UNESCO Institute for Statistics (2018)
IT Infrastructure	Fixed Mobile broadband Subscription	ITU World Telecommunication/ICT Indicators database (2020)

3.1   Manufacturing Capability

In order to implement I4.0, the nation's policymakers need to plan strategic turnarounds, leading to a global reconfiguration of manufacturing focused on high-tech products, low value-added, and low-profit margin productions [25]. The manufacturing capability can be used to demonstrate the country's industrial revolution, including I4.0, using a few indicators such as GDP, the percentage of GDP that comes from industry value added, foreign direct investment net flow, and high-technology exports. Among, in the current study, high-tech exports (% of manufactured goods) presented in Table 7 were only considered as an indicator to test the readiness of I4.0 implementation in African nations with emerging economies. High-tech exports include products such as computers, pharmaceuticals, aerospace, electrical equipment, and scientific instruments

Table 6. Top five African countries with high economic growth [Data source: The World Bank Data (2021)].

Global rank	Country Name	Economic growth: the rate of change of real GDP
3	Ethiopia	6.06
7	Benin	3.85
8	Niger	3.58
9	Egypt	3.57
14	Uganda	2.95

with high R&D intensity. From Table 7, it can be observed that Ethiopia has the biggest high-technology exports as a % of manufactured goods, accounting for 13.1 % the smallest belongs to Uganda, accounting for 2.1 %. Ethiopia's largest high-technology exports as a % of manufactured exports can be attributed to an increase in foreign investment. In conclusion, these data demonstrate that while the GDP of five African emerging economies is growing, high technology exports are low. As a result, these countries should be able to spend more in the creation of high-tech goods with a significant R&D aspect.

Table 7. African Countries with high-technology exports as a percentage of manufactured exports [Data source: The World Bank Data (2020); % of manufactured exports].

Global rank	Country Name	% of manufactured exports
36	Ethiopia	13.1
100	Uganda	2.1
92	Benin	2.68
40	Niger	12.23
93	Egypt	2.68

3.2 Research and Development

In this section, the R&D intensity of the considered African countries with emerging economies has been evaluated. For this purpose, two indicators such as the number of patent applications and expenditure on research and development have been used. An application for a product or process that offers a novel method of performing a task or suggests a novel technical solution for a problem and is submitted via a patent agency in order to acquire exclusive rights to an invention is referred to as a patent application. The research and development expenditure is shown in Table 8 as a percentage of GDP. It is important to mention that only two of the five chosen countries have the indicator data.

According to Table 8, Egypt spends more money on R&D than Ethiopia. In addition, Table 9 demonstrates that Egyptian citizens registered a higher number of patent applications than that of Ethiopian citizens. This shows that Ethiopia and Egypt rely on the production of low-tech content, and the country, need to do more to support the I4.0 goals such as high technology, innovation, and integration since R&D investment and activities are an important basis for the creation of their brands. It is important to note that the data in Table 9 are not organized according to the citizenship of the citizens; rather, the data only indicate the nation in which the patent is filed.

Table 8. Research and development expenditure as a proportion of GDP [*Data source*: The World Bank Data (2017); Expenditure on research and development].

Country Name	Expenditure on research and development (in percent)
Ethiopia	0.27
Egypt	0.68

Table 9. Number of patents filed by citizens [*Data source*: The World Bank Data (2017); Number of patents].

Global Rank	Country Name	Number of patents
101	Ethiopia	6
93	Uganda	13
33	Egypt	978

3.3 Human Capital

Human resource development is crucial for achieving I4.0's objectives. The practice of working with personnel with a commitment to the cause helps to create an adequate working environment for enhancing the creativity and innovation of human capital. Human capital is essential to foster research practices [36]. Human talent are essential for research and innovation, so it is important to develop human capital through high-quality education. I4.0 employees working on I4.0 are required to be trained in order to be able to run the system. Revival through education is an essential first move toward further growth. Policymakers must guarantee that there are enough researchers in their nations in order to improve knowledge societies. [26]. In the current study, the distribution of researchers per 1 million inhabitants engaged in R&D has been used to evaluate the human capital for the implementation of I4.0, as presented in Table 10, where data is available. It can be seen from the table that both countries have fewer researchers per million inhabitants. This shows that policymakers in these countries should consider creating labor demand for I4.0. Further, educational institutions should concentrate on cultivating and teaching college graduates to contribute to the implementation of I4.0, since the availability and skill of the workforce are important factors that have added to the competitiveness of manufacturing. Besides education, training is a requirement for the implementation of I4.0 because it calls for a different group of skills from the workforce. Several nations initiated skill development programs to develop the I4.0-required skills, including India, which has started an I4.0 skills development initiative called Skill India [17]. Similar to this, a working group on the development of I4.0 skills exists as part of the BRICS partnership with the goal of fostering digital skills among member nations [9]. In order to develop the necessary skill set, the government and private sector of African nations should actively engage in outreach and training initiatives.

Table 10. Researchers' distribution per million inhabitants [Data source: UNESCO Institute for Statistics (2017)].

Country	Researchers (in full-time equivalent) per million inhabitants
Ethiopia	90.5
Egypt	677.1

3.4 Information Technology Infrastructure

Information and Communication Technology (ICT) has been shown to be essential for success in the I4.0 arena as it enables quick responses to a dynamic market. ICT facilitates the use of information resources easier [20]. In the era of modern manufacturing, billions of digital devices have internet connectivity. This rapid growth has caused ICT to become the cornerstone of manufacturing systems, supported by modeling, simulation, and presentation tools, as well as digital and virtual production [10]. As a result of this rapid development, ICT has become the core of manufacturing systems, aided by tools for modeling, simulating, and presenting as well as digital and virtual production. Moreover, it has been reported that the impact of I4.0 technologies has led to a substantial increase in the availability of and delivery of digital economy services via digital media and mobile devices in developing nations like Africa [33]. Digital services include services offered by banks such as cell phone banking and new designs based on cloud-based computing such as mobile payments, digital platforms, and crypto assets [46], the African emerging economies can greatly benefit from this growth. In this study, the number of fixed-broadband subscriptions per 100 people at the end of 2020 has been used as an indicator to estimate the telecommunication/ICT infrastructure required for I4.0 implementation in the selected countries, as depicted in Table 11. From Table 11 it can be observed that Egypt has the highest rate of fixed-broadband subscriptions per 100 people compared to other countries. This indicates that Egypt has a better ICT readiness for the implementation of I4.0. However, the rest of the countries included in this study have the lowest readiness. Therefore, it is important that other countries focus on building ICT infrastructure for I4.0 implementation.

Table 11. Fixed broadband subscriptions per 100 people [*Data* Source: ITU World Telecommunication/ICT Indicators database (2020)].

Global Rank	Country Name	Fixed broadband subscriptions per 100 people
170	Ethiopia	0.18
176	Uganda	0.13
164	Benin	0.25
186	Niger	0.05
106	Egypt	9.14

In general, it can be seen from the case study that for the African countries included in the study, despite their growing GDP, which is a promising picture for I4.0 implementation, there is a problem with defining goals and ideas for I4.0 implementation. The challenges for I4.0 implementation include promoting technologically advanced new technologies through investment in research and development, increasing the accumulation of intellectual property, and the necessary human capital, and developing the "Internet plus" industry. The study also identified four key crucial actors that will influence and support I4.0 implementation in African emerging economies; these are manufacturing capabilities, R&D, human capital, and ICT infrastructure. In addition, it was noted that the countries included in this study are in need of qualified professionals who could contribute their experience and creativity to the I4.0 blueprint to sustain their growth. Further, the country's policymakers should consider ambitious strategic plans for implementing I4.0 to effectively use digital technologies to build new industrial environments, fabricate new products, and enhance well-known brands.

Furthermore, technologies associated with I4.0 will replace the low-skilled workforce, which is plentiful in Africa and shown in the current study with a highly skilled workforce, so African governments should invest in I4.0 education and training programs so that technology complements rather than replaces the workforce. Moreover, to get the most out of I4.0, African governments and entrepreneurs must recognize new industry niches and use them to achieve sustainable, inclusive growth and take bold steps to close gaps in infrastructure, digital skills, and R&D. Also, the study shows that access to I4.0 in Africa is limited by infrastructure parameters such as broadband penetration, resulting in a low number of mobile phone and Internet users. Thus, new strategies are required to modernize the ICT infrastructure in Africa.

4 Conclusions

In this study, the concept, key technologies, key factors, national preparedness, benefits, and challenges of Industry 4.0 were explored and presented using existing literature. A case study was then presented to analyze the challenges and benefits of implementing I4.0 in African emerging economies by selecting five countries based on their GDP, such as Ethiopia, Benin, Niger, Egypt, and Uganda, using indicators from various data sources. The study found that while the GDP of five emerging African countries is growing, high-tech exports remain low. The number of patent applications filed by citizens of the selected countries is relatively low, indicating that the countries rely on low-tech content production. In addition, countries have fewer researchers per million inhabitants and low levels of fixed-broadband subscriptions per 100 people. In general, the study noted that empowering manufacturing capability through R&D driven manufacturing, creating the necessary infrastructure, green development, optimizing the national industry, and increasing the necessary human capital should be the guiding principles for successful I4.0 implementation. Further, for emerging economies in Africa, it can be concluded that more work needs to be done to meet I4.0 requirements beyond their GDP growth to remain globally competitive. Furthermore, future studies could be conducted using different sub-categories of indicators to test the capacity of African countries to implement I4.0 along with the implications. Moreover, with regard to geographic coverage, more research is needed in regions that have contributed to the global economy beyond the considered major African emerging economies. In addition, a study of women's participation in the digital economy could be carried out in the future.

References

1. Alcácer, V., Cruz-Machado, V.: Scanning the industry 4.0: a literature review on technologies for manufacturing systems. Eng. Sci. Technol. Int. J. **22**(3), 899–919 (2019)
2. Anitah, J.N., Nyamwange, S.O., Magutu, P.O., Chirchir, M., Mose, J.M., et al.: Industry 4.0 technologies and operational performance of unilever Kenya and l'oreal East Africa. Noble Int. J. Bus. Manage. Res. **3**(10), 125–134 (2019)
3. Bag, S., Yadav, G., Dhamija, P., Kataria, K.K.: Key resources for industry 4.0 adoption and its effect on sustainable production and circular economy: an empirical study. J. Clean. Prod. **281**, 125233 (2021)
4. Bagheri, B., Yang, S., Kao, H.A., Lee, J.: Cyber-physical systems architecture for self-aware machines in industry 4.0 environment. IFAC-PapersOnLine **48**(3), 1622–1627 (2015)
5. Barbosa, G., Aroca, R.: Advances of industry 4.0 concepts on aircraft construction: an overview of trends. J. Steel Struct. Constr. **3**, 125 (2017)
6. Benešová, A., Tupa, J.: Requirements for education and qualification of people in industry 4.0. Procedia Manuf. **11**, 2195–2202 (2017)
7. Bersani, C., Ruggiero, C., Sacile, R., Soussi, A., Zero, E.: Internet of things approaches for monitoring and control of smart greenhouses in industry 4.0. Energies **15**(10), 3834 (2022)

8. Bodkhe, U., et al.: Blockchain for industry 4.0: a comprehensive review. IEEE Access **8**, 79764–79800 (2020)
9. Bongomin, O., Nganyi, E.O., Abswaidi, M.R., Hitiyise, E., Tumusiime, G.: Sustainable and dynamic competitiveness towards technological leadership of industry 4.0: implications for East African community. J. Eng. **2020**, 1–22 (2020)
10. Colin, M., Galindo, R., Hernández, O.: Information and communication technology as a key strategy for efficient supply chain management in manufacturing smes. Procedia Comput. Sci. **55**, 833–842 (2015)
11. Dalenogare, L.S., Benitez, G.B., Ayala, N.F., Frank, A.G.: The expected contribution of industry 4.0 technologies for industrial performance. Int. J. Prod. Econ. **204**, 383–394 (2018)
12. Erboz, G.: How to define industry 4.0: main pillars of industry 4.0. Manage. Trends Dev. Enterp. Glob. Era **761**, 767 (2017)
13. Erol, S., Jäger, A., Hold, P., Ott, K., Sihn, W.: Tangible industry 4.0: a scenario-based approach to learning for the future of production. Procedia CiRp **54**, 13–18 (2016)
14. Gillwald, A., Calandro, E., Sadeski, F., Lacave, M.: Unlocking the potential of the fourth industrial revolution in Africa (2019)
15. Hall, B.H., Maffioli, A.: Evaluating the impact of technology development funds in emerging economies: evidence from Latin America. Eur. J. Dev. Res. **20**(2), 172–198 (2008)
16. Hermann, M., Pentek, T., Otto, B.: Design principles for industrie 4.0 scenarios. In: 2016 49th Hawaii International Conference on System Sciences (HICSS), pp. 3928–3937. IEEE (2016)
17. Jujjavarapu, G., et al.: AI and the manufacturing and services industry in India. The center for Internet and Society, India (2018). https://cisindia.org/internetgovernance/files/AIManufacturingandServices_Report_02.pdf. Accessed 06 Jan 2019
18. Kamble, S.S., Gunasekaran, A., Gawankar, S.A.: Sustainable industry 4.0 framework: a systematic literature review identifying the current trends and future perspectives. Process Saf. Environ. Protect. **117**, 408–425 (2018)
19. Kang, H.S., et al.: Smart manufacturing: past research, present findings, and future directions. Int. J. Precis. Eng. Manuf.-Green Technol. **3**(1), 111–128 (2016). https://doi.org/10.1007/s40684-016-0015-5
20. Ketteni, E., Kottaridi, C., Mamuneas, T.P.: Information and communication technology and foreign direct investment: interactions and contributions to economic growth. Empir. Econ. **48**(4), 1525–1539 (2015)
21. Kim, J.: Are countries ready for the new meso revolution? Testing the waters for new industrial change in Korea. Technol. Forecast. Soc. Chang. **132**, 34–39 (2018)
22. Kolberg, D., Zühlke, D.: Lean automation enabled by industry 4.0 technologies. IFAC-PapersOnLine **48**(3), 1870–1875 (2015)
23. Kumar, A.: Methods and materials for smart manufacturing: additive manufacturing, internet of things, flexible sensors and soft robotics. Manuf. Lett. **15**, 122–125 (2018)
24. Kumar, N., Siddharthan, N.S.: Technology, Market Structure and Internationalization: Issues and Policies for Developing Countries. Routledge (2013)
25. Li, L.: The path to made-in-China: how this was done and future prospects. Int. J. Prod. Econ. **146**(1), 4–13 (2013)
26. Li, L.: China's manufacturing locus in 2025: with a comparison of "made-in-china 2025" and "industry 4.0". Technol. Forecast. Soc. Chang. **135**, 66–74 (2018)

27. Liao, Y., Deschamps, F., Loures, E.D.F.R., Ramos, L.F.P.: Past, present and future of industry 4.0-a systematic literature review and research agenda proposal. Int. J. Prod. Res. **55**(12), 3609–3629 (2017)

28. Lu, Y.: Industry 4.0: a survey on technologies, applications and open research issues. J. Ind. Inf. Integr. **6**, 1–10 (2017)

29. Maisiri, W., Darwish, H., Van Dyk, L.: An investigation of industry 4.0 skills requirements. South Afr. J. Ind. Eng. **30**(3), 90–105 (2019)

30. Maisiri, W., van Dyk, L., Coeztee, R.: Factors that inhibit sustainable adoption of industry 4.0 in the South African manufacturing industry. Sustainability **13**(3), 1013 (2021)

31. Mavrikios, D., Georgoulias, K., Chryssolouris, G.: The teaching factory paradigm: developments and outlook. Procedia Manuf. **23**, 1–6 (2018)

32. Monostori, L., et al.: Cyber-physical systems in manufacturing. Cirp Ann. **65**(2), 621–641 (2016)

33. Mpofu, F.Y., Mhlanga, D.: Digital financial inclusion, digital financial services tax and financial inclusion in the fourth industrial revolution era in africa. Economies **10**(8), 184 (2022)

34. Mueller, E., Chen, X.L., Riedel, R.: Challenges and requirements for the application of industry 4.0: a special insight with the usage of cyber-physical system. Chin. J. Mech. Eng. **30**(5), 1050–1057 (2017)

35. Peres, R.S., Jia, X., Lee, J., Sun, K., Colombo, A.W., Barata, J.: Industrial artificial intelligence in industry 4.0-systematic review, challenges and outlook. IEEE Access **8**, 220121–220139 (2020)

36. Popa, S., Soto-Acosta, P., Martinez-Conesa, I.: Antecedents, moderators, and outcomes of innovation climate and open innovation: an empirical study in SMEs. Technol. Forecast. Soc. Chang. **118**, 134–142 (2017)

37. Pradhan, A., Agwa-Ejon, J.: Opportunities and challenges of embracing smart factory in South Africa. In: 2018 Portland International Conference on Management of Engineering and Technology (PICMET), pp. 1–8. IEEE (2018)

38. Raj, A., Dwivedi, G., Sharma, A., de Sousa Jabbour, A.B.L., Rajak, S.: Barriers to the adoption of industry 4.0 technologies in the manufacturing sector: an inter-country comparative perspective. Int. J. Prod. Econ. **224**, 107546 (2020)

39. Rghioui, A., Oumnad, A.: Internet of things: visions, technologies, and areas of application. Technology **6**(7) (2017)

40. Rüßmann, M., et al.: Industry 4.0: The future of productivity and growth in manufacturing industries. Boston Consult. Group **9**(1), 54–89 (2015)

41. Santos, C.H.D., de Queiroz, J.A., Leal, F., Montevechi, J.A.B.: Use of simulation in the industry 4.0 context: creation of a digital twin to optimise decision making on non-automated process. J. Simul. **16**(3), 284–297 (2022)

42. Shamout, M., Ben-Abdallah, R., Alshurideh, M., Alzoubi, H., Kurdi, B.A., Hamadneh, S.: A conceptual model for the adoption of autonomous robots in supply chain and logistics industry. Uncertain Supply Chain Manage. **10**(2), 577–592 (2022)

43. Shvetsova, O.A., Kuzmina, A.D.: Development of engineering personnel in the era of the fourth industrial revolution. In: 2018 Third International Conference on Human Factors in Complex Technical Systems and Environments (ERGO) and Environments (ERGO), pp. 45–48. IEEE (2018)

44. Strozzi, F., Colicchia, C., Creazza, A., Noè, C.: Literature review on the 'smart factory' concept using bibliometric tools. Int. J. Prod. Res. **55**(22), 6572–6591 (2017)

45. Valdeza, A.C., Braunera, P., Schaara, A.K., Holzingerb, A., Zieflea, M.: Reducing complexity with simplicity-usability methods for industry 4.0. In: Proceedings 19th Triennial Congress of the IEA, vol. 9, p. 14 (2015)
46. Wube, H.D., Esubalew, S.Z., Weldesellasie, F.F., Debelee, T.G.: Text-based chatbot in financial sector: a systematic literature review. Data Sci. Financ. Econ. **2**(3), 232–259 (2022)
47. Zhong, R.Y., Xu, X., Klotz, E., Newman, S.T.: Intelligent manufacturing in the context of industry 4.0: a review. Engineering **3**(5), 616–630 (2017)

Classification and Detection of Prohibited Objects in X-Ray Baggage Security Images

Sintayehu Zekarias Esubalew[1]($\boxtimes$) (iD), Ashenafi Kifleyohans Birhanu[2](iD), and Fikir Awoke Fantahun[3](iD)

[1] Ethiopian Artificial Intelligence Institute, 40782 Addis Ababa, Ethiopia
sinte2119@gmail.com
[2] Commercial Bank of Ethiopia, Addis Ababa, Ethiopia
[3] Addis Ababa University, Addis Ababa, Ethiopia

Abstract. *Airport security* is strengthened by baggage screening to prevent potential threats and ensure safety. Researchers have been striving to create more precise models for baggage screening through the use of techniques such as fusion, denoising, and histogram equalization. While object detection in X-ray baggage images mostly relies on the Bag of Visual Words (BoVW) model, Convolutional Neural Networks (CNN) have also demonstrated potential. In recent studies, image projection and transfer learning in deep neural networks have been utilized to increase the accuracy of detecting potentially dangerous items. One study specifically improved the detection of obscured prohibited items by incorporating a De-occlusion Attention Module into a custom dataset of X-ray scanned images.

In this research, the focus is on exploring the potential of computer vision for prohibited item detection and classification through image enhancement using a custom dataset resembling X-ray scanned images, as the main contribution. X-Ray machines are commonly used at high-security locations such as airports to scan baggage for hidden prohibited objects, like guns, knives, and razor blades. The research team added new layers to a pre-trained model using transfer learning, manually labeled the images, and enhanced the contrast. The YOLOv2, YOLOv3 and YOLOV5 models were employed to classify X-ray baggage images and detect obscured prohibited items, resulting in a mean average precision (mAP@0.50) of 59.44%, 98.61% and 84.1% respectively. These outcomes indicate the practical applicability of the suggested strategy for real-time baggage screening systems.

Keywords: Deep learning · Baggage X-ray image · Occluded prohibited object detection · transfer learning

1 Introduction

Currently, in airports, train stations, embassies, hotels, banks, universities, and other public transportation hubs, the security detection of baggage and other items are mostly carried out by X-ray security technology in addition to manual detection by human inspectors. However, because there are so many different kinds of items that must be identified and some of them may be likely to be covered by other items, using only the human eye to identify every item contained within a bag is quite difficult. As a result, there may occasionally be false detection and missing detection in manual detection. Thus security inspectors struggle to detect prohibited objects that pose a serious hazard to the public. Upreti et al. [22] this procedure not only affects security but also requires a significant amount of time and manpower.

The advancement of artificial intelligence has made computer vision essential for intelligent manufacturing as it allows for automatic detection, recognition, and location analysis. This is particularly important as it enables the replacement of manual detection with automated processes, improving efficiency and accuracy. The object detection technique in computer vision is important for quickly and accurately detecting things.

In recent times, deep learning has shown remarkable results across various image-based applications. Among the different types of deep learning models, convolutional neural networks (CNNs) [15] have gained widespread popularity and are being employed in a diverse range of applications, including i) the Health sector, including breast cancer analysis [9,10], brain tumor analysis [5,6,14], and skin ii) Agriculture, including coffee disease detection [23], identification of bacterial wilt affecting enset crop [1] and cereal crops disease detection [24] iii)the Financial industry, including face identification [12,28], optical character recognition [20,21], employing chatbots to offer customer service [26] and other computer vision activities.

This study's primary objective is to examine a potential computer vision application called "Prohibited Items Detection and Classification with Image Enhancement." In this work, the researchers investigate the capability of computer vision algorithms to precisely identify and categorize items that are considered prohibited, such as guns, knives, and razor blades, in images that resemble X-ray scans. The researchers leveraged transfer learning techniques with YOLO to classify and detect objects in X-ray images for baggage security purposes. They employed deep Convolutional Neural Networks (CNN) with transfer learning to accomplish image classification and detection. The data used in the research was collected using Chrome Image Eye add on and consisted of 349 images of guns, knives, and scissors, with 279 being used for training and 70 for testing. The researchers manually labeled the images using LabelImg tool. The researchers trained the YOLO algorithm using pre-trained weights from darknet19448.conv.23 and darknet53.conv.74. After training, the researchers improved the image contrast using Gaussian Blur and Median Filter and integrated the models into the X-ray baggage scanning machine system. The final step involved feeding the X-ray baggage-trained model into the system for object detection and classification.

One of the key contributions of this research is the creation of our own dataset that has been specifically designed to mimic X-ray scans. The researchers will be using this dataset to assess the efficacy of computer vision algorithms, particularly YOLO, which they are currently testing. The researchers intend to ensure that the outcomes of their study are applicable to real-life situations where detecting restricted items is crucial by employing their own dataset.

The application of image enhancement techniques is another noteworthy contribution of this research. In computer vision applications, image enhancement plays a crucial role as it enhances the quality of images and renders the object features in the images more prominent and discernible. As a result, human inspectors have less work to do and detection is more accurate and effective. The paper is structured as follows: Sect. 2 provides a description of the related published articles, Sect. 3 details the methodology adopted, Sect. 3.5 presents the model evaluation parameters, Sect. 4 covers the experimental results and discussion, and Sect. 5 discusses the conclusions and recommends topics for future research.

2   Related Work

Baggage screening is believed to provide protection against threats and reduce security concerns [22]. For Image enhancement, identification, and threat detection of a passenger's baggage, numerous studies and projects have been conducted. In light of this, researchers are still developing new models that can produce a higher degree of accuracy. In the paragraphs that follow, the researchers have attempted to review a few of those papers.

The paper [7] proposed a combination of fusion, denoising, and image enhancement techniques to produce a clear and enhanced image for improved threat identification and object categorization. Additionally, Zhou et al. [27] introduced an image enhancement algorithm that combines histogram equalization with alpha-weighted mean separation to eliminate background noise and enhance the visual quality of images.

The majority of research on object recognition in baggage X-ray pictures is based mostly upon that the Bag of Visual Words (BoVW) approach [4]. It has received a great deal of attention in previous publications, although just a small amount of research utilizing various methods, such as automated checking from a single X-ray source [2].

In the context of X-ray baggage images, convolutional neural networks (CNN) are introduced by [2], where they are compared with a BoVW technique utilizing manual-based feature engineering and an Support Vector Machine (SVM) classifier. In keeping with [2,16] examines and compares CNN-based and conventional classifiers for the classification of X-ray luggage objects. As per [2], the research presented in [16] investigates and contrasts CNN-based classifiers with conventional ones for the categorization of X-ray baggage objects. In [3], transfer learning and image detectors are proposed, and CNN models such as sliding window convolutional neural network (SW-CNN), Fast Region-based Convolutional Neural Network (Fast-RCNN) [11], Faster RCNN [19], region-based fully convolutional networks (R-FCNN) [8], and YOLOV2 [17] are explored for object detection in X-ray baggage security imaging.

The idea provided by [3] gives an explanation on different CNN algorithms and how they contribute to comprehending object detection and classification, not only this but also clearly describes the various CNN layers as well as their usage in a particular X-ray image classification and object detection. According to [3], various CNN-based algorithms such as SW-CNN, RCNN, F-RCNN, R-FCN, YOLO v2, and BoVW with SVM classifier were used. Among these, R-FCN with YOLOv2 exhibited the best overall performance in terms of accuracy for X-ray object detection task.

Jain et al. [13] aim to implement a framework for threat item detection based on deep neural networks. The framework uses CNN-based methods like YOLO and FRCNN to detect threats from objects. A transfer-learning approach is also attempted in order to enhance model performance. Using the pre-trained Faster RCNN with residual neural network (RESNET) on the ImageNet dataset, 98.4% accuracy is attained.

According to a most recent study [22], image projection is an effective technique to give deep learning models more variation and increase their generalizability. They explored an approach to produce a large number of automatically labeled images with minimal resources to produce a synthetic dataset. These methods can eliminate the need for endless hours of labor-intensive human labeling. They employed the yolov3-tiny CNN model to detect the x-ray baggage. Each object was correctly classified by Yolov3-tiny, which was trained and tested on both real and synthetic data. Likewise, the study presented in [25] focuses on the detection of occluded prohibited objects by creating their own dataset, called Occluded Prohibited Items X-ray (OPIXray), which centers on the commonly found prohibited item "cutter". The authors proposed a De-occlusion Attention Module (DOAM), which can be easily integrated into popular detectors to handle occlusion in X-ray image detection. DOAM uses multiple appearance details of the prohibited item to generate the attention map, which sharpens the feature maps for general detectors. The detectors, such as single-shot detector (SSD), YOLOv3, and fully convolutional one-stage object detection (FCOS), demonstrated an improvement of 3.12%, 1.04%, and 0.39%, respectively, when DOAM was applied as a plug-and-play module.

The related research that is summarized in Table 1 focuses on various techniques used by various authors and the results they attained, with a particular focus on x-ray baggage detection and classification.

Table 1. Summary of related works.

S.No	Author	Methods	Result	Dataset
1	Bastan et al. [4]	Support Vector Machine (SVM).	Achieving performance of R = 0.7, P = 0.29, and AP = 0.57	
2	Upreti et al. [22]	Yolov3-tiny	Testing real dataset of - Gun:93.59% - Knives:94.82% - Razor:55.05% Testing Synthetic dataset of - Gun:93.59% - Knives:0%, and - Razor: 0.34%.	Real Dataset from GDXRay [300 images] and another model from our Synthetic Image Dataset [2000 images]
3	Chen et al. [7]	Background subtraction based noise reduction approach.	Reduced the likelihood of false alarms during X-ray luggage screening	
4	Zhou et al. [27]	Alpha weighted mean separation and histogram equalization enhancement approach.	Enhanced images by background noise elimination	
5	Akcay et al. [2]	AlexNet	Achieving performance of - TP = 99.26%, and TN = 95.92% - FP = 4.08% and FN = 0.7%.	The dataset comprises 9123 samples, including firearms (2847), firearm components (1060), knives (2468), ceramic knives (1416), cameras (432), and laptops (900)
6	Liu et al. [16]	Faster R-CNN	Achieve 77% mAP	This dataset comprises 32,253 images of baggage security screening at subway X-Ray stations
7	Akcay et al. [3]	YOLOv2	Achieve 88.5% mAP	
8	Jain et al. [13]	Faster RCNN with RESNET	Accuracy 98.4%	The model has been trained on four categories of threat objects: guns, shurikas, razorblades, and knives

3   Methodology

The YOLO algorithm has several advantages over other algorithms such as Sliding Window Convolutional Neural Network (SW-CNN), Fast Region-based Convolutional Neural Network (Fast-RCNN), and Faster RCNN. Firstly, it is designed for real-time object detection and has a faster processing time, which is critical in security applications where quick and accurate results are essential. Secondly, YOLO is an end-to-end system, which means that the model is trained directly on the output space without any intermediate representations. This makes it more efficient and reduces the computational time compared to other algorithms that require multiple stages [17].

Additionally, YOLO is a single-shot detector, which processes the entire image in one forward pass. This makes it faster and more efficient compared to algorithms that require multiple stages to detect objects. The researchers in the paper also used transfer learning for YOLO, where they added their own layers to a pre-trained YOLO model. This reduced the computational resources and training time required to train the model, making it more feasible for the research. Lastly, YOLO has been shown to have good results in object detection and classification tasks and has been widely used in many applications [17].

The researchers employed a Transfer Learning model trained on a dataset from the Darknet for item detection and classification using YOLOv3. The algorithm is designed based on 53 CNN layers which are Darknet-53 stacked with and have 106 layers. The detections are at layers 82,94 and 106. But due to the computational power and time needed to investigate all layers, the last layers are selected for our research. Deep Convolutional Neural Networks (CNN) with transfer learning were suggested by the researchers for image classification and detection in X-ray baggage security imaging. The following steps will be taken during data analysis (Fig. 1).

3.1   Data Gathering and Understanding

It is crucial to gather, understand, and organize the data in a way that facilitates analysis easier. The OPIXray dataset had been our suggested usage. But despite our best efforts, the researchers were unable to get the dataset. Therefore, the researchers used the Chrome Image Eye addon from Google to extract three types of occluded prohibited x-ray luggage images, including guns, knives, and scissors. Because, scissors, guns, and knives are common items that may pose a threat in certain settings such as airports or schools. Accurately detecting and classifying objects in X-ray images is crucial for ensuring the safety of individuals and preventing potential security threats. Additionally, these objects have distinct shapes and features that can be easily identified in x-ray images, making them good candidates for object detection and classification tasks.

3.2   Data Preparation and Preprocess

For this research, the researchers have collected 349 images that have guns, knives, and scissors after cleaning and deleting undesired images from the pre-

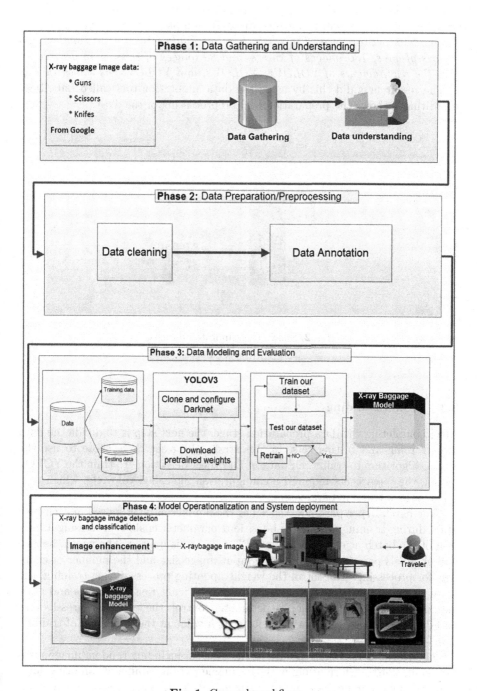

Fig. 1. General workflow.

vious stage. Out of the total, 279 samples are allocated for the purpose of training the model, while the remaining 70 samples are reserved for testing the model's performance. *The researchers manually labeled approximately 300 images of guns, 180 images of knives, and 80 images of scissors in accordance with the requirements of YOLOV2, YOLOV3, and YOLOV5, as shown in Fig. 2.* The researchers did this by using the data annotation tool called LabelImg. Algorithm 1 shows the preparation and preprocessing of the data.

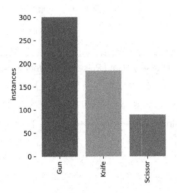

Fig. 2. Shows the annotated dataset.

3.3   Model Building

After completing the data preparation stage, the next step is to divide the data into training and testing sets. In this study, the researchers chose to use the YOLO algorithm to train their dataset for object detection. To train the YOLOv model, the researchers required a configuration file called yolov.cfg, which contains various training parameters.

The batch hyper-parameter specifies the number of images used in each iteration during training, and the subdivisions parameter enables processing a fraction of the batch at one time when GPU memory is limited. The width, height, and channels parameters specify the input image size and the number of channels for processing. To control the weight updating process during training, the momentum and decay parameters penalize significant weight changes and mitigate overfitting. The learning rate parameter controls the learning aggressiveness and decreases over time, starting with a high value at the beginning of training [17].

The researchers employed data augmentation, including random image rotation and color transformation, with the augmentation parameters and the aforementioned parameters used in Table 2 included in the configuration file, to maximize the quantity of training data available. The researchers also utilized transfer learning, which involves adding our layers to a pre-trained model. To this end, they downloaded darknet19448.conv.23, darknet53.conv.74 and yolov5s.pt to obtain the pre-trained weights for YOLOV2, YOLOV3 and YOLOV5, respectively. By using these previously trained weights, they were able to save significant time and computational resources compared to training the model from scratch.

Algorithm 2 outlines the steps for building the model by training the custom dataset with a pre-trained YOLOV model.

Table 2. Hyper-parameters configuration for this research.

S.No	Hyper-parameter	Value
1	batch	64
2	subdivisions	16
3	width	416
4	height	416
5	channels	3
6	momentum	0.9
7	decay	0.0005
8	learning rate	[0.001-0.0013]
9	max batches	6000 (2000*n), n = 3 number of classes
9	policy	steps
10	steps	4800, 5400
11	scales	0.1
12	burn in	400
13	angle	0
14	saturation	1.5
15	exposure	1.5
16	hue	0.1

3.4   Image Enhancement and Model Operationalize

After the researchers have completed their work, the models are integrated into a production environment. The researchers must integrate the models into the X-ray baggage scanning machine system and improve the image contrast using image enhancement techniques. To further refine the images, the researchers apply Gaussian Blur and a Median Filter to eliminate any noise or unwanted information that could potentially confuse the neural network. Finally, the researchers feed an X-ray baggage-trained model into the system to detect and classify any obscured prohibited objects, as depicted in the proposed architecture. Before object detection and classification, Algorithm 3 illustrates the process of improving the X-ray baggage images, while Algorithm 4 outlines the object detection and classification process using YOLOV3 (Fig. 3).

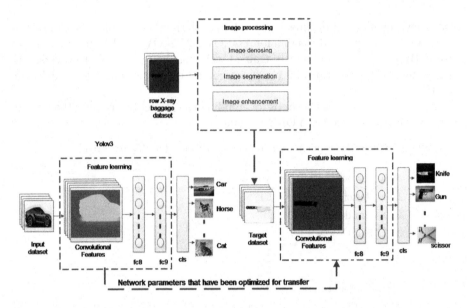

Fig. 3. Proposed Architecture for the transfer learning.

Algorithm 1. Data preparation and preprocess

Require: *ScrappedImages* ← download images from google using scrapping tool called image eye

1: Generate cleaned images from scrapped images
2: $N \leftarrow length(ScrappedImages)$
3: **for** $k \leftarrow 1$ to N **do**
4:     **if** $ScrappedImages_k$ is [gun,knife, scissor] **then**
5:         $CleanedImages \leftarrow ScrappedImages_k$
6:     **end if**
7: **end for**
8: Generate annotated images based on YOLOV requirement using LabelImg in CleanedImages
9: $N \leftarrow length(CleanedImages)$
10: **for** $k \leftarrow 1$ to N **do**
11:     $Class.txt \leftarrow CleanedImages_k$ [gun, knife, scissor]
12:     $image.txt \leftarrow CleanedImages_k$ [object_id, center_x, center_y, width, height]
13: **end for**
Ensure: CleanedImages with annotated data

Algorithm 2. Proposed Model Building

Require: *Googledrive* ← Upload the output of Algorithm 1

1: *Googledrive* ← Unzip the image dataset
2: Setting up google colab
3: *LocalMachine* ← Clone or download from githhub repository(git clone https://github.com/sintsh/X-ray-Baggage-detection-and-classification)
4: Open google colab
5: *GoogleColab* ← Upload YOLOv3_TransferLearning.ipynb file from the downloaded repository
6: *GoogleColab* ← Enable NVIDIA GPU
7: *GoogleColab* ← Mount your google drive
8: *GoogleColab* ← Clone darknet (git clone https://github.com/AlexeyAB/darknet)
9: *GoogleColab* ←Navigate to google drive to find darknet
10: Configure and compile : *OpenCV* ←1, *GPU* ←1, *CUDNN* ←1, *Make* ←Compile
11: Creates a copy of yolov.cfg file : *yolov_training.cfg* ←yolov.cfg
12: Configure yolov_training.cfg : *batch* ←16, *subdivisions* ←16, *max_batches* ←6000, *Classes* ←3 at line 610, *Classes* ←3 at line 696, *Classes* ←3 at line 783, *filters* ←24 at line 603, *filters* ←24 at line 689, *filters* ←24 at line 776
13: Create object.names train and test file : *obj.names* ← [gun, knife,Scissor], *OnYourdrive* ← Create train.txt and test.txt, *OnYourdrive* ← Copy obj.names
14: *img_paths* ← Get all paths to your images files
15: *data_size* ← length(img_paths)
16: *train_size* ← data_size *0.8
17: Save 80% of images path: *train.txt* ← img_paths[:train_size]
18: Save 20% of images path : *test.txt* ← img_paths[train_size:]
19: Download pre-trained weights for the convolutional layers file : *GoogleColab* ← darknet53.conv.74
20: Start training
21: **while** *loss* ≈ 0 **do**
        yolov3_training_last.weights ← ./darknet detector train /google drive/data/obj.data /google drive/yolov_training.cfg darknet53.conv.74 - dont_show
22: **end while**
23: *Measured_accuracy* ← ./darknet detector map data/obj.data cfg/yolov_training.cfg /google drive/yolov_training_last.weights
Ensure: yolov_training_last.weights and yolov_training.cfg

3.5   Model Evaluation Parameter

The YOLOv2, YOLOv3, and YOLOv5 models can perform inference on an input image and output a set of results that include an expected target class, a confidence rating (ranging from 0 to 1) that indicates the likelihood that a detected object belongs to the predicted class, and a set of coordinates that represent the predicted bounding box for all objects. The model, which has been trained on all accessible target class, assigns confidence scores to each one during the inference phase. The prediction with the greatest confidence score is the one

---

Algorithm 3. Image enhancement

Require: *Images_Path* ← load x-ray images

1: *enhanced_image_list* ← {}
2: Generate enhanced image using Gaussian and Median filter
3: N ← *length(Images_Path)*
4: **for** k ← 1 to N **do**
5:     *filename* ← split filename(*Images_Path_k*)
6:     *noisy_Image* ← read (*Images_Path_k*)
7:     *denoised_Image_gaussian* ← gaussian_filter (noisy_Image)
8:     *denoised_Image_median* ← median_filter (denoised_Image_gaussian)
        enhanced_image_list[filename] ← denoised_Image_median
9: **end for**
Ensure: *enhanced_image_list*

---

that is associated with each identified object. Algorithm 4 shows object detection and classification for YOLOV3.

In deep learning, there are numerous methods for evaluating model accuracy. Classification accuracy, mAP, and F1-score are a few examples. The accuracy of classification refers to the percentage of correct predictions made out of all possible predictions, where a prediction refers to the classification of an object inferred during the inference process. The use of classification accuracy as a statistic has been challenged in some applications due to imbalances in class occurrences during inference, which can lead to misleading results. As a result, various criteria were created for a more effective evaluation of model accuracy.

The accuracy of the predicted bounding box is measured using the mean Average Precision (mAP), which is calculated by determining the Intersection over Union (IoU) between the ground-truth box and the predicted box. IoU is obtained by calculating the ratio of the overlap area between the two boxes (Aoverlap) to the total area occupied by both boxes (Atotal), as shown in Eq. 1. The resulting value ranges from 0 to 1, representing the percentage of overlap between the two boxes. To categorize a prediction as a True Positive, mAP-50 employs an IoU threshold of 0.5 (50% overlap). The IoU is combined with a threshold to determine whether the prediction is a True Positive, True Negative, False Positive, or False Negative, and the Precision and Recall values are obtained from these assignments, as shown in Eqs. 2 and 3. These values are represented as a Precision-Recall curve, and the area beneath the curve represents the Average Precision (AP) of each class. The mAP is calculated by averaging the AP over all classes, ranging from 0 to 1. This approach is advantageous because the model has already been trained using the ground truth of each object's bounding box (Fig. 4).

$$IoU = \frac{A_{overlap}}{A_{total}} \qquad (1)$$

Algorithm 4. Object detection and classification

Require: $local\_project \leftarrow download(yolov\_training\_last.weights, yolov\_training.cfg)$
from Algorithm 2
Require: $enhanced\_image\_list \leftarrow enhanced\_image\_list$ from Algorithm 3

1: load trained model and configuration file
2: $net \leftarrow readNetwork(yolov3\_training\_last.weights, yolov3\_training.cfg)$
3: Object detection and classification
4: **for** $filename$ in $enhanced\_image\_list$ **do**
5:     $img \leftarrow enhanced\_image\_list[filename]$
6:     $height, width \leftarrow img.shape$
7:     $blob \leftarrow dnn.blobFromImage(img, 1/255, (416, 416), (0, 0, 0))$
8:     $net \leftarrow setInput(blob)$
9:     $output\_layers\_names \leftarrow net.getUnconnectedOutLayersNames()$
10:     $layerOutputs \leftarrow net.forward(output\_layers\_names)$
11:     $boxes \leftarrow []$
12:     $confidences \leftarrow []$
13:     $class\_ids \leftarrow []$
14:     **for** $output$ in $layerOutputs$ **do**
15:         **for** $detection$ in $output$ **do**
16:             $scores \leftarrow detection[5 :]$
17:             $class\_id \leftarrow argmax(scores)$
18:             $confidence \leftarrow scores[class\_id]$
19:             **if** $confidence \geq 0.2$ **then**
20:                 $center\_x \leftarrow detection[0] * width$
21:                 $center\_y \leftarrow detection[1] * height$
22:                 $w \leftarrow detection[2] * width$
23:                 $h \leftarrow detection[3] * height$
24:                 $x \leftarrow center\_x - w/2$
25:                 $y \leftarrow center\_y - h/2$
26:                 $boxes \leftarrow append([x, y, w, h])$
27:                 $confidences \leftarrow append(confidence)$
28:                 $class\_ids \leftarrow append(class\_id)$
29:             **end if**
30:         **end for**
31:     **end for**
32:     $indexes \leftarrow dnn.NMSBoxes(boxes, confidences, 0.2, 0.4)$
33:     **if** $length(indexes) \geq 0$ **then**
34:         **for** i in $indexes.flatten()$ **do**
35:             $x, y, w, h \leftarrow boxes[i]$
36:             $label \leftarrow string(classes[class\_ids[i]])$
37:             $confidence \leftarrow string(round(confidences[i], 2))$
38:             $color \leftarrow colors[i]$
39:             $draw \leftarrow rectangle(img, (x, y), (x + w, y + h), color, 2)$
40:             $putText \leftarrow putText(img, label + "" + confidence, (x, y + 20))$
41:         **end for**
42:     **end if**
43:     $Predicted\_output \leftarrow save(filename, img)$
44: **end for**
Ensure: Predicted_output

$$Precision = \frac{TP}{TP + FP} \tag{2}$$

$$Recall = \frac{TN}{TN + FN} \tag{3}$$

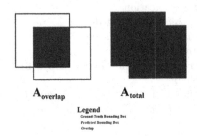

$A_{overlap}$ A_{total}

Legend
Ground-Truth Bounding Box
Predicted Bounding Box
Overlap

Fig. 4. Illustration of IoU for Detection Accuracy.

According to the equation in 4, the F1-score approach also uses precision and recall. In contrast to mAP, Eqs. 2 and 3 use the classification outputs of the discovered objects (like Classification Accuracy) rather than IoU to determine the number of True/False Positives/Negatives. The F1-score was created to strike a compromise between precision and recall in situations where there is an uneven class distribution in order to address the primary issue with classification accuracy.

$$F1 = 2\frac{Precision * Recall}{Precision + Recall} \tag{4}$$

4   Experimental Result and Discussion

The official YOLOV2, YOLOV3 and YOLOV5 model comes with a specified list of objects (a total of 80 objects), such as a car, person, cat, and dog. To detect and classify custom objects like guns, knives, and scissors using the official YOLOV2, YOLOV3 and YOLOV5 models, the researcher must train the YOLO custom object detection model by themselves. Google Colab was used to train the YOLOV2, YOLOv3 and YOLOV5 models to identify occluded prohibited objects in X-ray images.

For the training set, the researchers arbitrarily selected 80% of the clear subset's data, and for the testing set, they randomly selected 20% of the clear subset's data. This was done to determine how the detection performance is impacted by the size of the training set. For the YOLOV3 model, which has an 80:20 training/test split, the values of the mAP and loss functions are shown. After roughly 1200 iterations, the models showed no discernible gain in performance, proving that in this case, training the YOLO model on a small set of training images with few iterations is possible without dramatically decreasing the model's performance.

In Fig. 5 the confusion matrix provides a visual representation of the performance of a classification model. In this particular confusion matrix, the rows indicate the predicted classes, while the columns represent the actual classes. Each cell contains a count of the detections. For instance, for the "Gun" class, there were 100 true positive detections and 4 false positive detections. This implies that the model identified 100 objects that were truly guns and 4 objects that were not guns but were classified as such by the model. The "Knife" class had 23 true positive detections and 0 false positive detections, while the "Scissor" class had 22 true positive detections and 0 false positive detections.

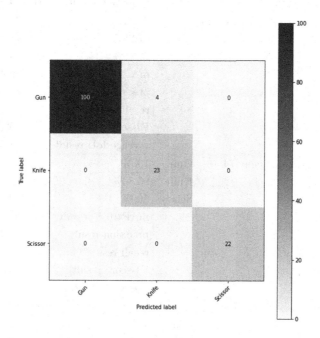

Fig. 5. Confusion matrix representation.

For YOLOV2, YOLOV3 and YOLOV5 the task of detecting three classes-gun, knife, and scissor-the achieved mAP after training were 59.44%, 98.61% and 84.1%, and the average IoU after training were 48.53%, 84.73% and 75.01%, respectively. For YOLOV2, YOLOV3 and YOLOV5, the average accuracy for the Gun class was 63.22%, 100% and 89.3%, the Knife class was 37.28%, 95.83% and 78%, and the Scissor class was 77.80%, 100% and 85%. Recall in this instance was 54%, 99% and 69.1%, and the F1 score was 59%, 99% and 76%. Both for YOLOV2, YOLOV3 and YOLOV5, respectively.

The experiment's findings show that the YOLOv3 model is effective at meeting the study's main goals, which include identifying and categorizing knives, weapons, and scissors in x-ray images of luggage. The occluded banned objects shown in an X-ray image's Average Precision (AP), mean Average Precision (mAP), precision, recall, F1-score, and average Intersection over Union (IoU) are shown in Table 3. Guns, scissors, and knives-all of which have distinct forms and dimensions–are among the items evaluated. According to the findings, the mAP parameter does not change depending on the size and shape of the object, as shown by the similar values of the parameter for all of the occluded forbidden items.

Table 3. Accuracy of detection of occluded prohibited items.

Model	Network	Name	Detection accuracy AP	TP	FP
YoloV2	darknet19_448.conv.23	Gun	63.22%	39	22
		Knife	37.28%	18	12
		Scissor	77.80%	13	3
			mAP@0.50 result	59.44%	
			precision result	65%	
			recall result	54%	
			F1-score result	59%	
			average IoU result	48.53%	
YoloV3	darknet53.conv.74	Gun	100%	100	4
		Knife	95.83%	23	0
		Scissor	100%	22	0
			mAP@0.50 result	98.61%	
			precision result	99%	
			recall result	99%	
			F1-score result	99%	
			average IoU result	84.73%	
YoloV5	yolov5s.pt	Gun	89.3%	87	1
		Knife	78%	52	4
		Scissor	85%	90	10
			mAP@0.50 result	84.1%	
			precision result	85.6%	
			recall result	69.1%	
			F1-score result	76%	
			average IoU result	75.01%	

In Table 3 YOLOv3 boasts several architectural improvements over YOLOv2, such as the incorporation of residual connections, skip connections, and multiple anchor boxes per grid cell. These enhancements enable YOLOv3 to more accurately capture object features and improve localization accuracy. Additionally, the quality and amount of the training data used to train the model greatly impacts performance. In order to increase the model's adaptability to new data, YOLOv3 was trained on a bigger and more varied dataset than YOLOv2 and made use of data augmentation techniques such random scaling and flipping. Moreover, the choice of hyperparameters used during training plays a significant role in a model's performance. YOLOv3's hyperparameters may have been better suited to the particular problem being solved. Besides, YOLOv3 introduces improvements in inference speed, making it more practical for real-time applications. It is also worth mentioning that YOLOv3 has been trained on a larger and more diverse dataset than YOLOv5, which could lead to better generalization and improved detection performance on new, unseen data [18].

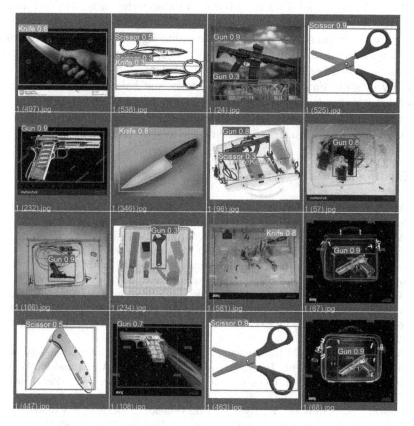

Fig. 6. This diagram illustrates the method proposed for detecting occluded prohibited objects in X-ray imaging.

Figure 6 displays several sample output images. occluded prohibited objects are bounded in a red box in the output images with labels and their confidence. Around 3 samples of data are used for the training on top of Darknet.

5 Conclusion

The primary contribution of this study, the researchers explore a potential computer vision application called prohibited items detection and classification with image enhancement in our own dataset that resembles X-ray scanned images. Security screening system depends on accurate threat detection since it tells us where and what kind of threat is hidden in the x-ray baggage. In exposed locations like airports, railway stations, etc., people's luggage should constantly be checked. The researchers use deep learning-based object detection algorithms like YOLOv2, YOLOV3 and YOLOv5 in order to automatically detect and classify baggage carrying concealed prohibited objects in the shortest period of time. In terms of 3-class object detection and classification, YOLOv3 generates 98.61% mAP based on internet data from our own dataset that was obtained utilizing a scraping tool from Google.

Future studies may use various deep learning algorithms to implement threat detection and classification for objects like weapons, knives, scissors, powders, explosives, and other items based on a local dataset from x-ray luggage. The majority of x-ray images of luggage are noisy and have poor visual quality. A novel image enhancement technique can be employed by researchers that integrates with object detection and classification-trained algorithms to enhance the visual quality of such images and simultaneously reduce noise.

References

1. Afework, Y.K., Debelee, T.G.: Detection of bacterial wilt on enset crop using deep learning approach. Int. J. Eng. Res. Afr. **51**, 131–146. Trans Tech Publ (2020)
2. Akçay, S., Kundegorski, M.E., Devereux, M., Breckon, T.P.: Transfer learning using convolutional neural networks for object classification within x-ray baggage security imagery. In: 2016 IEEE International Conference on Image Processing (ICIP), pp. 1057–1061. IEEE (2016)
3. Akcay, S., Kundegorski, M.E., Willcocks, C.G., Breckon, T.P.: Using deep convolutional neural network architectures for object classification and detection within x-ray baggage security imagery. IEEE Trans. Inf. Forensics Secur. **13**(9), 2203–2215 (2018)
4. Baştan, M., Yousefi, M.R., Breuel, T.M.: Visual words on baggage X-Ray images. In: Real, P., Diaz-Pernil, D., Molina-Abril, H., Berciano, A., Kropatsch, W. (eds.) CAIP 2011. LNCS, vol. 6854, pp. 360–368. Springer, Heidelberg (2011). https://doi.org/10.1007/978-3-642-23672-3_44
5. Biratu, E.S., Schwenker, F., Ayano, Y.M., Debelee, T.G.: A survey of brain tumor segmentation and classification algorithms. J. Imaging **7**(9), 179 (2021)
6. Biratu, E.S.S., Schwenker, F., Debelee, T.G.G., Kebede, S.R.R., Negera, W.G.G., Molla, H.T.T.: Enhanced region growing for brain tumor MR image segmentation. J. Imaging **7**(2), 22 (2021)
7. Chen, Z., Zheng, Y., Abidi, B.R., Page, D.L., Abidi, M.A.: A combinational approach to the fusion, de-noising and enhancement of dual-energy X-Ray luggage images. In: 2005 IEEE Computer Society Conference on Computer Vision and Pattern Recognition (CVPR'05)-Workshops, p. 2. IEEE (2005)

8. Dai, J., Li, Y., He, K., Sun, J.: R-fcn: object detection via region-based fully convolutional networks. Adv. Neural Inf. Process. Syst. **29** (2016)

9. Debelee, T.G., Amirian, M., Ibenthal, A., Palm, G., Schwenker, F.: Classification of mammograms using convolutional neural network based feature extraction. In: Mekuria, F., Nigussie, E.E., Dargie, W., Edward, M., Tegegne, T. (eds.) ICT4DA 2017. LNICST, vol. 244, pp. 89–98. Springer, Cham (2018). https://doi.org/10. 1007/978-3-319-95153-9_9

10. Debelee, T.G., Schwenker, F., Ibenthal, A., Yohannes, D.: Survey of deep learning in breast cancer image analysis. Evol. Syst. **11**(1), 143–163 (2020)

11. Girshick, R.: Fast R-CNN. In: Proceedings of the IEEE International Conference on Computer Vision, pp. 1440–1448 (2015)

12. Islam Chowdhury, A., Munem Shahriar, M., Islam, A., Ahmed, E., Karim, A., Rezwanul Islam, M.: An automated system in ATM booth using face encoding and emotion recognition process. In: 2020 2nd International Conference on Image Processing and Machine Vision, pp. 57–62 (2020)

13. Jain, D.K., et al.: An evaluation of deep learning based object detection strategies for threat object detection in baggage security imagery. Pattern Recognit. Lett. **120**, 112–119 (2019)

14. Kebede, S.R., Debelee, T.G., Schwenker, F., Yohannes, D.: Classifier based breast cancer segmentation. J. Biomim. Biomater. Biomed. Eng. **47**, 41–61. Trans Tech Publ (2020)

15. Krizhevsky, A., Sutskever, I., Hinton, G.E.: Imagenet classification with deep convolutional neural networks. Commun. ACM **60**(6), 84–90 (2017)

16. Liu, J., Leng, X., Liu, Y.: Deep convolutional neural network based object detector for x-ray baggage security imagery. In: 2019 IEEE 31st International Conference on Tools with Artificial Intelligence (ICTAI), pp. 1757–1761. IEEE (2019)

17. Redmon, J., Farhadi, A.: Yolo9000: better, faster, stronger. In: Proceedings of the IEEE Conference on Computer Vision and Pattern Recognition, pp. 7263–7271 (2017)

18. Redmon, J., Farhadi, A.: Yolov3: an incremental improvement (2018). arXiv preprint arXiv:1804.02767

19. Ren, S., He, K., Girshick, R., Sun, J.: Faster R-CNN: towards real-time object detection with region proposal networks. Adv. Neural Inf. Process. Syst. **28** (2015)

20. Srivastava, S., Priyadarshini, J., Gopal, S., Gupta, S., Dayal, H.S.: Optical character recognition on bank cheques using 2D convolution neural network. In: Malik, H., Srivastava, S., Sood, Y.R., Ahmad, A. (eds.) Applications of Artificial Intelligence Techniques in Engineering. AISC, vol. 697, pp. 589–596. Springer, Singapore (2019). https://doi.org/10.1007/978-981-13-1822-1_55

21. Tarawneh, A.S., Hassanat, A.B., Chetverikov, D., Lendak, I., Verma, C.: Invoice classification using deep features and machine learning techniques. In: 2019 IEEE Jordan International Joint Conference on Electrical Engineering and Information Technology (JEEIT), pp. 855–859. IEEE (2019)

22. Upreti, A., Rajat, B.: Automated Threat Detection In X-Ray Imagery For Advanced Security Applications. Ph.D. thesis, University of Alberta, Canada (2021)

23. Waldamichael, F.G., Debelee, T.G., Ayano, Y.M.: Coffee disease detection using a robust HSV color-based segmentation and transfer learning for use on smartphones. Int. J. Intell. Syst. **37**(8), 4967–4993 (2021). https://doi.org/10.1002/int.22747, https://onlinelibrary.wiley.com/doi/abs/10.1002/int.22747

24. Waldamichael, F.G., Debelee, T.G., Schwenker, F., Ayano, Y.M., Kebede, S.R.: Machine learning in cereal crops disease detection: a review. Algorithms **15**(3), 75 (2022)

25. Wei, Y., Tao, R., Wu, Z., Ma, Y., Zhang, L., Liu, X.: Occluded prohibited items detection: an x-ray security inspection benchmark and de-occlusion attention module. In: Proceedings of the 28th ACM International Conference on Multimedia, pp. 138–146 (2020)

26. Wube, H.D., Esubalew, S.Z., Weldesellasie, F.F., Debelee, T.G.: Text-based chatbot in financial sector: a systematic literature review. Data Sci. Financ. Econ. **2**(3), 232–259 (2022)

27. Zhou, Y., Panetta, K., Agaian, S.: Ct baggage image enhancement using a combination of alpha-weighted mean separation and histogram equalization. In: Mobile Multimedia/Image Processing, Security, and Applications 2010, vol. 7708, pp. 137–148. SPIE (2010)

28. Zinjurde, A.M., Kamble, V.B.: Credit card fraud detection and prevention by face recognition. In: 2020 International Conference on Smart Innovations in Design, Environment, Management, Planning and Computing (ICSIDEMPC), pp. 86–90. IEEE (2020)

Author Index

T. Girma Debelee et al. (Eds.): PanAfriCon AI 2022, CCIS 1800, p. 297, 2023.
https://doi.org/10.1007/978-3-031-31327-1

Printed in the United States
by Baker & Taylor Publisher Services